# TIMELESS MEXICO

*Other Books by Hudson Strode*

FINLAND FOREVER

SOUTH BY THUNDERBIRD

THE PAGEANT OF CUBA

THE STORY OF BERMUDA

IMMORTAL LYRICS: an Anthology of English Verse

SPRING HARVEST: an Anthology of Alabama Stories

# TIMELESS MEXICO

by

## HUDSON STRODE

972
St 87

NEW YORK

HARCOURT, BRACE AND COMPANY

PRINTED IN THE UNITED STATES OF AMERICA

27531

*For*
*Raymond Ross Paty*

*"Only the Timeless is true. Truths lie beyond history and life, and, vice versa, life is something beyond all causes, effects, and truths."*

# Contents

# Preface

Sharing a frontier of river water and silt more than a thousand miles long, Mexico and the United States are linked together willy-nilly by geography. "Geography does not argue"; as the late Dr. Nicholas Spykman said, "it simply is." The acceleration of modern mechanics, added to geography, has made the United States and Mexico more or less interdependent. A contented next-door neighbor, at peace with herself, in some degree of prosperity and looking forward to a reasonably happy future, is urgently desirable for the well-being of the United States. So particularly in this period of world strife and revolutionary change, is it of interest to the northern neighbor how the southern neighbor fares, how she ministers to the needs of her people, what direction she takes.

To deal sensibly and sympathetically with Mexico is a challenge to our understanding. To understand an alien nation it is essential to know its peoples' past, their struggles and their sacrifices, as well as their present desires. In order to comprehend Mexico it is as needful to know her history as it is to know what her leaders are trying to do and the obstacles that confront them. With this purpose in mind I have undertaken to write this book, revaluing afresh the story of the people of Mexico, who have already been the theme of so many excellent books. Since history is largely the record of the lives of the men, good and bad, who made it, I have put the emphasis on the individuals who helped destiny shape events. For as Hilaire Belloc says, "In notable achievements, one man generally stands at their origin."

Montaigne believed that history should be read as a discipline to the judgment. He felt convinced that Plutarch, the great biographer of the ancients, would prefer that we should applaud his judgment rather than commend his knowledge. So recalling Montaigne, while writing this history, I have endeavored to discern the motives of men, to see how their minds and emotions worked, and thus to interpret the manifold "facts" as set forth in the various, and often conflicting, chronicles. In selecting scenes and events for depiction I have tried to choose those which throw some special illumination on the complex character of Mexico. I have sought to catch gleams of that "inner light of actuality and attention" which floods life as men actually lived it. It has not always been an easy task, however fascinating; for Mexico is replete with secret contradictions as well as spontaneous variety.

Behind the alluring mask of Mexico there lies a grim reality. The basis for friendship depends on some knowledge of what lies behind the mask. Good will cannot be bought merely by lend-lease, artificial high prices for silver, or honeyed phrases in which the *norteamericanos* are bungling amateurs compared to the Latin Americans. The human approaches to the heart of Mexico must needs be improved.

Sympathetic understanding of alien fellow mortals is a rare gift. And by a consensus of opinion Mexico is one of the most illusive of nations to catch and catalogue. Even the Mexicans often give themselves up with a shrug and almost inevitably end with *"Quién sabe?"* As the Mexican poet sings, *"Quién sabe* from the cradle, *Quién sabe* to the grave."

Not without symbolic suggestion does the heart of Mexico beat in the shadow of volcanoes. For it is a land where strange violence in mankind and in nature seems to lie in ambush, where dire memories are rooted deep in racial consciousness. Yet despite the vehemence in the Mexican story, there is withal an amazingly submissive patience in the people that often passes beyond resignation and becomes sheer serenity. To strangers, even when the land lies under the most gracious spell of peace, Mexico sometimes seems faintly touched in the brain. The Mexicans like to say of themselves, "We exist close to music and madness." But the theme music of their *tierra* is the haunting dirge of the mourning dove. With all its flowery fiestas Mexico is not a joyous land. Its history is too deeply tinctured with blood. The tragic past is ingrained in the selfhood of its people, like the grace inherent in the movement of a puma. Mexicans are not oblivious of the crushing and ruinous rates they have had to pay for such benefits as have come with their "advancement."

The inimitable Charles Flandrau once asked a Mexican lady, "Does it rain here in summer as much as it does in winter?" After a thoughtful silence, she replied, "There are no fixed rules, Señor." And after several years' sojourn, in which he learned that theory and practice only occasionally coincide, the unorthodox Flandrau came to regard the lady's statement as a consummate epitome of the country. He found in this very unaccountability, in this "hazard of the unexpected," the indisputable charm of Mexico.

Mexico is a magnificent paradox. Its ironic story is strung with contradictions and incredible happenings. Prescott confessed that he found it difficult to treat such romantic subject matter according to the severe rules prescribed by historical criticism. In its dramatic struggles Mexico has known horrendous climaxes and the most ludicrous anticlimaxes. It is a tale of triumphal entrances and sudden flights, of clod-like inertia and lightning-swift violence, of vicious betrayals and heart-stirring loyalties, of mocking glee and grief too stark for tears. Since the Conquest, and even before, Mexico has been like a house divided against itself. Humboldt called it the land of inequality. Certainly human life there has been too much the sport of accident and ignorance.

What might have been an idyll in this strangely evocative land turned out to be a blood-stained cavalcade.

That pattern of paradox which is woven through the texture of Mexico's being and doing often makes truth seem as deceptive as marsh-lights. On the map one sees at once how the shape of Mexico resembles the horn of Amalthaea. But in this area of fabulous wealth dearth and privation are notorious. The abundance is extremely spotty. Deserts and mountains make up more than two-thirds of the topography. The graceful horn of plenty is sadly lacking in two essential gifts of providence: rivers and generous rainfall. There is not rain enough in the blue Mexican sky to water a tenth of the thirsty earth. There are no important rivers, and none is commercially navigable all the year.

It was Humboldt who revived the fallacy that Mexico is a land of unexhaustible riches. And many noted writers since 1800 have furthered the illusion that there is illimitable treasure to be had for the scratching or the digging. It is a paradox that opulent Mexico is poor. Except in fertile pockets of soil or in precious-veined strata, Mexico wrests a living by the hardest. "Until we realize that Mexico is poor," says the economist Ramón Beteta, "and plan our economy accordingly, we are not going to make sound progress." Seventy per cent of the people earn their living by agriculture. Only seven to ten per cent of the land is arable under present technical conditions and only twenty per cent could be arable under any conditions. Both the Atlantic and Pacific coastal regions are so swampy and full of tropical disease germs that effective drainage system on a large scale seems prohibitive because of cost.

Mexico is a crumpled land, like that piece of paper Cortés wadded in his fist and dropped on the table before the king of Spain, in answer to the question, "What is the country like?" Mexico is a land of ravines. Ravines are a wonderful feast for the eye, but an adversity for agriculture. Even in the purported halcyon days of the *hacienda* under Díaz, when the population was scarcely half that of today, Mexico imported beans, wheat, and corn.

It is true that the republic at present ranks first among the countries of the world in the export of silver and third in the export of copper. But the price of silver is an artificial one created by the New Deal administration to keep the American-owned mines going and to bolster the neighborly good will. The best answer to Mexico's reputation of being the "treasure house of the world" is that American economists would regard the hypothetical "taking over" of the republic as a decided economic liability.

In this fascinating, poor-rich land where the peasants are by nature as gentle as any people on the face of the earth, sometimes the peace has been broken by a single deed or word and the docile folk transformed to savage fanatics. Yet on the surface the peasants of Mexico seem to live more or less in a state of philosophical timelessness. They are inclined to accept without argument what fate brings them. They have little confidence, because they know that while providence gives with one hand it takes with the other. With only the most meager necessities of life they somehow manage to present a feeling of stability and blessed quietude in the midst of the stirrings and fluctuations of contemporary civilization. Flowers still have emphasis in the daily life of the most humble, as the first *conquistadores* discovered to their amazement. Music is not long absent even in squalor. A kind of listless mysticism beguiles and takes the edge off the daily bargaining. An apt wit mocks the most shocking misfortunes. The Mexican peasants know magnificently how to endure the inevitable. They exist as if their ancestors had overheard Buddha saying: "Overcome the will, renounce preference and you will have entered Nirvana." And perhaps this is why many a tense and flustered foreigner discovers an ineffable peace in the Mexican countryside. For despite all the disturbing elements that have plagued the nation, Mexico still has roots in its metaphysical past. One senses eternal perspectives in the Mexican landscapes. Even in those villages where civil strife swept with most venomous fury, the Indians kept their own private and silent sanctuaries.

The Mexican struggle for independence from Spain which began in 1810 and the Revolution of the people which began in 1910 both stemmed indirectly from the American Declaration of 1776. Our War of Independence was more or less ended in four years, but Mexico's Revolution is still in progress. Mexicans have been injected with a desire for both political and economic freedom. In their socialistic experiments for the general welfare we should wish them God-speed. And notwithstanding the differences in resources, technological equipment, and racial characteristics that are obvious between the two nations, we might well note the effect of the various reforms to see if this or that successful one might be applied with profit to some remediable defect in our own democracy. But the American reformer should be on his guard in evaluating the claims of progress. Though Mexico has produced some of the purest idealists that have ever devoted their lives to uplifting mankind, let him remember that Bertram Wolfe shrewdly defined Mexican socialism as "three parts genuine social reform, three parts bureaucratic corruption, and four parts demagogy."

It is quite true that the submerged man of Mexico has often been offered a faulty compass with which to find his way to greater happiness, and sometimes it has gained him nothing more than a restless and corroding discontent. The rhythms of Mexico cannot be and should not be accelerated too swiftly. As one cannot turn back the clock of progress without causing a noisy rupture, so it is not good to urge the natural speed of one country to match that of another. Many a visitor has remarked that, despite the imperative demands of modern civilization, it is far more charming to watch Mexicans indulging in *dolce far niente* than to watch Americans taut at an assembly line in an industrial plant. But one is conscious, too, that this evocative, habitual land, so strangely imbued with positive assertions of the past, still has an eye fixed wonderingly on the future.

If the United States, which professes to champion the rights of small nations, really wants to help Mexico, it must take the nation as it finds it with all its differences of temperament and tempo. Though since 1910 Mexico has been a battleground between ideas and individual rivalries, where each move in the march of time has left the land strewn with wreckage, the fundamental heart of Mexico seems little affected. The Indian continues to use household articles dating from thousands of years. He is born and dies on the same *petate,* woven of straw and reeds, as his ancestors did; the corn for his *tortillas* is ground in the same kind of *metate* and the food prepared and cooked in the same immemorial way. The form of the peasant dwelling remains unchanged. And the man himself is aware that life is something beyond all causes, effects, or truths.

North is North and South is South, when North means the Anglo-Saxon United States and South means Spanish-Indian Mexico. Though the twain are not ocean-cleft, but conjunctive, one has only to cross that arbitrary line called the Border to sense divergencies in the realm of spirit. Though men of two different kinds are ever separated, each in his own spiritual island, still one can strive to establish a mutual confidence, and confidence often leads to admiration. To have a steadfast neighbor is worth all the long patience and ceaseless vigilance necessary to bring about the consummation.

HUDSON STRODE

*Cherokee Road*
*Tuscaloosa, Alabama*
*May 15, 1944*

# TIMELESS MEXICO

# Prelude: Before Cortés

*"That which was yesterday is not today; and
let not that which is today trust to live tomorrow."*

NEZAHUALCOYOTL

One December evening in 1941 after an afternoon at his place
in Coyoacán, Diego Rivera brought me back to my hotel in
Mexico in his station wagon. We had begun to discuss the
Mongol origin of his Indian progenitors just before we arrived.
Standing there on the street below the curb in the space of illumination from the doorway of the hotel, with a flapping tweed
top-coat held about his expansive middle girth and a vast broad-
brimmed hat on his head, the artist seemed as huge and as Mexican as his own canvases. Then slowly he narrowed his great
bulging eyes and drew in his thick lips and became Mongolian
before my eyes. "We Mexicans are Chinese," he said persuasively,
in a voice hardly more than a whisper. "Of course we are
Chinese," he repeated softly with the quintessence of assurance.
And any passer-by at the moment might have said quite naturally, "Look at that big Chinaman in a Mexican hat." The migra-
tion from Asia by way of Alaska had always seemed to me the
right answer to the Western Indian's origin. Now Rivera's inner
conviction of his Mongoloid kinship which could so transform
his aspect and his aura added peculiar evidence to my belief.

There has been much contention among the anthropologists
and historians as to whence came the "natives" of Mexico. Direct
links with the ancient Egyptians have been claimed by some.
Evidence has been advanced to prove migrations from the other
side of the Atlantic over some submerged continent like the lost
Atlantis. Some believe the Mexican Indians came from Cambodia

3

along the chained islands of the equatorial Pacific. But the weight of what might go in the category of proof says they came along the Aleutian Islands and over the Bering Strait to Alaska and thence south.

By whatever route they came it is easy to believe that the Indians of Mexico are cousins to the Mongols. Though the color of one is yellowish and the other a coppery brown, there is affinity both in physiognomy and temperament. The biological structure of bone and skull of the Mexican Indian is more related to that of the Mongol than to any other race. And the Mexicans indubitably seem akin to the Chinese in spirit. Like the Chinese, they have "no modern servile and shallow worship of mechanistic and materialistic facts, accurately observed and well tabulated, seemingly sufficient unto themselves." They have little sense of the accuracy of facts and figures. They too know the value of things, no matter how high or how low the purchase price may be. Sooner or later with both peoples mysticism supersedes any kind of knowledge. And like the Chinese they are at once inscrutable and as simple as earth. They have the Chinese quality of extraordinary endurance and absorption. Although the civilization and the official language of Mexico have been Spanish for four centuries, the nation today remains Indian in blood and soul, as José Vasconcelos has said.

Yet however one may theorize, despite all the inspired and persistent delvings and compilations of the anthropologists and archeologists, the origin of the Mexicans remains a mystery. A plentitude of enigmas is left unsolved. The work of experts is entangled with contrary conjectures. Although several priceless codices of the Aztecs are extant, most of the ancient "manuscripts" are irretrievably lost. The records in picture writing found at the great library of Texcoco were burned in the public square by the first Christian bishop, the over-zealous Father Zumárraga. Only twenty-three manuscripts in Aztec escaped the flames. And in Yucatán the same sort of disaster befell all but a few of the

Mayan works by order of Father Landa. Though Aztec is still spoken in villages to the very edges of Mexico City, modern man has not yet learned to decipher the fragments in ancient Mayan.

The Indian writers of the sixteenth and seventeenth centuries, Ixtilxochitl, Durán, and Tezozomoc, are often as little in agreement as the Spaniards who played a part in the conquest, Cortés, Bernal Díaz, and de Tápia; or as those who sifted the records shortly afterwards, Sahagún, Motolinía, and, somewhat later, Dávila, Mendieta, and Torquemada. Notwithstanding the work of such scholarly and devoted contemporary archeologists as Vaillant, Spinden, Hewett, Morley, and Blom, with whole libraries of books and monographs by other scientists in ten different languages, the record before the fourteenth century is highly conjectural.

No certain date in Aztec history goes back farther than 1325. The city of Mexico, on whose pavements Diego Rivera and I were standing when he turned into a Chinaman, had been founded in that year. The founders spoke the Nahuatl or Aztec tongue and they came originally from the northwest in the direction of California and Arizona. They had come into what is now Mexico sometime in the twelfth century and wandered about, fighting both losing and winning battles, until they finally arrived at the southwestern edges of Lake Texcoco. According to legend, here they beheld an eagle perched on a branch of prickly pear projecting from a rock. Secure in its talons the bird held a struggling serpent. The oracle with them took this to be an auspicious sign for making a permanent settlement. They called the place Tenochtitlán—"cactus [prickly pear] on a stone."

The Aztecs had been preceded into the Valley of Anáhuac by several other tribes that had risen and fallen. By far the most important of these were the Toltecs, and they are the first mentioned in the annals. In the sixth or seventh century these more advanced people had come from the north into this fertile highland valley. They were the great builders who erected the massive Pyramid of the Sun at Teotihuacán and the temple to Quetzalcoatl at Cholula, which is over a thousand feet square at its base and more extensive than any pyramid in Egypt. To the Toltecs is attributed the Golden Age in pre-historic Mexico.

As the ancient people of Mexico had changed from a nomadic to a sedentary folk they had domesticated the abundant wild fodder grass, which became known as maize or Indian corn. On this corn they formed their culture. When the Toltecs settled down, they molded clay into pottery, took up weaving and metal work. With the years their endeavors revealed some artistic shape. They made sound laws and created just administration and enjoyed long periods of peace and plenty. Religion was a dominant feature of their culture.

It was the Toltecs who took the legendary Quetzalcoatl for their special patron and transformed him into a god. Like the Christ child, this Quetzalcoatl was purported to have been born of a virgin, though some claimed that he rose miraculously full grown out of a volcano flame, as Aphrodite did from sea foam. When he appeared as a human being among the ancient Toltecs his skin was not Indian-dark but fair, and he wore a beard, which was extraordinary among men whom nature had made beardless. His name meant "feathered serpent," derived from the brilliant *quetzal* bird and *coatl,* serpent. All good seemed to emanate from his intelligence and magnanimity. This god-like being banned human sacrifices and substituted reptiles and butterflies on the ceremonial altars. He invented a calendar and taught the people the art of picture writing. It was he who instructed them in weaving cotton, in firing pottery from clay, in shaping stone and fusing metal. He showed them how to improve the yield and quality of cultivated commodities. Corn grew so large that a man could hardly make his hands touch in an embrace about a single ear. One yellow squash would fill a small boat. Cotton grew in the fields already dyed in the luminous pastel shades of the rainbow.

Quetzalcoatl, the physically handsome and tall, stirred his people like the wizened Mahatma Gandhi of contemporary India. He, too, frowned upon acquisition by attack and violence and tried to create a kingdom of happiness out of simple things. As the human Gandhi represents the innermost desires of a vast body of India, so the superhuman Quetzalcoatl embodied the secret longings of the Toltec masses for peace, brotherly love, and abundance.

Then, according to the legend, some jealous god in the high heaven, looking down upon this paradise on earth, determined to ruin this demigod who had produced out of earthly materials such an ideal state of consciousness. They beguiled their victim to drink the intoxicating draught called *pulque* fermented from the juice of the ubiquitous maguey plant. They told him it would preserve his pristine youth and health. The draught made him drunk. He in turn made his sister drink to intoxication and took her to bed with him. The next morning his self-shame was so great that he felt unworthy to remain as the ruler. He burned his palace built of silver and sea shells, and, preceded by singing birds and flute players, he departed in voluntary banishment. In his odyssey he took up his abode in Cholula and remained as the ruler for twenty years. Then he journeyed on to visit the Mayas in Yucatán, where he directed the building of their templed cities. The Mayas knew him as Kukulcan—"feathered serpent" in their tongue—and he became the most revered of their gods and heroes.

At the end of his Ulysses-like wanderings, Quetzalcoatl made himself a boat of snake-skins and sailed off towards the rising sun. The legend ran that the white god promised to return to his people, when extraordinary need for him arose in the future. His cult spread to the far corners of Mexico, and he was worshiped as the god of life and as the morning star. Though the origin of the Quetzalcoatl myth is generally attributed to the Toltecs, the worship of the deific serpent who could fly was prevalent among the Indian people thousands of miles apart. In the symbol of earth, the serpent, and in the symbol of sky, the wings, was combined and unified the life force. The individual achievements in science claimed for Quetzalcoatl were symbolical; for the invention of a calendar and the discoveries of various principles of agriculture were the fruits of many men's work over a stretch of years.

After Quetzalcoatl's disappearance, the Toltecs continued to flourish for three or four centuries. Then they are supposed to have fought some unsuccessful defensive wars and to have been decimated by famine and plague. In his *Historia Chichimeca*, Ixtilxochitl, the Indian writer descended from the ruling house of Texcoco, attributes the downfall of the Toltecs to "rebellions, crop failures, and religious contentions." Before the end of the twelfth century the Toltecs' day was done. As a people they were dispersed. But they left behind them embers of a culture the Aztecs were later to stir up and use to their own glory.

After an interim of about a century tribes known as the Chichimecas moved into the Valley of Anáhuac. They were a crude, prolific people from the north who circulated about the region for about a century, apparently preferring nomadic to sedentary existence. At last came seven tribes who spoke the Nahuatl tongue. They often fought among themselves, until those who had settled at Texcoco became recognized as supreme, losing their prime importance only for a brief period early in the fifteenth century, then regaining it and retaining their high position until 1472.

The last of the seven tribes to arrive were those sometimes called today the Mexico City Aztecs. They were the lowest in estate and the weakest; but as the puniest petunia seedlings grow into the strongest plants when mature, so did these Aztecs. In the famous year of 1325 they set up their "frail tenements" of reeds and mud in piles on marshy islands in Lake Texcoco, where they got a haphazard living by fishing. A century passed during which the Aztecs were considered of smallest consequence. But houses and progeny multiplied. And by 1440 the Aztecs had formed a mutual assistance league with the neighboring cities of Texcoco and Tlacopán. This alliance gradually brought them stretches of conquered territory and made them masters of other peoples. The taste of organized battle developed a martial appetite. War had two special objectives: a ceremonial one, to bring back victims for the sacrifices; and a practical one, to gather tribute. By one of those unaccountable turns of fortune, the Aztecs were blessed with a series of chiefs who were as shrewd and able in civic organization as they were in military tactics. The rulers who brought their people with such extraordinary celerity to glory and masterdom were in succession: Itzcoatl, Montezuma I, Axayácatl, Tizoc, Ahuitzotl, and the most famous of them all, the unfortunate Montezuma II.

The great dynasty of the Mexico City Aztecs belongs to one family. The founder was Acamapichtli, reputedly a Toltec whom the tribesmen chose for their chief in 1375. (For the first fifty years after their settlement in the Anáhuac Valley, they were governed by a council.) The Aztecs wisely adopted a process for the succession of their leaders which was something like an elective monarchy, a policy which the ancient Scandinavians pursued. The chieftainship did not necessarily go in the line of primogeniture; but from among the members of the leading family the succeeding ruler was selected, sometimes a brother, sometimes a nephew of the chief. Acamapichtli was followed in turn by three of his sons. The last and by far the most important was Itzcoatl, his son by a slave mother. Itzcoatl became the head of the tribe in 1427, and though there is confusion in the annals before this date, the records are comparatively clear afterwards.

Itzcoatl built new temples, extended the town, and constructed causeways to the mainland. He ruled for thirteen crowded years and won many battles. Then in 1440 came Montezuma I. He was even more remarkable as a fighter, and he conquered towns in far-off territory in what are now the states of Vera Cruz and

Guerrero. He built the great aqueduct to bring sweet water from the springs of Chapultepec down to Tenochtitlán.

In 1469, after a long reign of twenty-nine years, Montezuma I was succeeded by his grandson Axayacatl, who went conquesting as far south as the Tehuantepec Isthmus. The famous Calendar Stone, twelve feet in diameter and weighing forty thousand pounds, was quarried and carved under Axayacatl. Three years after he acceded to the chieftainship his foremost Indian contemporary and the greatest of all Indians, Nezahualcóyotl, ruler of Texcoco, died. From 1472 the supremacy of the Aztecs of Tenochtitlán was indisputable.

Axayácatl's rule of a decade ended in 1479 and he was succeeded by his brother Tizoc. This chieftain's brief reign is most significant for the reconstruction of the Temple of Huitzilopochtli, which was completed under his brother Ahuitzotl. For the first two years of his administration the latter's prime function seems to have been in collecting prisoners of war for the gala dedication of the temple, which took place in 1487. At the ceremony, in the most awesome and horrible religious spectacle ever recorded in history, the palpitating hearts of twenty thousand victims were ripped out on the sacrificial stones. Of all the Aztec chiefs, this Ahuitzotl was perhaps the fiercest fighter. Though he had an insatiable appetite for warfare, he was also a great builder. The city spread enormously in his reign, which lasted until 1503—exactly a century before the death of Elizabeth of England.

Montezuma II, son of Axayacatl, succeeded his fierce and energetic uncle. He had been "king" for sixteen years when Hernán Cortés first set foot on Mexican soil. Strictly speaking, the Indians had no kings. The Aztecs used the term *tlatoani* to signify chief lord or overlord. (The word *cacique* is a West Indian word for chief, brought into Mexico from Hispaniola by way of Cuba.) But because the early Spaniards spoke of Montezuma as "emperor," he is generally so entitled in history. He was really a great chief rather than a king, though his person came to be considered sacrosanct and his government was virtually an absolute monarchy. He was the overlord of an extensive hegemony, not an empire.

Like the Romans the Aztecs went conquesting not only for sacrificial victims but to despoil other tribes of their most valuable possessions to advance their own standards of living. As with the Romans, military prowess became the principal objective in Aztec civilization, rather than the flowering of architecture and art as pursued by the more Grecian Mayas. Though the Aztecs were the militant business men of the time, they were able to absorb culture as well as possessions and domains. And just as the imitative Japanese formed their culture from that of the imaginative Chinese, so the Aztecs assumed the remnants of Toltec civilization and took on attributes of superiority they found among any conquered peoples. The Aztec energy and strength attracted many to their vassalage without even trial.

During the earlier years of the triple alliance, the Texcocans across the lake were considerably more important than the Aztecs of Tenochtitlán. Their influence reached its zenith in the fifteenth century under that great ruler Nezahualcoyotl, who is more honored in the chronicles than any Indian except Cuauhtémoc. Born in Texcoco about the year the poet Chaucer was dying in London (1400), he lived until 1472. His actual rule lasted some four decades, the early part of it as full of vicissitudes and turns of fortune as was Alfred's of England. Making use of the best that lingered on from the Toltec culture, this king created temples and great houses of stone, and gardens and steam baths, and he assiduously cultivated learning. In his own domain he was as famous as Solomon for his wisdom and for his sixty sons and fifty daughters by wives and concubines. He was such a wise lawmaker that his code was adopted by neighboring principalities. (Eighty of his laws exist in manuscript.) He made death the penalty for stealing produce in the open fields; but to avoid too severe an infliction of the law, he commanded that fields should be sown at the sides of the highways with foodstuffs for the distressed. To prevent bribery he ordered that the judges should be maintained and clothed according to their rank at government expense. He abolished human sacrifices; but later, "out of respect for the ancient religious system" and because of the clamoring of the populace, he was obliged to permit their re-establishment.

Besides being an able administrator and a statesman, like the Hebrew sage he was a poet of distinction. Through his verses run the recurrent theme of mutability, the impermanence of all worldly things. There is something of the fatalistic note of the Anglo-Saxon lyrists in his poetry. Dying just twenty years before Columbus discovered the New World and half a century before Cortés destroyed Tenochtitlán, Nezahualcoyotl seemed to sense the breaking of the power of the Indian alliance and the dissolution of his subjects.

In many lyrics like the following he reminded his people to be philosophical.

> And all the desires of this world,
> The riches and the dictates are but a loan,
> They are the stuff of make-believe,
> Shaded with rose-color.
> This is so true
> That you must answer me a question:
>
> What has happened to Cihuapán?
> To Quantzintecomtzin the brave?
> To Conahuatzin?
> What has become of these persons,
> Their voices?
> Where have they all gone?
>
> Please the gods, maybe now
> Those who are tied by the thread of love
> Which treasures friendship
> Will see the hard edge of death,
> Because there is nothing certain
> And everything changes with the future.

After observing the departure of many warriors and chiefs, he wrote again and again on the transitory nature of personal entity.

> The things of yesterday are no more today;
> And the things of today shall cease,
> Perhaps on the morrow.
> The cemetery is full of the dust of bodies
> Once quickened by living souls,
> Who occupied high places, presided over assemblies,
> Marshaled armies, subdued provinces,
> Arrogated to themselves worship,
> Were puffed up with vain-glorious pomp and power . . .
>
> But these glories have passed away,
> Like the fearful smoke
> That issues from the throat of Popocatépetl,
> With no other memorial to their existence
> Than the record on the stag skins of the chronicler.

Just before his death Nezahualcóyotl named his youngest son Nezahualpilli his successor, because of his virtues and talents. This son proved a good administrator, although the glory of Texcoco began to dim after the death of his great father. After a reign of forty-four years he died just before the arrival of Cortés and thus escaped the tragedy.

By the decade of Columbus' discovery the thrusting Aztecs had extended their domination to the Atlantic and the Pacific and as far south as the Tehuantepec Isthmus. From the subdued peoples of the hegemony they exacted a heavy tribute of foodstuffs, fruits, cereals, gold, silver, jadite, turquoise, pearls, and jewel-colored bird feathers. And with enforced labor, they built themselves palaces with fountained courts. They built a vast market place with colonnades and pavements of stone. They constructed greater aqueducts and causeways as their population increased. They continued to set up new temples to their various heathen gods. Religious ceremonial played an even larger part in the life of the ancient Mexicans than with their Catholic conquerors. Pagan temples called *teocallis*—"houses of the gods"—dotted the landscape as prodigally as do the Christian churches today. They were built of earth and stone in the form of truncated pyramids and on the flat areas of the tops were the altars and the sacrificial stones.

The Aztecs, like all the ancient inhabitants of Mexico—the Toltecs, Totonacs, Tarascans, Mayas, and the Zapotecs—were polytheistic. They deified natural elements: the sun, the moon, the wind, the rain. Their pyramids for worship were "pedestals on which to get into closer communication with the gods." Mankind and the numerous deities were interdependent. Without the godly beneficence mankind could not survive. But, on the other hand, the gods had to be fed by man, and their spiritual puissance was dependent on a diet of blood from human hearts. This monstrous belief led to their shocking living sacrifices. The sacrificial stone at the top of their pyramids was the focal point of their complex culture.

According to Sahagún, within the civic center of Tenochtitlán (where the Zócalo now is, but far more extensive in area), the temple enclosure possessed twenty-five temple pyramids, five oratories, fasting houses, sacrificial and penitential stones, seven skull racks, two ball courts, a well, three bathing places, a dancing court, nine houses for priests, a prison for the captive gods of conquered nations, and vast open spaces for the worshiping multitudes. On the summit of the great pyramid were temples to Huitzilopochtli and Tlaloc. Huitzilopochtli or Mextli, the god of war, was the chief deity of the Aztecs and dreadfully feared. The most popular god was Tlaloc, god of rain, who had authority also over clouds, mountain springs, and hail. Without his pleasure no agricultural crops could grow.

On the whole, the Aztec gods were a harsh and hideous lot, ever demanding their glut of blood, and reflecting the aggressive spirit of the people. Yet there were some sympathetic deities too, like the goddess of the cradle. Sometimes the Aztecs conceived poetic origins for their gods. One had descended from heaven by a ladder fashioned of spider webs. Another had been immaculately conceived when a woman picked up a little ball of feathers and tucked it in her bosom. The females of the hierarchy were not so deadly as the males. The wife of the ferocious Huitzilopochtli was believed to lead the souls of warriors who died on the battlefield directly to the House of the Sun, where she transformed them into hummingbirds.

From the beginning, the Aztec culture was a paradox in which complex social adjustments were interwoven with the barbaric practice of human sacrifices and the ritualistic feasting on human flesh. According to the present-day Mexican historian José Valades it was entering its decadence when Montezuma II ascended the throne at the beginning of the century. Within the briefest span, as history goes, the Aztec nation had reached the highest peak of culture in the hemisphere. Its incredibly sudden toppling was even more remarkable than its meteoric rise.

By one of those extraordinary historical coincidences, Hernán Cortés and his band of adventurers arrived in Mexico shortly after ominous portents had mystified the Aztec soothsayers and at the very time the seers had prophesied the return of Quetzalcoatl. Many Indians, sick of blood baths and dissensions, seized upon the report of palefaced men arriving from the east as if it were the god Quetzalcoatl returned to redeem his people. But the redeemer the natives welcomed turned out to be their destroyer. This first great irony in the Indians' traffic with white men was destined to have stalking behind it a whole battalion of other ironies.

# PART ONE

# THE CONQUEST

## 1. Beyond Audacity

*"I stood looking at it and thought never in the world would there be discovered other lands such as these."*

BERNAL DÍAZ

Though he was born with a lucky caul, like both the conquering Alexander and Caesar, and destined by his horoscope to vault to fame, Fate played capriciously with the youthful Hernán Cortés and almost cheated him out of his great adventure. Just before his scheduled departure for the New World with Columbus's successor, Don Nicolás de Ovando, the seventeen-year-old Hernán went to pay a nocturnal visit to a sweetheart. As he ascended a high wall to her upper window, by a ladder of plaited silk, the wall gave way, and Cortés plunged down two stories amid crumbling stone and mortar. If the young lover had broken his neck instead of some ribs, the chronicles of Mexico would have recorded a different tale, and the seed of Montezuma would have died out at a later date and under other circumstances.

As it was, Hernán Cortés was too badly injured by the fall to make the planned journey, but two years later he again essayed the western voyage with Alonso Quintero. This time Fate smiled on the ardent youth and sent him a sign he took to be from heaven. When his vessel was tossed by a violent tempest and given up for lost by the mariners, out of the sky fluttered a white dove, which perched like a symbol of hope on the mast. Then, preceding the ship, as if harbinger and guide, it winged its way to the island of Hispaniola. Cortés, ever as quick at snatching at signs as occasions, chose to look upon the dove as a favor from the Holy Ghost. So throughout his fabulous career he presumed to link himself with the silent partnership of Deity and to make use of the overt aid of the Most Holy Catholic Church.

This young man, who was to personify magnificently the age in which he lived, was born in the province of Estremadura, in 1485. His native town of Medellín lay thirty-odd miles to the north of Trujillo, the birthplace of Pizarro, conqueror of Peru, and sixty miles from the birthplace of Balboa, discoverer of the Pacific. It might seem as if some strange tonic wind had blown across the brown-sedge moors of Estremadura to fire with ambition this famous trinity of contemporary sons of Spain. As infant and child Hernán Cortés was frail, so his wet nurse selected for his patron the strongest of the saints, Peter. This proved a good choice, for by adolescence Cortés had developed into a supple youth, well formed, deep-chested. Though quick to learn what he thought significant, he was negligent in study and spent his chief hours out-of-doors improving his physique. When he had gleaned the best of what St. Peter could give him, he took the Virgin Mary as his special protector and adviser. Again and again in life it proved to be women who saved him in perilous situations. He stirred in them a passionate loyalty that transcended the masterful admiration he inspired in men.

In Hispaniola his letters of recommendation to his kinsman, the governor, provided him with a plantation and an allotment of Indian slaves, but the nineteen-year-old's contempt for this bounty is preserved to posterity in his first recorded words spoken in the brave new world. "I came," he said, "to gain gold with sword and shield, not to follow a plow like a peasant." Yet, biding his time, he did pursue agriculture for a space of years. He even made a success of growing sugar-cane and he introduced and bred Andalusian cattle. Later he went to Cuba with Diego Velásquez and got some much-desired practice in warfare by fighting the Indians. And because of his courage and his facile ability to make himself ingratiating, Cortés was made private secretary to Velásquez when the latter finally set up his office as governor of Cuba.

It was difficult, however, for the vital, sharp-witted Cortés to keep his talents long in subservience to his mentally inferior superiors. An open break came when he refused to take in marriage a distant relative of the governor's—the youngest of three sisters whom Velásquez had brought over from Spain as wards, and whom rumor said he had despoiled along with the other two. Dismissed in disfavor, Cortés soon became the nucleus of many malcontents. Fearing his persuasive opposition, the governor threw him into prison. Only the pleas of the frail girl whom he had scorned as wife saved the neck of Cortés from being broken by a rope. Thrice he wriggled out of manacles and escaped prison bars and thrice his audacity led to his recapture. After his third escape he lived for months in the sanctuary of a church. During his long self-incarceration, friends brought him continual gossip as well as food. And then one momentous day an old man came with marvelous tales of a land called Mexico. A piratical expedition under the command of Grijalva, the governor's nephew, had returned, bringing a small quantity of gold. The governor was seeking for a worthy commander to head an expedition to conquer the whole unexplored country.

Fired with excitement, Cortés cried, "I must go to Mexico!" and straightway rushed out of sanctuary to confront the governor who had sworn to hang him. On the hope of getting to Mexico, Cortés promised to marry the governor's kinswoman, defiled or virgin. Velásquez, inwardly applauding the three daring escapes from prison and the consummate impudence of a condemned man rushing unannounced into his apartment, fell, laughing and crying in reconciliation, about the neck of Cortés. And that sultry afternoon Cortés took his siesta on the same couch as his recent mortal enemy. Shortly it was officially announced that Hernán Cortés had been appointed captain-general of an expedition to Mexico.

On the tenth of February, 1519, with a fleet of eleven small ships, Cortés sailed from Cuba on his great adventure. The muster roll listed one hundred and ten mariners and five hundred and fifty-three soldiers, of whom thirty-two were crossbowmen and thirteen arquebusiers. Besides the white men there were some two hundred Indians and a few Indian women menials. The navigation was under the direction of a skilled pilot who had sailed with Columbus on his last expedition and who had been to Yucatán with Grijalva. It seemed in the first months that the mission was directed by divine providence, for even events that promised unhappily turned out to be of special beneficence.

A tropical storm swept the fleet south of its intended course, and Cortés landed on the Isle of Cozumel. While ships were being repaired, a Spaniard who had been captured by the Indians eight years before appeared and dropped to the ground with joy on beholding fellow Christians. Cortés raised him and embraced him with affection, scarcely considering what a treasure he had found. For this man, Jerónimo de Aguilar, was to prove worth many times his weight in gold as an interpreter. Cortés bought him from his *cacique* employer for a handful of trinkets and kept him close by his side, plying him with questions as they sailed along the coast of the mainland.

On Palm Sunday, some days later, there was a noisy battle with hostile natives of what is now Tabasco. The Indians fought fiercely, despite their terror of the cavalry. They had never before seen horses and they thought man and beast were deminatured in one monster. And it appeared to them that these strangers were directly allied with the gods, because they held the instruments of thunder and death-dealing lightnings in their own hands. Bare-skinned men with clubs and sticks affixed with stone blades could not do much against soldiers in armor. When the battle was done, eight hundred Indians lay dead on their own soil. With his sword Cortés cut three notches in a tree trunk and formally took possession of the land in the name of the Spanish king.

After their crushing defeat, the Indians became so submissive that they accepted immediate Christian conversion, whatever they may have understood it to mean. As a further conciliatory gesture, they brought offerings of cotton, foodstuffs, some rude golden ornaments, and twenty Indian slave girls. In this grab-bag assortment was a grand prize—the key that was to unlock the treasure house of Mexico. She was a damsel called Malinche. She knew the Aztec tongue as well as the Mayan, for she had been born along the southeastern border of the so-called empire of Mexico. Her father, who died when she was a small child, had been a rich and powerful chief. Her widowed mother re-married, and in order that Malinche's inheritance might come to the son of the second marriage, she had sold the girl to traders who had resold her to the Tabascan *cacique*. When pre-sented to the Spaniards, she was a virgin of fifteen, uncommonly pretty and of extraordinary natural intelligence. But Cortés, with his mind on sterner matters at the moment, passed her on to one of his lieutenants for a concubine.

In a brief time, however, he learned that her value was beyond rubies in her understanding of both Aztec and Mayan. When Mexicans spoke in Aztec, she would translate to Aguilar in Mayan, and he would interpret to Cortés in Castilian.

It was through this girl, who was baptized Marina, that Cortés was able to converse with the next Indians he met. When the fleet anchored off the shore of what is now Vera Cruz in the evening of Holy Thursday, friendly natives in pirogues put off from the mainland and brought fruit and flowers to the flagship. Through the double interpretation of Marina and Aguilar, Cortés learned that these shores and these people owed allegiance to a great monarch named Montezuma—far beyond the mountains—and they themselves were directly subject to a governor called Teuhtlile. Cortés gave them trifling presents and requested a meeting with their chief.

Delighted with the friendly manners of these natives and the information that there was much gold in Mexico, the commander decided to disembark when dawn came. The day was Good Friday, which fell in that year of 1519 on April twenty-first. The place of first encampment was near the spot where the city of Vera Cruz now sprawls. In a plague of gnats and mosquitoes the soldiers began cutting down small trees and bushes to rear temporary protection from the elements. Amiable natives flocked to see the strangers who had arrived by the great "water-houses." They brought tropical fruits, corn cakes, wild turkeys, and armfuls of flowers.

On Easter morning, the *cacique* Teuhtlile arrived with a train of attendants. Cortés received him like a prince and Teuhtlile listened politely to a celebration of the Mass. Then through the interpreters, diplomatic conversations ensued. The presents Cortés had brought for the emperor were set forth, among them an ornately carved and richly painted armchair. To impress the strangers with the affluence of the Aztecs, Teuhtlile had brought a quantity of fine cotton fabrics, mantles wrought of bird feathers, and a basket of ingenious ornaments of gold. Noting a helmet of one of the soldiers gleaming brazenly in the sun, the chief expressed a desire to send it to Montezuma for examination, since it resembled the headdress their god Quetzalcoatl wore when he departed for the east. In his most charming manner, Cortés presented the helmet and ingratiatingly suggested that it might be returned filled with gold dust, so that he could compare the quality of the metal with that of Spain. "The Spaniards," he explained to Teuhtlile—on whom the wit was lost—

"are troubled with a disease of the heart for which gold is a specific remedy."

This confession rather surprised the chief, for to the Indians gold was the dung of the gods. To the Spaniards it was to prove not heart's ease but veritably "that precious bane that grows in hell."

When Cortés saw some Indians painting on cloth details of Spanish costume and arms and learned that it was a report in picture-writing to be sent to Montezuma, he decided to make a spectacular showing. He ordered horsemen to race on the hard beach, to make their charges rear and plunge, and to brandish their weapons ostentatiously. The cannon were charged with an extra loading of powder to create more noise and flame when fired. When the cannon balls shot above the heads of the crowd and tore out the tops of trees, the Indians were as wonderstruck as terrified. All these phenomena the amazed picture-writers got onto their rolls of cloth and sent by runners to Montezuma. When the reports and paintings were received by the emperor, he was filled with dismay and foreboding. The newcomers, he felt, were omens of disaster. He refused to see them. He only wanted their absence from his country, and asked them to leave at once. To speed the departing guests he sent them fabulous gifts in gold and silver, including a great golden wheel like the sun and an enormous silver disk, large as a cartwheel, representing the moon. No gesture could have been more perfectly calculated to magnetize the Spaniards to Mexico. When the gifts were unwrapped and spread before him, Cortés's resolution was fixed. He would meet the reluctant and sacrosanct monarch face to face. He would capture him and subdue his empire. He sent word graciously requesting an audience.

Cortés had not come to Mexico hungering for gold only. Wealth without renown would never have brought satisfaction to his ambitious heart. He wanted fame and prestige. He was a man, too, who was uplifted by the wonder and mystery of the new and the strange. A sense of danger and odds against him fired him with enthusiasm. A challenge to his wits or his fighting arm stirred his blood more than gifts of golden platters. And he was not to be contented merely with renown in this earthly world. He played, too, for heavenly recognition and honor, and he never failed to make opportunities to propitiate his Catholic God. Sometimes it seems that he looked into the future when his immortal self would be relating to the Majesty of Heaven, before an admiring throng of prominent saints, the details of deeds in Mexico he had done for the glory of God. He ever went about his business bolstered by faith in his own high destiny. In hours of transient doubt, however, he consulted his astrologer and had his horoscope cast and the propitious days predicted.

But, possessing an acute sense of timing, Cortés generally knew when to act and when to wait. Like a stage star to whom that sense of timing—knowing when to speak fast or slow, how long to pause—is a chief requisite for success, he had a dramatic instinct which stood him in good stead in crises. He also had the knack of seasoning his speech with salty jests and homespun wit. Judging by its effect, his smile was one of the most potential weapons in his armory of talents. It could stir to loyalty as could an alarum bell to war. Countless times it completely disarmed his adversaries.

Along with his boundless imagination to conjure up great enterprises, Cortés possessed such a practical sense of reality that men trusted his judgment as well as his vision. His richly gifted nature was blessed with a superb sense of balance. A sensual man, whom women of every class found fascinating, he indulged in amours with zest, but he could abstain with chilled indifference when some business of state was under consideration. He drank wine with gusto, but never did he let drink interfere with important matters. He had the facility of expression not only by word of mouth but by pen, and he could write with as much ardor as logic. This dream-inspired man of action proved himself as skillful in administrative statesmanship and economics as in warfare. Rarely have so much acumen and charm of personality been commingled with so stout a courage.

While Cortés awaited royal permission from Montezuma to visit him in person, the adventurers encamped on the blistering sand dunes began to chafe from inaction. Some came down with tropical fever. In others, tortured by the sweltering heat and the insects, mutinous thoughts began to incubate. Continually radiating cheer, Cortés made two moves calculated to relieve the boredom and to strengthen his own power. He decided to establish a town and thereby change the status of the encampment from a military to a civil community. By doing so, he renounced allegiance to Governor Velásquez and put his forces directly under the protection of the king. Everything was done according to rule and notarized. Cortés was elected captain-general. The position gave him supreme power, as well as one-fifth of all the treasure acquired. A town site to be used as a base for operations was selected near the shore. The name of the projected town was to be La Villa Rica de la Vera Cruz, "The Rich Town of the Holy Cross." Material and religious promise were thus wedded in the name, as symbolic of the motives of the expedition. A ship was dispatched to Spain to report to the king what had been done.

Just as this business was being settled, some visitors from a people called Totonacs arrived. They wore blue stone rings in their ears and noses, and a golden leaf attached to their lower lips. They came with invitation from their chief to visit him at his capital of Cempaolla. Cortés was not unimpressed by the glint of gold in the lip ornaments, but he was deeply excited to learn that the Totonacs loathed the Aztec yoke. He thrilled to hear that there were as much division, hatred, and jealousy among the barbarous infidels as among the Christian nations of Europe. Immediately he divined that out of a thirsting for revenge against Montezuma's tyranny he might create a net of confederacy that could catch them all, foe and friend alike. First he would unite the weak against the strong, act as their champion, and lead Indian against Indian.

With high heart, he set off northwest to Cempaolla, to win his first ally. The troops revived in leaving the burning coastal sands to traverse a shadowy jungle masked with beauty. The forest was draped with orchids and luminous blue morning glories. Heavy-scented honeysuckle rioted with wild roses in the thickets. Tropical birds outdid the luxuriant vegetation with the brilliance of their plumage and the virtuosity of their song. "It is as wonderful as paradise," toughened soldiers said to each other.

As they approached the city itself, a curious populace came out to welcome them with bouquets and wreaths. They hung garlands about the horses' necks and a wreath on Cortés's helmet. The Spaniards were surprised at this passion for flowers in the savage heart. (After centuries it is still a trait in the Indians that neither oppression nor civilizing time has diminished.) Cortés and his men remarked that the houses had palm-thatched roofs above walls of stone or stucco, and made note of native architectural principles for the town they were to set up in the forthcoming weeks.

The fat *cacique* received the white men with cordiality, and began to relate his tribulations under the vassalage to Montezuma. Enemy states on the fringes longed for the downfall of their powerful Aztec neighbor, he told Cortés. Too long their youths and maidens had been snatched from them for living sacrifices to insatiable Aztec gods. They lived in continual fear of raid and rape. The oppressed tribes welcomed a strange ally as a gift, legitimate or illegitimate, from heaven. The *cacique's* story was sweeter music to the ears of Cortés than a garden of nightingales.

In the midst of the conferences, Montezuma's tax collectors arrived with their train. Holding roses to their refined nostrils, they gave cold and supercilious looks to the white men, and arrogantly demanded twenty youths for human sacrifice as part of their tribute, because of Montezuma's displeasure with the Totonacs for entertaining the strangers. (In his capital on the high plateau beyond the mountains, the monarch knew everything through fleet messengers who furnished him with news from every corner of his domain. These political runners were even swifter than those who ran daily with fresh seafood from the ocean for the royal tables.)

The perturbed Totonac chief would have given up the twenty for the sacrifice, but Cortés peremptorily ordered him to seize the proud tax collectors and bind them. Astounded at such daring against the majesty of Montezuma, the chief obeyed with fear and trembling. Cortés set his own guard over the tax collectors, but in the night he arranged their escape, and sent them back to their lord with protestations of friendship. By this clever duplicity, Cortés began that artful dissembling in which he was super-adept when occasion demanded. Now with the imminent wrath of Montezuma threatening direst revenge, the Totonacs' only recourse was to make active alliance with the Spaniards. Indian had become the accomplice of the white man against his brother Indian. In this bond the doom of the dark-skinned race was sealed.

Having dared so far, the Spaniards dared farther. As they witnessed human sacrifices in which the beating heart was torn from the split breast of the victim, the hard-boiled soldiers were so revolted that fifty of them rushed up the temple steps at Cempaolla and stopped the ceremony. They toppled over the hideous stone idols and rolled them to the ground. The people looked on in dumb horror when they saw that their gods could not protect themselves from profanation. Yet when Cortés set the image of the Virgin on the bloodstained altar, they brought armfuls of flowers until the Lady was almost submerged in blossoms. Mass was celebrated, and the savages were considered converted. But as the wise and good priest, Father Olmedo, remarked wistfully to Cortés, "Of what use is it to overturn the altar, if the idol remains enthroned in the heart?"

After preparations for the allied march to Tenochtitlán were discussed, the Spaniards began the hasty construction of the town to be known as Vera Cruz. The Totonacs helped enthusiastically in the construction. Many of the Spanish soldiers lost their restlessness in the activities, but there were some who had little faith in this grandiose conception of a handful conquering a million in an unknown terrain beyond the mountain rim. These wavering ones conspired to steal part of the fleet and return to Cuba.

When Cortés learned of the conspiracy, he determined to burn his bridges behind him. Under pretext that five of the ships were unseaworthy and a liability, he had the movable gear and fixtures, the instruments and the iron brought on shore. Then the ships were scuttled. The soldiers took the action in good faith. But when Cortés proceeded to have four of the remaining five ships condemned and destroyed, there rose a threatening fury of protest.

Cortés tamed his companions by his honeyed eloquence, and offered to let the faint-hearted among them renounce the glorious adventure just ahead and return like cravens to Cuba to report that they had deserted their commander in his hour of greatest need. He fired them with admiration for his audacity and courage. As one said, what he had done was worthy of a hero of mythology. Intoxicated by their leader's invincible optimism, the men began to shout "To Mexico!" and forgot the dangers and hardships they were to face.

On the nineteenth of August, in 1519, the little band of warriors began its heroic march to fame. In their troop they had thirty Totonac nobles as guides and hostages, and two hundred porters. Marina went along like a lady of great estate, because she had now become the captain-general's beloved bedfellow as well as his invaluable interpreter.

Had Cortés not convinced himself that he had heaven's blessing on his enterprise, his march against Mexico would have seemed the great impudence of all times. With four hundred Spaniards, fifteen horses, and artillery pieces that could be counted on the eight fingers of two hands, he started up a wall of mountain to conquer an empire vaster than Spain.

## 2. Garden of Gardens

*"When I beheld the scenes that were around me, I thought within myself that this was the garden of the world."*

BERNAL DÍAZ

The troop went by way of the Tlascalan country, for the Tlascalans were a people who had stubbornly maintained their independence from Montezuma. But the Tlascalans were not inclined to be friendly. They looked upon the white intruders with as much suspicion as Montezuma did, though without his foreboding and superstition. Their territory was defended by a nine-foot stone wall between mountain and mountain. Behind it they lay in wait for the strangers. The gate Cortés's men approached was left unguarded purposely, as a trap. The Tlascalans hoped to take the white men alive as a rare sacrificial treat for their gods. After the weary soldiers were all inside the boundaries the Tlascalans set upon them with howls of zest. They fought sportively and then furiously, for the Spaniards with their firearms and horses proved a hundredfold more formidable than any other foe the brave Tlascalans had ever faced. Battles were lost and then renewed. The carnage was frightful. Finally, after several fierce days of combat, the Tlascalans realized they were thoroughly whipped. They took counsel, and decided that with their combined strengths the white men and they might rout the mighty Montezuma. Anticipating both the sport and the profit, they offered to be confederates with Cortés.

While resting in the capital of Tlascala from the vicissitudes of the march and the fighting, the Spaniards received emissaries from Montezuma. The monarch knew everything that had occurred. When he had learned that the white men were coming by way of Tlascala he had rejoiced, for he felt sure that way meant death to the strangers. But now that they had defeated a people Montezuma himself had not been able to subjugate, he was deeply troubled. He began to believe these strange men from the east might really be descendants of Quetzalcoatl. Five of his nobles brought to Cortés three thousand ounces of gold ore and other presents, along with congratulations on his success. But they urged him to proceed no farther, because Montezuma's subjects were unruly and might do great harm to the white men. When Cortés proved adamant in his determination to behold Tenochtitlán, Montezuma offered annual tribute to the king of Spain and large bribes to Cortés and his captains, if they would stay away from his capital.

Many of the most loyal among Cortés's men, as well as the grousing malcontents, were all for accepting the tribute and returning to the coast. Even the stoutest heart among them could not foresee how they could reach Tenochtitlán. But Cortés, so ill with fever now that he could scarcely sit straight on his horse, went about spreading cheer and courage, ever holding out the golden promise just ahead. He refused to listen to any suggestions of halting in his purpose. He sent word to Montezuma he was coming.

Now changing his tactics, Montezuma pretended to be willing to receive him, but told him to come by way of Cholula, where preparations had been ordered for his entertainment. But the emperor begged Cortés not to enter into an alliance with the untrustworthy Tlascalans. The latter warned Cortés not to trust in Montezuma's fair words or his gifts. They urged him not to go by way of Cholula. They said the people of that place, though not valorous, were exceedingly tricky. The Spaniards learned that a large armed force of Aztecs was unaccountably encamped not far from Cholula. But Cortés, not wanting to reveal the slightest apprehension, declared he would go by

Cholula. The town lay twenty miles south of Tlascala, and the city of Mexico was some seventy miles to the northwest.

Cortés selected six thousand from the volunteer Tlascalan warriors to accompany him on his march to Mexico. Beyond the rugged Tlascalan country, where the people were inured to scanty living, Cortés's band came upon irrigated plantations of maize, aloe, chili, and maguey. They encamped in the woods for the night. The next morning, leaving the new allies outside, Cortés and his Christian army entered the city between silent rows of wondering citizens, who threw flowers in their path. The soldiers were so amazed by the reception that they lost count of the three or four hundred towers gleaming in the sunlight.

But they learned that Cholula, the great commercial center of the Puebla plateau, was the city sacred to Quetzalcoatl. Here the legendary god had lived for twenty years, giving sweetness and light to the citizens. Besides the refinements of civilization, he had taught them that sacrifices should be of fruits and flowers and not of human flesh, even of their worst enemies. The colossal truncated pyramid erected in his honor was the focal point for pilgrims who came to worship at his temple.

The Christians were quartered in the courts and buildings of one of the greater temples. At first the atmosphere was all cordiality. Then, with the arrival and conference of messengers from Montezuma, it perceptibly cooled. Cortés's suspicions were aroused by both a furtiveness in action and a niggardliness in provisions. His Cempaollan porters reported preparations for treachery and ambush. Marina discovered the conspiracy from the wife of a *cacique* whom Montezuma had bribed, among others. The woman had taken a fancy to Marina and sought to spare her from the planned massacre of the Christians as they passed out of the city. Marina, having learned the art of dissembling from her lord, feigned secret hatred for the Spaniards, got the details of the whole plot, and relayed everything to Cortés.

The two thousand Cholulan porters who were to escort the Spaniards to the Aztec capital were to be secretly armed and to set upon the Spaniards just outside the city. The twenty thousand Aztecs encamped nearby were to rush in on the kill. Cortés made a quick and bloody decision. He would trap the intended Cholulan murderers.

On the morning set for departure, Cortés drew up his forces around the walls of the court and set his guns at the entrances so that no one from the city could get into the enclosure. When the *caciques* and the troop of two thousand porters arrived and were all within the gates, Cortés accused the Cholulans of the most hideous perfidy. Amazed at such prescience, the Cholulans confessed and laid the blame on Montezuma. But Cortés declared such double-dealing should be punished as a warning to other tribes. At a signal shot from an arquebus the massacre of the bare-breasted Indians began. By musket, pike, and sword they were mangled and torn, until there was no life left in any of them. The townspeople trying to get into the temple to rescue their fellows were met by slaughtering blasts from the cannon and then thrown into confusion by the charging cavalry. The Tlascalan allies, their brows bound with sedge grass for identification, rushed to attack the Cholulans from the rear.

Soon the wooden structures of the town were afire, and the flames added to the havoc of battle. At last, in response to pleas of Montezuma's ministers, Cortés called a halt to the carnage. He contented the vengeful Tlascalans with the spoils of richer clothing and provisions than they had ever known. The crushed Cholulans, submissive now, returned to their homes and began to clean up the city under Cortés's direction. When order and a semblance of the wonted way of civil life were restored, Cortés took up the march to Mexico.

The way lay spectacularly between two volcanoes crowned with a perpetual glory of snow—Popocatépetl and Ixtaccíhuatl.

The conquerors wound their way along the gorges in a terrain wildly picturesque but painful to traverse. Then they climbed laboriously into the rarefied atmosphere that made their hearts pound menacingly and their heads turn giddy with lightness. At last, panting with exertion, they reached a crest and stood dumb before the spell-binding panorama.

Shimmering in the light of afternoon lay the enchanting valley of Anáhuac—white cities, brown hamlets, and five great silvery lakes surrounded by natural opulence and tilled fertility. Beyond the towers and temples rose the mass of Chapultepec with its groves of gigantic cypress trees, hazy against a backdrop of blue porphyry hills and a luminous, azure sky.

Enraptured by the beauty, the warriors gazed as if they had been transported to the boundaries of some mythical realm. But as the first spell of enchantment subsided and dusk began to rub out the vision, the men drew together with a new fear. They distrusted the evidences of a superior civilization. They began to mutter that they would not proceed into the alluring maw of the Aztec nation. They urged return to the security of Tlascala, where they might gather fresh Indian allies or await reinforcement of European troops.

Cortés, who had nipped mutinies in the bud before with his dauntless faith, now employed the witchery of his eloquence to stir the imagination of his men. This City of Mace-Reeds that lay before them was an El Dorado other men reached only in their most extravagant dreams. They would all dare together to share in the glory. His enthusiasm rallied the faltering like the strains of martial music.

While Cortés was sleepless because he ached so to possess the riches of the valley, Montezuma was sulking in the splendor of his palace like Achilles in his tent. He had come to trust none of his courtiers and to take no joy in anything except music, which his faithful, aged music master arranged for his delectation. In his presentiment of doom, Montezuma called on all his dabblers in the occult arts, but from them he received no real cheer. The ghost of a god returned to tell him that all the other gods had abandoned him and that his glorious city would shortly be an ash heap. Calling his nobles into assembly, the emperor urged them to confront bravely the destruction that seemed destined. Then he commanded that the warriors' lances, shields, and arrows be made bright and ready.

Making their easier way now through beauty and abundance, the Spaniards stopped from time to time to receive delegations from towns and settlements, who brought them propitiating gifts. All the Indians had learned of the Spanish appetite for gold. As Cortés accepted the gifts with his most responsive smile, he listened sympathetically to complaints of Montezuma's tyranny.

At length the Spanish adventurers reached the town of Iztapalapán on the edge of the salt lagoon. It was the last large town before Montezuma's capital. Here they were ceremoniously received by Cuitláhuac, the emperor's brother, who presented golden and feathered gifts, and slave girls for their diversion. They were housed royally in a palace with a roof of scented cedar and inner walls hung with feather-work tapestry. They wandered in gardens under centuries-old cypress trees festooned with wild orchids, where silver pheasants and gilded butterflies flashed through the dappling sunlight. Again the Spaniards marveled at the Indians' love of flowers. They admired the aviaries and the vast fish basins. But their thoughts were on the morrow. Tenochtitlán was only a few miles away. Its towers and pyramids glimmered in the setting sun and were reflected in the lake's blue mirror.

On the morning of November eighth Cortés and his soldiers awoke to greet an adventure such as few mortals ever experience. They were the first Europeans to march into the fabulous Aztec capital. They were less than four hundred in number. As they left the North Gate of Iztapalapán the little band of white men seemed so small to face the throngs of dark ones that Cortés sent lieutenants back to see if any stragglers had remained behind.

The approach to the south entry of Tenochtitlán was a two-mile stone dam. Over this causeway the Spaniards made their way between walls of gaping spectators who had never before looked on white faces. The shallow lake waters along the edges were matted, as thick as water hyacinths, with canoes loaded with the curious.

From the suburb of Coyoacán another stone dam to Tenoch-titlán joined the dam from Iztapalapán and became a single causeway with cuts spanned by wooden bridges. The Spaniards did not fail to remark and applaud the geometry and engineering of the construction.

The preternatural excitement of the Spaniards' march through this maze of half-dream, half-reality did not entirely numb them to the perils of retreat. "Now we are in the mousetrap," murmured one of the horsemen to his companion, as they left the first wooden bridge behind them. But at the fortress of Xoloc the Spaniards were halted and treated with a welcome such as Caesar never saw. In a smoky atmosphere of incense that misted the golden morning, to the piping of flutes and the hypnotic pounding of drums, Mexican nobles, waving fans and little flags, came to announce the approach of the emperor himself. Four thousand of them passed, their bodies naked except for their blood-red or goose-white loin cloths and their mantles of bird-feather embroidery.

The armored Cortés rode out ahead of his chief officers to greet Montezuma. But the Christian possessed nothing remark-able with which to compete with the pagan splendor of the Indians except his sleek black horse. The emperor had never before seen a horse. Yet though he marveled inwardly, his face remained as impassive as a copper mask.

In litters of flower-embossed gold, canopied with feathers and sprinkled with jewels, Montezuma and two kinsmen kings were borne by nobles of the highest caste, who walked barefoot. When the emperor descended from his chair a cotton carpet was rolled out before his privileged feet. He advanced with his elbows resting in the palms of a nephew and a brother, the kings of Texcoco and Iztapalapán. The populace knelt and touched the paving stones with their heads. Cortés leaped from his horse and came forward. Shrewdly he began to measure his adversary, by his features, his attitude, his fantastic costume of bejeweled cotton cloth and feathers. Smiling with dignity the while, he carefully noted details. The emperor's mantle and sandals were embroidered in pearls and emeralds. On his head he wore a diadem of green plumes that floated down his back. He was paler than the other Indians and taller. Though slender, he was well knit. The expression of his regular-featured face was grave, and Cortés was surprised to note a certain benignity.

Making a profound bow, the Spanish commander stepped forward to embrace the monarch in the European manner. Swift as a released bow-string, two Aztec lords thrust themselves before their master to prevent contact. Cortés bit his lip at the rebuff; he did not know that to touch the divine personage was an offense calling for death. Then the lords moved aside, and the two great leaders smiled at each other politely, their eyes searching for the key to each other's nature.

Montezuma, seeing that the stranger was offended, hastened to make amends. Summoning one of his retinue, he took some orchids and presented the blossoms to Cortés. With as much cavalier éclat as if he had been offering a string of matched pearls, the Spanish leader presented the emperor with a necklace of sparkling glass beads. In return for the imitation jewelry, the emperor hung about him two heavy chains of pure gold skillfully fashioned as a linked procession of sea crabs.

It was an exchange symbolical of the majority of trades to ensue between Spaniards and Indians for centuries. Out of the mines of Mexico were to be extracted the precious metals to enrich Spain. On the return trips, the treasure vessels brought cargoes of tinsel and shoddy for the natives.

# 3. Entertaining the White God's Children

*"You should not let into your house a man
who may push you out of it."*

CUITLÁHUAC, CACIQUE OF IZTAPALAPÁN

After the withdrawal of Montezuma, Cortés and his force were escorted down the broad central avenue lined by the houses of the upper classes. They were built of reddish stone topped by parapets and flat roofs on which gardens bloomed. Crossing more wooden suspension bridges over canals, the Spaniards came upon a pyramidal pile that covered two acres and rose to almost a hundred feet. It was the temple of Huitzilopochtli, the Aztec war god, prime in the pagan Olympus. When word passed along the ranks that twenty thousand human victims had been sacrificed at its dedication, involuntary shudders ran through the soldiers. They were to reside in the very shadow of the blood-stained temple. On its western side stood the vast range of one-storied buildings which had been the palace of Axayácatl, father of the emperor. It was commodious enough to house the white men and all their Tlascalan allies.

The guest house Montezuma had presented the strangers was stout as a fortress. Cortés saw that the walls and towers were solid enough to withstand a siege. Within, the furnishings were Spartan. The beds were mats of straw on piled palm leaves. Besides some wooden stools and dyed cotton hangings, there was little else in the way of comfort or elegance. Before he took food Cortés set up his guns strategically and admonished his sentinels to be unusually vigilant.

That afternoon Montezuma paid a formal visit. He asked numerous questions, gave gold ornaments to the captains, and presented a cotton costume for each of the guests. At dusk, to make the Spanish presence more impressive, Cortés ordered a discharge of all the artillery at once. The citizenry were as awed as if the gods had thundered at them in their native tongue.

The next morning the captain-general returned the state visit of the emperor. He was received in an atmosphere dense with incense, but except for the wall tapestries of ingenious feather work, there was little to justify comparison with Oriental magnificence. Cortés explained his mission as one of bringing knowledge of the true faith. He sought Montezuma's conversion. Montezuma listened with respect to Marina's abridged interpretation, as Cortés expounded the theology of the Incarnation and the Atonement. But, protested Montezuma, his gods had been so good to him that he had no desire to renounce them. He admitted, however, his full belief in the story of Quetzalcoatl. The Spaniards might be descendants of the White God. Perhaps they had as much right to the land he ruled as he did. Montezuma had so convinced himself of the fulfillment of the prophecy that he even declared: "I know your sovereign across the water is the rightful lord of this empire. I merely rule in his name. You will share with me in everything." Then he distributed more golden chains among those who had accompanied Cortés on this matutinal visit. The soldiers were much impressed not only with the munificence but with "the gentle breeding and courtesy of the Indian monarch."

Cortés was shrewd enough to take the implied capitulation of Montezuma as part superstition, part courtesy, and part guile. Yet he intended, as far as he was able, to direct the affairs of the land as a power behind the throne. And in this face-to-face interview, Cortés felt convinced that he would conquer the melancholy monarch. Though he beheld this Indian arrayed like Solomon in his glory against a background of the most invincible fighters in the New World, he divined that the man lacked that prime quality Solomon had devoutly prayed for—wisdom.

Cortés soon became absorbed in learning the personal history of the bizarre figure he was to outwit. And through Marina he pieced together the portrait. Montezuma was a complex character of changeable temperament. As a youth he had appeared uncommonly modest. He possessed a kind of subtle, almost feminine charm that went hand-in-hand with awesome daring and ferocity in battle. Yet until he was chosen ruler he disdained all outward honors and rewards. At the time of his election he was serving as high priest in the temple of the war god. This combination of militaristic prowess and ritualistic devotion was admired above everything else by the Aztecs. Like the Emperor of Japan, their ruler became more and more an object of religious adoration.

After he was enthroned, Montezuma straightway set off to subdue a rebellious province, and he returned with a vast string of captives to grace his coronation with their sacrificial blood. In his first years he proved his astuteness in organization and administration. He furthered public works on a large scale, reformed the law courts, founded hospitals.

But shortly he began to display not only a consuming desire for power, but a passion for pomp. He was most careful of his toilet, bathing several times a day, and never putting on the same garment twice. He chose his daily fare from a banquet of fifty dishes. For the luxuries of the court, the people were burdened with staggering taxes. Besides developing a colossal arrogance, Montezuma cultivated a seemingly insatiable lust. By "divine right" he had the choice of all high-born maidens in the land, and he made his selections from among them when they reached proper age. During the first half of his reign, he was rumored to have as many as a hundred and fifty girls big with his offspring at one time. Perhaps it was due to an early sexual surfeit that he became neurotic and the victim of fits of melancholy. With everything his heart could desire in the orbit of his world, he had grown satiated and bored. His courtiers and advisers came to treat him as a brain-sick child who had to be constantly diverted. Yet they continued to pay him as much ceremonious respect as if he had been divine.

Cortés, in analyzing his adversary, comprehended that it was not cowardice that motivated Montezuma, but a compelling sense of fatality. He knew well enough that Montezuma, with his overwhelming numbers, could annihilate the whole Spanish force, or, merely by shutting off provisions, starve them to death. But he felt sure that neither would happen. He believed in his own lucky star, and his sanguinity was prepared to overleap any obstacles. He determined to play the rôle of Quetzalcoatl's descendant for all it was worth. This Aztec superstition was to prove a metaphysical aid as potent as firearms and horses.

With Marina as his voice, Cortés asked innumerable questions when he and his captains were taken on an inspection tour of the city. The Spaniards were mightily impressed with the state of civilization which the so-called savages had achieved. It seemed all the more remarkable to them because the Indians had no iron, no steel, no lead, and no beasts of burden for hauling.

The main part of the capital was laid out with that innate sense of design and form for which the Indians are noted. The main streets were wide and well cared for. Flares lighted them by night. A sanitation squad cleaned the streets thoroughly. There were public toilets and public baths. The Spaniards were more impressed by the great market than by anything else they saw. It was three times as large as the famous one at Salamanca. Here commercial representatives from all the Aztec provinces brought their wares. Like the bazaars of the Arabs, there were various quarters and alcoves assigned to different types of merchandise. The Spaniards remarked gold jewelry intricately designed, fine woven cotton splendidly dyed, hatchets, medicinal herbs, razors and mirrors of obsidian, skins of wild animals, silver receptacles, pottery vases, quilted armor, fresh lake fish, exotic fruits from

the hot coastal swamps as well as local fruits, mantles and cover-
lets of bird-feather embroidery, an infinite variety of green vegetables, dressed turkeys, frothed chocolate sold by the cupful, stone
and timber for building, freshly cooked corn cakes, a profusion
of flowers for pure decoration as well as sale, chained wild beasts,
chained slaves.

Most of the exchange was done by barter, but little cotton
sacks of cacao and goose quills filled with gold dust were used
as currency. Every fifth day was market day. In the clean and
orderly precincts of the market as many as forty thousand citizens
came together at a time. But these warlike people were a peace-
able lot in their own city. The police on guard had little to do,
and a small tribunal set up at one end of the market immediately
settled disputes and dealt summarily with misdemeanants. Cortés
noted the significance of the social aspects of the market, where
men and women who neither bought nor sold haunted the square
to satisfy instincts of gregariousness.

On the whole, the people were well governed. Private property
was recognized and protected. At the same time, other land was
held communally, with certain sections allotted to families for
working, and all sharing in the fruits and benefits. Taxes were
paid not in coin but in produce. The government had its ware-
houses stored with foodstuffs and other commodities, both as
precaution against bad seasons and for commerce with other nations. The old and the indigent were provided with charity hospitals. As much was done for the health and general welfare of
the citizens of Tenochtitlán as in any European city at the beginning of the sixteenth century. In the court there was as much
attention given to protocol and ceremonious language as in the
European courts at the same period.

As Cortés went about during his first week, he noted well
the discipline of the subjects, the general submissiveness to an
absolute authority. This pattern of unquestioned obedience to
superiors he would turn to his own good use. In the meantime,

despite the outward show of friendship from Montezuma, he knew the Spaniards' position was in no way secure. The royal favor might sour at any time. The arrival of messengers from Cholula announcing that there had been trouble between some Aztecs and the Spaniards near Vera Cruz and that nine Spaniards had been killed gave him the occasion he wanted. After pacing the floor all one night in coming to a decision, he boldly resolved to use the news as a pretext for kidnapping Montezuma.

Accompanied by a heavily armed bodyguard, Cortés paid another visit to the monarch. For some time he indulged in an affable conversation until sufficient groups of his warriors by fours or fives had dropped into the palace halls as though out of curiosity. Then he confronted his host with accusations of treachery, claiming that he had been responsible for the death of the Spaniards. Montezuma professed innocence. To prove his good faith, then, Cortés insisted that he must come with him to the Spaniards' headquarters to remain as their guest until the guilty Aztecs were brought to the capital and the investigation concluded.

Montezuma went pale with astonishment at such a monstrous proposal. With all his magnetic persuasion, Cortés tried to convince him that he would not be a prisoner in any sense, but that he would be merely changing his seat of residence. Montezuma protested that his subjects would never endure the degradation.

After two hours of argument, one of the cavaliers, realizing they were all lost now if the attempt failed, vehemently urged seizing the royal person immediately, without more ceremony. Marina pled with Montezuma to come quietly, to prevent any damage to his person, and assured him of the most honorable treatment. Believing that destiny had renounced him, Montezuma wavered and at last gave in. His nobles were dumbfounded when he ordered the royal litter. As a muttering mob gathered along the way, Montezuma assured his people that of his own free will he was going to pay a visit of some days to the white men. But as he was borne through the portals of the Spaniards' quarters, he felt his doom was sealed. Cortés had sprung his great trap.

Montezuma was treated by the Spaniards with ceremonious respect. He was allowed to choose his apartments and to furnish them with pieces from his own palace. His favorite wives and pages and nobles were installed to serve him. He gave audiences and conducted affairs of state in the usual manner. Cortés and his captains uncovered before him every morning and asked his orders. They sought to divert him with Spanish music and stories. They learned to play Aztec ball with him. When especially distinguished visitors came to interview the monarch, they redoubled their efforts to make the situation seem like one grand house party. But noting the heavily armed guard of thirty at the front door and thirty at the rear, the populace was aware that their lord was a prisoner. Yet they could not act without risking the life of the sacred hostage.

At length the Aztecs who had been responsible for the death of the Spaniards near Cholula were brought to trial. The leading *cacique* did not deny his guilt, but when he and the sixteen with him were condemned by Cortés to be burnt alive, as an example, he accused Montezuma of instigating the trouble. So, for his share in the guilt, Cortés ordered shackles put on Montezuma's ankles until the public execution in the courtyard was concluded. The monarch's horrified wives fell on their knees and put their soft scarves between the iron bands and the royal flesh.

When the men were burnt to ashes, Cortés with his own hands unloosed the fetters, embraced the monarch, and declared he loved him like a brother and was ever in his service. But Montezuma was so stunned by the ignominy of fetters that he never regained his pride. Though he was no longer to be deceived by the Spaniards' sweet talk, from then on he was in such despair of spirit that he little cared how the white chief governed in his name.

Under Cortés's order vassal kings were sent for. Those from a far distance, who had heard only snatches of the momentous happenings, were astounded to behold the plight of their omnipotent ruler. They were even more stupefied when he asked them to swear allegiance to "the great king beyond the water" and to render the tribute they were accustomed to bring him to the king's representative, Cortés. Even the most doughty of the Spanish warriors was moved by the spectacle of the weeping Montezuma and his subject kings taking an oath of allegiance to an unknown sovereign to whom they attributed supernatural power.

Thus, without striking a blow in the capital, the audacious Cortés had formally gained Mexico for the crown of Spain. Soon from all parts of the realm of Montezuma the tribute began to arrive—gold and silver, foodstuffs, bales of woven cloth. The treasure room where the wealth of Montezuma's father was hoarded was now unsealed and the Spaniards told to help themselves. A dream beyond their most fantastic imaginings had come true. "It seemed to me," wrote Bernal Díaz as he beheld the stock of gold and silver in bars and ore, the jewels, the ornaments, the fabrics, "as if all the riches of the world were in that room."

But though Cortés could report by letter to Spain that Mexico had become a vassal state, he and his men knew that the affair was far from settled. Except for their possession of the trump ace in the person of the monarch, every other factor manifested their danger. If the Aztecs were willing to sacrifice Montezuma, the Spaniards could be trapped at the drawbridges in an attempted escape. To prevent this catastrophe, Cortés decided to build brigantines so that his men could escape across Lake Texcoco if necessary. Montezuma, intrigued at the prospect of beholding a winged water-house, accommodatingly furnished porters to transport ship gear, sails, and tackle from the coast to the capital, and he provided timber and workmen for the construction under the Spanish shipwright. When two boats large enough to accommodate the Spaniards had been furnished and armed with little cannon, the invaders breathed easier and Montezuma's spirits revived when he was taken for a pleasure ride seated under a canopy bearing aloft the flag of Castile.

In the meantime, while Montezuma was being beguiled of his despair, certain chiefs formed a confederacy to march upon the capital, rescue their monarch and drive the invaders from the land. Through Montezuma's own spies and through plots, Cortés got possession of most of the confederate chiefs, including the leader Cacama, the proud young king of Texcoco and the emperor's nephew. When these most formidable enemies were chained under his roof, Cortés sent one hundred and fifty of his small band under Velásquez de León to form a colony and a fortified post about one hundred and eighty miles south of Vera Cruz. Others he sent searching for gold mines.

Everything seemed to be succeeding for Cortés except the avowed purpose of the expedition, conversion of the natives to the Catholic faith. Neither Montezuma nor any of his people seemed impressed by the new religion. But at last Cortés boldly asked Montezuma's permission to turn the temple of Huitzilopochtli into a Christian shrine. Horrified at the awful prospect of vengeance from his gods, Montezuma refused. Cortés then said his men would be satisfied to have one section of the temple. If this were denied, he threatened, the temple would be razed and the idols destroyed. With a groan, Montezuma could only consent.

When the shrine had been scrubbed and scoured of its dried blood, the band of Christian soldiers, singing lustily, marched up the one hundred and twenty steps behind their priest. While hideous idols glared viciously at them, Mass was celebrated.

Below, the dark-skinned populace muttered menacingly at this new profanation.

The atmosphere chilled perceptibly. After a series of grave conferences with priests and nobles from the city, Montezuma summoned Cortés. Their gods had told the priests, he said, that the white men must leave the city at once or be offered as living sacrifices upon the altars they had profaned. Montezuma wished them to go in peace. He reminded Cortés that at a lift of his finger the Aztecs would rise in a body and tear them to pieces.

Really perturbed now, Cortés temporized. Calmly and ingratiatingly he said he would regret to leave in such haste since there were no vessels at the coast in which to make the return trip to Cuba. He added cunningly that if he went immediately he would be obliged to take the royal personage with him as hostage to insure safe conduct.

In his dilemma Montezuma promised that the Spaniards might remain until the vessels were built. He sent a large force of Indian workmen along with the Spanish shipwrights to Vera Cruz to begin the construction. Cortés dispatched private word urging all the delay possible.

It was May now, and the Spaniards had been in the capital for six months. As unrest among the Aztecs became more threatening the Spaniards slept in their armor and performed every function of their daily routine within reach of their weapons.

On top of his apprehensions and worries close at hand, disturbing news reached Cortés from his commander at Vera Cruz. Pánfilo Narváez had arrived on April twenty-third with a fleet of eighteen vessels, nine hundred men, and eighty horses. The expedition was excellently equipped with guns and war gear. Narváez had been sent by the irate Governor Velásquez of Cuba to glean the spoils of Cortés's conquest and to bring the rebel back to justice. Cortés was in a quandary. Here was an obstacle that would be hard to overleap. With the whole Aztec nation now muttering at his back, he had to face a white enemy more than twice his strength in men and equipment. At first he played his usual skillful game of temporization and conciliation. He received Narváez's emissaries with warm affability, showed them the treasure presented by Montezuma and the tributary chiefs. He bestowed rich gifts upon them. They were as charmed by his manner as his munificence. The conceited Narváez was not gifted with the art of winning friends. For all his courage, he was both arrogant and niggardly. Cortés promised that Narváez's men would share with his soldiers if they would throw in their lot with him.

In the meantime, he had sent his good priest Father Olmedo to talk with Narváez, who was encamped at Cempaolla. The priest enthralled groups with fascinating tales that bespoke the sure promise and the rich bounty of Cortés—how he was adored by his followers, how approachable and heart-warming he was. Like Cortés, Olmedo possessed a honeyed tongue, and by clever insinuations he achieved the disaffection of a group of Narváez's followers. But one of the lieutenants boasted that he himself would cut off Cortés's two ears and eat them broiled for breakfast. As Narváez began to make plans for the attack on the Spaniards in Tenochtitlán, he proclaimed to the Indians that he was coming to deliver Montezuma from the criminal rebels.

In the extremity of the crisis, Cortés made one of his masterly, quick decisions. He could not let Narváez come to the capital. He had to intercept him with celerity before he gained allies. He chose Pedro de Alvarado, his most valiant and favored captain, to command the capital in his absence. To hold the fort against the most powerful nation north of Panama, he left one hundred and forty white men and some Tlascalan allies. Then he set off with seventy Spanish soldiers to meet the nine hundred of Narváez. His men traveled light, in armor of quilted cotton, not steel. They had only five horses among them, and no artillery whatsoever.

It was mid-May, and the Valley of Anáhuac had never looked

more desirable than when Cortés and his intrepid band made a forced march across it and up the azalea-dotted western slopes of the mountains. In a few days they had reached the river three miles from Cempaolla and here they were joined by the men Cortés had sent under Velásquez de León to found a settlement in the south. Sandoval, too, with his few men from Vera Cruz was waiting to meet him.

In his contemptuous complacency Narváez had not measured his man—he was planning to take Cortés in his own good time. Vigilance and discipline had been relaxed in the Narváez camp. It was a night of terrific thunderstorm, and again Cortés felt as if heaven had bestowed a special benison on him. In a cloudburst his soldiers forded the river, and only three were swept away. The crashes of thunder and the downpour of water drowned out the sounds of the troop movements. It was after midnight, when, dragging through the deep mud, they came to the edges of the town. One of the weary rain-soaked guards they captured without a struggle; the other escaped to tell the news.

The men at headquarters thought the excited guard was having hallucinations—Cortés was surely far away in Tenochtitlán. Besides, no one could cross the river in such a storm. If he was on the way they would battle with him in the morning. They plied the guard with liquor and went back to bed.

As the troops of Cortés moved noiselessly under the pouring rain, the town was shrouded in the silence of sleep. A single light burned in the quarters of Narváez in one of the towers of the temple. "Get Narváez!" was Cortés's brief command to Sandoval.

As they approached the temple enclosure where the enemy was encamped someone gave the alarm. A trumpet blared. The roused soldiers sprang to their posts, the artillery opened fire. But Cortés's men hugged the walls, and the cannon balls went down the middle of the street. They beat down the cannoneers and took possession of the guns. Sandoval and his detachment stormed up the temple steps to get the commander. Narváez fought violently, but a copper-pointed lance tore through his left eye. "Holy Mary," he cried out in agony, "I am slain!"

The men of Cortés began to shout "Victory!" at the top of their lungs, though they did not abate their fighting. The rain stopped suddenly, and out of the darkness came thousands of those gigantic tropical fireflies called *cocuyos* with their brilliant, intermittent flames. Narváez's men took them to be approaching soldiers with matchlocks. As Cortés trained the enemy's own artillery against them, he called on them to capitulate, promising complete amnesty and bounty. After one round of firing, they surrendered. The enemy arms were stacked and the nine hundred men filed past Cortés to take oath of allegiance to him as captain-general.

When morning came, the forces of Narváez were amazed to discover the slimness of the victorious army. Cortés himself hardly knew how victory had been achieved with such celerity against such odds. He gave the credit to his protector, the Mother of Christ. The men of Narváez seemed little depressed to change masters. Some could not conceal their pleasure when Cortés turned his warming smile upon them. Narváez and the boastful chap who was going to broil the captain-general's ears were brought before him in chains. Cortés had balm applied to their physical wounds and sent them under guard to Vera Cruz. He also sent two hundred men to dismantle Narváez's ships and bring the sails and movable gear on shore.

Hernán Cortés was again master of Mexico, and he had gained a reinforcement of white men almost double his own force and an equipment vastly superior to that he had brought with him. Now the complete conquest of Mexico should be easy, he said. Through Heaven's blessing, life was at its sweetest.

In the midst of the celebration of his great triumph, disturbing news came from Alvarado. The Aztecs had risen against the

Spaniards. They had burned the brigantines and were besieging the Spanish barracks. Cortés was urged to come quickly or all would be lost. He had no choice. Before his fatigued soldiers had had time to recover their wind, he commanded a second march on Mexico.

# 4. The Sad Night

*"Doubt not that the Almighty will shield you,
for your cause is just, and you are fighting
under the Banner of the Cross."*

HERNÁN CORTÉS

Cortés sensed the chilling hostility as he recrossed the Valley of
Anáhuac. The citizens of the hamlets turned away, closed their
doors. No hospitality was offered. Under compulsion, provisions
were set forth grudgingly. When the troops arrived in Tenochtitlán no armed force barred the Spaniards' way, but the city was
ominously silent. The streets were empty, the market deserted.
The atmosphere was so foreboding that Narváez's men had
strange attacks of the creeps.

In the Spanish headquarters Cortés learned the cause of the
change. The impetuous captain left in charge had played the
consummate fool and all but ruined everything the captain-
general had achieved.

Alvarado had given permission to the Indians to hold a ritualistic celebration in the temple enclosure. They had pledged themselves to go unarmed and to indulge in no human sacrifices.
Several hundred young men of noble families gathered for the
ceremony clad in loin cloths and bejeweled feather mantles and
bearing wreaths of flowers. Alvarado's full-armed men stood
about the walls and at the entrances. When the religious dancing
was reaching a climax, the Spaniards unsheathed their swords,
rushed upon the unsuspecting Indians, and began hacking them
to pieces. They killed every breathing man and then like ghouls
grappled among the slain in the welter of blood and broken
blossoms to salvage the jeweled ornaments. It was the most in-

defensible act in the conquest of the New World. Alvarado tried to excuse the massacre by saying he feared another Cholula and that if he disposed of the young nobles the rest of the Aztecs would not dare rise against the Spaniards. His psychology could not have been more stupid. Cortés knew that no insinuating eloquence could ever hoodwink the Aztecs again. For the first time in his life he became so angry he completely lost control of himself. "You have acted like a madman," he shouted at Alvarado. "You are no longer fit to be a captain."

The Spaniards were in a desperate plight for food. For a fortnight before Cortés's return, the Indians, in retaliation for the massacre, had blockaded their enemies from supplies. Cortés accused Montezuma of planning to starve them to death. Montezuma said he was powerless, his people had renounced him. The only man who could possibly influence the populace and obtain food was his brother, Cuitláhuac, whom Cortés held as another royal hostage.

Cuitláhuac was released with instructions to open the market. The market was not opened and the prince did not return. He became the people's champion, inciting them to rise and finish off the white impostors. On the housetops warriors gathered with stones and weapons. Again and again they stormed the palace. Twice they set fire to the wooden parts of the structure. They were killed by the hundreds, but two sprang up for every one that fell.

At last Cortés made a sortie in an effort to rout them and put everlasting terror in them. The Aztecs fought in the streets with a ferocity that amazed even the captain-general. Because of their earlier submission, ordered by Montezuma, he had miscalculated their ingrained temper. Though he fired blocks of houses, where many civilian inmates were burned to death, his terrorizing did not intimidate the Indians.

Soon the Spaniards were face to face with actual starvation. They were more than willing now to depart in peace with their lives and their booty, if the Aztecs would let them go. But the brigantines had been burned, and the canals and lakes swarmed with armed warriors in canoes. Escape by the causeways would be perilous, for if the wooden drawbridges were withdrawn the Spaniards could be trapped and captured alive for the human sacrifices.

In his desperation, Cortés turned one last time to Montezuma. But the disconsolate monarch was no longer to be beguiled by smooth words. In his disgrace he wished only to die. Yet to rid his capital of the perfidious white men he consented to ask his people to let them go. To give a semblance of former majesty to his presence, he resumed again his imperial robes and trappings. As Montezuma appeared on the terrace of the central turret, an awed hush fell over the battle-yelling crowd. Out of habit they bowed before his sacrosanct figure. Then the emperor began to speak of the strangers as his guests. "Let the white men depart in peace," he urged; "return your weapons to the armory." The people raised their heads and as one voice roared out against him. They reviled him with epithets of "coward," "weakling," "woman." One of his own nephews hurled the first stone. Missiles began to fly from every direction. A stone struck Montezuma's forehead and he fell unconscious to the floor. At the sacrilege the mob dispersed in panic. But within an hour they had gathered together again to plan sure death for the Spaniards.

Montezuma lay in physical and mental anguish on his bed. He refused to be treated for his wound. He tore the dressing away. He would not take nourishment. He begged to be allowed to die.

Cortés racked his brain to devise a way out. He knew the Aztecs had long since stopped believing that the Spaniards might be descendants of Quetzalcoatl. But in his desperation he tried to play on the Indian superstition by storming the war god's shrine atop the pyramids. His soldiers captured two of the priests, killed scores of defending Indians, left the shrine in flames. The

Aztecs became only the more furious and determined. In a parley Cortés made threats as well as promises. His enemies laughed scornfully. "Your men are dying of hunger and disease," they cried. "The bridges are destroyed. There is no escape. You shall be sacrificed alive to the vengeance of our gods."

All the food was gone now except scanty corncakes. The men were faint with hunger. The rents and breaches in the fortifications were gaping wider. Little ammunition was left. The confused and disappointed men of Narváez began wildly to talk mutiny. Fear gripped the entire company. Under severe punish- ment from the darts and slings of the enemy, the Spaniards tried by night to fill with timber and debris the gaps in the canals which the drawbridges had spanned. The Indians tore them out by day.

There were agonizing decisions for Cortés to make. To attempt to escape in any direction bespoke disaster. Should he abandon the treasure completely or try to salvage the cream of it? Again he temporized.

It was the death of Montezuma that accelerated the decision. The wound in the emperor's head proved fatal on June thirtieth. Cortés and all the captains and all the soldiers who had known him wept for him. "Nor is it to be wondered at," said Bernal Díaz, "considering how good he was." His death was a major misfortune to the Spaniards; they had lost their royal hostage. Now they had to make as quick a getaway as possible; the last decision was whether the escape was to be attempted by day or night.

Cortés now sought the advice of Botello, "a soldier of respecta- ble demeanor," who was gifted in astrology. Botello consulted the stars and his charts and decreed, "At night, this very night." If they delayed another day not one would be left alive. But the signs were mixed, malevolent and benevolent. Great trouble and sorrow in any case. As Botello read his own personal horoscope he foresaw his own imminent death. "I myself shall not survive the night," he said. His prediction proved correct.

Cortés hastily went about arranging the treasure, while carpenters finished making a portable drawbridge. The king's fifth, mostly in gold and silver bars, was loaded on horses and put under strong guard to go through first. When the vast deal of undivided treasure lay heaped upon the floor, Cortés called his common soldiers and told them to help themselves. But he cautioned them, "The fastest traveler in the night is the one who travels lightest." His own men took only what would not weight them down. Narváez's men overloaded themselves.

When the soldiers were ready to march, a midnight Mass was celebrated by Father Olmedo. Then, in the darkness of the early morning of July first, in a drizzle of rain, the Spaniards, with their thousands of starving Tlascalan allies, emerged stealthily from the gate. Porters groaned under the heavy weight of the portable drawbridge, which Cortés intended to fit into each of the gaps in the causeway as they came to them. The streets were so silent, the Spaniards breathed prayers of thanksgiving for their deliverance. But the wily Aztecs were not napping. When a third of the procession had passed over the drawbridge set into the first gap and Cortés himself was on it, a wailing tempest of battle cries rose from the waters. Soon the canals became masses of slithering war canoes. Drums of stretched snakeskin began to sound alarums with barbaric pounding, as arrows and hurtling stones began to rain on the fugitives. The portable bridge was so tightly wedged by the weight of the passing cannon and cavalry that the stoutest soldiers and porters could not dislodge it though they ruptured themselves in their frantic bursts of energy. Now the whole army was caught on the island beyond the first gap. Their retreat was blocked by the oncoming hordes of aroused warriors on foot. To the right and left of them the canals were choked with boatloads of spear-throwers and archers.

The Spaniards were caught in the "mousetrap." Disorder broke the ranks. It was every man for himself. Those behind pushed those in front. At the second gap all the men except those who made it on the backs of horses were forced to swim. Soldiers played mortal leapfrog with one another. As Spaniards and Indians fell wounded their comrades in arms used them as fords and crossed on their struggling bodies. From their boats the Aztecs would grab the fugitives by the ankles and drag them into the water and crack their skulls with war clubs. Some Indians struggled to haul the Christians alive into their canoes to save them for the sacrifices. Amid the savage whoops of vengeance and the screams of agony that rent the air rose the softer pleas to the Holy Mother for pity's sake.

Along with the cannon and wagons that dropped into the second causeway went most of the treasure, the bales and coffers, the gold and the silver. The mass, loosely cemented by the dead and the helpless wounded, formed an unstable but passable bridge for men behind. At the third breach the horses were encouraged back and forth like ferries and many who could not swim clung to the manes and tails.

Cortés's magic voice of command was drowned out in the demented noise of battle. Yet he dashed back and forth on horseback assisting the hard pressed, rescuing, encouraging. His favorite page was struck down dead by his side. With his own eyes he saw the prophesied end of Botello, his astrologer. Marina was saved. But all the other concubines except one were lost, and she slashed her own way through a mass of Indians with a broadsword she had retrieved from a dying soldier. Half of Narváez's men were lost and most of the Tlascalan allies. The golden loot in his doublet dragged many an adventurer to muddy death. And the cream of the treasure of Montezuma's empire sank in the black bottomless ooze—never to be recovered.

The fighting continued until dawn broke. The first glimmer of morning light was reflected like myriads of fireflies in the blades of obsidian glass topping the Indian spears. The canals were still choked with canoes. But the Spaniards who were destined to escape the trap had already reached the mainland to the northeast. Alvarado, who had fought like a demon to make up for his criminal stupidity in the temple massacre, was the last to go over. He had remained on the last island as long as there was any living person to be saved. Now, as the Aztecs in their boats closed in upon him by water and others came at his back, his friends watching from the mainland thought his end had come. But the agile Alvarado plunged his long lance deep into the brink of the causeway and vaulted through the air. To the amazement of friend and foe he landed clear on the other brink. The distance of the leap has never been accurately ascertained, but Bernal Díaz reports that it was impossible for a mortal man to make, and he refuses to believe the god-like feat. The site of the fabulous leap has been preserved in Mexico City, though filled in now as have been the canals.

Slowly the torn and battered remnant of the army moved on away from the lost city. The Aztecs did not pursue them beyond the two-mile limit of the causeway, for they had stopped to celebrate their triumph, to gather up the discarded Spanish weapons, to rescue oddments of spilled treasure.

At a safer distance beyond the suburb of Tacuba, the Spaniards halted to recover their breath and nurse their wounds. Cortés sat down and leaned back against the vast trunk of a cypress tree. He put his hand over his eyes and frankly wept. It was the first time his men had ever seen him weep. This night of June thirtieth was the saddest of his crowded life, and in the chronicles it has ever since been referred to as *la Noche Triste*.

For some hours the aching men, coated with salt ooze and coagulated blood, remained in a kind of stupor. The few banners that had come through were in shreds. All the artillery, the baggage, and most of the treasure were irretrievably lost. The ammunition was exhausted. Not one musket was left. Only the battered swords remained for the army's defense. Forty-six of the cavalry were dead, leaving only twenty-three. Four hundred and fifty of the Christians had perished. It was the most disastrous rout the arms of Spain had sustained in the New World.

The night had proved lucky and unlucky, as Botello had predicted. At least the great captain-general and half his soldiers, together with Marina, the interpreter Aguilar, and the invaluable shipwright Martín López, had escaped the death trap. But on that fateful night posterity, as well as Cortés, sustained a priceless loss. All of his papers, including his day-by-day account of the conquest from February tenth, 1519, the day he left Cuba, to June thirtieth, 1520, were gone. He sighed for this loss, among the others.

But as he leaned inert against the cypress and his breathing became more regular, he began to consider what was saved. As he remarked the salvage, the flame of his indomitable courage revived. Reckoning the damaged blades, the lacerated horses and the prostrate, groaning soldiers, the defeated leader began to speculate on how he would reconquer the kingdom.

At length he ordered the famished men to march on and bear the incapacitated in litters. There was no succor in any of the villages. The inhabitants had left the houses deserted and carried off all the foodstuffs. Stalwart soldiers fainted with hunger and fatigue. The men gnawed ravenously at cornstalks left standing in the fields. They feasted on bits of wounded horse they killed. They ate of green gourds. Then in one blessed place they came upon thickets of wild cherries that had just ripened. It was heaven-sent manna in their extremity. They called a long halt and gorged themselves on cherries.

In their depleted condition they had covered no more than thirty miles in seven days. But they felt delivered. Then as they wound a circuitous route into the valley of Otumba, to their consternation they discovered an enormous host of Aztec warriors in full battle array. They had reason to believe their end had come when the enemy swooped down upon them. They had nothing with which to defend themselves against the countless hordes—estimates ran as high as two hundred thousand—except their hacked swords and their weakened right arms.

In the fury of the fight, when it seemed that there was not the faintest hope for the Spaniards, Cortés, as had Elisha, closed his eyes and called on heavenly aid. On opening them he discovered in the distance the Aztec commander, full panoplied, directing the fight from his litter. Following his rule of "Get the leader," Cortés passed the word to the nearest cavalrymen and they dashed at the Aztec chief, trampling his men in the way. The commander's guards were overturned and he himself was struck to the ground.

The cry that their chief was killed passed like a whirlwind among the Indians. In panic, they stampeded. Against tremendous odds, Cortés had won again.

As his men and the remnant of Tlascalans gathered up the plunder, the discarded arms and the ornaments torn from the dead warriors, Cortés wondered at his reception in Tlascala. He feared it might be hostile. But when at last the troops arrived, the hill people received them kindly. They fed the famished and ministered to the wounded.

Cortés himself had been wounded in the knee, the hand, and twice in the head. Like the doughty fighter in the Scotch ballad he had merely paused "to sit and bleed awhile" and then had risen to fight again. Surgeons had to remove a piece of split bone from the skull. For days he lay desperately ill with a fever. But both in and out of delirium he planned the new conquest.

The old *cacique* of Tlascala was most willing to continue the alliance. "We have common injuries to revenge," he said. But when Cortés was mended enough to walk about he was confronted with a new, grave problem. Disaffection had infected the troops. A large proportion demanded to be allowed to return to Vera Cruz and ship to Cuba. Again Cortés employed the

witchery of his tongue to dissuade them. And as he wrote to
King Charles of his ingrained conviction that "Fortune favors
the brave," the winds of fortune blew beneficence from unexpected quarters. A vessel sent by the governor of Cuba and filled
with stores for Narváez's force arrived at Vera Cruz. Cortés
beguiled the crews to join with him and appropriated the welcome supplies. A second vessel-load of men and stores from Cuba
was won to his cause. Three ships sent by the governor of
Jamaica to establish a colony north of Vera Cruz arrived, and
their men, too, were persuaded to become companions in adventure with Cortés. The captain-general now had a hundred and
fifty fresh soldiers, twenty new horses, and a stock of arms and
ammunition. On top of all, a trading ship from the Canaries
arrived in Vera Cruz offering military supplies for sale. With
Aztec gold Cortés purchased the ship as well as the arms and
persuaded the entire crew to join him.

With the augmented forces to back him he began to win
over tribes under vassalage to the Aztecs. Those who did not
succumb to his persuasion fell before the Spanish and Tlascalan
arms. By mid-December he had done all the necessary conquest
of neighboring provinces. He had drilled Indians in battle forma-
tions and instructed the newly arrived Spaniards in the special
sort of warfare they would taste. He prepared for reconquest with
scrupulous care. As a master stroke, he ordered thirteen brigantines to be constructed in Tlascala. The war vessels were to be
transported on Indian shoulders sixty miles over the mountains
and put together on the shore of Lake Texcoco opposite Tenochtitlán. The gear and rigging from dismantled ships were brought
up from Vera Cruz. Martín López, the shipwright, instructed
Indians who had never seen anything larger than a canoe to
build brigantines. Cortés did not hesitate to conceive other Herculean tasks. When he found himself short of gunpowder he sent
a group of cavaliers to the crater on Popocatépetl, where by turns

they lowered each other down hundreds of feet into the smoky bowels of the volcano to collect sulphur by the bucketful.

By the end of the year 1520, Cortés had again amassed an army of nine hundred white men and so many thousands of Indians that no two chroniclers agree on the aggregate. He had conquered every province and tribe between the seacoast and the Valley of Anáhuac. And when he reached the valley he took the towns one by one. He made his headquarters in Texcoco. Iztapalapán, the city beautiful, where the troops had been entertained the night before their first entrance to Tenochtitlán, refused to surrender. So the soldiers of Cortés looted and burnt and massacred, but they in turn lost their plunder and barely escaped drowning when the dikes were cut and the ruined city was flooded. The former lord of Iztapalapán, Cuitláhuac, who had led the uprising against the Spaniards and had succeeded Montezuma on the throne, was not alive to suffer for the loss of his lovely city. After a brief reign of four months, he had succumbed, not to Spanish might but to a disease hitherto unknown in Mexico, which had been brought in by a Negro slave in Narváez's force. It was smallpox. It had spread from Cempaolla across the mountains and killed Indians by the thousands, among others the great old *cacique* of Tlascala.

In the place of Cuitláhuac now reigned Montezuma's nephew, a young man of twenty-four named Cuauhtémoc, who was married to a daughter of Montezuma. This youthful Aztec was a match for Cortés in dauntless spirit. He hated the Christians with a diamond-hard fury. He knew it was a fight without quarter, so he prepared his defenses with ingenuity and studied care. And he ordered every white man taken alive to be sacrificed on the altar of the war god.

Awaiting the arrival of the brigantines, Cortés spent his time annoying the Aztecs and blockading their food supply. He carried his blockade as near as Cuernavaca and the vegetable gardens of Xochimilco. When the brigantines arrived on human shoulders—the procession took six hours to pass through the main street of Texcoco—it was a day of triumphant celebration. In three weeks the ships were assembled and launched in the three-mile canal which had been dug between the town and the lake. Cortés was now ready to attack.

On the twenty-eighth of April, 1521, the captain-general mustered his troops in the plaza of Texcoco. Now, besides tens of thousands of Indian fighters, he possessed eighty-seven cavalrymen and eight hundred and eighteen foot soldiers, of whom one hundred and eighteen were arquebusiers and crossbowmen. His artillery numbered eighteen pieces. He made a shrewd, inspiriting speech, in which in return for valor he held out the promise not only of temporal fortune and fame, but immortal glory in the life to come. He emphasized the Christian aspect of the crusade, and assured the soldiers that Heaven smiled on their great quest.

Cortés's plan was to attack Tenochtitlán from the water and three ways by land—one by the causeways from Tacuba, one by Coyoacán, and one by Chapultepec. He himself took charge of the fleet and its three hundred men. The Indian allies were apportioned to the three land captains in detachments that approximated twenty thousand each.

On May tenth the march to the various places of attack began. First, the aqueduct to Chapultepec that supplied the citizens of the capital with fresh drinking water was broken. After destroying hundreds of war canoes, the brigantines soon had complete control of the lake. Except for stray boats that slipped across the lake from the mainland in the night, food supplies were cut off.

The Aztecs had prepared to use the parapets and roofs of the houses as fortifications from which to hurl stones and missiles. So Cortés ordered the Indian allies to destroy the buildings section by section as they gained ground. The breaches in the causeway were filled with the debris. The Tlascalans took fiendish delight in joining in the work of vandalism, of leveling the principal structures of their proud enemy. As the palaces of the princes were fired and then demolished, Cortés grieved for the ruin of "the most beautiful city in the world," as he called it. Each tumbling building took away from his ultimate triumph as well as from the value to history. Yet he saw no other way to defeat the enraged and stubborn Aztecs, who fought with a ferocity that won his admiration. The young Cuauhtémoc revealed in his command the military astuteness and courage that had made his ancestors the masters of Mexico.

But the Aztecs, already weak with malnutrition, were reduced to eating insects, tree bark, and the flesh of their fallen comrades, while Cortés's men were supplied with plenteous food by their Indian allies. And now that the Spaniards seemed to be winning, more Indian reinforcements joined them. By Cortés's own estimate, one hundred and fifty thousand warriors came to his aid to revenge past grievances against the haughty men of Tenochtitlán.

Without fresh water, without wholesome food, the Aztec strength began to dwindle, though by their spirit the enemy could not notice it. Cuauhtémoc saw pestilence spreading among his people, who did not have time to bury the festering dead. Though he listened to offers of generous terms of capitulation sent by Cortés, Cuauhtémoc had no faith in the words of Christians. He had witnessed their perfidy. He marveled how his brain-sick uncle Montezuma could ever have been so deceived by these white fiends of hell as to believe them kinsmen of Quetzalcoatl. He determined to carry on the fight as long as his warriors had strength to lift their battle arms, even though he saw thousands of former vassals in the ranks of the white men.

Despite certain success, the Spaniards suffered many setbacks. Again and again they found themselves in tight places and forced to fall back. The materials thrown into the breaches by day would be torn out during the night by the Aztecs. Without surcease the fight continued on the causeways, on the lake, in the city. Twice

Cortés barely escaped death. Once the Aztec warriors actually laid hands on him and in the melee he was thrown to the ground, while lieutenants fought for his life. In this same engagement his chamberlain, while assisting Cortés to his saddle, was seized by the enemy and taken off prisoner in a canoe. Along with innumerable allies, seventy-two Spaniards were captured and rushed off to be sacrificed in the Aztec manner. The horrified troops saw their comrades in arms forced to dance naked about the idol of the war god, with plumes on their heads and fans in their hands. Then they were bent backwards over the convex stone, their breasts were ripped open with obsidian knives, and their hearts were torn out from the living flesh. The ceremony done, their bodies were hurled down the temple steps to be seized and eaten by the hungry hordes. The stirring account of the ghastly procedure by the eyewitness Bernal Díaz ends with a casual masterpiece of understatement: "When I saw the sacrifice of our seventy-two countrymen," he writes, "and their hearts taken out palpitating and offered to the war god of the Mexicans and their legs and arms cut off and eaten, I had a sensation of fear."

When Cuauhtémoc received assurance from the priest that Huitzilopochtli would give them victory within a week, the allies of Cortés began to desert in the night. But the blockade was not relaxed, and the Aztecs within the city began to die of starvation. The systematic destruction of the principal buildings went on. By the first week in August three-fourths of the capital was in ruins. The northwestern corner of the city with the great market of Tlateloloc was all that remained intact, and here the Aztec forces were concentrated.

When the week passed and the deserting allies saw that the prophecies of Christian defeat had not come true, they began to return to the aid of the white men. Now Cortés determined to sacrifice the entire city, and he began to fill up the canals with the materials of palace and hut alike. One last time he begged Cuauhtémoc to capitulate. He praised his valiance. He promised him confirmation of his authority, but under the protection of Spain. Yet Cuauhtémoc refused to consider surrender. "We can at least die like warriors," he told his people.

At last the Spaniards stormed the sacred pyramid in Tlateloloc and fired the sanctuaries built of wood. A few days later Cortés planted the flag of Castile on the temple top.

Though citizens dropped from disease and hunger and died in their tracks, Cuauhtémoc would not surrender. The siege went on. The living lay down to rest on the festering bodies of the dead. As Cortés said, "A man could not set foot down unless on the corpse of an Indian." The August rains descended and brought drinking water, but the wetness alternating with hot sun brought quick putrefaction. Spaniards almost fainted at the city's stench. In the midst of the horror some of the entrapped sufferers became mad with hallucinations. A group of nobles sought Cortés and begged him to finish them off and put an end to their suffering. But the indomitable young Cuauhtémoc never lost his courage. He inspired famished women and hollow-eyed children to take up arms in the last attack of the Christians. Starving boys and girls threw stones from housetops with all their feeble might.

When Cortés gave up hope of moving Cuauhtémoc, he determined on the havoc of total defeat. He called on all his forces and his brigantines to attack from every possible angle at once. On August twelfth cannon roared intermittently, muskets sent forth continual fire. The slaughter was so merciless that the dead were heaped up in mounds and the blood turned the remaining canals the color of wine-dregs. Cortés offered mercy to those who would give themselves up. But the Indian enemies of the Aztecs, frenzied with excitement of the blood, got completely out of hand and butchered women and children as well as men.

To stop the carnage, Cortés ordered the trumpeter to sound re-treat again and again. The estimated dead that day—by his own report—numbered forty thousand.

The end came the next day, on August thirteenth, the feast of Saint Hipólito. When the Aztec ruler still refused to parley, after waiting several hours, Cortés gave orders to proceed with the carnage. The rumor reached him that Cuauhtémoc was going to escape by water. Boats which began pushing off from the shore were chased or shot at by the brigantines. One large pirogue was pursued by a swift sailer. The Indians rowed with super-human energy, but the Spanish boat overtook them. The captain ordered his men "to level their crossbows." Before they could shoot, the young lord, to save his wife and attendants, stood up and confessed he was Cuauhtémoc and the prisoner of Cortés. "Let no harm come to my followers," he asked. It was a rich haul. The foremost nobles of the Aztecs who were still alive were among the twenty aboard.

Cuauhtémoc was brought before Cortés on a house roof gar-nished for the occasion with red carpets. His presence and his dignity excited admiration among the Spaniards. "Cuauhtémoc," says the eyewitness Bernal Díaz, "was of noble appearance both in person and countenance; his features were rather large and cheerful, with lively eyes; his complexion very fair for an Indian." The defeated young monarch spoke first. "I have done my best to defend my people," he said with profound feeling. Then touching the dagger in Cortés's belt, he asked to be rid of life at once.

Cortés gave his word that Cuauhtémoc should be treated with all the honor that befitted a valorous warrior. A banquet was ordered served on the roof. It was late evening. Dark clouds covered the paling sky. Then rain began to fall. That night nature completed the Christians' ravages on the Aztec capital. A tropical storm rent the valley with fearful thunder-rolls and lightnings, and the wind sent partly demolished buildings crashing to the ground.

The next morning at Cuauhtémoc's request, the remaining Aztecs began their departure from the city. For three days the procession of some tens of thousands of dark-skinned wraiths made their exits over the various causeways. The white men's day had come in the brave new world.

The savage siege of Tenochtitlán had lasted for almost three months. Besides the hordes who died of starvation and pestilence, more than a hundred thousand Indians had fallen in battle on both sides. The Christians had lost a hundred of their men.

Never in history had the dissolution of an important civilization been so thoroughly and quickly wrought as in the conquest of Mexico by the little band of Spanish adventurers. No conqueror's record is more remarkable than that of Cortés. His conquest was successful not primarily because of its Catholic faith, as de Madariaga says—though belief in heaven's auspices did play an indispensable part—but because of other more significant factors. On the material side were the horses and the superior arms and military discipline. There was Cortés's genius for organization, and beyond that his superb gift for diplomatic subterfuge. On the metaphysical side were Aztec superstition, their half-belief in the white gods, and their monarch's fatalistic acceptance of his country's doom. If Montezuma's brother, Cuitláhuac, had been on the throne, Cortés and his men would doubtless have perished at their first entrance into Tenochtitlán, for Cuitláhuac had urged his bewildered brother to mobilize his forces and destroy the intruders without delay.

The really decisive factor of the conquest was the division among the Indians themselves and the eager Fifth Columnists within the tribes. The vassal people oppressed by the tyranny of the Aztecs were ready to do anything to humble their hated overlords. Cortés skillfully marshaled Indian against Indian, just as revolutionary patriots and foreign exploiters have recurrently done since. It was the aid lent to Cortés by the tens of thousands of Indian allies that finally wrought the ruin of the Aztec nation. Yet taking into consideration every factor, profane or sacred, of chance or of design, the conquest of Mexico remains unparalleled in history.

# 5. Treasure Hunt and Phantoms

*"I have labored hard and have staked all in this undertaking for the love of God and renown—the noblest recompense of man."*

HERNÁN CORTÉS

When the peace came, the Spaniards celebrated drunkenly in the midst of the spectred ruins. They postponed division of the spoils until the Indian allies departed for their homes, rejoicing in the downfall of the men of Tenochtitlán. These Indians did not suspect the terrible thing they had done to their race. Few had the wit to note the paradox by which they had put themselves, as well as their defeated foe, under the foreign yoke.

After the loot was assessed and divided, a howl of protest rose from the common soldiers. Each had expected a grandee's wealth for himself and what he got "was not worth stooping for." As they demanded more, they began a treasure hunt that tore up floors, dragged the lake, exhumed the dead. They accused Cortés of perfidy, of holding back valuables, of secret understanding with Cuauhtémoc. The muttering against him grew so menacing that to pacify the disgruntled men Cortés did the most unforgivable act of his life. To satisfy them as to whether or not Cuauhtémoc and the king of Tacuba possessed undivulged treasure, he allowed the Aztec nobles to be put to torture. Before a slow fire the royal feet were roasted in an agony prolonged by the anointment of oil. Cuauhtémoc had no revelation whatever to make. He endured the excruciating pain with extraordinary fortitude, and when his elder companion groaned aloud in anguish, the young man reproved him by saying, "Do you think I myself am enjoying the pleasure of my bath?"

In the meantime, out of the basic materials of ruined Tenochtitlán Cortés began the construction of the City of Mexico. First he had the aqueduct restored so there would be plenty of water for drinking and cleansing and mortar mixing. Then he divided the area into plots for churches, for monasteries, for public buildings and plazas. On the very site of the temple of the war god a cathedral dedicated to Saint Francis was begun, the foundations laid with the stones of broken idols. One of the corners of the great square was reserved for a Franciscan monastery, to be erected. Cortés built himself a mansion on the plaza where Montezuma's palace had stood. Along the main thoroughfare the Spanish officers built houses of stone with beams of cedar. To the Indians—they returned within two months—was given the district of Tlateloloc around the site of the old market for their dwellings.

In the years immediately following the surrender, Cortés proved his masterly qualities of organization and administration as well as initiative, daring, and diplomacy. In searching for tin to use as an alloy with copper for cannon, he discovered iron deposits, of whose use the natives knew nothing. And, more significantly, he discovered new rich veins of silver.

By blandishments or force of arms he began to bring hostile tribes into line. He found it rewarding to invite envoys of distant tribes to visit him and his new capital, where he dazzled their eyes with Spanish pageantry, treated them to sham fights, and their first sight of prancing horses. He feasted them with Spanish cookery and pressed heady wine upon them. At length, in amiable befuddlement, they promised to receive with open arms whatever colonists he might desire to settle in their domains.

Over the whole face of Mexico the Spaniards began to establish their homes. They became squires of vast areas and masters of hordes of workmen under the vicious *repartimiento* system, which virtually enslaved the Indians. Agriculture, in greater or less degree, was compulsory according to the extent of the grant.

Cortés urged the crown to require all vessels leaving Spain for Mexico to bring European seeds and vines. He introduced sugar cane and raised it on his estate at Cuernavaca where he established the first sugar mill on the continent. He imported the olive as well as the grape, and oranges and almonds, which were not native to the New World. He established a series of inns between Vera Cruz and the capital, and even prescribed how the pigs and poultry were to be kept separate from the horses, so that the mangers should be clean. He constructed a hospital, the Hospital of Jesus, not far from his original meeting place with Montezuma, and in his will he provided for it in perpetuity. Besides the horse and hog and the chicken, Cortés brought the first cows and sheep to the New World.

To encourage domestic morality—or, at least, give it a face value—all married settlers were ordered to bring their wives to New Spain within a year and a half. Bachelor estate owners were obliged to marry within the same length of time or lose title to their property. Many chose the Indian girls with whom they were then living. Cortés, practicing what he preached, sent to Cuba for his wife—that Catalina Suárez whom he had wed to get to lead the expedition to Mexico. He was far from jubilant at her coming, but on her arrival she was treated like one of the great ladies of the world. As wife of the supreme *conquistador,* Catalina walked about in an incredible dream—for three months. Then one evening, "in smiling health," she attended a banquet, and the next day she was dead.

Along with the wives from Spain came shiploads of artisans to whom Indians were apprenticed so that they might learn useful skills. With their aptitude for imitation the Indians soon became proficient.

Cortés attempted to curb not only gambling, but also extravagance among the settlers. A decree was passed prohibiting the dressing in brocades and velvets for all except men of special rank. However, the captain-general himself continued privately to indulge his own desire for gambling, and he dressed with the richness that befitted his position.

To carry out the holy aspects of the conquest, Cortés requested the king to send him a band of Franciscan brothers to convert the heathen and to impress upon them the virtues of humility and obedience. The friars were eminently successful, for the poverty of their dress and their bare feet had a profound influence on the Indians. And the good men made wholesale conversions and began to establish small schools about the land.

While Cortés was struggling to settle New Spain on a sound and forward-looking basis, at the court in old Spain the intrigues against him waxed viciously. As his influence and power increased, so did his enemies.

Meanwhile, conquesting forays and explorations went on. Cortés himself built a squadron and explored the coastal territory of the Pacific, ever hopeful of finding the real El Dorado, which, for all its bounty, Mexico was definitely not. Hearing of a land to the south so rich in gold that common fishermen "used golden weights on their nets," he sent an expedition under Cristóbal de Olid to follow the gleam. In Honduras, de Olid decided to carve out a realm for himself and renounced the authority of his master, as Cortés himself had renounced that of Velásquez.

On October twelfth, 1524, with a large and well equipped force augmented "by musicians, a buffoon, a juggler, and a puppeteer," Cortés went after de Olid. He took along the hopelessly lamed Cuauhtémoc and his companion in torture, the king of Tacuba.

Everything went wrong with the expedition. It was as if the presence of Cuauhtémoc with his charred feet—a constant reminder to Cortés of his broken pledge and his cruelty—put a blight on the venture. Ever since the disgraceful foot-burning episode, Cortés had kept the closest watch on Cuauhtémoc because he feared an Indian uprising. He took him on horseback when he went riding or had him carried in a chair when he went walking a considerable distance. His distrust of Cuauhtémoc seemed subtly mixed with his own bad conscience, as if he must needs have his victim at his side like a burr to prick and sting him.

In Tabasco the Spaniards were obliged to cross fifty little rivers within a hundred miles and construct bridges for each of them. Their supplies gave out completely. They got lost in jungles so thick that they could not see the sun at noon. They bogged down in swamps. Guides deserted, and Indian auxiliaries dropped and died of starvation.

In the midst of the misery, it was reported on flimsy evidence that Cuauhtémoc had formed a conspiracy to massacre the white men. The young man stoutly denied the accusation. Nevertheless, Cortés decreed execution. Cuauhtémoc and the *cacique* of Tacuba were hanged together on a limb of a giant ceiba tree. The last words of the young king were to be remembered by Cortés until death. "I knew what it was to trust your false promises from the first," the Indian said. "I knew you intended this fate for me. Your God will demand of you why you killed me so unjustly." As he glanced down on his ruined feet, the neck of the last of the Aztec rulers was broken.

The killing of Cuauhtémoc did not rid Cortés of either his difficulties or his bad conscience. He knew that most of his men thought he had done wrong. His sleep was tormented. He would rise from his pallet and pace about in the night. Once in the darkness he walked off a stone platform, dropped twelve feet and suffered a concussion of the brain.

Some spark of genius had gone out in the great commander. He was no longer so astute in his decisions and judgments. His magnificent physical strength and endurance had passed their zenith. He could not stand grueling hardship with such fortitude as formerly. For the first time in his life he became moody and irritable.

Shortly after the end of Cuauhtémoc, Cortés gave up Marina forever. For five of the most exciting years any woman in history has ever lived, Marina had been the conqueror's devoted companion. She had been his very voice. Without her guardian angelship, Cortés might have failed in his conquest. In her native province of Coatzacoalcos, through which the expedition passed, he left her and endowed her "with great estates" after giving her in marriage to one of his cavaliers, Juan Xamarillo. Their natural son, Martín, had remained with his nurse in Mexico. (If the boy ever saw his mother again, history does not record it.) Marina herself was still hardly more than a girl, barely twenty-one. But from childhood her life had been one of extraordinarily romantic adventure, and she remains the most famous woman of the Indian race, even if she was unwittingly the first Fifth Columnist in the New World. There is no parallel to her case in history, where a girl shares so intimately the vicissitudes and triumphs of her warrior lover. Though her earthly record after twenty-one is a blank, in the Indian folk tales Marina has become the white phantom, Llorona, "the one who weeps." She is said to move like a white mist through the night, a restless soul for eternity, wailing softly for having betrayed her race to the Spaniards.

After Cortés set Marina aside, the sufferings and privations of the expedition became worse. Finally, after seven of the most ghastly months any men, Christian or heathen, ever endured, the survivors, half crazed with fevers and starvation, reached the Spanish colony on the Golfo Dolce to find the settlement suffering from famine. Yet Cortés, with his indomitable optimism, began to plan exploratory expeditions through the swamps, as preparation for the conquest of Nicaragua.

But disturbing news from Mexico reached him and changed his course. Two of his appointees had seized power and set themselves up as rulers. They had given out that he was dead, had held ceremonial funeral services and divided his estates among fellow conspirators. Twice Cortés set sail to claim his own, and twice he was shipwrecked. A tropical fever then laid him low. He became cadaverously thin and so profoundly despondent that he ordered his burial robe. When his companions had despaired of his life, a letter from his favorite captain, "Son" Sandoval, rallied his spirits. He rose from his bed and sent word he was returning.

It was almost five months before he reached the capital, where he was treated to a fanatical ovation. Once more he took charge of affairs in Mexico, but he was never quite the same again. The old stamina and zest were gone. Arch-enemies close by and at the Spanish court continued to eat at his reputation as termites do in timber. But he knew one happy month of supreme command. Then in July he learned that the Spanish sovereign had deputed others to take over his great office. He retired in high dudgeon to his beautiful place in Coyoacán, where others among his loyal captains had built themselves mansions.

Two years later the king allowed Cortés to return to Spain. At the court he summoned up his old-time charm and captivated them all. He refuted the calumnies with consummate skill. Basking in the royal favor and recounting the incredible stories of the conquest with easy art, Cortés became the man of the year. He handled himself and his case so well that the king bestowed on him the title his heart craved. He was created Marqués del Valle de Oaxaca. Besides considerable estates in the capital of Mexico and at Cuernavaca, he was assigned so much territory in the province of Oaxaca that his possessions embraced "twenty towns and hamlets and twenty-three thousand vassals." He was also proclaimed "Captain-General of New Spain and the Coasts of the South Sea," and he was to rule over such new lands as he would explore and colonize. But nothing could persuade the king to entrust Cortés with the government of New Spain, which he had won for the mother country.

Now forty-five, rich, famous, ennobled, Cortés was eminently eligible as a husband for a daughter of one of Spain's best families. He chose for his bride the niece of that nobleman, the Duke of Bejar, who had supported him at court through all the calumnies. Juana de Zuñiga, daughter of the Count de Aguilar, was a young girl of indifferent charm but considerable spirit, and in her veins flowed the royal blood of Navarre. In the spring of 1530, with his bride, his aged mother, and a princely retinue, Cortés set out for New Spain.

Though he was received everywhere with joyous demonstrations by the people, even by the Aztecs of the capital who poured out to greet him at Texcoco, Cortés was not to know contentment. He chafed at not having control of the government. He quarreled with the *audiencia* and indignantly left the capital. For a while he pursued the delights and endured the trials of a gentleman farmer. Besides sugar cane, he cultivated mulberry trees, imported silk worms and instructed the Indians in their culture and the making of silk. He made a real success of agriculture. But at heart he was an explorer and a conqueror, and he could not stay at peaceful pursuits long, although he had an heir now—also named Martín, like his bastard son by Marina—to inspire the acquisition of a greater fortune. Soon he was building ships and exploring the Pacific coast. He went on expeditions by land and sea, and though what he found was good for cartographers and Spain, it profited nothing for him. After nine years of ship-building and of equipping expeditions, he had spent three hundred thousand *castellanos* of gold, pawned his wife's jewels, and was deep in debt.

By 1538 Cortés was asking the king to relieve him "in order that he might live." With his power and prestige mere relics of their former high estate, he set sail for Spain in 1540 to lay his problems before the sovereign in person. He was never to return to Mexico.

When he arrived in Europe, accompanied by his legitimate ten-year-old son Martín and his illegitimate son Martín, almost a man now, Cortés was received with a show of warmth. But when it came to a settlement of his affairs his case was handled with cool formality. In the end he realized he was entirely outside the radius of royal benediction. Like Columbus and Balboa and other great discoverers and conquerors who had played leading parts in the drama of Spain's glory, Cortés found himself at the end of his life relegated to a distinctly minor rôle. When an expedition was sent against Algiers he volunteered to accompany it. But when affairs were going badly in the siege, the great strategist was not even asked to attend the council. Once when he thought aloud how his stalwart soldiers from New Spain could easily have taken the Algerian fortress, he was greeted with supercilious smiles and the reply that he would find the Moors a more formidable foe than a bunch of naked savages.

With his prestige shrunk almost to *persona non grata* dimensions, after waiting in anterooms for years, Cortés determined to return once more to Mexico. Broken in spirit, he made his farewells to gentlemen who wished him God-speed with lip-courtesy only. On his journey to the ship he was stricken. The legitimate Martín, now seventeen, removed his father to the village called Castillo de la Cuesta. Here on December second, 1547, in his sixty-third year, Hernán Cortés died. His body reposed in the monastery at San Isidro for a time, until Martín had it sent across the sea for burial in Texcoco. Thence it was moved to various places in and about Mexico City. Where his bones lie today no one knows, just as no one can say with assurance whether the mortal remains of Christopher Columbus repose in Cuba or Santo Domingo. The great discoverer and the great conqueror, who both loved nothing better than to dare the uncharted and to test the mystery of things, continued their earthly travels after death and left unsolved riddles in their wake.

Cortés, more than Columbus, was the superb epitome of his age. Though he possessed the defects of his brilliant qualities and some of the bad as well as good manifestations of the times in which he lived, he is one of the world's indisputable heroes.

## PART TWO

# COLONIAL NEW SPAIN

## 6. Spain Builds and Mexico Drowses

*"No country in the world has ever been so completely ruined as Spain by the avoidable faults and follies of its governors."*

DAVID HUME

The men who conquered Mexico were not allowed to rule the land they had won. New Spain, as the land was now called, was administered by a bureaucracy appointed by the crown. First there was an *audiencia*, and then in 1535 arrived Antonio de Mendoza as the first viceroy. From this date until the achievement of independence in 1821, New Spain was governed by foreign-born viceroys. The colonists had virtually nothing to say about their own government.

Mendoza was one of the very best in the long line of rulers, mainly indifferent and bad. He was able and conscientious, cautious and just, and even progressive. It was he who sent the first colony of Spaniards from Mexico to Manila across the Pacific. He was wise enough to leave the Indian villages under the administration of the Indian *caciques,* each village to retain its communal acreage or *ejido,* which was at length legally established at something like ten square miles. In 1536 a public mint was established, and later in the year the first institution of higher learning in the New World.

If New Spain had been ruled by a series of Mendozas, the colonial state would have had a very different record. But in the twenty-eight decades following there were few among the viceroys whose names are even worth remembering. Most of them came solely to line their pockets for the homeward voyage. They lived in regal splendor and ruled like absolute monarchs, accounting only to a sovereign five thousand miles away. And for almost three centuries the Spanish crown made the dependence of Mexico on the mother country as complete as possible.

To Cortés's men had been given extensive tracts of land and a quantity of Indians to work for them in field or in mine under the *encomienda* system practiced in Cuba and Hispaniola. The wording of the grant *encomienda* read thus: "Unto you, ——, are given in trust, under chief ——, with the chief, so many Indians, for you to make use of in your farms and mines; and you are to teach them the things of the holy Catholic faith." But the hardened soldiers were far less zealous in pious instruction than in grinding out money from native labor. Some of the war-scarred adventurers stayed at home overseeing the running of their new estates and laying the foundations of the future aristocracy of Mexico. But many, lured by rumors of richer kingdoms to despoil, went off conquesting afresh, and left the management to stewards.

While Cortés was wasting his wealth in fitting out fruitless squadrons on the Pacific, other *conquistadores* were nosing to the north. The mountainous territory above Mexico City was still largely unexplored and unconquered. Some of the natives only a few days' march beyond the capital were nomadic savages. The tribes in the Zacatecas mountains refused to be subjugated and proved the ruin of many an expedition sent out against them. But, stimulated by tall tales of riches, the Spaniards pushed on. To rid themselves of the ravaging invaders, the Indians would point to some fantastic region of gold and precious stones, to the north, the north-east, the north-west—always beyond. Francisco

Vásquez de Coronado, who had started out magnificently equipped not only with Spaniards and Indian allies but with a thousand horses and great flocks of sheep and droves of cattle, conquered the Indians of New Mexico and reached as far as the plains of Kansas. But he returned with empty hands and a sadly reduced force. The cattle had been lost along the way—to multiply and to form the basis of future fortunes in the limitless pastures of Sonora and Chihuahua.

While attempting to subdue the Zacatecans, Spaniards discovered extraordinarily rich deposits of silver in 1548. Soon they were building a road to transport the silver to Mexico City. As other silver mines were found, the white men began enslaving more and more Indians to work in the mines. The baptizing friars could not save their converts from the killing fate of beasts of burden under inhuman loads and inhuman treatment. As the Indians died like flies, their places had to be constantly filled, and slave hunting became something like a sport. Along with work too heavy to be endured, the natives suffered from new diseases the Europeans had brought—smallpox, tuberculosis, and influenza. To escape the pains and dangers of the white man's civilization many Indians preferred to flee to mountain or jungle and live as isolated savages.

Never in any other period of history did daring youths have such opportunities to test their mettle. Shiploads of younger sons came out from Spain for the sport, and many a rakish ne'er-do-well learned to endure rank hardship. The "youngest conquistador," Francisco de Ibarra, was made governor of all northwest Mexico at the age of sixteen. Zestfully he set forth to find silver and subdue natives who opposed the Spanish rule. For twenty years he roamed and ranged. Though the precious stuff he found was paltry, he and some of his fellows made fortunes out of the wild herds descended from Coronado's strayed cattle.

Throughout New Spain in the sixteenth and seventeenth centuries, spasmodic rebellions continued to break out. Punitive expeditions were ever and again on the march. The troublesome Indians who were caught were branded on the face and sold as slaves. Many of them changed masters often, and with each exchange they had the hot iron applied with a different marking. Some of them had so many scars of letters and symbols that the entire face was written upon, and, as one chronicler said, "they carried their history on their countenances."

All during the subjugations and explorations, Franciscan and Dominican brothers pursued their work of conversion. Two priests reported that they had baptized and anointed more than fourteen thousand Indians in five days and declared that it was "very exhausting work." In friendly Tlascala, three priests claimed—with considerable exaggeration—to have baptized over a million Indians during their sojourn among the hill people.

The more sagacious of the church fathers were quite aware that conversion came too easily. But if the new attitude was really pagan at heart, they argued, it would come right in time. Wherever possible the clergy set up their churches on sites of heathen temples where the people had been wont to congregate. And on feast days it was not altogether unseemly for Indians to pay passing tribute to their dethroned divinities, while making obeisance to the saints of the new religion. Whenever the Indians could transmute and fuse ancient symbolism with new, the priests with their shrewd psychology never said them nay. For the natives to identify the Holy Ghost with the sacred eagle of the Aztecs was quite natural and pardonable. It was better, the priests reasoned, that they should be gently weaned away from false gods. But now today, after four centuries, the Indians have not completely renounced pagan adoration.

Yet within a decade after the conquest the understanding fathers granted the Indians their own special protectress, a Virgin who performed a miracle for the most humble of men. On the hill of Tepayac at Guadalupe, a few miles from the capital, had once stood a temple to the gentle Indian goddess of corn called

Tonantzin, who preferred sacrifices of doves and pigeons to human beings. An Indian, renamed Juan Diego, who had listened to doctrines explained in simple language by the Franciscans, was signally honored by this appearance of the true Holy Mother. She intercepted him as he crossed by the mountain of Tepayac and told him to inform the Bishop Zumárraga that she desired a church erected on the spot. The bishop was not impressed, and asked for some token from the Virgin. When she appeared next time before Juan Diego and he demanded a sign, she told him to go to the top of the barren mountain and gather an armful of roses. But he reminded her that this was the twelfth of December, and nothing but cactus had ever grown on the mountain top even in May. Nevertheless, he obeyed and found the roses. On his return the Virgin wrapped the blossoms in his *tilma,* or mantle, and sent him to the prelate. When he came into the bishop's presence, he loosed one end of the *tilma* and the roses fell to the floor between them. But what astounded the bishop was an image of the Holy Mother painted on the coarse cheap cloth. There she stood in the curve of a moon in a pale golden aura, her pink gown dusted with gold, and the expression on her face exceedingly sweet. How the painting came about the bishop could not or would not say, but when he had taken counsel with himself and others a miracle was proclaimed. Soon was begun the construction of a beautiful church in honor of the patroness of the Indians. It paid blessed dividends. The Virgin of Guadalupe did more to reconcile the Indians to the Christian conquest than any other agency. When one of the intellectual churchmen of the end of the eighteenth century had the temerity to deny the miracle in public, he was exiled for thirty years for his lack of tact.

In towns and villages and sometimes even in a wilderness, almost immediately after the conquest, the friars began building great churches of stone. As soon as an Indian was Christianized his labor was commandeered to help to build a place of worship.

Without benefit of beasts to draw loads, the natives formed lines like rural bucket-brigades for firefighting and passed the great stones by man to man from quarry to church site.

Besides saving souls and building churches, the indefatigable friars strove to educate their dark charges. Perhaps the most remarkable in education among the Franciscan teachers was a friar named Pedro de Gante. He came from Ghent in August, 1522. This begging friar had royal blood in his veins, being related illegitimately to the Emperor Charles V. At Texcoco he established himself and immediately began to study the Aztec language. By 1524—perhaps through secret imperial patronage, since the Franciscans declined state subsidies—Father Gante was able to create a school large enough to instruct a thousand Indian children at a time. Here besides the catechism the pupils learned to read and write in Spanish and to reckon. Some with proper aptitude were taught drawing and music. Some were instructed in weaving and leather work after the Spanish models. Others were trained in masonry and carpentry. Father Gante himself is recorded as teaching sculpture and painting. When they had finished their simple courses of instruction these Indian youths were sent abroad in the land to teach others and to help in the construction of churches, convents, and schools.

Artisans from Spain had been imported not only to ply their trades but to teach the Indians the Spanish skill. The Indians learned so quickly that the Spaniards at length refused to teach them since the amount of their own wage went down. Often the friars themselves were the sole teachers of crafts. The most famous among these beneficent clergymen was Vasco de Quiroga, who settled at the picturesque lake town of Patzcuaro and later became the first bishop of Michoacán. In 1533 Quiroga wrote of the Tarascans: "They own things as one another and these men of nature do not have, and never had, king or master over them, nor hereditary successor, but designate him by election— and there are not true slaves or serfs among them." This good intellectual, who had read Sir Thomas More, experimented with his own Utopian ideas, and aimed to order society so that the Indians might live "without need, insecurity or laziness, and removed from danger and infamy." The bishop was an inspiriting pastor to his flock, which had been dismayed by the brutality of the vicious administrator Nuño de Guzmán, who tied their Tarascan chief to the tail of a horse and dragged him over the rocks before burning him. Quiroga encouraged one special kind of trade or industry in each separate village for the benefit of all. So agreeable is custom to the Mexican Indian that after four centuries the same trades are pursued in the same villages. Tourists today visit them and take note. In Uruapan, the finest lacquer ware in the hemisphere is still made, and the formula of the varnish is yet a secret. In Parocho the Indians still specialize in guitars. In Santa Clara they produce copper ware; in Tzintzuntzán, pottery; in Teremando, shoes. In Capula, the natives work in wood; in San Felipe, in iron. And in the town of Cocupao, renamed Quiroga after the good bishop, they pride themselves on painted boxes. Though he died in 1556, Quiroga's memory is still revered by the Indians today.

Another zealous friend of the Indians was that staunch enemy of imperialism, Father Bartolomé de las Casas, who believed that all aggression was evil except that which was evangelical. By word and by pen he insisted that the sole purpose of expeditionary forces should be to convert the heathen to Christianity. His idealism was not altogether without influence on the Emperor Charles, but Spain was far away and the monarch's commands were winked at by his avaricious agents. However, Las Casas was largely responsible for the new law of 1542 by which *encomiendas* could not be inherited. Stirred by Las Casas, the Spanish crown sought from time to time, even after his death, to restrain abuse of the Indians, but the protective laws were usually ignored or circumvented.

The colonization by the British in North America was something quite different from that of the Spanish, in motive and manner. The Englishmen who first settled along the Atlantic seaboard came as neither gold seekers nor missionaries. They came to save their own skins and to worship God in their own way. They set forth as pioneers to carve new homes out of a wilderness. But they showed far less concern for the preservation of the Indian than did the Spaniard, who set up his house in the midst of the Indian population, for convenience and exploitation. The Englishmen cheated the nomadic redskins out of their lands for jugs of rum and pushed them farther and farther inland from the coast. Those they did not exterminate the Americans finally corralled in reservations. There was scarcely any inter-racial marriage. On the other hand, many of the Spaniards who first settled in Mexico married Indian girls. Others cohabited promiscuously with natives. For better or worse, Spain brought forth a new race, the fusion of Iberian blood with native Indian, called the *mestizo*. One thing is certain, that the mixed-blood people bore in their hearts the seeds of conflicting emotions and potential future explosions. From the beginning, however, the Spaniard in Mexico seemed to regard the native masses principally as work beasts. The Indian's inferiority and lack of ability were taken as matters of fact. The Spanish policy in general was to stifle native talents and to keep him in a state of physical, mental, and spiritual subjection.

Yet one cannot discount what Spain did in creative building and organization. It is to her everlasting credit that, with the marvelous help of her early friars, she laid a kind of luster on colonial Mexico. It is true the Aztecs had achieved a comparatively high civilization. But the conquest of the New World was inevitable, and the Spanish were energetic colonizers as well as great conquerors. Without that influx of Iberian blood and energy and gift for architecture, Mexico would be minus a patina that makes it one of the most evocative lands in the world. In all the Western Hemisphere only in the city of Lima did civilization approach such a scale of grandeur as colonial Mexico knew in the eighteenth century. Significantly, it was in those two countries, Peru and Mexico, that the native culture of the pre-Columbian era reached its most brilliant flowering, as blood-soaked and sinister as both were.

Almost like magic, throughout Mexico, towns with churches and plazas to last for generations began to occupy the sites of native villages. The early Spanish architects, both ecclesiastical and mundane, seemed to have planned for the delectation of posterity. At first the churches and monasteries and even private homes possessed qualities akin to fortresses. And then after subjugations were completed came a lavish outpouring of decoration. Only in architecture did "the two somnolent centuries," following the energetic sixteenth, contribute much to the lasting glory of Mexico. But in that branch of creative art the heritage is uncommonly opulent. And there the Indian was allowed to make consummate use of his talent. Both façades and interiors of the magnificent, solid Spanish conceptions were overwrought with memorials of Indian ingenuity.

Cities beautiful, such as Oaxaca and Morelia, took form, softly luminous with the green or pinkish stone of their regions. Streets with gracious mansions stretched out longer. Boulevards were widened and enriched with planting. Aqueducts paraded in great, chained arches into the cities, bringing spectacular beauty along with water from the heights. A profusion of flowering shrubs was set out to grace fountained patios. Plazas and green parks for refreshment of body and spirit became as customary as the town wells. Everywhere the eye looked there were great churches to dramatize the religion of the simple Nazarene. By the end of the eighteenth century Mexico had some ten thousand Christian churches. The great, well ordered piles of pink or dove gray or mushroom yellow stone, with their heaven-ascending towers, gave the variegated Mexican landscape a kind of characteristic Spanish harmony and a richness that made the United States seem raw and homespun beside it.

There is significant truth in Sylvester Baxter's remark that "New Spain never experienced the long period of colonial simplicity of the English possessions. . . . Thanks to the startling energy of the conquerors, greedy for wealth and power, animated at the same time by a profound faith, the New Spain became flourishing within a few years."

As time went on, silver in greater and greater quantities was dug from the bowels of the hills. Indians sweated, groaned, and died in increasing numbers under the strain, as individual Spaniards made tremendous fortunes. By 1750 the yield from the silver mines was reckoned at more than thirteen million pesos annually. Towards the end of the eighteenth century Humboldt remained for weeks at Moran and Real del Monte, inspecting the methods of mining. "The hardest part of the work," he wrote, "was performed by the native Indians, who carried the metals out on their backs, in loads of from two hundred and fifty to three hundred and fifty pounds at a time, ascending and descending thousands of steps of an inclination of forty-five degrees, where the air was from seventy-one to seventy-three degrees [centigrade]." Better off by far were the peons who cultivated the corn and cotton for the great plantation owners.

In the eighteenth century the country estate became a focus of social life as well as an economic factor. Certain idle society groups spent their time revolving about a series of house parties. But the *hacienda* had never quite the significance of an antebellum Southern plantation home in the United States. In the South the owner and his family usually lived on the plantation, scorning the more vulgar civilization of the towns. In Mexico the plantation owners generally lived in the cities and went out to the plantation for a holiday, for the shooting, or the country air. The management of the estate was rarely a burden on the *hacendado*. An overseer ran the place, and his job was to extract as much labor as possible from the peons. The peons' welfare was rarely considered as was that of the Negro slaves of the better Southern plantations. The vicious absentee-landlord system, which has been the curse of all Latin America, became more and more accepted.

During the colonial period, almost all of the important offices went to Spaniards from Spain, who came merely with the intent of acquiring money. And Spanish business men, too, had no original intention of remaining longer than to gain the sum they had set their hearts on. But many found the life so much easier and less competitive in Mexico than in Spain that they remained. A new social order emerged.

Yet within two generations after the conquest a Spaniard cobbler or mule driver just over from Europe would set himself up as superior to a Mexican-born Spaniard. The haughty Spaniards came to be called *gachupines,* "men who wear spurs." The descendants of the Spaniards who were born in Mexico were known as *criollos.* These creoles were of pure white blood. The *gachupín* held himself socially superior to the *criollo,* who in turn felt immoderately above the *mestizo,* who looked down on his darker Indian cousins with contempt, and the latter in turn often renounced the half-blood. By the seventeenth century this caste system had four distinct classes, though exceptions occasionally blurred the differences.

Through the seventeenth century New Spain was almost as much a closed book to Europe and the British colonies in North America as was Japan. The only Englishman who got into Mexico and lived to return home to write first-hand impressions about the fabulous land was a man named Thomas Gage. In England he had become a Dominican friar, and as a missionary to the Philippine Islands he "had got himself conveyed to Mexico" where he paused en route and remained for almost a dozen years. On his return to England he renounced the Catholic faith and became a Puritan preacher. He gave such a glowing account of Mexico, that according to Bullock, Oliver Cromwell in the period of his Protectorship thought of adding New Spain to the British dominions. At any rate, he sent an expedition under the command of Penn and Venables to have a look. And though nothing came of the venture so far as Mexico was concerned, on the return trip the British took over the valuable island of Jamaica.

Friar Gage gives a very lively account of Mexico City in the second quarter of the seventeenth century. He seems particularly impressed with the coaches, the ostentation of dress and the prevalent passion for gambling, for he refers to these things again and again in his book, which was published in London in 1648.

The streets are very broad, in the narrowest three coaches may goe, and in the broader six may goe in the breadth of them, which makes the city seeme a great deal bigger than it is; in my time it was thought to bee of between 30 to 40,000 inhabitants, Spaniards, who are so proud and rich, that half the city was judged to keepe coaches, for it was a most credible report that in Mexico in my time there were above fifteen thousand coaches. It is a by-word, that in Mexico there are foure things faire, that is to say, the women, the apparel, the horses, and the streets. But to this I may adde the beauty of some of the coaches of the gentry, which doe exceed in cost the best of the court of Madrid, for they spare no silver, nor gold, nor pretious stones, nor cloath of gold, nor the best silkes of China to enrich them. And to the gallantry of their horses, the pride of some adde the cost of bridles and shooes of silver. . . . Above all, the goldsmiths' shops and workes are to be admired. The Indians, and the people of China that have been made Christians, and every yeere come thither, have now perfected the Spaniards in those trades . . .

To the by-word touching the beauty of the women, I must add the liberty they enjoy for gaming . . . nay, gaming is so common to them, that they invite gentlemen to their houses for no other end:— to myself it happened that, passing along the streets with a friar . . . a gentlewoman of great birth, knowing us to be chapetans, from her window called unto us, asked us if wee would come in and play with her a game at primera.

Both men and women are excessive in their apparel, using more silkes than stuffes and cloth; pretious stones and pearles further much this their vaine ostentation; a hatband and rose made of diamonds, in a gentleman's hat, is common, and a hatband of pearles is ordinary in a tradesman; nay, a blackmore or tawny young maide and slave will make hard shift but shee will bee in fashion with her neckchaine and bracelets of pearles . . . The attire of this baser sort of people (which are of a mixt nature of Spaniards and blackmores) is so light, and their carriage so enticing, that many Spaniards, even of the better sort (who are too prone to venery) desdaine their wives for them . . .

Thomas Gage did not spend all of his time in the capital, but roamed as far away as remote Chiapas and the borders of Guatemala. As a friar he was *persona grata* everywhere. As an Englishman he made the mistake of calling a *mestizo* or anyone with part Indian blood an Indian, but his comments attest to the fact of the importance of *mestizos* in some provinces. "No town hath so many Dons in it of Indian bloud as this. Don Felipe de Guzmán was Governor of it in my time, a very rich Indian, who kept commonly in his stables a dozen of as good horses for public shewes and ostentation as the best Spaniard in the country. The Indians put on sham sea-fights, horse races and were clever at all manner of Spanish dances, instruments and music, as the best of Spaniards . . . As for the acting of playes, this is a common part of their solemn pastimes; and they are so generous that they think nothing too much to spend in banquets and sweetmeats upon their fairs and neighbouring towns, whensoever they are minded to shew themselves in a publick feast. The town is very rich, and many Indians in it trade about the country as the Spaniards do."

While wealth accumulated and sons of the wealthy decayed with a dry rot of nothing useful to do, some Indians existed with barely enough necessaries to hold body and soul together. Not until 1720 did an actual end come to the *encomiendas*. But soon the Indians suffered a new kind of slavery—that of perpetual debt to the landlord. And the ecclesiastical order in Mexico, having gradually added its weight of domination to that of the state, began to batten on the ignorance of the people. Mexico suffered generations of corrupt church politics. After the hard spadework of inaugurating a new religion was done by the selfless friars, Spanish priests arrived bringing their trained political astuteness and their shrewd schemes for collecting money. There were unceasing demands for fees. It became costly—sometimes ruinous—to be born, to marry, or to die. By gift, by legacy, by mortgage foreclosures, by instilling fears of purgatorial fires, the church came into possession of some forty to fifty per cent of the real and personal property of the land. The archbishop and the bishops received princely salaries, as high as 130,000 pesos a year, and vied with the viceroys in ostentatious display. While hard-working, self-sacrificing rural priests often lived on a pittance, idle city prelates often lived in stuffy self-indulgence without the faintest effort at constructive work.

The great Spanish nation which had reached such a climax of dynamic expansion in the sixteenth century became exhausted before the eighteenth century. Its body politic began to suffer from a dry rot that attacked it at the top. And to keep her sickness undivulged, by a show of material well-being, she ever demanded more of her colonies, and in return gave less and less. In time the Spanish crown seemed to lose interest in everything except revenue from monopolies and taxes. There were sixty different kinds of taxes by the end of the eighteenth century. Monopolies for the benefit of the few multiplied on the body of Mexico like plague sores. The populace was sucked and drained by every conceivable leech of duties, royalties, taxes, fees. The crown reserved for itself the fat monopolies of gunpowder, salt, tobacco and the lotteries, but it was not too lofty to keep also for itself even much lesser monopolies as packs of playing cards, cockfights, and even the God-given mountain snow utilized in refrigeration. Paradoxically, the gold and silver that poured into Spain was the precious bane that undermined the monarchy's constitution and brought on a kind of fatty degeneration.

In Mexico, commerce was deliberately hamstrung. Local industries and manufacture were regulated or forbidden, for the profit of business men in Spain. The Mexicans were not permitted to trade with any other except the mother country. All Mexican trade, both import and export, was compelled by law to pass through ports in Spain. The retail prices of hundreds of articles became thrice those of the same things in European shops. Except for the native foodstuffs, living costs were higher than in any other country in the world. In the early nineteenth century the leeching of Mexico brought Spain half of its income. No such profiteering had been known. The privileged Spanish merchants in Mexico lived in blazing magnificence. But since many of the *gachupín* business men in Mexico were often uneducated and uncouth as well as rapaciously aggressive, they came finally to be looked upon with contempt by the creoles, who never had been allowed the advantages of commerce and who, like many gentlemen of England, came to look upon work of any kind as degrading. Even in agriculture, Spain made its prohibitions for the benefit of Spaniards at home. Crop cultivation was reduced to a minimum of a few staples, like corn, beans, chili, cotton. In some years, plantation owners left eighty per cent of their holdings to grow up in weeds.

Bribery and the law's delay were accepted conventions. Justice was a commodity to be bargained for. Accused men languished for years in jail and in many cases died before the court ever got around to trying them. Graft was as prevalent as termites in the hot lands. Custom officials held out a palm and winked an eye at smugglers. Petty officials robbed and cheated the Indians and gave a rake-off to men higher up.

Communications continued to be hopelessly inadequate. Traveling was dangerous because bandits lurked by the roads and trails. Education retrogressed and became increasingly an affair for the well-to-do. The schools the friars had set up for the Indians were taken over by the creoles, who came to resent

learning in the natives. Spanish artisans, who had been niggardly about teaching Indian apprentices their skills, gradually
caused Indians to be prohibited from practicing certain crafts.
Experimentation in any field was frowned on. There was nothing to foster ingenuity in either the Indian or the *mestizo*. Since
there was virtually no market for Mexican goods, there was no
incentive to produce. Only those persons talented in architecture,
painting, or sculpture could find proper outlets of self-expression.

Humboldt, in speaking of the Academy of Fine Arts in 1803
—and giving it credit for much that had been done before it
came into existence—wrote:

It is impossible not to perceive the influence of this establishment
on the taste of the nation. This influence is particularly visible in the
symmetry of the buildings, in the perfection with which the hewing
of stone is conducted, and in the ornaments of the capitals and stucco
relievos. What a number of beautiful edifices are to be seen in
Mexico! Nay, even in provincial towns like Guanajuato and Querétaro! These monuments, which frequently cost a million and a
million and a half of francs, would appear to advantage in the finest
streets of Paris, Berlin, and Petersburg. M. Tolsa, professor of sculpture at Mexico, was even able to cast an equestrian statue of King
Charles the Fourth; a work which, with the exception of Marcus
Aurelius at Rome, surpasses in beauty and purity of style everything
which remains in this way in Europe. Instruction is communicated
gratis at the Academy of Fine Arts. It is not confined alone to the
drawing of landscapes and figures; they have the good sense to employ
other means for exciting the national industry. The academy labors
successfully to introduce among the artisans a taste for elegance and
beautiful forms. Large rooms lighted by Argand's lamps contain every
evening some hundreds of young people, of whom some draw from
relievo or living models, while others copy drawings of furniture,
chandeliers, or other ornaments in bronze. In this assemblage (and
this is very remarkable in the midst of a country where the prejudices of the nobility against the castes are so inveterate) rank, color,
and race are confounded: we see the Indian and the *mestizo* sitting
beside the white, and the son of a poor artisan in emulation with the
children of the great lords of the country. It is a consolation to

observe, that under every zone the cultivation of science and art establishes a certain equality among men, and obliterates for a time, at least, all those petty passions of which the effects are so prejudicial to social happiness.

With little to anchor their days to, besides horseback riding and the pursuit of sexual adventures, the creole sons, who had no talent for the plastic arts, grew up shiftless and irresponsible. They attained a certain grace in lolling and swaggering. But because of the purposelessness of their routine, the colonial polish, however charming, was thin indeed. And existing side by side with the white and the *mestizo* civilization, the Indian, with rare exception, was a complete outsider. But he had one unadulterated blessing from providence—the introduction of the burro to lighten his unbearable burdens.

The one supreme blessing allotted to Mexico, above all European nations and the North American Thirteen Colonies, throughout the eighteenth century, was peace. But the country was sealed against the intrusion of new ideas. Literature was rigorously censored, and through the Inquisition the church effectively and painfully stopped the mouths of heretics and liberals.

Yet in the last quarter of the eighteenth century the American Revolution and the French Revolution began to be discussed clandestinely. Liberal philosophies were smuggled into Mexico by contraband book and proscribed conversation. In the sociological set-up, lawyers gradually became significant, and it is they particularly who began a struggle for state reforms, as they were later to lead in the overthrow of the power of the church.

During the reign of the enlightened King Charles III (1759-1788), His Majesty sent an investigator to Mexico to make a full report on the conditions. As a result, administrative reforms were introduced, and the Indians were relieved of considerable unlawful oppression. Trade and tariff regulations were modified, so that the economic structure was improved. A school of mines was established. Viceroys of considerably better caliber were sent to rule. But the reforms only scratched the surface of Mexico's real needs, and at the end of the eighteenth century there was not a single free elementary school in Mexico, and such schools as existed were run by priests, good, bad, or indifferent. The next King Charles was a nincompoop who undid all the good of his intelligent father's reign. His stupidity helped to precipitate the fight for freedom against the mother country which came early in the next century. But whatever the state of things that mark an advancing civilization, in 1800 there was no other city in the New World so beautiful as Spanish Mexico, in spite of her contrasts in riches and misery.

## PART THREE

# INDEPENDENCE

## 7. Patriot Priests

*"Despair not the obliquities of younger ways,
nor despair of better things whereof there is
yet no prospect."*
SIR THOMAS BROWNE

Between the great conqueror, Hernán Cortés, born in 1485, and
Miguel Hidalgo, a parish priest born in 1753, no name of prime
renown appears on the Mexican scene. The lack of well-known
personages shows how completely Mexico was subjugated to the
will and interest of Spain during the three centuries of colonial
rule. The desire for independence was not born with the passionate cry for "liberty" that it later employed, but it grew
rather out of a long-suffering need of reform. And though there
was no conceivable intention of breaking with the orthodox
church, paradoxically it was a priest who launched the rebellion
against the established authority.

Father Hidalgo was as beloved as Chaucer's poor parson. Not
only was he a shepherd of great heart who practiced the good he
preached, but he was a man capable of fiery action and a thinker
who read philosophies forbidden by the Inquisition. Like Bishop
Quiroga, he tried to better the rude standards of living of his
poor parishioners at Dolores, not only by aiding them in rudi-
mentary education but by establishing local industries so they
might employ their stifled talents. He set up a small textile

99

works. He established a place for tanning hides and another for fashioning better earthenware utensils. He encouraged bee and silk-worm culture. He planted vineyards on the hillsides. When the grapes were ripening, Spanish officials ordered the Indians to uproot the vines, so that wine monopoly in Spain might lose no jot of revenue. Father Hidalgo protested in vain. The tearing up of the vines from the soil tore at the heartstrings of the priest, and he resolved to do his mightiest to strike off the Spanish yoke.

In the nearby city of Querétaro was a group of thinkers and army officers who belonged to a literary society founded to discuss, in secret, revolutionary sentiments. Their ideas of reform were mild enough. They did not desire to establish a republic, but merely wanted Mexico to be governed by men born in Mexico and not by officious Spaniards. Hidalgo was invited to meet them. Prominent in the group was an eager young captain named Ignacio Allende, who was also a landowner and devotee of bull-fighting. Another member was Josefa Ortiz Domínguez, the wife of the mayor. Both Allende and Señora Ortiz Dominguez were sincerely interested in the welfare of the Indians. But the chief concern of the society was to expel the sucking *gachupines* from their land. They hoped to win over the creole army officers in various towns so that the riddance could be accomplished without bloodshed, if possible. They purposed to make their formal declaration of independence in December at the fair of San Juan de Lagos. But their activities were treacherously disclosed to the government. Before the leaders could be arrested, however, the mayor's wife discovered the danger at a secret conference in her own house at which her husband was present. She tapped on the floor to a servant waiting in a room beneath for the signal. He rushed to inform Captain Allende. The latter rode through the night to Dolores to warn Father Hidalgo and ask his advice. It was the night of September fifteenth. The aroused priest listened to the captain and made a swift decision. Although there was no time now to win over the creole army, he would appeal directly to the Indians.

Before dawn the church bell began an insistent ringing in a new way. Those who were not already awake were aroused by the clamor and dressed hurriedly. The church was soon overflowing. As the sun broke, Hidalgo, his eyes lighted with seraphic fire, took his place in the pulpit. He offered his dark-skinned children freedom if they were ready to fight for it. "Will you make an effort to regain the lands the greedy Spaniards stole from your forefathers three centuries ago?"

As the good man spoke, with prophetic zeal, the words "liberty" and "emancipation" took on a kind of magic. On inspiration he seized the church banner bearing the image of the Indian Virgin of Guadalupe and elevated it before them. The Lady was to be their conquering symbol. The congregation began to shout, "Long live independence!" Holding the banner aloft, he marched down the aisle and out of the little church. The Indians followed, ready to dare anything. Though they had no firearms—for these were forbidden to them by the authorities—they seized machetes, pitchforks, scythes, clubs. Indians from the neighboring villages joined them with makeshift implements of war. By noon, a troop of ill-equipped but passionate crusaders was on the march.

Within two months the army had grown to almost a hundred thousand. At first, the rebels met with success. Totally unprepared for such an insurrection, the Spanish authorities lost town after town. The clergy became alarmed. Monks armed with pistols and crucifixes galloped on horseback, like so many Paul Reveres, ahead of the oncoming rebels and begged the common people not to join the accursed ones. But they had little or no effect. The ragged bands took possession of strings of towns. In Celaya rioting and pillaging began. The lowest of the population rose to batter down the doors of Spanish residences. Well-to-do creoles were not spared. Their town houses also were looted. This was not at all what Allende and Hidalgo had planned. The peasant army got utterly out of control. The leaders could not stop the disorder. They were horrified to realize that they had stirred up not so much a fight for independence as a class conflict. Revenge for centuries of oppression became rampant. And as their followers razed creole *haciendas,* seized cattle and foodstuffs as it suited them, the leaders foresaw they would lose the support of those upper-class native-born whites on whom they had counted. Now that the tide of revolt had started rising, however, it could not be checked. Hidalgo, deploring the method, yet saw that the freedom of Mexico would come this bloody way—by Indian uprising and the terrorization of the *gachupín.*

The city of Guanajuato fell after a terrific slaughtering of Hidalgo's Indians by artillery fire. Then, in turn, the Indians massacred as many of the Spaniards as Hidalgo could not save. From Guanajuato the rebel forces marched to Valladolid and took it without a struggle, as the Spaniards fled pellmell.

The news of the revolt and the successes spread like a grass fire. Sympathetic bands flaming with patriotism or a mere desire for loot sprang up mushroom-like, won over villages, and swept into towns. *Gachupines* and bishops fled to safety as they could. Northern Mexico was soon completely in control of the insurgents.

While the white-haired priest of Dolores under the grandiose title of "Captain-General of America" had subdued the governmental forces in the north, another younger priest was organizing an army in the south. José María Morelos had been a pupil of Hidalgo's when the latter was rector of the little College of San Nicolás at Valladolid. He was the son of a poor village carpenter. A *mestizo,* he was reputed to have also a strain of Negro blood which came from African slaves brought into Michoacán in the early part of the seventeenth century. From his Indian ancestry he inherited his shortness in stature; he stood barely five feet tall. But his shoulders were extraordinarily broad, and though subject to recurrent attacks of migraine and stomach upsets, he was a human dynamo. He had been born behind the front door of a small house in Valladolid, when his mother, who had come to town to market, was suddenly stricken with labor pains in the street. As a youth he had suffered the hunger and privations of the Mexican poor. Before he began working his way through school he was employed as a mule driver. Yet his energy and his inspiration marked him for leadership among men. And this obscure Michoacán priest rose meteorically to be in his time the first name in Mexico.

Hidalgo had dispatched Morelos with two dozen men and no firearms to foment rebellion in the south. Before the end of 1811, in the mountains between Taxco and Acapulco the twenty-five had increased, like the Biblical loaves and fishes, to nine thousand. Morelos won consecutive victories.

Frightened by the mass uprising and the seizure of their property by the Indians, the independence-seeking creoles began to desert the cause and to long for the success of the Spanish soldiers so that order might be restored. Almost all the landowners and creole officers who had earlier favored rebellion now began to throw their support back to the Spanish government.

In the north, Hidalgo and Allende had mobs to back them, but no trained forces and few arms. Their hordes were really no match for Spanish artillery and Spanish discipline, when met with face to face. The Indians could not make up, by their valor, what they lacked in war gear. Though they intrepidly approached the flame-spitting cannon and tried to stop its wholesale destruction by pressing their flimsy sombreros against its mouth, it would no more be stopped than an erupting volcano. Indians were sacrificed by the thousands, but as they fell others appeared to carry on the fight.

When a ragged rebel force of eighty thousand appeared at the approaches to Mexico City, the Spaniards were dismayed, for the biggest part of their army was in the north trying to recapture San Luis Potosí. The desperate viceroy ordered the doll image called the Virgen de los Remedios to be brought by carriage from its mountain shrine to the great cathedral. This Virgin, which was reputed to have saved Cortés once, was now invoked again to save the Spaniards from the avenging Indians. In view of a packed congregation the viceroy knelt before the doll and prayed for the city's deliverance. Then, climactically, he publicly proclaimed the blank-eyed image "Commander of the Spanish Army." This white Virgin was now pitted against the brown Virgin of Guadalupe.

Oddly enough, the event coincided with the turning point in the war. While Allende urged immediate attack, Hidalgo temporized. Either he dreaded the slaughter of his forces by Spanish cannon or he feared that if his undisciplined horde got loose in the city and started pillaging, he could never get them together again. Against all advice, he decided the time was not ripe for taking the capital, and ordered a circuitous march to Guanajuato. This fatal withdrawal lost the revolution.

In furious disappointment, peons as well as creoles began to desert in shoals. Hidalgo's baggage trains and what cannon he had were seized by the Spanish General Calleja, who was returning from the north. Allende was separated from Hidalgo. While Allende carried on the actual war, which became more bloody with merciless reprisals on both sides, Hidalgo went on to Guadalajara and prepared to set up his own government.

With his forces shrunken to less than half, Hidalgo announced his emancipation proclamation, by which all slaves were freed and the lands were to be restored to the Indians. As defeats came one after another, Hidalgo continued to proclaim his constructive program for the future. "Crafts will be stimulated, industry will come to life. In a few years the inhabitants of this fertile land will enjoy the benefits which the Sovereign Author of Nature has poured over this vast continent."

At last Allende and Hidalgo once more joined forces. But again Hidalgo's military judgment was bad, and their troops were shot to bits. The final undoing came from treachery, after the pattern of Mexico's sad history. One of his own creole officers tricked Allende and destroyed his remaining forces. The gallant young leader was captured and shot in the back as a traitor. Shortly afterwards Hidalgo too was captured. He was first degraded by the church and then executed. The heads of both the aged Hidalgo and the young Allende were severed and forwarded to Guanajuato. There, atop the fortress wall, they were set up as grizzly souvenirs. In wet or burning weather, for ten long years, the heroic heads remained, darkening and shriveling before the public gaze. Not until 1821, when independence was actually achieved, were the ghastly masks removed. But even though Hidalgo's mortal head suffered a decade of indignity as it moldered mutely on a fortress wall, his *Grito de Dolores* and his summoning bell on that mid-September dawn in 1810 went echoing down the corridors of history.

That other fighting priest, José María Morelos, still held the field in the south. His power grew as political events in Spain swung pendulum-like from right to left and left to right. Besides the crusading zeal of Father Hidalgo, Morelos possessed qualities of military strategy and a statesmanlike mind which the older priest lacked. Having seen that the cotton-suited Indian mob, armed with farm implements, could never defeat Spanish artillery, Morelos created small, well-disciplined army units equipped with guns captured from the Spaniards. He proved such a genius for strategy that he was able to capture city after city—Orizaba, Oaxaca, Acapulco—and he was as adept at maintaining order as he was at fighting. He gathered to his ranks bands of horsemen, including creole landowners about Chilpancingo. Morelos had the skill, too, to pick worthy lieutenants. Among the most valuable was an illiterate *mestizo* peasant named

Vicente Guerrero who was to carry on the fight alone after his commander was killed.

When the little military dictator felt he had won sufficient victories to warrant the establishment of a legal government, he called a congress of delegates at Chilpancingo. Here he laid before them his plans for independent Mexico. The country was to be a republic, where the will of the majority would dominate. "Laws must extend to all alike, without exception or privileges," he declared. "Those which our Congress shall enact must be such as to moderate opulence and penury, and so augment the wages of the poor, in order that they may improve their habits." He advocated racial equality and the division of the large landed estates into small holdings for the peasants. He would abolish all special privileges for army officers and clergymen. He decreed a general redistribution of wealth; the property of the rich Spaniards was to be taken over by the government, half of it to be used for expenses and public works, and half to be distributed among the poor. He advocated suppression of government monopolies and the sales tax. He asked that all adults be obligated to do useful labor. Though a good Catholic himself, he declared for the confiscation of the accumulated church funds to the uses of the general welfare.

The amazed delegates to this congress in 1813 listened to proposals of radical reforms that were a century before their time. And even a century after the revolutionary padre, only a fraction of the socialistic ideology embodied in his program had been achieved in Mexico. Except for Juárez's reform laws in 1859, not until the new constitution of 1917, adopted under the Carranza administration, was anything approaching the ideas of Morelos really attempted. And not until the regime of Lázaro Cárdenas—1934-1940—were they put into actual practice. Even at the end of the Cárdenas administration the social progress envisioned by the little *mestizo* priest was a long way from realization. But this aim set by Morelos at Chilpancingo in 1813 was something all future reformers were to look to as a gauge and a light.

By the time the congress had drafted its constitution, however, the reinforced Spanish forces began driving the rebel troops out of the cities. The church decreed excommunication and eternal damnation to anyone who even read the new constitution. Most of the well-to-do began to withdraw their support, because the price of independence seemed too costly to their class. Doubtless Morelos should have waited until he had won his war, to set forth all his war aims. And taking time out from winning victories to establish a constitutional government gave the enemy a considerable advantage. While Morelos was busy in the south creating a republic, General Calleja, given full command as viceroy, had subdued and pacified the north. Now, by December of 1813, Calleja was ready with almost the full might of his army to strike at the south. Morelos gathered his conglomerate forces and went north to retake Valladolid in Michoacán, his birthplace, which he had selected for the permanent capital of his republican government.

Here on the historical scene dashed a young cavalry colonel who also had been born in Valladolid. But this man sprang from a well-to-do family, which sought to deny its strain of Indian blood. He was Augustín de Iturbide. Favoring independence, he had yet so feared the social revolution stirred up by the humble priests that he had offered his able services to the hated royalists. Now he seized the chance to break the backbone of the rebellion by attacking Morelos's forces on a rocky hilltop. In the dusk he led a daring cavalry charge up the steep hill, and, taking the camp by surprise, scattered the rebel forces. Morelos was forced to flee with the rest.

In January, Iturbide won another significant battle. Then victory after victory for the royalists followed all over the country. But no Spaniard proved more relentless in bloody execution than

Iturbide, who merrily chased down *guerrilleros* and shot his prisoners by the hundreds.

Too much of Morelos's valuable energy was spent in saving his congress, which he had brought along with his troops. As he was conducting his legislators to a retreat at the rebel town of Tehuacán, Morelos risked his life by a feint to get the enemy off their trail. Forced to take refuge under some bushes, he was captured by a lieutenant who had formerly served under him. Brought before the viceroy in Mexico City, Morelos was ordered to be shot, "as secretly as possible in the outskirts of the city," so as not to tempt a general uprising. His jailer offered him escape, but he would not accept the offer.

After Morelos's execution, at the end of 1815, the priest-inspired revolt for independence was soon over. The only significant leader who retained sufficient power and enough men to be called an army was Vicente Guerrero, in the southern mountains. The new viceroy, Apodacá, offered him a military command and a sum of money if he would give up the struggle. But Guerrero was too imbued with Morelos's high principles. With his mountaineers he continued to defy Spanish rule in the rugged province that immortalizes his name. Except for this courageous and incorruptible peasant who was to live to see himself the second president of the republic, the immediate struggle for independence was over.

# 8. Upstart Emperor

*"Consider what men are when they are eating, sleeping, generating, easing themselves and so forth. Then what kind of men they are when they are imperious and arrogant, or angry and scolding from their elevated place. But a short time ago to how many they were slaves and for what things; and after a little time consider in what a condition they will be."*

MARCUS AURELIUS

Morelos had overreached himself by his radical ideology. If he had concentrated absolutely on running the *gachupines* out of Mexico before he promulgated his democratic plan, Mexican independence might have been achieved with reasonable facility. But he had frightened and alienated the powerful upper classes by putting emphasis on racial equality. As it was, independence was merely delayed for six years after the death of Morelos in 1815.

In the interim there arrived stimulating reports of the success of the great South American patriots Bolívar and San Martín, who were struggling to liberate a continent. In Mexico the watchful Augustín de Iturbide was biding his time to strike on his own for independence. And when occasion knocked, the alert opportunist was ready. With his shrewd political sense to back his militaristic talents, he brought about the "liberation" in nine brief months.

Because of his decisive defeat of Morelos, Iturbide had been made commander of the army in the north and appointed governor of his native province. It was a swift rise for a young man who had been a mere lieutenant in 1810. But from his childhood Iturbide was enamored of tales of warfare and he had intended to rise. Born in the city of Valladolid—subsequently called Morelia—on the twenty-seventh of September, 1783, he had entered military service at the age of fifteen. Iturbide was an odd-looking fellow with luxuriant "sideburns" curling in half-moons almost to the corners of his mouth. With the years his right eye had become considerably smaller than his left, as if narrowed by perpetual scheming. His fearlessness and devil-may-care charm, however, made him a hero to his soldiers, notwithstanding his vicious treatment of his enemies.

Now he was hero to the royalist administration and the church also. But his conduct shortly became so reprehensible that he was recalled, charged with unnecessary cruelty and flagrant embezzlement. The case against him was dropped, ostensibly because of his war record, but really because too many high-ups in government were parties to his thefts. Yet he was not permitted to resume any of his commands. Having spent his gains in reckless extravagance, he retired temporarily to private life not only under a cloud but in much reduced circumstances.

Then, after a plausible interval, he did what many a shrewd politician has done—he professed piety. Moreover, he sought a holy retreat in which to prove his contrition and devotion. For his worldly cleansing he was careful to choose a monastery, La Profesa, that was popular with the highest among the hierarchy. Here Iturbide would pause in his prayers and penances to listen to the reactionaries arguing advantages to themselves to be gained by Mexican independence. They did not like what was going on in the mother country. To keep himself on the throne, the Spanish King Ferdinand had been forced to accept a liberal constitution, which was anathema to the clergy in Mexico. They looked with horror on such things as freedom of the press and any nibbling at church properties by the state. So a direct break with Spain seemed the only course by which they might continue to wield their extraordinary power.

Iturbide's dynamic personality soon attracted the bishops, who became thoroughly convinced of his conservatism and his Catholic loyalty, however dubious an eye they may have cast upon his piety. He seemed the ideal champion to fight the dragon of social reform spawned by those dead and excommunicated priests, Hidalgo and Morelos. His abilities were recommended to the viceroy, Apodacá, who recalled his bloody war record. Soon he was commissioned to lead a force against the rebel, Guerrero, who was still invincible in the south. The new levying of troops was to a degree a pretext for proclaiming the absolute power of King Ferdinand, as against the new liberal constitution in Spain.

When Iturbide met with military defeat, he trickily decided to turn it to victory by pretending to be converted to the rebel cause. To catch Guerrero—as well as the attention of all Mexico —he conceived his own plan of independence, read it to his soldiers, who swore allegiance to it. By its terms Mexico was to become independent, but as a constitutional monarchy, not a democracy. The throne was to be offered to Ferdinand or some other member of European royalty. The Catholic church was not to lose any of its extraordinary privilege, and its property was to remain intact. There was to be equality between *gachupines* and *criollos*. Officials of all categories, ecclesiastical, military, and civil, were to remain in office, if they agreed to the plan; if not, they were to be dismissed. Former rebels were to be forgiven. This shrewd, statesmanlike declaration, known as the Plan of Iguala because it was drafted in that town, more or less embraced everything that the literary society of Querétaro had envisioned before Hidalgo's stirring up of the Indians had made the movement a social revolution. It was a far cry, however, from the redistribution of wealth and the racial equality promulgated by Morelos at Chilpancingo. The catchy slogan was

"Liberty, Union, and Religion." In his most conciliatory manner, Iturbide besought an interview with Guerrero to beguile him into accepting the "Plan of the Three Guarantees." Guerrero, after long debating with himself, came to believe that joining forces with Iturbide might be the quickest way to rid Mexico of Spanish overlords. So he agreed to support his former enemy's cause.

Since there was only gain in the Plan for them, the creoles were ready adherents. And after an initial hesitancy many royalist officers began deserting and taking their troops with them to Iturbide. With the aid of the most formidable insurgent, linked with that of all the creoles and many Spanish officers, Iturbide had almost everything he needed for victory except money. Securing money presented no serious obstacle to the resourceful schemer. He first got a moderate sum by furnishing convoy guards for a silver train from Mexico City to Acapulco, whence 500,000 pesos were to be shipped to Spanish merchants in Manila. Pocketing the commission as small change, Iturbide himself seized upon the whole fortune he had been paid to safeguard, as the mule caravan wound over the mountain pass. With the stolen silver he paid his soldiers enough to hold them in arms.

By summer only four cities still proclaimed allegiance to the flag of Spain. When a new viceroy arrived in July at yellow-fever-infested Vera Cruz and saw how the wind blew, he agreed to support Iturbide to save his own skin and the lives of his staff. So he was allowed to proceed to Mexico City and take nominal charge, while the creole commander further strengthened his grasp. Iturbide had played his cards so skillfully that there was little bloodshed in the last stage of the rebellion. The Spanish army in the federal district marched quietly down to the sea and shortly sailed for Spain. Now, as master of Mexico and styling himself "Liberator," Iturbide mounted a black charger and at the head of armed forces made his triumphal entry into the capital on the twenty-seventh of September. The date marked his thirty-eighth birthday.

Mexico's independence was an accomplished fact. The movement Father Hidalgo had generated, and nourished with his life's blood, had been achieved—with a big difference. Though it meant independence from Spain and Spanish extortion, the liberation was merely the change of one set of reactionary masters for another. Now there were no royal edicts to prevent the privileged from preying upon the people's ignorance to their hearts' satisfaction. All the good intentions for the general welfare promulgated by the two patriot priests were discarded. The unpossessing ninety per cent of the population had seemingly gained nothing from their years of insurgence and sacrifice. Instead of the republic Morelos had wanted, with class distinctions eliminated and the vast differences between the very rich and the very poor considerably leveled, Iturbide set about to create a "constitutional monarchy."

This move was one of the most mocking in the long history of Mexican anti-climaxes that range from the ludicrous to the ghastly. A rubber stamp of cynical, hypocritical demagogy was cut, to last many decades. The gullible, helpless masses were so frequently deluded that betrayal became an infectious virus and instability the accepted order.

During the fifty-five years between 1821 (Augustín de Iturbide) and 1876 (Porfirio Díaz) Mexico was ruled by forty presidents, two emperors, and a few provisional governments and regencies. Interlarding the governmental changes were insurrections, *pronunciamentos,* barrack switches, sudden flights, sudden deaths, and complete reversals of governmental policy. Mexico was like the centipede on its back distracted to consider which foot came first and which came next.

Ensconced in the capital as head of a Regency of Five, Iturbide, as one of his first patriotic acts, had himself voted a salary of one hundred and twenty-five thousand pesos a year for life.

Next he gave over the idea of offering a Mexican crown to some
European prince. Seeing himself as a New World Napoleon, he
hired a claque to call on him to be emperor. After a show of
declining the clamoring offer, he reappeared on his balcony and
suffered himself to be drafted to the throne. On May eighteenth,
1822, the formalities of his election by an unenthusiastic and
divided congress were completed. In July the coronation took
place, amid gaudy festivities. A little dressmaker who had once
been attached to Napoleon's court gave advice and direction as
to *mise en scène,* costumes, deportment. It was necessary to create
a new aristocracy. Iturbide's old father and mother did not mind
being addressed as prince and princess, but they felt like amateur
play actors simulating royal behavior. The seven Iturbide children were in high fettle at becoming princes and princesses of
the royal blood, like boys and girls in fairy tales. Protocol was
a bit ragged, however, and a subject of venomous contention.

Followed by their new-titled relatives and retinue, Iturbide
and his wife drove in royal procession through the decorated
streets. Their smiles glittered like the fake crown jewelry with
which they were bedecked. (The real jewels demanded of the
director of the national pawn shop had been refused.) In the
great cathedral, where High Mass was celebrated, not one
bishop, but four, presided. Señor and Señora Iturbide were duly
anointed and crowned. Bells pealed with brazen joy. The mob
made drunken merriment. The air was rent by salvos of artillery
fire saluting Emperor Augustín I.

For a few dazzling months the Iturbides lived in high estate.
Then Nemesis appeared, in the guise of a septuagenarian friar,
Fray Servando de Teresa y Mier, who returned from an exile
that had lasted almost three decades. An intellectual of strong
opinions, he had been deported for his heresy in tactlessly denying
the miracle of the Virgin of Guadalupe. Straightway elected to
congress, he immediately began to make a joke of the Iturbide
pretensions. With mordant wit he mocked the emperor's arro-

gance and the court's affectations. Ridicule has an especially keen edge in Mexico and many a puffed-up fellow has cut his throat against its blade. Congressmen began to grin. Waves of laughter ran through the populace like an infection. Even the jailing of Fray Servando, along with several disaffected congressmen, did not stop the jeers.

When Iturbide could get no concerted action out of his balking legislators, he took unto himself dictatorial powers. He counted on the backing of his army. But often army officers in Mexico were ardent only so long as the salaries were forthcoming. The cupboard was now bare of cash. The mere breath of praise and promise was too aerial a coinage to keep generals content. As they began to hand in their resignations, there popped up another opportunist as ambitious as Iturbide and as gifted in personal magnetism and duplicity. This was a youngish army officer of strong conservative convictions, named Antonio López de Santa Anna.

Seizing upon the word "republic" as a symbol to rally the enemies of Iturbide and the tinsel monarchy, this handsome creole instigated a rebellion at Vera Cruz. The former insurgent leaders against the Spaniards were quick to emerge to take up the fight against Emperor Augustín. Guerrero, realizing how he had been duped by Iturbide, joined forces with Santa Anna— only to be duped by him, in turn, later. Soon the entire army went over to the new cry for "freedom." And those very generals who had propped Iturbide on the throne now helped topple him off. The monarch had hardly got used to the set of his imperial garments before he had to cast them aside and don traveling clothes for exile. On March twenty-ninth, 1823, he offered to abdicate. He chose Leghorn, Italy, as the seat of his retirement and he accepted an annual allowance of $25,000 as befitting an ex-emperor's state.

Feeling abominably mistreated and misjudged, and believing he could still regain his power, Iturbide could not acclimate

himself to Leghorn. He soon left for London, where he published a statement. Without waiting to hear the reaction in
Mexico, he took ship on May eleventh and sailed for home,
confident of his retrieved high destiny. Meanwhile, congress
had declared him a traitor and an outlaw and even passed the
death sentence on him if his banished carcass were ever found
on Mexican soil again.

When Iturbide arrived, ignorant of the act of outlawry, he
disembarked in disguise and proceeded to the town of Padilla.
Here he was recognized and arrested—the day was July nineteenth, 1824—and shot immediately, without ceremony. Iturbide's downward plunge from an imperial throne to an obscure
execution was more swift than his compatriot Morelos's rise to
power had been. The cruel irony of his end made him a prime
national hero in the eyes of the clergy and many of the upper
class. Today he is fondly spoken of as "the Liberator" by die-
hard conservatives in Mexico. And, beyond doubt, without Iturbide the coming of Mexican independence would certainly have
been delayed. But, as Bertram Wolfe so aptly pointed out, "independence as a political preliminary to social change had been
converted into independence as a preventive for social change."

With the abortive empire dissolved, a republic so-called was
established. With the conservatives split both over the rise and
fall of Iturbide, the more liberal elements were able to control
the new congress, which met in November of 1823 to adopt a
constitution. When the elections took place next year, the rebel
*guerrillero,* Guadalupe Victoria, was elected president by the
state legislatures. Here now was the great chance for liberalism
to follow through with the best that Hidalgo and Morelos had
envisioned for the salvation of Mexico. But the intrepid fighter
had small talent for statesmanship and he muffed his great opportunity, despite the fact that during most of his term of office
Mexico was at peace. Apparently the peasant president forgot

Morelos's promise of land for the peasants. He sought to retain
his power by not offending the plantation owners. Church lands
and *haciendas* not only were not confiscated, they were not
taxed. To meet the vast annual deficits, Guadalupe Victoria began borrowing money from abroad, thus starting the promiscu-
ous mortgaging of Mexico at exorbitant rates to foreign powers.

From the earliest period to the last day of her possession of
power in Mexico, Spain had zealously kept from the rest of the
world information relative to New Spain, and, conversely, the
Mexicans were woefully ill-informed about other men and lands.
In the years immediately following independence, the foreigners
who were admitted to Mexico were astounded at the general
ignorance concerning the state of Europe. As one British com-
mentator who arrived during the regime of the first president
wrote: "Both men and women in general—believe the continent
to be under the domination of Spain; that England, France, Italy,
Holland, Germany are only so many paltry states or provinces
to which the King of Spain appoints governors, who superin-
tend the manufactories for the benefit of that country. I found it
dangerous to contradict this flatly. One lady asked me where a
muslin dress had been made? 'in England,' 'and how came it
here?' 'probably through Spain,' I replied: 'well then, what is
England but the workshop of Spain?' Many think that the riches
of Spain enable the others, and as they call them, 'the poorer
parts of Europe,' to live."

Great Britain was overjoyed at the liberation of Mexico and the
other Latin American countries one by one. She had long had an
eye on the trade of the Spanish colonies. Now, when independence was achieved, she moved to get a foothold in their commercial development.

The man responsible for the immediate British penetration
into Latin American commerce was the ultra-shrewd and far-
seeing George Canning. He had been made foreign minister in
1822, just as Iturbide was finding his seat on the imperial throne

anything but comfortable. Perhaps better than anyone else, Canning realized the advantage to England of Latin America's rebirth as a series of independent republics. He saw, too, that the other great European powers should be kept out of range of influence. So England was the prime supporter of the Monroe Doctrine of 1823. With British ships to back United States fighting men when either were necessary, the way was cleared for Great Britain to make investments in virgin territory. When the central European powers threatened to assist Spain to regain her American colonies, Canning strongly hinted that they would first have to sink the British fleet.

Among the Englishmen who came to observe Mexico at first hand in 1823 was Mr. W. Bullock, who had been proprietor of the London Museum. For six months he wandered over the country and made comments on the natural productions, the state of society, antiquities and manufactories. The last of these, in which he was especially interested, took up no more than half a dozen pages in his five-hundred-page book on Mexico, which John Murray published in 1824. The reason, of course, was that the manufacture of goods in Mexico was a rarity because of Spain's prohibitions, and new industries had not yet got started, partly because of a general abhorrence of factory life. Bullock wrote:

The account of manufactories of New Spain will occupy but a small space. The practice of the mother country in keeping the colonies dependent on her as much as possible induced her to frame strong laws for this purpose. . . . A few coarse woollens and cottons, amounting in the whole country to scarcely a million and a half sterling, were, it appears, formerly made; but during the revolution even these have diminished.

The wretched system in which public manufactories are conducted is of itself sufficient to disgust even the most degraded and lowest of human species. Instead of encouraging the love of labor and industry, as the means of obtaining comfort, wealth and enjoyment, it is here accompanied by slavery, poverty, and misery. Every manufactory that requires many hands is strictly a prison, from which the wretched inmates cannot remove, and are treated with the utmost rigor. Many of them are really confined for a number of years for crimes against the laws; and others, by borrowing a sum of money from the owners, pledge their persons and their labors till they redeem it, which it often happens is never done. The proprietor, instead of paying in money, supplies them with spirits, tobacco, etc., and by these means they increase, rather than liquidate the original debt.

At one of these places, near the city, where woollens are made . . . they have mass said for the wretched inmates on the premises; but high walls, double doors, barred windows, and severe corporal punishments inflicted in these places of forced industry, make them as bad as the worst-conducted gaol in Europe. As the people receive their ideas of manufactories from such place, can we wonder at the detestation in which they are held? What must their opinion of Europe be, which they are taught to consider as the place where all the manufactured articles imported are produced, and, as they suppose, carried on by the same system? But this state of things cannot long remain; a liberal Government like the present will surely devise a remedy for so great an evil, while the introduction of artisans from Europe, and the steam-engines which are now erecting at two of the mines, will give the natives an idea of our mechanical knowledge, and tend greatly to prepare them for improvement.

Mr. Bullock listed lacks and needs and tastes of the citizens, so that English industrialists might know what would make profitable business. But he cautioned his countrymen against coercion and made it clear that the Indian workmen were unusually averse to innovation. "A common wheelbarrow is much too complex a machine to be used in removing rubbish from the mine, and the superintendent was obliged to submit to two men dragging about half as much earth on a raw hide as one could have removed with ease on a barrow." Yet he sanguinely opined that he had no doubt they would gradually be brought to know the superiority of the English mechanics.

Mr. Bullock's book was one of several produced by Englishmen in the first decade of the republic to attest to the growing importance of Mexico to the commercial enterprise of Britain.

He was so optimistic over prospects that despite the predilection for French silk stockings and Swiss watches and German linen, he wrote: "But, in a short time, I have no doubt that little else will be seen in Mexico but English manufactured goods and English fashions."

The first British chargé d'affaires to Mexico, Mr. H. G. Ward, did his country signal service. Possessing charm as well as shrewd business sense, he captivated Mexican society and established British commercial interests on such a basis that for six decades Great Britain was to hold undisputed first place among foreign capitalists. (The United States did not begin its flush time of investment until the middle of the 1880's, after Porfirio Díaz had become dictator.) Suavely Mr. Ward added fuel to the smoldering fire of suspicion Mexico now held of the United States as a potential aggressor, desirous of more territory.

The first American minister to Mexico, Dr. Joel Poinsett of South Carolina, was no match for the British chargé in diplomatic adroitness. As to his background and qualities Poinsett seemed an ideal choice, though he himself was far from eager for the appointment. Poinsett was a gentleman and he had had the advantages of a European education, having studied at Woolwich Military Academy and the University of Edinburgh. He had traveled in Russia and Asia and fulfilled diplomatic missions in Argentina and Chile. He spoke Spanish fluently and had been a strong supporter of the Spanish-American struggle for independence. Only two years previously he had been to Mexico as a special agent of his country at the court of Iturbide, to whom he expounded his ideas of democracy. Robert Owen, the famous British philanthropist and socialist, who met Poinsett in Mexico, was so impressed by his qualities and his ideas that he spoke of the South Carolinian as more of "a citizen of the world than anyone else I know." Yet Poinsett did not succeed in Mexico. Part of the failure of his mission was due to circumstances over which he had no control and part to his over-zealous actions to assist Mexico to be a thoroughgoing democracy. Where the Britisher Ward played a masterly and subtle game, Poinsett in all good faith directly meddled in the internal affairs of Mexico.

At this time the new Mexican government was largely made up of army officers drawn from all factions. The two most important groups were members of rival branches of Freemasonry. The Scottish Rite Masons were largely conservatives who favored a monarchy. In the York Rite Masons were the liberals both creole and *mestizo* who would tolerate nothing but a Republican form of government. Dr. Poinsett supported the *Yorkinos* with undisguised ardor and alienated completely the other powerful group. He made no diplomatic pretense of being neutral. In his zeal for democracy he saw himself a Mexican patriot. Branded by the conservatives as a rank radical, the Southerner could harᵈly have been anything more radical than a Jeffersonian democrat. While the British chargé flattered, Poinsett warned the Mexicans of internal dangers and of certain unprincipled elements within the population that should not be encouraged and stirred up. "Under strong governments these bad elements turn to crime," he said, "and under weak governments, to revolution."

Nicolás Bravo, the vice president who belonged to the Scottish Rite group, had been against Poinsett from the first. In 1827 this former patriot, who had fought beside Morelos and who had escorted the Emperor Iturbide to his embarkation for exile, was beguiled into accepting the leadership of a conservative revolt against President Guadalupe Victoria. In his *pronunciamiento* Bravo demanded among other things the abolishment of secret societies and the departure of Minister Poinsett. Again it was Vicente Guerrero who rose as leader of the popular forces. He put down the revolt before it was fairly started and sent the turncoat Bravo to his own exile. But even with the strengthening of the liberal forces, and though Vicente Guerrero himself was the Grand Master of the York Rite Masons, Poinsett did not become popular.

Already on his arrival in 1825, Mexico had changed her cordial attitude of the first two decades of the century and now regarded her northern neighbor as a natural enemy. The growing suspicion increased. Poinsett did all in his power to disabuse it. But after March, 1827, when he was instructed by Secretary of State Henry Clay to make Mexico a cash offer for Texas, the Mexican government distrusted the United States more keenly and was in less mood than ever to accept the good offices of her envoy. In this same year almost twelve thousand American colonists settled in Texas, despite Mexican immigration restrictions and the demand of allegiance to the Roman Catholic faith.

Living in a thinly concealed hostile atmosphere was too depressing to Poinsett's disposition. He asked to be recalled. But President John Quincy Adams preferred to hav˞ such a powerful friend of Andrew Jackson out of the country as election time drew near, and he refused to recall him. Poinsett took solace in pursuing his hobby of horticulture. He had red clover seeds brought from Long Island and introduced the succulent legume to Mexico. He sent back to the United States seeds of Mexican oaks, nutmeg, and cloves. And he immortalized his name by introducing to the world the Mexican shrub that blooms at Christmas, called "Fire Plant" and "Painted Leaf," but christened "poinsettia" in the botanic lexicon.

Even the most material-minded traveler to Mexico in the 1820's and 1830's was profoundly impressed by the variety and abundance of the flowers in Mexico. But it is Mr. Bullock, the flower-lover, who gives us perhaps the best *coup d'œil* of the city houses, and it is he who emphasizes the sad change in the furnishings when the opulent Spanish residents returned to Spain and took their treasures with them rather than exist under upstart governments, either imperial or republican. Mr. Bullock wrote:

Many of the streets of the capital are nearly two miles in length, perfectly level and straight, and with the ends terminating in the view of the mountains that surround the valley. Most of the houses are of the same height, generally three stories, highly decorated, and ornamented with two rows of balconies of wrought iron, painted or gilt, and some of bronze. The stories are very lofty, the apartments being from fifteen to twenty feet high. The first or ground floor is entered by a pair of large folding gates, ornamented with bronze, often thirty feet in height. These lead into the courtyard, surrounded by the house, filled with trees and flowers, and having a gallery to each floor, offering so many separate promenades under shelter from the sun and rain. The lower apartments are generally occupied by the porter and other servants; the floor above is often let; but the highest, which is the principal, is occupied by the family themselves, having a separate stone staircase of great magnificence leading to it.

The fronts of the houses are in general white, crimson, brown, or light green, painted in distemper, and having a pleasing appearance; and the dryness of the atmosphere is such, that they retain their beauty unimpaired many years. Many of these fronts have inscriptions upon them taken from scripture, or stanzas addressed to the Saviour or his divine Mother. . . .

But the furniture and internal decorations of most of the houses ill accord with their external appearances. The closing of the mines, the expulsion of the rich Spanish families, and sixteen years of revolutionary warfare, with all the concomitant miseries, have wrought a melancholy alteration in the fortunes of individuals, and in the general state of the country; and in this the capital bears no inconsiderable share. The superb tables, chandeliers, and other articles of furniture of solid silver, the magnificent mirrors and pictures, framed in the same precious metal, have now passed through the mint, and in the shape of dollars are circulating over Europe and Asia; and families whose incomes have exceeded half a million per annum can now scarcely procure the means of a scanty existence.

However much there was of decline in the luxury of private living, divine service in the churches was still celebrated with wonted glory. A procession which Mr. Bullock saw from the cathedral far exceeded in order and regularity, in the grandeur of vestments, in gold and silver, anything he had ever seen. "The processions of Rome suffered by comparison." Coming from England, he was particularly impressed with the utter democracy of the congregation, of the lack of distinction of pews and seats, so universal in his country. "Here on the same floor, the poorest Indians and the highest personages in the land mix indiscriminately in their prayers to that being to whom earthly distinctions are unknown."

But though on the Mexican church floor all class distinction was forgotten, in the political as well as the social arena, the complexion and the degree of breeding still figured. In 1828 when the popular hero Guerrero, "an ignorant man of the lower class," ran against an educated white man, Manuel Gómez Pedraza, class distinction did enter in the voting. The latter won by a majority of one state legislature's electoral votes out of the nineteen. The election was appealed, but congress sustained the Gómez Pedraza victory. The Guerrero supporters decided to resort to arms.

Seizing the contentious occasion, the reactionary Santa Anna, who wished to be known as founder of the Mexican republic since he had been the prime instrument of Iturbide's downfall, turned liberal. With high-flown sentiments and a show of arms he espoused the cause of Guerrero. Though he was defeated himself, he had stirred up the mob and enough of the army to create general confusion and a new outburst of looting. When the smoke cleared, Guerrero took office as the second President of the Mexican republic. Santa Anna smiled deceptively and awaited the psychological hour to create, or take advantage of, the next crisis.

For all his sterling qualities, the rugged Guerrero unfortunately was no more prepared to administer a nation than Guadalupe Victoria. Because of his lack of education, his country manners, his reputed Negro blood, he was held in contempt by the upper-class society of the capital. The conservatives chose to regard him as a triple-blooded outsider. Those not on his salary list plotted his ousting, while those on it juggled for more power.

In December, 1828, when street fighting occurred between the York and the Scottish Masons, and Poinsett's life was endangered, Guerrero asked President Jackson to recall him. In his last address to the Mexicans, Poinsett pled for a spirit of kindliness towards the United States. His words fell mostly on deaf ears. When he left Mexico he felt he had accomplished nothing except to have had definite influence on the noted physician, Valentín Gómez Farías, who came to be looked upon as the leader of the liberals during a struggle of three decades, which was to reach its vindication with Benito Juárez and the constitution of 1857. Poinsett admitted frankly the failure of his mission, but W. R. Manning wrote, in the *American Journal of International Law,* "no other man of the time could have filled the post."

Having sent Mexico one of her best sons as minister, the United States government followed him with a chargé of the worst possible type: a spoils politician, an unprincipled "bully and swashbuckler," whom Jackson himself finally called a "scamp." For five years he remained in Mexico, a "national disgrace." And by the time this Anthony Butler was recalled in 1835, the relations between the adjoining republics were in most deplorable disrepair.

Opposing Gómez Farías, the intellectual leader of the conservatives was Lucas Alamán, a remarkable man of high integrity and the most able scholar and historian of his day. By profession this cherubic little gentleman with gold-rimmed spectacles was a mining engineer. In statesmanship he was as shrewd and determined as he was soft-spoken and shy in daily manners. Alamán did not believe in the rule of the masses. He thought Mexico could best succeed as a monarchy. And in lieu of that he advocated a strong centralized government, with a military dictatorship if necessary. Believing that the rising power of liberalism would completely disrupt Mexico, he joined forces with the creoles, the clergy, and the army. The intensely pro-Spanish Lucas Alamán was foremost among other cultured creoles who could not bear the idea of being governed by an unlettered *mestizo* like Guerrero, who butchered the Spanish language.

In Vicente Guerrero's second year of office the army revolted. Again it was the vice-president—this time Anastasio Bustamente —who led the troops under cover of night into the capital and seized the strategic strongholds. Guerrero fled to his native mountains. Here on ground where he had defied the Spanish army for four years and carried on the struggle for Mexican independence almost single-handed, the former rebel resisted those who now rebelled against him. But once again Guerrero was tricked by his incorrigible trust in men. At the port of Acapulco he was beguiled to visit an Italian trading vessel, where he was seized, bound, and declared captive. The insurgent government paid the shipmaster fifty thousand pesos for him. In a farcical show of justice Guerrero was pronounced mentally deficient. Then to make his incompetence incontrovertible, he was shot for a traitor.

Guerrero's death marked the end of the great four who were chiefly responsible for Mexican independence—Hidalgo, Morelos, Guerrero, the three selfless strugglers for liberty, and Iturbide, the self-seeking egoist. Bullets from firing squads made periods to the earthly careers of all four. But in the Mexican chronicles of the first three centuries after the great Cortés himself, these four oddly assorted contemporaries have the most illuminated pages.

# PART FOUR

# THE REPUBLIC

## 9. The Tragi-comedy of Santa Anna

*"What do you want? Souls of rational men or irrational? Souls of rational men. Of what rational men? Sound or unsound? Sound. Why then do you not seek for them? But we have them. Why then do you fight and quarrel?"*

SOCRATES

The first five-year period of independence brought small joy and no serenity to Mexico. Involving political intrigue, desertions, party switches, and civil strife, it was largely a free-for-all between the *criollos* and *gachupines* for material benefits. In 1827 the last Spanish officeholders and business men were urgently invited to leave the country. But instead of their departure bringing peace, the new republic was thrown into a financial panic because the Spaniards took so much capital with them.

With the offending *gachupines* out of the picture, the white Mexicans and an increasing number of *mestizos* began to scrap among themselves for position and privilege. Despite the constitution of 1824, there was little political stability. Whichever party was defeated in an election fomented revolt. Elections were fraudulent on both sides, and for a bellyful of pulque the ignorant Indians could be persuaded to vote as their benefactors commanded.

After the downfall of Iturbide in 1824, for more than a quarter of a century the reactionary Santa Anna, who had expediently proclaimed a republic, was more or less the strong man of Mexico. But he had to wait until the elections of 1832 before he was actually called to be the country's president. In January, 1833, as Iturbide had done, Santa Anna staged a triumphal entry from the east. Now in his fortieth year, he was seen by the public as an imposing and gravely handsome figure on horseback. He possessed the animal magnetism and Latin charm to catch the imagination of both the street mob and the drawing room. But because liberalism—which he had espoused but really despised— was in the ascendancy, Santa Anna found it expedient to be ill at his country place when inauguration day came. Most of the time he remained at home while his vice-president, Valentín Gómez Farías, a true liberal, worked with congress to enact reforms. A few of these measures hit at the church and sheared it of some power and revenue. Others curtailed the special privileges of the army officers. An uproar of protestation rose from the church, the army, and all conservative *criollos*. Santa Anna played a wily game, temporizing to see which way the cat would jump. He did not overtly oppose the reforms of his vice-president and congress, but he gave sympathetic audience to the outraged churchmen and military.

Calculating the psychological time aptly, the president selected the last day in May, 1834, for his *coup d'état*. He audaciously shooed his congress from the Sessions Hall, locked the door, pocketed the key, exiled his vice-president, and made himself dictator. All the reforms directed against the church were voided and the special privileges of army officers restored. *Te Deums* were sung in the cathedral and a chorus of prayers for Santa Anna's immortal soul went up from pious beadsmen about the land. Recalcitrant liberals were suppressed with a bludgeoning ruthlessness worthy of an Iturbide.

Ironically, the man whom the liberals had elevated to the presidency put Mexico into a vise of conservatism so pressing that it was more than two decades before she could breathe freely again.

The struggle for the spoils of freedom was unceasing. Like the disgusted rank and file of Cortés's army at the division of Montezuma's treasure, almost everyone in independent Mexico felt cheated. There were jostling and screaming for sinecures, pensions, indemnities. Chicanery, fraud, and treason developed artfully. Swaggering army officers found outlaws useful in their employ. The church was in a stew of political manipulations. Many idealists gave up in despair; a few over-sensitive ones committed suicide.

A new centralist constitution was promulgated on December thirtieth, 1836, to nullify the constitution of 1824 devised by the liberals. By its terms the franchise was so restricted that power lay wholly with the privileged classes. Liberal supporters of the former constitution in various states put up a stout resistance. The wrangling reached its climax a few years later in Texas, when colonists from the United States, after a series of protests against the centralist powers, created a revolt and finally seceded.

During the long chain of ill-starred events in which Mexico marked time in its growing up, Antonio López de Santa Anna created for himself a spectacular career and had a marvelous time in the rôle of leading man. The life history of this amazing fellow was like a prolonged tragi-comedy overloaded with intrigues and counter-intrigues. The plot shifted as lesser characters sparred for personal advancement. The spotlight touched here and there, and moved on. It was the most thoroughly self-seeking and confused period in Mexican history. In between flurries of insurrections, society indulged in gaudy interludes. In the paradeful and shallow-brained hero the glittering façade and the inner corruption of Mexico were neatly personified. Yet from the callous viewpoint of historical entertainment, the scene was dull when the pretentious hero was off stage.

Like a chameleon, Santa Anna could change his coat to match the color of the hour, but in the hard core of his heart he was an indelibly dyed reactionary. Shrewd, with a disarming melancholy courtesy, he was adroit in his political twists. Inordinately conceited, with an eye and a nose for the ladies and a passion for gamecocks and fine coaches, he possessed what journalists would call a front-page personally. In every emergency Santa Anna bobbed up like a *deus ex machina* with his grave, purposeful countenance and his readiness to promise anything.

His life was a series of exiles and recalls. By turns he was disgraced and elevated. Seven times he was Mexico's chief executive. His single famous victory at Tampico in 1829 against reconquesting Spaniards, who surrendered because they had stupidly cut off their own supply line from Cuba, made him accepted as a military genius. Though his defeats and retreats were far more sensational than his successes, facts could not rub out the public opinion that he was the ablest soldier in Mexico. It is true he did possess a keen sense of military strategy. But he was careless of preparation and criminally negligent about equipment and supply. However, no matter how disastrous the rout, how flagrant the blunder, he always managed to give defeat some aspect of victory.

Corruption was never ranker in the corrupt political history of Mexico than during the quarter century of Santa Anna. A continuous graft gouged at the vitals of the Mexican treasury. The government was generally controlled by the army officers, who persuaded themselves that the republic was created for their special indulgence. Though the army budget was proportionately very large, the bulk went into officers' pay checks and left little enough over for guns and only a pittance for clothing and feeding the common soldiers.

Santa Anna's bad statesmanship and his military misjudgments largely caused the loss of half of Mexico. The trouble began with Texas. A Connecticut Yankee named Moses Austin, who was engaged in mining in Missouri, had secured from Iturbide permission to bring a group of Roman Catholic colonists from Louisiana. Though he died before he could get the colonization started, his son, Stephen F. Austin, took over and brought the first American settlers into Texas. Because the Mexican government regarded the plains of Texas as valueless from the point of view of real estate, they asked the settlers an absurdly small price for acreage and granted them immunity from taxes for seven years. Through the 1820's so many more thousands of Americans came that Mexico became uneasy. Though the immigration laws of 1826 demanded allegiance to the Roman Catholic faith, that did not deter the Americans. Many came in and settled with a rifle instead of a title to the land they took. In 1830, under the colonization law proposed by Lucas Alamán, foreign minister, settlers were forbidden to bring slaves in with them. But the Protestant colonists, who had readily subscribed in name to the Roman Catholic faith, facilely changed the status of their Negro slaves to that of indentured servants. By 1833 some twenty thousand settlers had crossed into Texas, and already they were talking of independence and refusing to pay Spanish customs duties on goods brought in from Louisiana. In 1835, during one of his recurrent periods of dictatorship, Santa Anna sent troops to collect these customs fees. But his soldiers met hot opposition.

In December, General Cos and his army stood off a five-day siege at San Antonio, but at length retreated across the Rio Grande. The Texans, thinking the shooting was all over, returned to their agricultural pursuits. They were taken by surprise in February when the famous Santa Anna himself appeared at San Antonio with three thousand troops.

William Bartlett Travis was in command of the Texans, who numbered only one hundred and fifty. They quickly readied the old Spanish mission called the Alamo, and prepared to withstand Santa Anna's attack. Though outnumbered twenty to one, the American refused to surrender. From the nearest church tower the red flag of no quarter flew, and the Mexican band played the piece called *Degüello* (the cutthroat). For a fortnight the Americans put up superhuman resistance. The desperately wounded fought from their cots until the last remaining ones were massacred. Because not a single American lived to tell the tale, no authorized report of the battle can be given.

The only persons within the Alamo who survived were two illiterate Mexican women servants and a Negro boy. What they recalled from their terror makes the record heroic if confused. At the end three Mexicans burst through the heavy doors, shortly followed by a horde. Bowie, desperately wounded, sat up in his bed for a last fight before he was beaten down. He was firing both his pistols when he was killed. Davy Crockett was using his rifle as a club when he was finished off. Major Evans was shot just in the nick of time, as he was on the point of firing the magazine, which would have blown the building to rubble, and spoiled for posterity Texas' most historic shrine. The heroism of the Texans is today attested to by the epitaph carved on the monument: "Thermopylae had its messenger of defeat. The Alamo had none."

The Americans who had refused to surrender were prepared to take what they got. The Alamo was not the worst slaughter, however. The affair at Goliad was not so spectacular, but it was an unmitigated disgrace to Santa Anna and General Urrea. There, surrounded by an overpowering force, and when food and ammunition were completely used up, three hundred and forty-seven Texans did surrender. The terms of surrender were duly signed by both sides. The wounded were to receive medical attention and the fit were to be paroled on the pledge they would not fight against the Mexicans again. The Mexican generals carried out their obligations by ordering the active to be shot or bayoneted and the wounded to be butchered in their beds. Three hundred and twenty men perished in the mass killing.

Twenty-seven escaped into the woods and sought their way to Sam Houston to tell the gruesome tale.

The slaughters at San Antonio and at Goliad were to cost the Mexican government a pretty penny. While the siege was in progress at the Alamo, other Texans in the eastern part of the territory had called a convention and drawn up a declaration of independence. Sam Houston, whose life had already assumed legendary lumination, had recently arrived and had been elevated from his self-created position of a Cherokee Indian chief to the command of the rebel Texans. Unprepared yet for battle, Houston sent word everywhere for the American soldiery and all civilians to retire as rapidly as possible out of Mexican reach. Santa Anna pursued the general retreat. Houston kept everybody on the hopping move until he was ready. At last, near Lynchburg ferry, on the San Jacinto River, the doughty frontiersman made his stand and gave final instructions.

On the afternoon of April twenty-first, 1836, armed literally to the teeth since some had bowie knives between them, the Texans emerged from the oak forest to the music of fife and drum. The tune the two-piece band played was perhaps not so appropriate as "The Cutthroat," which the Mexicans had played as accompaniment to the Alamo massacre, but it was a great favorite with the boys. They knew the words by heart, though this time they sang them under their breath:

> Will you come to the bow'r I have shaded for you?
> Your bed shall be roses bespangled with dew.
> Will you, will you, will you, will you come to the bow'r?
> Will you, will you, will you, will you come to the bow'r?

The sentiment better suited the sweetness of the season and the lulling spring fever in the air than imminent death. Santa Anna and his foot-weary soldiers were indulging in a long siesta. The Mexican cooks were already preparing a high-flavored stew for the evening meal. Suddenly the little band stopped its music. Two cannon, donated by sympathizers in Cincinnati and affectionately called "the twin sisters" by the troops, loosed a volley of scrap iron and stones into the Mexican camp. The Americans began yelling like Comanches. Shouting "Remember the Alamo!" they charged. The Alamo carnage was revenged four for one. With six hundred and thirty of their men killed, the remaining Mexicans surrendered. The Texas losses were six killed and twenty-five wounded. Santa Anna escaped in carpet slippers. Next day he was captured hiding in sedge grass. To save his own skin, on May fourteenth, 1836, by the Treaty of Velasco, he signed away Texas.

This time Santa Anna's eloquent tongue could not twist into victory such a defeat. Though the Mexican congress refused to recognize Texas independence, the army did not pursue the fight. Texas was to remain for some years the "Lone-Star Republic." She petitioned the United States government for annexation, but the northern anti-slavery senators voted against it for political reasons. In the meantime, pioneers poured into the big, empty spaces.

Back in Mexico, after months of detention and a pleasant visit to Washington, Santa Anna prudently remained out of the limelight, biding his time for the next spectacular opportunity. It came in a most unexpected manner. A French fleet arrived to collect damages to French shopkeepers incurred in a riot ten years previously. The Mexicans belittled the episode by calling it "the Pastry War," because a French *patisserie* had been wrecked by drunken officers and the proprietor was howling for restitution. Santa Anna rushed to Vera Cruz to assume command of the defense. This time he was nearly caught, not in carpet slippers, but barefooted and with his pants off. He fled in his underclothes. The next day, however, superbly groomed, he appeared on horseback leading his troops. In an instant he had the bad and good fortune to have his leg torn off by a French cannonball. The loss of his leg brought him into popular favor again. And when the enemy fleet sailed off after receiving some guarantee of payment, Santa Anna proclaimed a military victory.

After his brief and nearly fatal new sally into public life, Santa Anna retired to his estate at Manga de Clavo ("spike of clove") to recuperate and to gather wind for the next dramatic move. It was in this period that he entertained Angel Calderón de la Barca, the newly arrived first Spanish ambassador, and his lively Scottish wife, the author of those remarkable letters which gave a more vivid picture of Mexico than anything else since the publication of Bernal Díaz's personal reminiscences of the conquest.

After passing through miles of enchanting natural garden, all the property of Santa Anna, the Calderón de la Barcas arrived at five in the morning at Manga de Clavo. The tall, thin Señora de Santa Anna received them at that early hour in white muslin, white satin slippers, and diamonds. Madame Calderón de la Barca wrote:

In a little while entered General Santa Anna himself, a gentlemanly, good-looking, quietly dressed, rather melancholy person, with one leg, apparently somewhat of an invalid, and the most interesting person in the group. He has a sallow complexion, fine, dark eyes, soft and penetrating, and an interesting expression of face. Knowing nothing of his past history, one would have said a philosopher, living in dignified retirement, one who had tried the world, and found that all was vanity, one who had suffered ingratitude, and who, if he were ever persuaded to emerge from his retreat, would only do so, Cincinnatus-like, to benefit his country. It is strange, how frequently this expression of philosophic resignation, of placid sadness, is to be remarked on the countenances of the deepest, most ambitious and most designing men.

The Calderón de la Barcas were entertained at a breakfast served in white and gold French porcelain, and after the meal Señora Santa Anna smoked her little cigar taken from a gold cigar case with a diamond latch. Santa Anna showed the visitors his favorite old war-horse, a white charger, and his prize game-cocks. When Madame Calderón expressed surprise that there was no special garden connected with the house, the general protested truthfully that the whole estate, which was some forty miles square, was a garden.

On departing, the perspicacious lady prophesied to her husband that the general "would not long remain in his present state of inaction." Her quick perception judged correctly. Shortly Santa Anna and two other important generals bombarded the capital in an unscrupulous revolt against the incumbent president, because he was not sufficiently proficient at tax-gathering. When the shooting was over and the president in hiding, Santa Anna in his coach and four drove into the city and resumed the rôle of dictator. He quickly revealed his talents at extracting money. And in three years, between 1841 and 1844, he commissioned 12,000 army officers. The military was gratified with the trust they had put in him. To show their appreciation the officers brought the amputated leg from its resting place at Manga de Clavo and honored it with ceremonious interment in the cathedral itself.

In the capital of the young republic of Mexico, Madame Calderón de la Barca found an atmosphere "as anti-republican as one could wish to see." There was "hardly a connecting link between the blankets and the satins, the poppies and the diamonds." But the City of Mexico was exciting in its difference, and, by dawn or moonlight, noble-looking with its silhouettes and solidity. The almost overpowering odors of rose and jasmine, honeysuckle and heliotrope suggested to her the blissful Elysian Fields. Yet Mexico seethed with intrigue and parvenu display. The cost of living was remarkably dear. House rent was absurdly high—"nothing tolerable to be had under two thousand five hundred dollars per annum, unfurnished." Beggars infested the capital and made the air discordant with their choruses of whines and supplications "for the love of the pure blood of Christ." Professional mendicants were inspired in artful dodges. One day, as an image of the Virgin was being passed through the streets to be kissed, one *lépero,* affecting intense devotion, bit off a large pearl that adorned the bejeweled girdle and escaped in the crowd before the theft was discovered. Street murders were everyday occurrences, and the crowd would look on with curious non-interference while a killing took place. Occasional dead bodies would sprawl on prominent streets like unconsidered trifles. Soldiers in long, yellow cloaks and priests in their shovel hats would step around the cadavers and go on their own personal ways.

Indians selling green vegetables came gliding on the canal along the Viga in their flower-embowered canoes, with plaintive songs on their lips. The most prevalent objects in shop windows were prayer books and rosaries, daggers and spurs, and prodigious sombreros weighted with silver embroidery. The displays themselves offered keys to an understanding of Mexico's quality of civilization.

And through the shifting kaleidoscope of color contrasts, from dawn to nightfall came the varying cries of the street venders, chanting their wares like the priests intoning prayers in the church, but with more enthusiasm and persuasion. Each type of vender had his special cry and his favored hours for business. Earliest came the charcoal sellers, then the lard and suet women, then the peddlers of needles and pins, then the makers of meringues and honey-cakes. In the late afternoon the chants of "hot roasted chestnuts" were wafted with the pungent odor. And in the evening came the most enticing cry of all from those who sold roast duck: "Ducks, oh, my soul, hot ducks! Come, young señors, come!"

The nights were punctuated with spurs striking sparks from the pavements, as adventurous officers swaggered to rendezvous of dalliance or plot. When darkness fell on the market place and

the shops and stalls were closed, the arcades would be metamorphosed into political clubs. Officers and civilians would stroll
about discussing the current revolution, the one just past, or the
one to come.

Though the street scenes by day or night resembled a Venetian
carnival masquerade, society and etiquette in Mexico were no
less fantastic. No lady ever paid Madame Calderón de la Barca
a morning visit without diamonds and satin slippers. And in the
afternoons and evenings the élite would use five and six brooches
instead of one to fasten their mantillas. Gold chains wrapped
three times about ladies' necks reached to the knees. At the theater the boxes glittered with "a monotony of diamonds and crepe
de chine shawls."

The grand old ladies of the viceregal court were fast disappear-
ing by 1840, and their place in society was being filled by the
amiable but uncultivated wives of upstart generals. The town
houses were elaborate with gilt cabinets and bric-a-brac, but the
furnishings could not measure up to the lace and embroidery and
spangles and fringe of the costumes. When formal invitations
came for receptions or bullfights or celebrations of Mass for the
repose of a dead soul, they were written on blue satin bordered
with silver lace and tassels. The elaborate invitations were in
keeping with the dazzling suits of the matadors, and with the
private masses when the great churches were hung with crimson
velvet and lit with thousands of wax tapers, where whole orches-
tras played while a hundred white-robed friars prayed in unison
for a young girl's soul.

Ladies went to afternoon bullfights in full evening décolle-
tage and smoked their cigars in the open as freely as they did in
intermissions at the theater or in their carriages on the Paseo.
This was the golden age of the carriage, when one's social standing was often gauged by the elegance of the equipage. On the
afternoon drives the ladies always appeared "in full toilet," but
without mantilla, their dark hair interwoven with jewels and

jasmine. Officers on prancing mounts rode by their side, while gallantry and coquetry gracefully leaped the conventional interval. Sometimes ladies driving alone in the suburbs were undone because of their jewels. A cavalier permitted to leap from his horse to a seat beside a girl for a rendezvous repaid the courtesy by running his saber into her side and relieving her of her diamonds, much to the astonishment of the family coachman when he awaked from a nap under a roadside tree.

Yet with the excitement of the unexpected at any turn in the street or at any hour of the day, Madame Calderón de la Barca found Mexican compliments uncommonly tiresome. Though she reported the Mexican woman the most amiable of all her kind in the world, as Lady Mary Wortley Montagu did the Turkish woman, she remarked they had no conversation beyond the formula:

After having embraced each lady who entered, according to the fashion which after all seems cordial to say the least of it, and seated the lady of most consequence on the right side of the sofa, a point of great importance, the following dialogue is *de rigueur.* "How are you? Are you well?" "At your service; and you?" "Without novelty (*sin novedad*), at your service." "At your disposal; and you?" "A thousand thanks, and the señor?" "At your service, without novelty," etc. Besides, before sitting down, there is "Pray be seated," "Pass first, señorita." "No, madam, pray pass first." "Vaya, well, to oblige you, without further ceremony; I dislike compliments and etiquette."
The first visit over, the ladies re-embrace, the lady of the house following her guests to the top of the staircase, and again compliments are given and received. "Madam, you know that my house is at your disposal." "A thousand thanks, madam. Mine is at yours, and, though useless, know me for your servant, and command me in everything that you may desire." "Adieu, I hope you may pass a good night." At the bottom of the first landing-place the visitors again turn around to catch the eye of the lady of the house, and the adieus are repeated.

During this period, though the social life of the city was incessant, that of the *hacienda* was in eclipse. The country houses were largely empty because of the continual rounds of revolutions and counter-revolutions. A countess assured Madame Calderón de la Barca that she had twice completely furnished her place, but that in two revolutions everything had been thrown from the windows and destroyed. In the future she had resolved to confine herself to *le stricte necessaire.* So half the bedrooms in her great house were bare of furniture, and the others reduced to green-painted bedsteads and washstands and chairs, with no rugs on the elaborately painted brick floors. On the whole, the country houses at this time were used more as occasional summer retreats than for entertaining. To foreigners they seemed crosses between fortresses and barns.

Many of the convents were far more luxurious than the *haciendas,* for rarely were they molested during uprisings. One that Madame Calderón de la Barca visited in 1842, the Convent of the Incarnation, was in fact like a palace. She wrote:

> Each nun has a servant, and some have two. . . . The convent is rich; each novice at her entrance pays five thousand dollars into the common stock. . . . Having visited the whole building and admired one virgin's blue satin and pearls, and another's black velvet and diamonds, sleeping holy infants, saints, paintings, shrines and confessionals . . . we came at length to a large hall, decorated with paintings and furnished with antique highbacked arm-chairs, where a very elegant supper, lighted up and ornamented, greeted our astonished eyes; cakes, chocolate, ices, creams, custards, tarts, jellies, blancmanges, orange and lemonade, and other profane dainties, ornamented with gilt paper cut into little flags. I was placed in a chair that might have served for a pope. . . . The elder nuns in stately array looked like statues in stone. A young girl, a sort of pensionnaire, brought in a little harp without pedals, and while we ate, sang different ballads with a good deal of taste.

The magnificence of the church in contrast to the rags of the Indians continued to amaze Madame Calderón de la Barca's Scotch sense of proportion. Again and again she was struck with wonder at the bishop's "blaze of gold and jewels" and the dazzling display of silver and gold and crimson velvet and jewels in churches. At the consecration of a new archbishop of Mexico, "the bishops were arrayed in white velvet and gold and their miters were literally covered with diamonds. . . ."

It was to keep the gold candlesticks and golden holy-water basins secure and in good repair that the clergy supported the unprincipled Santa Anna. Next to the bishops, the generals had the pick of the fruits of the land, and it became a diverting sport to seize upon the coveted estate of a political opponent and to shoot him for a traitor to the republic if he put up defiance.

The popularity of Santa Anna ran according to pattern and lasted only so long as there was cash to meet the officers' salaries. Though the schemer proved adroit at extraction of taxes, the treasury was kept bankrupt by the rapacity of the officers. In 1844 General Paredes revolted, and while Santa Anna went off to quell the rebellion, his liberal enemies in Mexico took over, and elected a new president. In trying to regain his power Santa Anna was defeated, and skipped to the hills. Here he was rescued and captured by enemy troops, just as cannibalistic Indians were preparing "to stew him for dinner." The government banished him "forever" and permitted him to choose Cuba for his exile.

# 10. "Green Grow the Rashes"

*"The morrow of the victory has more perils than its eve."*

MAZZINI

Sam Houston had been inaugurated as President of Texas, the "Lone Star Republic," on October twenty-second, 1836. Nine years passed before Texas's petition for admission to the Union was finally granted on March first, 1845. The Mexican government had never ratified the Treaty of Velasco or recognized the independence of Texas. But though Mexico had not taken up arms to dispute the annexation, it had continued to harass the Texans. Sporadic raids into Texas, with Santa Anna's sanction, had continued. Now the Mexican minister in Washington promptly demanded his papers and called the annexation the most unjust act of aggression in modern history. The United States minister to Mexico was speeded home. Though Mexico was totally unprepared for war and a house divided against itself, her journalists and orators began to shout for a vindication of national honor.

They ignored the fact that the Mexican treasury was worse than depleted and there was a large foreign debt to meet. France and England were demanding payments on debts, in threatening notes. The latter's claims were based on outrageous speculations in Mexican bonds, which the British had paid for at twenty-five cents on the dollar, for which they demanded payment at face value plus generous interest. In an arbitrated counter-damage-claims case, umpired by the Prussian king, the United States had recently been awarded $2,500,000. Though the budget of the Mexican army was greater than that of her northern neighbor in 1845, only a meager proportion of it went into arms and equipment and the training of soldiers. Most of it went into fat salary checks of officers. Mexico was devoid of matériel.

The United States had long cast amorous glances at California. Some of her congressmen had sought assiduously to find justifiable and noble reasons for acquiring the territory willy-nilly. In October, 1842, in the Tyler administration, Commodore T. A. C. Jones had impulsively and imprudently seized Monterrey, California, in the belief that war was inevitable. Though ordered to withdraw with apologies, he had stirred up the worst suspicions in Mexico. But it was April of 1846 before war was loosed, with a *casus belli* that satisfied the majority.

General Zachary Taylor was in command of the American army at Fort Jesup on the western boundary of Louisiana. On July thirtieth, 1845, "Old Rough and Ready" was ordered "to defend Texas as far as occupied by Texans." He moved his forces down to Corpus Christi. In March, 1846, he proceeded westward to the east bank of the Rio Grande across from Matamoras, just as regulars of the Mexican army were ordered to the frontier. While Taylor was getting established much nearer to war, President Polk sent John Slidell of Louisiana to treat with President Herrera, who believed a policy of appeasement could best serve Mexico. Slidell had been authorized to offer $5,000,000 for the loss of Texas and $25,000,000 for California. However, the sale of neither territory was to be made a condition of peace negotiations. Secretary of State Buchanan had said to Slidell: "The President is sincerely desirous to preserve peace with Mexico. Both inclination and policy dictate the course."

But by the time the stage was set for negotiations to proceed, General Paredes, a Yankee-hater, had overthrown the moderating Herrera, who departed posthaste with all that remained of his government, in one vehicle. Paredes was not in conciliatory mood, and did not disguise his disdain. The Slidell mission flatly failed.

On April twenty-fifth, 1845, the war actually began when a

small body of Taylor's dragoons was ambushed and destroyed
by Mexican cavalry in disputed territory. The Americans maintained that the destruction occurred in "a tax district of the United
States." So in his message to congress President Polk described
the ambuscade as "the shedding of American blood on American
soil." Though Polk's message was stigmatized as "untruthful and
frantic" by his more bitter opponents, only two senators out of
forty voted their disapproval of it, and fourteen representatives
out of one hundred and seventy-four. Though many private
citizens denounced what they called "the foul dealing of the
United States towards Mexico," the war was launched.

In May, General Arista's six thousand Mexicans fell back before the marksmanship of the Americans. Taylor crossed the Rio
Grande and took Matamoros. By river boats the troops went four
hundred miles to prepare to march overland to Monterrey in
Nuevo León. There was a lull of two months, while the Americans fell victims of Mexican dysentery and a virulent epidemic
of measles. The chief occupation was handling the corpses of the
thousands who died. To cheer each other in their illness and
convalescence, the boys did a lot of singing. A favorite which
they sang with especial gusto in the arid plains of north Mexico
was "Green Grow the Rashes, O," Robert Burns's poem set to a
lively tune. The Mexicans listening to the chorus, hearing "Green
grow" repeated over and over and trying to catch some significance in the words, began muttering, *"Gringo, gringo,"* and at
length applied the name *gringos* to the Americans who sang
about the *gringo*. The word came to embrace all the opprobrium
the Mexicans stored up in the word *gachupín,* something similar
to the hate and contempt Southerners came to put into the word
"Yankee."

In 1846 the opponents on both sides professed and expressed
more contempt than hate for the other. The Mexican newspaper,
*El Diario del Gobierno,* gave its disdainful view of the American
soldiers: "The American army is made up of adventurers who

have no country, no political or religious creed, no moral principles or sentiments; for whom there are no priests or magistrates,
and for whom the house of God, the Senate, a drawing room,
a theater, and a circus, are all the same."

The *Washington Union* attempted to season its contempt with
a dash of moral righteousness: "We must teach these Mexicans
that we are superior to them in energy as well as military skill.
We must impress them with a deep conviction that their true
interest is peace with us—now, and in all future time. Acting
upon these high principles, we will prosecute the war with
greater means, a sterner will, and with irresistible vigor. If they
are not sufficiently beaten to make them seek for peace, we must
beat them again and again—coerce them at every available point,
scatter their *guerilleros,* occupy their towns, and levy more contributions upon their inhabitants."

However much the Mexicans despised the Americans, their
soldiers were no match for the guns of the American adventurers.
When his boys were strong enough to be on the march again,
General Taylor proceeded to take the city of Monterrey with
ease.

While Taylor was on his way south, another revolution took
place in the Mexican capital and another change of government,
with a restitution of the constitution of 1824. President Paredes,
who had adamantly opposed appeasement, had found the conduct of war too difficult and had taken to drink. Amid the consternation and confusion in Mexico City the name of Santa Anna
was loudly voiced. As in other national emergencies, he was recalled from exile in Cuba. But the American fleet in the Gulf
blocked his way. By a clever deception, the slippery Santa Anna
persuaded President Polk to let him through the American blockade to Vera Cruz to stop the war. He proposed to make a good
American peace at the first opportunity, "after the Mexicans had
been slightly chastised for their misdeeds."

On his arrival, the liberal congress in power once more gave

Santa Anna command of the army and expected him to go straight off to halt the Americans. But the war stood still for several months while Santa Anna collected an army and Taylor's men further recuperated from the ravages of disease. In the interim General Winfield Scott, "Old Fuss and Feathers," was put in command of half of Taylor's army and ordered to effect a march on the City of Mexico by way of the seaport of Vera Cruz. Taylor, against orders, moved down to Saltillo at the end of January, 1847.

At the head of 25,000 ragtag and bobtail troops, Santa Anna drove off from San Luis Potosí in his mule-drawn coach, with a crate of his favorite gamecocks, to meet the Americans. Taylor's force, reduced by the withdrawal of soldiers under Scott, was only a third the size of Santa Anna's.

This time, after all the long waiting, it was Zachary Taylor who was caught napping. Leaving a quantity of his supplies in smoking ruins, he withdrew helter-skelter for some ten miles to the *hacienda* of Buena Vista. The fighting on the two days of February twenty-second and twenty-third was bitter and bloody. It ended in a draw. The three-to-one numerical advantage of Santa Anna, plus his better strategy, was offset by the aim of American artillery fire. The ragged Indians soon got enough of it and said they wanted to go home. Their women—those *soldaderas* who always accompanied their husbands to the Mexican battles to cook for them—gathered pots, pans, and babies together and agreed that this cannon fire was too rough. Santa Anna turned tail in the night after ordering a stealthy retreat. Leaving his conscripts to fend for themselves, he drove off in his coach, proclaiming his success in every town and displaying two captured American flags as evidence of victory.

The next morning, after a miserable night, General Taylor and his men, who thought they had been whipped, were flabbergasted and delighted to find the Mexican army had vanished. While Santa Anna was waving his captured standards and being hailed as a hero, the president in Washington was duly informed of an American victory.

The Mexican commander, like his soldiers, was unwilling to face more of Taylor's artillery until he was better equipped. So the liberal congress timorously passed a law authorizing the conversion of church properties up to the value of 5,000,000 pesos—if funds were not forthcoming elsewhere. The churchmen were willing to offer generous prayers for victory, but were indignant at the thought of contributing to the war effort. Some of them cried aloud, "Death to the government!" To many of the clergy, the Yankees were the less of two evils. Several priests were accused of conspiring with secret agents to surrender the capital to the Americans. Insurrection broke out, and the liberals were ousted from the government.

By mid-March Santa Anna again held the balance of power. But he had no time for further politics, because the Americans under General Winfield Scott had captured Vera Cruz on the ninth and were on the march to Mexico. At the pass of Cerro Gordo on the road toward Jalapa, Santa Anna set up fortifications and felt confident he could hold out against any American attack. But Scott's soldiers, aided by disaffected Mexicans, made a flank attack on April seventeenth, and on the eighteenth Santa Anna's troops retreated to Orizaba. In mountainside encounters, with native guides to assist them, the Americans outmaneuvered as well as outshot the Mexicans all along the way. Many of the survivors rushed back to the capital, every man for himself.

As Indians who hated the Aztecs had made conquest easier for Cortés, so did members of opposing factions make the way less tedious for the Americans. Puebla, stronghold of Catholicism, capitulated without a shot being fired. General Scott was cordially entertained. The deplorable division in Mexico was expressed by *El Diario del Gobierno:* "The internal enemies of the country, the secret agents of our external enemies, those who are laboring to open to United States soldiers the gates of the capital, neglect no means, however criminal, of fomenting dissensions and distrust among us; as more favorable to the designs of the invader is our own disunion than all the disasters we can suffer in combat." In the City of Mexico even Santa Anna himself was accused of betraying the Mexican cause to the Americans, and temporarily lost his political control. Pandemonium was loosed as various generals thrust themselves forward as potential saviors. But as always in the crises, Santa Anna proved the strong man.

Now he vigorously prepared for the defense of Mexico City, while holding off the Americans who were encamped and billeted at Puebla by intimating that the Mexicans would soon be ready to make peace. Hoping that a quick peace could be obtained without an attack on the capital, President Polk had sent Nicholas B. Triste to negotiate with the Mexican government from General Scott's headquarters. Through his commissioners Santa Anna had the gall to plead the immediate necessity of ten thousand dollars to speed his peace movement. The cash was actually forwarded to him from American headquarters at Puebla. After three months of dickering, while the defenses of Mexico City were being strengthened, when peace did not come General Scott decided to hasten the Mexicans' decision by advancing on the capital. By the tenth of August his forces were within striking distance. Still there was no peace. The Mexicans demanded the return of the north bank of the Rio Grande and California and indemnification for invasion damages. Scott gave the command to capture the city.

The populace of Mexico now seemed for the first time united in the cause of defending their capital against the invaders. All men from fifteen to fifty were under arms. For three weeks the volunteer recruits withstood the Americans with stubborn bravery. In this period Santa Anna displayed his best talents in leadership and personal courage. When excessively hard pressed he asked once more for a truce to discuss peace terms. In the interim of armistice, which was obligingly granted, he repaired his broken defenses. Then he declined the peace offer.

The Americans finally shot their way into the city, and on September thirteenth attempted to storm the fortress of Chapultepec, high above on its porphyry hill. Here they met with fierce opposition from the heroic young cadets of the military school. Disillusioned with their country's betrayal and ruin by their elders, the youths fought like tigers to redeem the honor of Mexico. When the castle was irrevocably lost and almost all of their young comrades lay dead all about them, the last boys wrapped Mexican flags about their bodies and leaped to their deaths over the precipice, defiantly shouting "Viva Mexico!" The Americans stood dumb with admiration before such valor.

In the early morning of September fourteenth, General Scott and his battle-stained troops drew up in the great plaza before the cathedral, the white flag of surrender fluttering high above them. The capital was theirs. The American boys believed the war was over and turned their thoughts to getting home.

But while peace negotiations were again in progress, sporadic fighting continued throughout the fall and winter. The elusive Santa Anna, who had escaped by withdrawing to Guadalupe, was for continuing the war. The majority was against him. Mexico was without leadership. Bandit gangs on the prowl not only ambushed Americans but looted well-to-do Mexicans. The conservatives were for peace and order at any price. At length they ousted Santa Anna, who hid in the mountains until the Americans promised him safe conduct. This time he chose Jamaica for his exile, and American officers at Vera Cruz gave a farewell party for him before he sailed.

Constituted authorities of the two nations now went on with peace negotiations. The terms were exceedingly bitter to Mexico. The United States demanded almost half of her territory, everything north of the Rio Grande from Louisiana to the Pacific: Texas, New Mexico, Arizona, California. In return the United

States would pay fifteen million dollars and wipe out the long-standing damage claims. While some of the American press was ringing with a popular clamor for annexing the whole of the Mexican territory, the new president of Mexico, Manuel de la Peña y Peña, and his congress agreed to the hard terms. The Treaty of Guadalupe Hidalgo was signed on February second, 1848. It was ratified in Washington on March tenth. The last American soldier departed in July. Hatred smoldered in Mexico and humiliation left its corroding marks. In the United States the acquisition of so much new territory increased the growing hostility between the North and the South over slavery and was a potent factor in bringing on the tragic War Between the States.

Mexico was so stunned by the result of her disastrous little war with the United States that she stayed quiescent for five years. She entered a frugal period and cut the army appropriation about seventy per cent, without arousing a revolution. In the sobering interval more and more men came to consider the grasping military and the church as incubuses to be thrown off, if Mexico were ever to progress or relieve the distress of her people. The moderate liberals began to see that drastic measures were necessary, that only in becoming extremely radical could they achieve anything of real value. So the defeat was in a sense the stimulus to a nationalistic feeling, a desire to regain self-respect as an independent state, an awakening of consciousness of the rights of Indian citizens.

All about the country provincial intellectuals were stirring, and making up programs for reforms. Students and literary men, becoming acutely nationalistic, sought to undermine conservative ideas in prose, poetry, and oratory. For the public's edification they revealed how not only political life had retrogressed, but how agricultural, mining, and commerce had lost impetus since colonial days. They pled for a complete re-estimation of values and some immediate relief for the pitiable condition of the masses.

One of the most forceful of these promising radicals was the governor of the state of Oaxaca, Benito Juárez. He was a pure-blooded Zapotec Indian who had begun his "civilized" life as a house boy. Before that he had known dire poverty at first hand, but he had been fortunate in coming in contact with a kind cleric who recognized his youthful abilities and arranged for his education. From a humble law office, Juárez rose to be governor. And because neither he nor any official directly under him profited financially by his position, his almost unprecedented honesty became proverbial throughout Mexico. A naturally taciturn man, every word he did speak or write carried conviction. He came to be recognized as that liberal leader who had the clearest conception of democracy.

In desperation at the prospect of losing their power because of the growing popular nationalistic movement, the conservatives cast about for a king from Europe to head a Mexican monarchy. In the interim they decided on the expedient of a military dictatorship. By a concentrated effort they threw out the liberals. Once more Santa Anna was offered the dictatorship on a silver platter. With almost immodest haste he arrived from his exile to take it with both hands. After a prolonged royal progress from the coast, he was solemnly sworn in as "president with dictatorial powers" on April twentieth, 1853.

Lucas Alamán became chief of Santa Anna's cabinet and drew up an excellent program for the dictator, including the construction of roads, the installation of telegraphs, and the development of unoccupied lands. But the admirable Alamán died suddenly in June, and Santa Anna was left with no check on his external conscience. The death of the honest-purposed Alamán was the worst blow that could have befallen the conservative party. He had thought that under the dictatorship of Santa Anna, guided by himself, the country could be readied for a monarchy, to be furnished with a Catholic prince from a foremost house in Europe.

Though his term was set for one year only, Santa Anna secretly reckoned on the rest of his days. To avoid future annoyance, the new dictator cleared all offices of remaining liberals, though most of the important ones had already fled. Juárez was among those who sought refuge in New Orleans. Here the former governor rolled cigarettes to make a living for his family.

Despite the ruptured economy and the staggering debt-pile, Santa Anna now tried to outdo Iturbide in creating a glittering court. His fondest dreams were now about to be realized. He had everything his way. So he confiscated, levied, plundered. But he was so tender with the church that the bishops supported him with all their temporal and spiritual power. A church-inspired claque soon hailed him as "Perpetual Dictator," and on December sixteenth, 1853, he actually proclaimed himself Perpetual Dictator. He came to be addressed as "Most Serene Highness," and began to create about him a society worthy of his supreme position. He took an enormous house and furnished it richly. He had resplendent uniforms specially designed for the officials surrounding him. Attracted by the bushy beards of the Czar of Russia's guards he saw in pictures, he decided that his beardless Indian guards should have them too. So he got them enormous false black ones, and when he attended the opera his retinue was a sight to behold. In the midst of his gala circle Santa Anna himself dressed in grave but expensive simplicity, for contrast. But he drove in a variety of elegant coaches. And he decreed that his cabinet ministers should ride in coaches of various colors —canary yellow for one ministry, mauve for another, emerald green for a third, and so on through the spectrum. The poor ministers had not only to ride in them, but they had to buy them and provide the satin liveries for their grooms.

For two years the Perpetual Dictator lived in mimic greatness, with his fighting cocks to amuse him and a succession of amorous adventures to relieve the tedium of statecraft. He never failed under any circumstance to pay obeisance to his religion. The bull-fights he attended were always "in honor of the Virgin." He opened the cockfights with the chant: "Hail, most Holy Mary, the cocks are coming." Then, despite his tributes to heaven, suddenly the jig was up. The treasury was again bare. In an effort to save himself (less than six months after Lucas Alamán's death) he had sold a strip of territory, south of Arizona, known as the Mesilla Valley to the United States for ten million dollars. But this cash had not lasted long in Santa Anna's extravagant hands, and the act was more unpopular than anything Santa Anna ever did in his misguided career. Generals and officeholders turned against their chief, as the republicans of Guerrero under the aging Juan Alvarez already had done the year before, when they launched the Plan of Ayutla. Scenting the imminent whirlwind, Santa Anna made a quick getaway to the coast. At Perote he paused to release an abdication. On August seventeenth he shipped from Vera Cruz. By grim coincidence the boat that took him to exile was named after that upstart emperor whose downfall he had plotted. The *Iturbide* bore him to Venezuela and colorless obscurity. His country never again recalled His Most Serene Highness to the political stage.

For two decades, however, Santa Anna figuratively lingered in the wings, straining to hear a cue. He made one abortive entrance, when he appeared to offer his services to Maximilian. But the French swiftly shifted him away. Finally, in the early Díaz days, as an old man, he was allowed to return to the capital, where he mingled with the mob completely unrecognized. As an unconsidered supernumerary the old-time star eked out a shabby existence, and he died unmourned in 1876.

Santa Anna made a more spectacular mess of his life than any of the other prominent historical figures. During the quarter century of his interrupted ascendancy, instead of progressing with the new, hard-earned independence, Mexico floundered in civil broils concocted by cynical selfishness. Repeatedly looked to as the savior of his country, Santa Anna was its chief wrecker. Not only did he lose half the territory of Mexico, but he was the agitator of bloody revolts that left his country prostrate and virulent with animosities. Madame Calderón de la Barca had shrewdly discerned on that early morning visit at Manga de Clavo "the lurking devil in Santa Anna's eye." But neither any casual observer nor his close friend who early remarked that he had within him "a principle of action forever impelling him forward" foresaw the destructive potentialities of his misguided ambition. If this sinister figure had possessed half as much constructive ability as he had genius for intrigue, Mexico's sequent history would have run differently.

## PART FIVE

# JUÁREZ AND MAXIMILIAN

## 11. Indian in Command

*"How close is the kinship between a man and
the whole human race, for it is a community,
not of a little blood or seed, but of intelligence."*
MARCUS AURELIUS

With Santa Anna's precipitate exit in 1855, the Mexican stage
was again in chaos. But out of the confusion there emerged a
purposeful liberal movement, with some men of good will to
lead and inspire. For twelve years, however, a kind of social
revolution waxed and waned—a revolution of the *mestizo* bourgeoisie rather than the masses. The *mestizos* rose rapidly in
political power and laid the foundations for economic development. The period is known as the Reform. Its prime objectives
were the destruction of feudalism and the weakening of the
temporal power of the church. The Reform was only partially
successful, but it gave birth to forces that were to come to dominate in Mexico more than a half century later. In its own time
it met with envenomed opposition, and it would most likely have
been blotted out if it had not been for one man—the Indian,
Benito Juárez. Juárez is the hero of the Reform.

In the new governmental set-up, at a *junta* in Cuernavaca on
October fourth, Juan Alvarez, the doughty warrior chieftain of
the southern mountains, was made temporary president. It was

this old Indian with Negro blood who had initiated the revolt—on February twentieth, 1854—that finished the political career of Santa Anna. He had fought by the side of Vicente Guerrero, his idol, and for forty years he had been a leader in every important rebellion. In succeeding against Santa Anna in the south he had been aided by Ignacio Comonfort, a creole gentleman of mildly liberal tendencies who commanded the forces at Acapulco. Comonfort was made minister of war in the new cabinet. To Benito Juárez was given the post of minister of justice, and an opportunity to initiate reforms.

On November fourteenth Alvarez made his entrance into the capital, fantastically attended by a bodyguard of bizarre Indian warriors. White Mexicans and *mestizos* alike were filled with apprehension at what they regarded as a portentous racial gesture. While they jeered openly, they feared in private. And many of the intellectual liberals looked with frank distaste on the presidency of the dark, uneducated chieftain. They did not feel antipathy, however, to the full-blooded Benito Juárez, whose intellectual caliber was superior to that of most of them. Juárez was a thinker, not a soldier, and a man of such integrity and austerity of character and habits that he commanded instant respect.

Nine days after Alvarez had set up his presidential office in the capital, Juárez, as minister of justice, made a bold move. He decreed (November twenty-third, 1855) the abolition of the special privileges of the church and the military. Priests and army officers were to be brought to civil justice as were any other citizens. Such a tempest was created by the church and the army that the liberals who opposed Alvarez took the opportunity to persuade him to relinquish the presidency to the more moderate Comonfort. The old fighter was not reluctant to return to the mountain farm he plowed with his own hands when he was not in revolt. He realized his incapacity to steer a ship of state as fully as he knew he was without a peer in guerrilla fighting. He left for Guerrero on December twelfth, having been chief executive of Mexico for two months and a week.

Though the troubled waters were somewhat stilled by Alvarez's departure with his Indians, the move to end clerical domination did not subside. And on June twenty-fifth, 1856, a climactic stage was reached when the *Ley Lerdo* was passed by a more than five to one majority in the congress. The law was named after Miguel Lerdo de Tejada, the secretary of treasury, who drew up the document. By its articles all the church properties except the actual houses of worship were to be sold. It was made illegal henceforth for the church to own agricultural land. But the law was not confiscatory, in that the church was to receive the purchase price less a substantial tax paid to the government. The liberals had expected the land-hungry people to buy up the land in small tracts. But the priests frightened the poor and humble out of desire to buy, whereas members of the new rich bourgeoisie bought up vast estates intact.

The church was not really damaged economically by the law, though its prestige had been assaulted. And the church was further humiliated when the control of cemeteries was taken from it and entrusted to a department of public health, which had just been created. The church was not only accused of gross carelessness of hygienic considerations in burials, but it suffered the loss of the lucrative burial fees.

The *Ley Lerdo* and the *Ley Juárez* together raised such violent opposition from the church that friars began to store arms and ammunition in some of the monasteries. A revolt of clerical-conservatives broke out in Puebla. The infection spread, and it was March, 1857, before peace was restored. Comonfort may have been wrong in pardoning all the captured insurrectionists, for worse trouble was to come later.

The new Reform constitution, which had been in preparation throughout most of 1856, was completed on February fifth. It included among its articles both the abolition of the special dis-

pensations from civil justice for clergy and military and the pro-
hibition of future land ownership by corporations. The churchmen now became frantic, for they recognized that a new era was
being born. The pope himself damned the Reform constitution
and all its ratifiers and supporters. Any person who swore allegiance to it or bought church property was to be denied Christian burial. When a certain signer governor was assassinated, the
church refused to bury his corpse until his family had suffered
it to be scourged penitentially in public, and had paid a tidy sum
to the church for the ceremony of chastisement.

A prime object of the Reform constitution was to break up
land concentration and to put the entailed estates of the church
to use for the general welfare. Tenants living on church properties had the right to buy them at a fair price, according to the
rents they were paying. But few enough tenants had any capital,
and those with money dreaded the threatened excommunication.
So when the church lands were put on sale, or "denounced," a
troop of American, British, French, and German capitalists
rushed to buy the properties. In the effort to breathe life into the
*mortmain* estates of the church, the Reform lost many of the best
to foreign absentee landlords.

By forbidding the ownership of land by civil corporations, the
new laws broke up the *ejidos,* those community-owned lands on
which the Indian peasants largely made their living. This proved
to be a most unfortunate procedure, although the family heads
of the villages now individually owned their private parcels. The
*hacendados* began to buy up many of these parcels, and their
agents became adroit in cheating the Indians. For a handful of
cash and a drenching in *aguardiente,* Indians could be persuaded
to sell their new private property.

It had seemed a logical part of the program to give every man
his own plot of ground. But it simply did not work; the Indians
were subject to the dictates of human nature, and many did not
care to save themselves from themselves for themselves. So, para-

doxically, the land reform so beneficently conceived for the general welfare merely brought about a greater land concentration. And the provision that dissolved the time-honored *ejido* proved the chief bone of contention in the revolutionary years to come.

Under the new constitution, Comonfort had been duly elected president and Juárez made chief of the supreme court, which was equivalent also to the vice-presidency. By autumn, in the thick of the increasingly bitter animosities, to try to avoid civil war by appeasing the conservatives Comonfort asked his party for a more moderate revision of the constitution. The liberal congressmen, distrusting his desire for conciliation, withdrew to Querétaro and renounced him, leaving him in the capital a president without a party. In its renunciation of Comonfort, congress automatically made the Indian Juárez president of Mexico. Completely rid of military men in the high offices, Mexico was now governed mainly by lawyers and writers, with more Indian blood in the ruling body than since the days of Cuauhtémoc. But it was not for long. The conservatives took possession of power in the capital, and the appeasing General Comonfort went off sadly into exile. The church-backed conservative army set about to wipe out the new liberal government. Juárez escaped to Manzanillo on the Pacific coast and shipped to Panama and thence to Vera Cruz, which had remained loyally liberal. For three years Juárez conducted his liberal government from Vera Cruz, refusing to accept defeat, while the whole land was rent with a most vicious civil war.

While the church was opening its coffers munificently to the reactionary armies, Juárez was appropriating the customs duties at Vera Cruz. Although the anti-liberal forces were successful in most of the cities and large towns, the constitutionalists held the countryside by the most devilish sort of guerrilla warfare. Vera Cruz withstood successfully two major attacks from the reactionary troops. And through the whole nightmarish three years— with the conservatives winning all the other major engagements

—it was the integrity and inflexibility of the little Indian tha‌ kept the ideal of democracy glowing. His simple words of profound import stirred the people as no Spanish rhetoric could have done.

In July of 1859, realizing that the power of the church had to be radically broken if Mexico were ever to have peace and economic stability again, Juárez issued his famous Reform laws. All church property was declared confiscated. Monastic orders were to be broken up and convents dismantled with the decease of present occupants. Seminaries were prohibited. Freedom of worship for all religions was decreed. Marriage was made a civil contract. Priests and nuns were prohibited from appearing on the streets in their religious vestments. Besides the strictures against the Catholic Church, freedom of the press and the right of assembly were written into the bill. All titles of nobility were abolished. The democracy of Mexico was emphasized in the sentence: "The national sovereignty is vested essentially and originally in the people." For these democratic reforms, Juárez has gained the title of "Thomas Jefferson of Mexico."

The public proclamation of the Reform laws was the signal for increased fury in fighting on both sides. When undefended by reactionary troops, church property was ruthlessly seized and the churches themselves were sacked. Priests who refused to give the sacrament to dying constitutionalist soldiers were shot. As that very able historian, H. B. Parkes, sees the radical decree: "It was a salutary severity, cleansing the country of the miasmas which had accumulated through three centuries of clerical control; it weakened the powers of religious superstition and taught the Mexican people that one could lay hands on the clergy without being smitten with wrath from heaven."

The proclamation of Juárez's anti-ecclesiastical measures was really the turning point in the war. Though the better equipped reactionary forces continued to win victories for a year, the waxing strength of the liberals became obvious as their civilian lead-

ers learned better how to direct the fight. The need of funds
drove both sides to desperate remedies of ruinous debt contracts
and dangerous treaties with foreign powers. The country was
bleeding to death. The intrenched interests, leagued with the
retrograde church, were not easily to be dislodged without super-
sacrifice and persistence. But Juárez never once wavered in his
abiding faith that democracy would triumph. He himself possessed in concentrated form the endurance and patience of the
Indian. He was a pure product of the soil; his humble origin
had brought him so close to life's immediacies that he was never
to be thrown off base by nonessentials or superficialities. The
steady flame of inspiration that refused to recognize defeat kept
the civilian soldiers uplifted in faith as well as courage.

While the European powers had recognized the conservative
Miramón as president of Mexico, the United States had acknowledged Juárez. But to forestall the menace of a European invasion,
that seemed likely, the government at Washington considered
United States intervention. With the threat of intervention dan-
gling like the sword of Damocles, to buy off the United States
Juárez agreed to the notorious McLane-Ocampo Treaty of December, 1859, by which the United States was to have in perpetuity a right of transit between the oceans across the Isthmus of
Tehuantepec and the right to send soldiers onto Mexican soil
to protect American property. Juárez's government was to receive
two million much-needed dollars in cash, and two more millions
were to be applied to American private damage claims against
Mexico. Many Mexicans were indignant at this smirch on their
national sovereignty and protested vigorously and with passion.
In the end the United States Senate refused to ratify the treaty,
largely because the Northern senators suspected it would help
the South in the struggle that seemed so imminent in 1860.

Even though some of his own followers opposed the treaty,
Juárez had agreed to it because his financial situation was so
desperate. Later he wrote an apologia and said it was his love

of liberty in the face of desperation that compelled him to take the step. "God knows the sacrifice it caused me," he said.

When Abraham Lincoln became president in 1861, the tone of United States diplomacy changed. "Be just, frank, and magnanimous," he instructed his first envoy to Mexico. "Gain the confidence of the people, and show that your mission is earnestly American, in that continental sense of the word, and fraternal in no affected or mere diplomatic meaning."

In the fall of 1860, Juárez had put a new man in command of his troops, General Ortega. The tide began to turn. After a series of liberal victories, three days before Christmas Ortega inflicted a decisive defeat on the conservative forces. On New Year's Day, 1861, he entered the capital with his victorious army. Ten days later Juárez, dressed in sober black, arrived from Vera Cruz to take up the Herculean task of administering a prostrate nation. The treasury was more than empty. European nations were already clamoring for debt payments and shortly threatening intervention.

In March, Juárez was re-elected to the presidency as the only one who could possibly revive the mangled land. All his splendid dreams for using the *mortmain* church properties and the hoarded capital for the general welfare had come to nought. Instead of going into schools and roads and irrigation projects and railways, the ecclesiastical wealth had gone the way of civil strife. In his desire for harmony and co-operation, Juárez made two mistakes: He declared an amnesty for all his enemies except a few dangerously powerful generals, and he permitted his congress to have more power than it has ever had under any other executive. This congress was filled with radical orators who had never had such a royal chance to extend their personalities. They continually criticized and condemned, proposed and counterproposed. Instead of being a help to the president, who was already enduring the tribulations of Job, they were an additional plague.

A little more than a month after Juárez's re-election, while desultory civil war was still going on in Mexico, news came that the United States was engaged in a war between the North and the South. None dreamed the indirect but momentous consequences of that war to Mexico. But in France the crafty little Napoleon III thought he saw an opportunity he could turn to his imperial credit. While the United States was too absorbed in its own tearing troubles to concern herself with Latin American affairs, Napoleon determined to create the nucleus of a new empire in the Western Hemisphere.

Payment on a calamitous loan negotiated by Juárez's chief opponent, General Miramón, was now demanded by the French government. The loan had been made by a Swiss banker named Jecker and taken over by a bastard kinsman of Napoleon who now claimed the total amount of 15,000,000 pesos, although only 1,500,000 had been paid before Jecker went bankrupt. Napoleon decided to make the claim a justifiable reason for occupation.

In the debt and damage claiming, Spain and England joined with France. Fleets from all three nations, with expeditionary troops aboard, arrived at Vera Cruz like *zopilotes* at a death in the swamp.

To try to keep peace in his queasy land, Juárez was forced to acknowledge not only the just claims, but many of the unjust ones. Payment, however, had to be deferred. The English and Spanish negotiators, convinced that Juárez was not dishonest, turned tail and sailed home, leaving France to do what gouging she would.

Napoleon had been fervently assured by refugee Mexican conservatives that the populace would welcome French intervention with expansive embraces. Juárez was pictured as a scheming, low-bred cutthroat. The annual revenue of Mexico and its potential wealth were made to sound like the fabulous tales of Montezuma's treasure. The exiled Mexicans were burning with desire to sell their country out to some alien prince supported by Napoleon's troops. They were delighted when the choice fell on a Hapsburg, the young Archduke Ferdinand Maximilian, brother of the Emperor of Austria.

Shortly, by way of prelude, another French army arrived at Vera Cruz, to reinforce the debt-collecting expedition, and the interventionists were ready for their march on the capital. They were joined by Márquez, the bloodiest of the reactionary generals, with the tattered remnants of his church-blessed troops.

With superlative self-confidence and colors bravely flying, the French set out for Puebla. On May fifth the invaders assaulted the city's fortifications and met with such a resounding defeat that the *Cinco de Mayo* became a national holiday and the subsequent name of a street in almost every Mexican town.

Napoleon was astonished beyond measure at the repulse of his soldiers. But, having launched his magnanimous regeneration of Mexico, his honor would not let him welsh now. He sent an abler general and thirty thousand fresh troops across the Atlantic to teach the Mexicans differences. It was a whole year later before Puebla finally capitulated, on May sixteenth, after a calamitous siege of two months in which starvation took its toll in miseries. After the bulk of the Mexican army had surrendered at Puebla, the defense of the capital was not feasible. With what was left of his army, Juárez and his government withdrew to San Luis Potosí in the north. The French took possession of the capital on June tenth, with a bought-and-paid-for floral demonstration. The jubilation in the churches, however, was as sincere as ardent. Were not the good Catholic French come to restore all their lost property?

But the joyous anthems died away, for the French commander decreed that the present owners of former ecclesiastical lands and possessions were to keep them. Nothing was to revert to the church. Nor did the French intend to hand over the rule of the country to those impatient conservative exiles who had returned with them from Europe. With considerable astonishment, the Mexicans who had encouraged the French intervention now saw that its regenerative qualities looked suspiciously like mere foreign domination. Yet to the young Maximilian was ceremoniously offered the crown of Mexico.

# 12. Pale Interloper

*"You think my life a music box that plays gay
tunes."*

JOSÉ RUBÉN ROMERO

A committee of exiled Mexican notables waited upon the Hapsburg prince at Miramar, his castle on the Adriatic, and invited him to become Emperor of Mexico. Maximilian modestly explained that he was not the sort to intrude where he was not wanted. He would accept only if he could be assured by a plebiscite that the populace wanted him. Of the utter farce of Mexican voting he was unaware. When informed in due time that he had been chosen emperor by a tremendous majority, he agreed to come.

Napoleon too had been deceived, not about the plebiscite but about the wealth of Mexico. Through the bragging and romancing of the Mexican commission, he was carried away with fantastic imaginings. He was not altogether insincere when he told Maximilian he was giving him "a throne on a pile of gold." But he was too suave a diplomat to add that he regarded the prince as a debt collector and a tool of imperial ambitions.

Maximilian set out in good faith as a benevolent ruler, not as the head of the conservative party. He had dabbled in the study of liberalism and had discussed the merits of socialism with that good Utopian Robert Owen in England. He wrote amiably to the austere Juárez, naively asking his help and assuring him of his appreciation of his patriotism.

The ocean voyage on the *Novara* passed blandly and full of golden expectation. The liberal Maximilian beguiled the weeks of crossing by preparing a lengthy compendium on court etiquette. He and his young wife Carlotta saw themselves in a rosy haze, receiving their due meed of royal courtesy from a grateful people. And, spurred by his princess, the prince conjured up a glamorous vision of himself as a kind of White Knight bringing blessings. The young hearts fluttered with intense anticipation as they approached the harbor of Vera Cruz on May twenty-eighth. Was not the whole world watching their historic landing and reception?

After the ship noises of casting anchor ceased, a profound and ominous silence held the sultry air in thrall. There was no reception committee, no martial music, no banners, no garlands. The only sign of life was the scavenger vultures, the *zopilotes,* swooping about their repulsive personal affairs. It was as if the sordid seaport had been deserted by a populace fleeing from a plague. In her overwhelming disappointment, the high-spirited Carlotta could not restrain a flood of tears.

Napoleon had ordered an expensive reception and a regal banquet. But something had gone wrong. After wandering dismally about the blistering streets, the royal party had to return to the ship for a savorless supper. With typical Mexican casualness about appointments, General Almonte, the acting regent, had miscalculated the time of their arrival. Hours late, he finally dashed into town from Orizaba. At his orders the fortress guns now let off a welcoming salute. Still the populace did not stir to cheer or even to look. Vera Cruz was overwhelmingly liberal in sentiment, and took malicious satisfaction in ignoring the pretensions of an emperor. The royal couple's night was filled with dark forebodings. Had they been deceived? Were they really wanted? How would it all end?

The next day, when they were resting at La Soledad from the first stage of their overland journey, a messenger arrived with a note from Juárez himself. Maximilian grasped it eagerly. But what he read chilled his heart. The very brevity of the message added to its import.

It is given a man, sir, to attack the rights of others, seize their goods, assault the lives of those who defend their nationality, make of their virtues crimes, and of one's own vices a virtue, but there is one thing beyond the reach of such perversity—the tremendous judgment of history.

Maximilian turned pale. It was as if an honorable enemy had presented a man with a loaded gun and suggested that he blow his brains out to forestall a greater catastrophe. The scales dropped from the Austrian's eyes. This Indian Juárez, who had been pictured to him as a vicious ignoramus, was obviously a man of parts and doubtless a sincere patriot. Had he himself not been tricked into coming to this most alien land as a savior?

Though the roads were so dreadful that one wheel of the royal coach was irreparably smashed, Carlotta endured the calamities of the progress with uncommon fortitude. She remarked the wonder of Mexican scenery. She noted the donkeys loaded with bags of vanilla that scented the air about their trail like sweet incense. She delighted in the brilliant-feathered cocka-toos perched among the pendent orchids. Again and again she called her husband's attention to the bronzed Indians in their white cotton suits and enormous straw hats, making fascinating pictures whether they moved or stood still. Like many another person through the ages who has lost the sense of his perturba-tion in the spell-binding beauty of Mexico, Carlotta, tired to the bone, took courage from the wild harmonies of nature as the party was forced to traverse the rim of the mountain on horse-back. What an odd way, she remarked, for a princess to spend her twenty-fourth birthday! The date was June twenty-fourth, 1864.

Five days later the royal party paused at the church of Guada-lupe for a blessing and to behold the shrine of the Virgin of the Indians. They were met by a cortège of conservative notables and their wives, all resplendently dressed. They took some heart as they proceeded the last three miles into the poplar-bordered avenue in Mexico City that led them to the great cathedral on the Zócalo. Here they were so quickly crowned that the proceedings seemed positively furtive. But the throngs in the plaza cheered lustily, and all the church bells in the capital pealed as the royal couple walked over to their new domicile, the vast National Palace with its more than a thousand windows. The desperately weary pair looked forward to nothing so devoutly as a night's tranquil sleep. But even this simple boon enjoyed by shepherds under the stars was denied the emperor and empress. Bedbugs roused them from their slumber. They were forced to seek out a billiard table on which to rest their imperial flesh.

Carlotta could not bear the cheerless palace. So the court removed to the summer castle at Chapultepec, high above the city. Here on this spot Montezuma had spent the best days of his fabulous reign. Maximilian began to remodel the building, to refurnish and decorate it. He planned a boulevard from the hill to the cathedral square, four miles away. Loggias and walks and intimate patios were conceived and executed. In the munificent climate, the new flowering shrubs and vines were quickly abloom.

Carlotta chose her ladies-in-waiting from the most prominent conservative families. And while she shocked the languid señoras by trotting about on jingling muleback among the thousand-year-old cypresses of Montezuma's park, her husband on horseback braved all kinds of weather to survey his new domain, to speak in halting Spanish to his new subjects, and to learn truth at first hand. On September sixteenth, Independence Day, he appeared at Dolores and risked assassination by appearing on Father Hidalgo's balcony and making a speech on liberty. The glaring Indians gave over their sullenness and admired his courage and even found him *simpático*. The legend of Quetzalcoatl had been revived among them. And some of them who looked upon the tall, fair giant with the parted golden beard were willing to believe there might be truth in the tale of the god's return. Because they cheered him with enthusiasm, the emperor believed the rest would be easy for him.

Maximilian came to have a fondness for the Indians. He liked their quiet ways, their patience and philosophy. He began to see himself as their protector, and he determined to abolish peonage. It was on the Indian that the emperor fixed his faith—they would be the foundation and mainstay of his empire.

"This continent is very progressive in a political sense," the emperor wrote to his younger brother. "All the stilted trumpery with which we so stupidly encumber ourselves in Europe, and shall continue encumbering ourselves for centuries, has been discarded over here." In another letter, he wrote: "Ours is a healthy democracy. We live here in a free land among free people and under enlightened principles such as you at home cannot ever dream about . . . in social questions we are far ahead of Europe."

The conservatives resented Maximilian's democratic attitudes, his big sombrero, his efforts to please the Indians. And the church party was highly displeased with their minion. The pope sent a nuncio across the seas to demand, among other things, the absolute annulment of Juárez's Reform laws, the restoration of monastic orders and the restitution of church properties. Carlotta herself interviewed the nuncio and backed her husband's liberal position in strong phrases. Neither side would give in an inch. The liberal press shouted that the Juárez doctrines had triumphed. Rome was mortally offended. Carlotta wrote indignantly and pertinently to the French empress: "To expect this country—burning with resentment against theocracies—to return the enormous holdings of the clergy would be not only blind and irrational, but silly beyond compare."

At last one of the most astounding of all Mexican paradoxes gradually became apparent on both sides of the Atlantic. The

Catholic prince of the most royal Hapsburg dynasty was championing the liberal cause. The realization dumbfounded the creoles as well as the clergy. Conservative society began to cast cold looks on Chapultepec. Carlotta's ladies-in-waiting became constrained in their politeness, when it was their duty to appear in court. To clear the social air of bad feeling, the emperor and empress tried the time-honored royal dodges of creating orders of merit and giving elaborate parties. For the titillating honor of the new decorations the piqued and the pouting seemed willing to brush aside their differences.

Mexico had never before known such state dinners, nor has it known such since. They began at three-thirty in the afternoon and lasted into the evening. Wines from Hungary, France, and the Rhineland brought spots of joy into the sallow cheeks of Mexican society and a headache to the treasury department. The wine bill exceeded one hundred thousand pesos the first year. And Maximilian in a private letter home contemptuously commented: "The diplomats gulp and guzzle so strenuously that after dinner they can do nothing but lisp inarticulate nonsense." Some of the dowagers snoozed audibly to the lullaby of after-dinner music by the Viennese orchestra. But catnapping and nonsense-babbling were not unamiable manifestations. And Maximilian was happy to endure both as long as he was looked on in friendly wise.

Dinners, suppers, musical soirées followed one another in succession. Life in the court must have seemed as aimlessly idle as it was extravagant. But Maximilian was not idle. He had become more and more fascinated with ideas of reform. And while soothing the members of the upper crust by pinning on decorations, he spent his work hours vaguely planning for the general welfare. One night, taking his aide and his Mexican private secretary with him, he visited the city bakeries, because he had heard "the employees were treated like slaves." Another night he made a surprise tour of the prisons, inspected each cell and dormitory, questioned some of the prisoners, and "exhorted them, on their release not to go back to crime, but to lead hard-working, honest lives." He sketched schemes for education of the masses. He started a national art gallery and purposed to create academies of science. He saw in the future the construction of a great Mexican navy. But whatever nebulous progressive measures Maximilian had in his mind, they were hamstrung by a subject to which he gave only the faintest consideration—finances. There was no money in the treasury, nor had a cent of his and Carlotta's personal salaries yet been paid.

Maximilian had not examined closely the realities of the rôle he had assumed. The agreement between him and Napoleon, known as the Convention of Miramar, was simple: A French armed force was to be maintained in Mexico until the end of 1867, and Maximilian obligated himself to see that Mexico paid her foreign debts and the entire expense of French intervention. Before leaving his own terrace on the Adriatic, Maximilian had burdened Mexico with a debt far beyond its capacity to pay.

Through one long, grueling night he sat up with his cabinet, learning from one after another the excessive deficits in their departments. The internal debt looked as hopeless as the foreign debt, which had been tripled by the French intervention. In an agony of headache, though realizing their economies would hardly be a drop in the empty tub of debt, Maximilian and Carlotta began cutting expenses right and left. They canceled parties, dismissed a large portion of their retinue, and took to the simple life with avid relief.

The new economy gave him an excuse to spend much time away from Chapultepec in Cuernavaca. His Mexican secretaries were delighted because they nearly roasted from the heat of the stoves he kept burning in the offices in Mexico. Maximilian disliked the chill of Mexico City's climate and kept the temperature as hot as a Turkish bath. At Cuernavaca the air was semi-tropical and very pleasant, and Maximilian and Carlotta found a measure of contentment. After a hard week's work, the emperor would seek diversion in picnics in the woods. He found a site that particularly appealed to him, and out of his inherited income he built Carlotta a house in Pompeian style and called it El Olvido, "Forgetfulness."

But there was little personal peace for the emperor and empress, for the leaders of the royalist party began to make incessant demands for an heir. What, nine years of marriage and no conception yet? Tch, tch, tch! Had Mexico gone to so much trouble and expense to procure an emperor, only to have the imperial line cut off so short? They urged Maximilian to bestir himself. Embarrassed and perturbed, Maximilian tried to be amiably evasive. But soon some venomous clergymen began to circulate the report that the failure was due to venereal disease contracted in the emperor's youth. Then Carlotta was shamed with the accusation of barrenness. Whisperers brought reports to the empress of infidelities on her husband's part. Scandal-mongering was rife, and for a period blighted their rather idyllic love affair. At last, as a gesture to satisfy the public, the royal pair adopted one of Emperor Augustín de Iturbide's little grandsons and made him heir to the throne. With the passing of the Austrian the rule of Mexico would again go back to the Mexicans. The idea was promulgated partially as propaganda to win over *juaristas*. But it had little effect on either their loyalty to democratic principles or their shouting.

King Leopold I of Belgium, Carlotta's worldly-wise father, watched the Mexican experiment with dubious interest. He sent two brief letters of special advice. He cautioned his daughter against harsh measures towards papal nuncios in particular and the church in general. "The clergy may become dangerous," he warned her. The other advice concerned the importance of the military command. He recalled to them the great Napoleon's aphorism: "God is always on the side of the heavy artillery."

But the trusting and honest Maximilian completely lacked

any of the Machiavellian astuteness of his father-in-law. In his efforts to do the decent thing as he saw it, he antagonized the pope, Napoleon III, the Mexican clergy, and the conservative creoles. And in the field of battle his *juarista* enemies were any-thing but pacified. Except in the capital there was little peace in the land. Guerrilla bands roved the country. The French troops did not know how to fight against ambush in the hills. The republican forces were merciless to the supporters of the monarchy when they caught them. Maximilian grieved for the agonies men endured for his sake.

By the first of April, 1865, however, the French seemed to have the situation under control. Juárez and his army had been pushed to the very edges of north Mexico. General Porfirio Díaz had surrendered in the south. The best of the *juarista* army officers and political leaders who were not dead were in exile or prison. Juárez stood almost alone. Maximilian longed to meet him. "It was the Emperor's great illusion," wrote his Mexican secretary, "that if he could talk to Juárez he could attract him to his cause, make him his ranking minister, and, aided by him and freed of the intervention of the French, he could govern the empire wisely and inaugurate for Mexico, in its entirety, an era of peace, progress, and well-being."

Just when Maximilian believed that all would come easier, the surrender at Appomattox occurred. The North had won the War Between the States. By the end of the summer much of the unused ammunition and equipment were at the Texas bor-der, and the *juaristas* were being reinforced by filibusters from both the South and the North.

Now that the United States had ended its own internal strife, the government was able to turn its attention again to interna-tional affairs. The most pressing extraterritorial problem was that the French were entrenched among the next-door neighbors. Secretary of State William H. Seward lent his shrewd intelligence and power to helping Juárez expel the French and put down local opposition.

Juárez's government had become peripatetic. His black carriage was often to be seen moving in a direction contrary to his desires. After Morelia, Querétaro, and Guadalajara had been surrendered to the French and the Mexican conservatives, and the combined forces had approached San Luis Potosí, Juárez and his government had left for northern Durango. Then he had been forced farther north into Chihuahua. And as the empire prospered he continued to make removals towards the north, until by the autumn of 1865 he made his last stand at Paso del Norte (afterwards known as Cuidad Juárez), at the very edge of Mexico and within rifle-shot of El Paso, Texas. General Bazaine stopped short of Paso del Norte. He did not want to risk trouble with Washington and give an opportunity for accusations that he had trespassed on United States soil. To come too near the Texas border would have inflamed the American public. Already there was a clamorous advocacy in the United States for turning the victorious Union forces into a punitive expedition to drive the French invaders from Mexico.

When Maximilian had sought representation in Washington, he had been coolly informed that Juárez, the president of Mexico, already had his minister there. In Paris, the United States minister now pointedly called on Napoleon III to ask how long the French tricolor would be in Mexico. He implied that the Monroe Doctrine was becoming extremely restive with a European flag flying so near the southern border of the United States.

Napoleon squirmed. He knew the Mexican venture had failed. He did not want to face a clash with the United States, particularly at a time when an inimical Germany at his border was growing menacing. In a last, vain effort to bring about the pacification of Mexico, the French put fierce energy into their punitive expeditions. Against all his instincts and principles, Maximilian was coerced by General Bazaine into signing a proclamation by which anyone caught fighting against the imperial forces would be shot as a traitor. The bloody executions that followed the decree stirred up tremendous ill-will against Maximilian, and turned the tables against him when he himself was captured by the enemy.

By the beginning of 1866 the recuperative forces of government in the United States were sufficiently stabilized and strengthened for Seward to issue an ultimatum to the French. On February twelfth, without further ceremony, he demanded the exodus of French soldiers. The French emperor decided to wash his hands of his imperial experiment in the Western Hemisphere. He prepared to bring his troops home, and wrote Bazaine immediately to that effect.

Though Napoleon was pledged to keep troops in Mexico until the end of 1867, Bazaine began to withdraw his forces from the north in March of 1866. As the French withdrew, the *juaristas* rushed in to fill the gaps. Meanwhile, a native army composed largely of illiterate Indians was being trained to protect the government after the French exodus.

Napoleon really expected Maximilian to leave with the army. Feeling betrayed by France, and realizing his powerlessness, Maximilian was not altogether averse to abdication. But Carlotta was determined they should yet succeed. She decided to intercede personally with Napoleon.

Risking capture by guerrillas, she dared the atrocious roads between the capital and Vera Cruz in the dreaded rainy season. Her humble entourage was attacked by bandits, who took the mules from her carriage and left her party on the roadside to walk to the next station in a drenching downpour. Here she was rescued by a young Irish-American engineer named Braniff who had recently arrived in Mexico. Braniff hired a high, open buggy, and drove the empress the rest of the way to Vera Cruz.

At Paris the embarrassed Napoleon tried to avoid seeing Carlotta. The importunate woman threatened to force her way into the palace. At last the French emperor and empress saw her three times and listened to her pleas and her vituperation. Both Napoleon and Eugénie were touched. They both wept at their impotence to help further. There was nothing to do, they said, but call the deal off and have Maximilian return to the serenity of Miramar. In her frustration, Carlotta became frantic and rushed to Rome to throw herself at the feet of the pope. Her wits began to turn on the way. She declined food and water, suspecting a Napoleonic plot to poison her. When the pope received her, she went stark mad in the holy presence. In a fit of frenzy she refused to leave the Vatican. She pled so piteously that the Pope had two cots prepared for her and her Mexican lady-in-waiting. They were the only women ever known to have slept in a pope's anteroom. At the urgent papal plea, Carlotta's brother came posthaste from Belgium. He took her to a guarded retreat and wrote Maximilian the tragic news.

By the time the letter got across the Atlantic, the *juaristas* had gained ground everywhere. Maximilian decided he might as well go to his wife, for the interlude of empire seemed destined to a speedy end. He packed and sent his luggage on to Vera Cruz. He wrote out his edict of abdication and left the capital for Orizaba. Here he vacillated for six weeks, coming more and more under the influence of his confessor, a Texas-born priest named Fischer, who, having failed to wrest a good living from ranching and gold-digging in the States, had taken holy orders in Mexico. Like Rasputin, this adventurous Fischer had a sinister attraction, though a disarming one, and Maximilian had found him diverting as he conversed with him in his native German. Fischer's slick tongue finally persuaded Maximilian to remain in Mexico, despite Bazaine's last entreaties for him to abdicate. To make the emperor see the folly of remaining, Bazaine destroyed all military equipment he could not take with him. But now Maximilian would not budge, for the reactionaries who had grown lukewarm about him passionately pressed him to remain. They were terrified of Juárez. Maximilian was haunted by fear that abdication would dishonor him. The priest had emphasized the dishonor, while laying on the unction of foolish hope with a lavish hand. In March, Bazaine sailed from Vera Cruz with the last of the French forces, leaving the emperor to Fischer and fate.

To forestall further threats of abdication, the conservative leaders now thrust Maximilian forward as supreme commander of the imperialist Mexican army. In a way he was flattered. On the thirteenth of February, having exchanged the imperial family silver for food supplies, Maximilian set out for Querétaro escorted by fifteen hundred soldiers. It was also the thirteenth day of the month when Carlotta had embarked from Vera Cruz on her vain and tragic errand. Maximilian's faithful secretary, José Luis Blasio, could not help but make a note of the coincidence. At Querétaro Maximilian took charge of the nine thousand troops with the other three M's—Miramón, Márquez, and Mejía—as his generals.

The city was gradually surrounded by forty thousand *juaristas*. Food supplies and water were cut off. The Austrian hussars left in the capital were sent for again and again, but the scouts were always captured and killed before they reached Mexico. Márquez and a strong detachment finally cut through the enemy ring. But they, too, were defeated, and could not return. Help did not come.

Maximilian played his soldier rôle nobly, as one who knew the eyes of future chroniclers were upon him. But the contemporary eyes certainly applauded his democratic soldiery, his denials, his courage, his willingness to undergo the hardships of his men. He wrapped himself for sleep in his blanket like an Indian. He ate the coarsest food. He recklessly exposed his person. Though weakened by dysentery and wasted with fever, he went about trying to spread courage and cheer. He suffered for the miseries his army's presence had brought upon the townspeople.

The heat that came with May made the situation less endurable as the putrefaction of corpses polluted the air. Many called to mind the horrors of the siege of Mexico City under Cuauhtémoc, though this time it was a European prince rather than an Indian who was the principal object of the attack.

In the ghastliness of the ordeal, Colonel López, a dashing courtier who had won the affection of both Carlotta and her husband, decided that Maximilian and he should live. He slipped through the lines to negotiate with an enemy commander. When the hour came, he had the guards removed, so that enemy forces could steal unmolested into the town and to the convent where Maximilian had his quarters.

In the tumult, the *juarista* officers pretended not to recognize the tall Austrian and did everything they could to permit his getaway. Maximilian found excuses to delay. He stopped to commiserate with Miramón, whose face had been split open in the struggle. And then, instead of escaping as López had planned, he went to join the Indian general, Mejía, encamped with scanty forces on the Hill of Bells. He stood boldly on the eminence waiting for the rebel infantry to charge the hill. He hoped to be killed in battle. But the enemy came forward without firing. The officer leading them halted before the emperor and announced hesitantly, "Your majesty, you are my prisoner." There was a rattling of his comrades' sabers, but Maximilian ordered them to put up their blades. Quietly he mounted his white horse and rode down to present his sword to the rebel commander, General Escobedo.

To his captor, Maximilian gave his beautiful horse for his courtesy in not parading him through the main street to risk the derision of the mob. All the rest of his possessions, except the clothes he wore, were pilfered by the passing lines of curious soldiers who came to view the fallen emperor as he lay wracked with fever on his convent cot.

Shortly Juárez ordered the sick man moved to another monastery and incarcerated in the dank crypt. Despite the emperor's dysentery and high temperature, Juárez commanded that he be put on prison rations. Defying Juárez's commands, the rebel general at Querétaro out of pity had the emperor subsequently removed to a room on an upper corridor where the other important prisoners were kept.

When Europe learned of Maximilian's plight, half the royal heads began soliciting President Johnson to intercede with Juárez. Although the new American minister had been appointed to his post more than a year before, he had not yet got to either Mexico City or San Luis Potosí, because of the disruption in the land. Now, when ordered to confer at once with Juárez, he claimed illness, resigned his office, and remained in New Orleans.

A committee of European diplomats visited Juárez to plead for Maximilian. They were met with the Indian's proverbial impassivity and told that the trial would begin on the twelfth of June. Juárez did not say that the trial was merely a formality and that the imperialist leaders had been doomed since the hour of their capture.

A jury of six republican captains, with a lieutenant colonel as foreman, was selected. The aristocratic Miramón, horribly disfigured in the face, and the stolid Indian Mejía were on view at the trial. But Maximilian did not appear in his own defense. Because of his illness he was allowed to be tried by proxy. Miramón and Mejía received their death sentences with celerity, as they had expected. But they waited half hopefully for the verdict on the emperor's fate. Maximilian's lawyers prepared and delivered an eloquent and able defense. The jury conferred in the lavatory.

After a lengthy session, they reached a divided verdict. Three were for perpetual banishment. Three were for execution. The foreman's vote settled the matter. He decreed death. The date of execution was fixed for June sixteenth.

The spotlight of the world's attention now concentrated on the taciturn Indian sitting in his Spartan-bare quarters at San Luis Potosí. He was the most significant Mexican Indian in history since Montezuma and Cuauhtémoc. In these momentous hours he was the most important man in the universe. On his desk lay imploring cables from all the ruling houses of Europe. Spilling over to the floor were stacks of individual letters and long scrolls of signed petitions. Foreign ambassadors and ministers and agents besought interviews. Victor Hugo sent an eloquent appeal. Even that great champion of the people, Garibaldi, put in his plea of mercy for the formerly hated Austrian. Beseeching Mexican ladies added their pleas for mercy. The fantastic New England-born Princess Salm-Salm, whose adventurous German husband was one of Maximilian's aides, literally threw herself at Juárez's feet and offered her body when other entreaties failed.

Juárez sat inflexible. But he was not untouched by the attention he received. There was a bitter-sweet satisfaction in the situation. The proud Indian who had been degraded and reviled for more than three centuries was having his hour of triumph. The blandishments of the white men, the humility of their kings and queens, did not move the implacable Juárez to spare Maximilian's life. He read or listened to their petitions in stone-image silence. When strongly pressed for some word, he would reply, "It is not I, but my people and the law who do this."

If he let the foreign interloper escape, Juárez reasoned, might there not be other alien princes who would make a bid for a Mexican throne when occasion served? Maximilian had to die to prove to the people that they themselves and Juárez, their elected leader, had the authority in their own nation. But many white Mexicans murmured among themselves, "It is Cuauhtémoc taking revenge on Cortés."

Paradoxically, however, by setting Maximilian before a firing squad, Juárez did him the best possible turn historically. It mitigated that judgment of posterity of which the Juárez note had warned him on his arrival three years before. To have been sent home in exile, well spanked for his thrusting impudence, would have been an anticlimax to mock a Hapsburg for the rest of his life. Receiving death in the breast from Mexican bullets gave a tragic aura to the emperor's story.

Execution finally took place on the nineteenth. The three condemned leaders had been given a three-day respite because Mejía's wife was having a baby, and the Indian general had asked for postponement until he beheld his child. It was one of those incredibly lovely days that come to Mexico in June. "I could not have chosen a better day on which to die," Maximilian exclaimed as he beheld the glory of the early morning. On the Hill of Bells, against an adobe wall of makeshift fortification, the prisoners were lined up. With his unfailing courtesy Maximilian insisted that Miramón have the place of honor in the center, since he was a Mexican who had once been chief executive of his own country. Mejía stood at Miramón's right and Maximilian took his place at the left. Just before the rifles were raised the emperor walked down to the nervous riflemen and presented to each some money in gold. He begged them to aim at his breast and to spare his head, so that the sight of his dead face be not too shocking to his family in Europe. Then he gave his hat and his handkerchief to his adoring Hungarian cook, who had followed him to Querétaro. Returning to Miramón's side, the pale towering prince made a speech that lasted only a few seconds. His last words were: "May my blood that is about to flow be for the good of this land." It was sincere, for he had come to have a great fondness for Mexico.

At the signal from the officer's sword, the shots rang out. Maximilian dropped. But he was not dead. Even in his execution there was blundering. Nothing had been clean-cut since the untimely hour of his arrival in Vera Cruz. Lying on his face on the ground, he cried out in astonished pain, *"Hombres!"*—as if to say, "Men, how could you?" His writhing body was turned over on its back. One bullet loosed by either a nervous or a malicious hand had plowed up his forehead. The horrified officer pointed directly at the heart and signaled again. This time one well aimed bullet snapped the cord of life cleanly.

As the instrument of France and that scheming "meddlesome mediocrity" Napoleon III, the mission of Maximilian had been a ghastly failure. Yet despite his shortsightedness and inadequacy, one is bound to have pity for the well-meaning aristocrat. There were few men alive equipped to undertake the rule of the most unstable and unaccountable country in the world. It is doubtful if even a much abler prince under the mentorship of Machiavelli himself could have succeeded. The strongest of alien interlopers would have been doomed, because the United States would not long have tolerated a European-controlled government at her side door.

As far as Maximilian was personally concerned, his life drama was ended at Querétaro on that historic day in June. The month of June, Carlotta's birth month, had coincidentally been pregnant with significance in the ill-starred lives of Maximilian and Carlotta. On June tenth, 1863, the French had taken possession of Mexico City. On June tenth, 1864, the royal couple had been crowned. On June thirteenth, 1866, Carlotta had sailed from Mexican shores on her frantic, fruitless mission which ended in her madness. On June nineteenth, 1867, Maximilian was executed.

But the drama in which he was the luckless hero was not entirely finished until he was laid away in a Hapsburg tomb many months later. In the interim another series of blunders and delays occurred. The embalming of the royal person was done by inexperienced local doctors, who did not have the essential chemicals. Eyes of black glass, the right size but the wrong color —taken from the image of an Indian Virgin—were substituted for the Austrian's broken blue ones. When Juárez came to Querétaro to look upon the dead prince he had never seen in life, for some reason he decided to keep the body in Mexico, either as a hostage or as a souvenir of triumph. From the end of June until November negotiations for the remains went on. In order to obtain them, Austria had recognized the government of Juárez. But when an Austrian admiral came for them, he was held up with red tape for weeks. In the meantime the body, which had turned black, was re-embalmed. Finally, so much international pressure was brought to bear on Juárez that he released the royal corpse. On November twenty-fifth, the *Novara,* the same vessel that had brought Maximilian so hopefully to Mexico, took him back to Europe.

But even after his interment in the family vaults, the story was not quite done. Carlotta lived on in her dream world until her eighty-seventh year. In a lonely castle in Belgium, with intervals of apparent sanity, she fed on her memories and watched dynasties pass. Emperors and kings departed forever—from Brazil, from France, from Russia, from Germany, from Austria, from Spain. Old Empress Eugénie clung to life until she was ninety-five, having lived long enough to see her hated Germany humbled by the treaty signed in the halls of Versailles, where she had once been the beauteous mistress. Carlotta did not die until sixty years after her husband's execution. She had lived so far into another age that she had become a romantic legend even to herself. At the time of her death in January, 1927, Mussolini had been dictator of Italy for five years. Hitler was writing *Mein Kampf*. In Mexico, a strong president named Plutarco Elías Calles was just beginning to slow down the revolutionary program and a young man named Lázaro Cárdenas was secretly planning to accelerate it if he ever got in power.

# 13. Reconstruction

*"That bitter hopelessness that comes over people who know Mexico well."*

D. H. LAWRENCE

Two days after Maximilian's execution, the conservative forces in Mexico City capitulated to the youngish General Porfirio Díaz, who had also won the siege of Puebla. President Juárez, still at his headquarters in San Luis Potosí, received the cheering but expected news with no show of emotion. What is called in history the War of the Reform was over. The republican cause was victorious. But the cost of victory had been great. Juárez had high cause to bear resentment. The French intervention had not only bloodied the land and stirred up vicious animosities, but it had retarded Mexico's growth by many years. The prime consolation lay in the fact that Mexico had been preserved as a sovereign state. The forces that had opposed liberalism—the church and the conservative party—emerged with their prestige draggle-tailed. The great majority of the people were now united to back the liberal constitution and the Reform laws. A new kind of patriotism had been forged. Though he had done no real fighting himself, Juárez was aware it was his indomitable spirit that had preserved Mexico in her most critical years.

The president wound up business in his makeshift capital and prepared for the southward journey. He sent word to the capital he would stop briefly at Querétaro and arrive in Mexico in good time. On July fifteenth, to greet the returning president whose way he had swept for him, Porfirio Díaz had arranged a spectacular welcome and spent money lavishly on floral decorations and the preparation for a banquet. At the head of a triumphant procession he rode on horseback to meet Juárez at Tlalnepantla above Mexico City. As the victor of Puebla and Mexico, Díaz not unnaturally looked for some token of appreciation from his Oaxacan compatriot and former law professor. He frankly expected the honor of being asked to sit beside the chief executive in the carriage the last few miles into the capital. As the presidential black vehicle lumbered into the village, Juárez, dressed in his customary sober black, looked as forbidding as he was solitary. But, with heart charged with the emotion of the hour, Díaz rode eagerly up to salute him. The unsmiling Indian acknowledge his foremost general with a perfunctory nod. Then, without further ado, he ordered the coachman to proceed. As Díaz whirled his horse about, in his disappointment and chagrin, there was conceived a consuming hatred for Juárez. Díaz had his heart set on the presidency, and he had expected to become immediately heir apparent. Now he determined to get the top place as soon as possible on his own resources. Juárez had alienated a powerful ally.

Arriving in Mexico City the dour president put a quietus on show and triumphant demonstration. Grimly he took up his work of reconstruction, which had been interrupted five years before by the foreign intervention. For the second time he had inherited an exhausted, bankrupt country, but this time conditions were far more chaotic than before. Since he did not work by witchcraft, he knew the problems of reconstruction would be long and arduous. "When a society like ours," he said, "has had the misfortune to pass through years of internal upheavals, it is seamed through with vices whose profound roots cannot be extirpated in a single day nor by any single measure."

He had hardly got himself established in the executive office when in August general elections were called for. Not all the liberals were in favor of Juárez. Some wanted to support the thirty-seven-year-old hero, Díaz. Others were in favor of Sebastián Lerdo de Tejada, intellectual younger brother of Miguel, the author of the *Ley Lerdo*. Juárez expressed a special desire for re-election, that he might be vindicated for having kept the presidency after the expiration of his regular term in 1865, when no elections could be held because of the war in progress and when constitutionally the office should have been assumed by the chief justice, General Ortega. In the October elections Juárez received seven-tenths of the remarkably small number of votes cast, less than 18,000 in the entire nation. The electorate seemed to say, "If Juárez is determined to be chief executive there is no use to vote either for or against him." His new term of office as constitutional president was to continue for four years, until November thirtieth, 1871.

Faced with manifold obstacles as he was, Juárez saw that Mexico's foremost job was to uplift her masses. In that significant year of 1867, a Jew in Germany named Karl Marx was publishing his *Das Kapital,* which was to have potent influence in diminishing the power of aristocracies and in raising the common people. Juárez had not heard of Karl Marx and his theories, but he knew that he must arouse the Indian to self-respect, "not only individually but as a social unit." He did not quite know how to go about it, but he knew that education must be a basic factor.

"The man who cannot supply his family with food," he wrote, "views the education of his sons, not only as something remote, but as a positive impediment to his struggle for existence. Instead of sending them to school . . . he hires out their frail labor-power to alleviate, even if only to a slight extent, the misery which engulfs them. If that man had a few conveniences, if he could squeeze the least profit from his toil, he would from that day on be eager to educate his children and provide them with a solid instruction. The desire to learn and to become illustrious is innate in the heart of man. Strike off the fetters of misery and despotism that oppress him and he will naturally achieve greatness. . . ."

Juárez ordered estate owners and municipal administrators to build primary schools. By the end of his third term the number of these so-called schools was estimated at eight thousand, and one-sixth of the Mexican children of school age were declared to be enrolled for some part of the year. The direction of education Juárez more or less entrusted to Gabino Berreda, who had been a disciple of the dry Auguste Comte in France. Berreda tried to impress upon the poorly trained teachers in backward Mexico the philosophy of positivism, which dealt only with positive facts and the properties of knowable things and which made no inquiry into causes. With positivism was brought into the liberal camp Comte's emphasis on "authority and a graded hierarchy." Though Juárez never seemed to understand positivism very well, some of its implications accorded well with his own inclinations.

The president himself was shortly called despot and accused of betraying freedom by his dictatorial methods. Juárez had hoped to govern without too heavy an executive hand. Doubtless he would have liked to be a true democrat, in action as well as theory. But liberal democracy in a land with unlettered Indians and self-seeking politicians simply could not function properly. Because of both stubborn and feckless oppositions in various quarters, Juárez assumed more determined authority. The work of reconstruction was balked by a series of niggling revolts in a number of states. Some of these might have been avoided if Juárez had taken more thought of his demobilized soldiers when the war was ended. The liberal army had been cut down by two-thirds. Because of the empty treasury, the soldiers had been sent home without a centavo to tide them over, and no provision whatever was taken as to the means of fitting them again into civilian economy. Revolts of ex-soldiers who felt they had been badly treated ensued. They were put down with more uncompromising harshness than had been meted out to the reactionary leaders who had fought with the French against their own people.

Hated by the conservatives, Juárez lost favor not only with the more radical liberals, but with many of the moderate liberals. He constantly alienated men in authority by slights, as he had the ambitious Díaz. He was never inclined to pass out favors and rewards. Though his admirers believed in his ideas and his integrity, they had little affection for him. He had no intimates. He liked to stand alone. There was nothing *simpático* about his personal presence. He was one of those men who was more inspiring unseen than seen.

Juárez shone more as an idealistic theorist than an administrator. But he did establish order in his own land, if only for a time, and he resumed friendly relations with European nations. He was on excellent terms with the United States and he freely confessed the importance of the moral and material support the United States had given him. (In 1869 William H. Seward, the recent secretary of state whose assistance to Juárez had been indispensable, paid Mexico a visit.) Juárez saw the earlier mistake in taking the *ejidos* away from the Indians and transforming them into privately owned parcels, and he did what he could to rectify it, despite the *Ley Lerdo*. He saw, too, the need for railroads and he proceeded with building the line from Vera Cruz to the capital which had been begun in 1850 and had been interrupted by the intervention. He made plans for Mexico's economic development. He envisioned a free-school system that was to make all Mexico literate. But his program needed many decades to reach fruition.

Now his third term was nearly up. Against the advice of many of his friends he asked for re-election to a fourth term as president. Instantly, from Sonora to Yucatán, there arose accusations of permanent dictatorship. This time not only his *mestizo* enemy Porfirio Díaz stood for the presidency against him, but his trusted friend and most important member in his cabinet, the creole Sebastian Lerdo de Tejada. The liberals who were bound to win the election were split three ways: For Juárez, the Indian; for Díaz, the *mestizo;* for Lerdo de Tejada, the creole. The supporters, who in no wise lined up according to complexions, were more or less evenly divided. In the elections there was no clear majority. The decision as to who would lead Mexico for the next four years devolved upon congress. Congress chose Benito Juárez. Lerdo de Tejada was consoled with the presidency of the supreme court, which carried with it the succession to the highest office if the incumbent died or resigned.

On November eighth, Porfirio Díaz, who got nothing, "pronounced" against the Juárez administration from his *hacienda* La Noria. In the ensuing revolt there was some serious fighting in four states. Díaz's brother Felix, who led the revolt in the home state of Oaxaca, was killed. In a vain hope that Mexico City would rally to his support, Porfirio made a cavalry dash to the suburbs. But he and his horsemen rode away faster than they had come. Finally, to escape capture, Díaz assumed the disguise of priest and sought refuge with a bandit in the mountains of Nayarit. The former hero was now at his lowest ebb in fortune.

By April, 1872, with the Díaz insurrection crushed, Juárez prepared to put all his progressive ideas into operation. But fate allowed him only three months more of service to his country. Sitting at his desk, on July eighteenth, he suddenly slumped forward unconscious among his papers. Taken home and put to bed, he died later in the night. Presumably he had suffered a heart attack. The symptoms, however, were somewhat strange for a fatal heart disorder. So men said, as whispers about poisoning buzzed furtively. But no accusations were formally made. No documentary proof whatever of foul play has ever come to light. Yet today, in discussing Juárez, many Mexicans are likely to say, "Of course, you know he was poisoned."

Die-hard reactionaries today seem to enjoy believing in the

poisoning theory. Others look upon the passing of Juárez as untimely for Mexico as Lincoln's assassination was for the war-scarred United States. Certainly, as Henry Bamford Parkes says, "with Juárez was buried the last hope for at least half a century of combining peace with freedom."

The name of Benito Juárez will ever stand as one of the greatest in Mexican chronicles. But threescore years after his death, his value is a subject of controversy in Mexico. His heroic figure is tarnished in the eyes of a large body of Mexicans by certain documented dickers with the United States. "It was Juárez," accuses José Vasconcelos, "who started the policy of delivering the resources of Mexico to American capital." Benito Juárez is no more wholeheartedly admired by the Mexican upper classes than Abraham Lincoln is by Southerners. Today the conservative upper classes and many passionately devout Catholics regard the great patriot sourly. For his expropriation of church property, for his agreeing to the McLane-Ocampo Treaty, for his early misjudgment in making *ejidos* illegal, they continue to accuse him. But to the populace at large his Reform laws, his final winning out over the French interlopers and saving of Mexico for Mexico put Juárez among the top of the national heroes. The people refer to him as the father of Mexican democracy, and he is called both the Jefferson and the Lincoln of Mexico. Yet in the accepted United States sense of the term, Juárez was hardly a democrat. It is true he had ultimate hope in the electorate of the people. But though the matter is not clear, he appears to have been imbued with the doctrines of the French, rather than the American, Revolution. He seemed to believe in the European idea of Absolute State, which he attested to by his state legislation in regard to religion. Oddly enough, in some phases of their liberal ideology, Juárez and Maximilian were not far apart. Yet in attitude Juárez, the democrat, was more of a dictator than the emperor.

Besides ridding Mexico of alien masters, the actual material good Juárez accomplished for Mexico in his own time is not impressive when catalogued. But considering the overwhelming adverse conditions against him, his achievements in imponderables were remarkable. Though the great Indian himself was unable to gain much for the Indians in his day, it is from the magic of his name that reformers in the twentieth century draw inspiration in working to alleviate Indian distress. The impassive Juárez emerges into history more as a symbol than as a human man.

# PART SIX

# DICTATOR BEFORE THE WORLD

## 14. Peace with an Iron Hand

*"If the crops of men fail, it is worse than when the crops of the country fail. For a country can be relieved, if things are well in the neighbouring countries, and experienced men manage the imports from them. But if the crop of men fails, if the morals of the people fail, the worst miseries must follow, because nobody can buy from a neighbouring country morals and manly discernment, if such of it that once was found in our country has been destroyed or dissipated."*

THE KING'S MIRROR (THIRTEENTH CENTURY)

According to constitutional authority, Sebastian Lerdo de Tejada assumed the presidency, and on October twenty-sixth elections for president were held, at which he was overwhelmingly elected according to the total votes cast, less than 11,000 out of a population of ten million. Díaz had accepted amnesty, but shortly after the elections Díaz's friend, the Nayarit bandit, Lozada, raised a revolt which ended with his capture and execution the following July. A breathing spell of peace came to disturbed Mexico, and during this time congress officially incorporated the laws of Reform in the constitution on November twelfth, 1874. This was the most significant event in the regime of

Juárez's successor. It had taken years of bloody strife to break the political and economic domination of the church. Public opinion had come over to the liberal cause.

But for all his brilliant intellect and oratorical virtuosity, Lerdo de Tejada no more possessed the essential qualifications for an administrator of discordant Mexico than had the pale Hapsburg prince. When he announced in 1876 that he would stand for re-election, Porfirio Díaz decided the hour to strike had come again. Upon the plank of "effective suffrage and no re-election" he made his chief stand. Current malcontents flocked to his standards. And while the United States government tactfully looked the other way, he gathered volunteers as well as capital across the border. Lerdo de Tejada had committed the indiscretion of being inimical to American financial interests. He had refused to allow American railway contractors to build a line from the Texas border to the Mexican capital. Because he distrusted the United States, he regarded the dreary stretches of northern waste land as Mexico's best safeguard against further depredation. His refusal to deal with United States business hastened his undoing. But he was able to hang on until November. Twice the federal forces routed the Díaz rebels, but when his own president of the supreme court created another personal rebellion against him, Lerdo de Tejada had no chance of survival.

On November twenty-first, Díaz made his entrance into the capital, a few hours after Lerdo de Tejada had precipitously departed for Acapulco and exile in California. Without any ceremonious to-do, Díaz seized control. On May second, 1877, his presidency was recognized by congress. He who had instigated three revolutions against the constitutional government set himself up as the great defender of democracy and constitutional rule.

Because he had ever fought valiantly on the liberal side, many of the advanced thinkers had faith in Díaz and gave him fervent support when he first went into office. The Indians who had suffered and bled for promised improvement in their lot gave devoted service to this *mestizo,* whom they believed to be their zealous advocate. But the hopeful smiles soon died on the faces of the betrayed. With his own hands this former soldierly comrade of the people barricaded all roads that might lead to reform. This burning liberal, who came into power under the slogan of "no re-election" was to rule with an iron grip for a third of a century. Except for a break of one term—following his first—he continually re-elected himself until he was in his ninth decade Though he cleverly covered the mailed fist with a variety of velvety gloves, his control was no less absolute. Democratic principles were thrown into the discard, and everything staked on economic development and peace.

In Porfirio Díaz was exemplified again the curious paradox that continually recurs in Mexican history—and is moreover too often a world truth—the radical democrat in power turned to arch-conservative dictator. The career of this man was of the stranger-than-fiction sort. Few leaders have left reputations more lauded and vilified. Few have inspired biographies written from such passionate viewpoints. The complexities of his *mestizo* character and his own reversals in political principles make him difficult of appraisal. But he can no more be categorically condemned than wholeheartedly praised. As a historical figure of Mexican history, for good or ill, Díaz looms large—like a monarch whose name symbolizes an age—like Elizabeth of England or Louis Quatorze of France. Paradoxically, the age of Díaz is held up as the best and the worst Mexico has known.

Señor José Valades, the brilliant young Mexican historian, sees Díaz as driven by the mysterious forces of his environment. Tolstoi once looked upon Díaz as a veritable superman. Henry Cabot Lodge spoke of him as the compendium of all virtues. Typical of the egregious extravagance of praise lavished upon the dictator by foreigners is the dedication in a book called

*Picturesque Mexico* by a lady named Marie Robinson Wright. In phrases out-Latining any Latins, she chants ecstatically:

To Señor General Don Porfirio Díaz, the Illustrious President of Mexico, Whose Intrepid Moral Character, Distinguished Statesmanship, and Devoted Patriotism Make Him the Pride and Glory of His Country, Is Dedicated This Volume, Describing a Beautiful and Prosperous Land, Whose Free Flag Never Waved Over a Slave, and Whose Importance As a Nation Is Due to the Patriot Under Whose Administration Mexico Now Flourishes and Holds Its Proud Position Among the Republics of the World.

Among a host of others who examined the picture critically, Blasco Ibáñez saw in Díaz simply a tyrant. But he forced himself to admit that however great a misfortune politically and spiritually Díaz was for Mexico, "as far as material progress went Mexico never had another ruler to compare with this man."

To the unprejudiced student of history, no matter how much bad is to be found along with the good, one fact stands out boldly like a promontory above a stormy sea. Díaz did what no one else had been able to do successfully since 1810—he maintained peace. And that achievement alone in a people as trigger-conscious as Mexicans should mitigate several lists of accusations. Blasco Ibañez is justified in declaring that "the peace that Díaz maintained for thirty years was secured by wholesale executions, ordered without due process of law, and by violations of the liberties of the individual." Yet no matter how hard and bitter for some was the price of peace, Mexico at this period needed peace above all else.

Like Benito Juárez, Porfirio Díaz came from the south, from the very same province, Oaxaca. But the blood of Juárez was all Indian, while in the veins of Díaz the Indian mixed with the Spanish on both sides of his ancestry. Juárez was all of a piece and he never changed. Díaz's complex character underwent a metamorphosis. Whereas Juárez's desire for power seemed austerely impersonal, that of Díaz was peculiarly personal. Juárez, though implacable, was guided by integrity. Díaz was willing to compromise to his own advantage, and he possessed craft and guile completely foreign to Juárez. Yet in his earlier days Díaz achieved a well-deserved reputation for honesty; when his heroic fight against the French was won he returned to the national treasury the 87,000 pesos he had not used. And according to his own interpretation anything he did subsequently that went into the category of the shady was for the good of the commonwealth. He persuaded himself that his country's supreme need was for a master, and he felt stirring within himself the qualities to command such a position.

In 1830 Porfirio Díaz made his advent into this hazardous world amid the confusions of civil war and a raging cholera epidemic. His birth took place in the city of Oaxaca in a third-class inn run by his industrious mother and his father, a horse doctor. He was christened speedily so that if he succumbed to the plague his immortal soul would be saved. The day of the christening was September fifteenth, exactly twenty years after Father Hidalgo had been awakened in the dead of night and made his decision to ring the Dolores church bell to announce the rebellion against Spain. Díaz chose to make the celebration of his birthday correspond with Mexico's national holiday.

Young Díaz was an apt and personable lad, full of high spirits and curiosity, but with a certain gravity that made him impervious to teasing by the mule drivers with whom he associated in the inn's courtyard. He was a normal boy in his play, and fearless; but though he was a dare-devil, he was never a show-off. He learned to be a good marksman by shooting wild game when poverty necessitated that every shot must kill. He accepted his share in the family responsibility—his father died of cholera when Porfirio was a child of three—and helped his widowed mother by earning money at carpentry and shoemaking. As a lad he made his own shoes from goatskins and was quite content in his blue denim jumper suit and his homemade worsted hat. His mother, who eked out the family resources by teaching neighborhood children at fees amounting to about five cents each a week, was determined that he and his brother should have an education. Because she set her heart on Porfirio's being a priest, the boy duly entered the local seminary. His manners and personality endeared him to his schoolmasters, but he never became really proficient in grammar or any other form of book learning. When he gave up the idea of priesthood, however, and went to the Institute to study law and military science, he discovered his extraordinary aptitude for the latter.

Blessed from birth with health and superhuman endurance, Porfirio was even-tempered and dependable. He possessed in heaping measure providence's most useful gift, common sense— a quality often lacking in the romantic Spanish-Indians. He was inherently cautious. There was little of the demagogue in him. He never swept mobs by impassioned oratory. Only on the rarest occasions did he ever display great passion or even great enthusiasm. The secret of his successes in life was largely due to his superb self-discipline and his coolness in climactic situations. In a picture of him done in 1860 when he was thirty, the outstanding feature is the large, dark eyes, sympathetic, brooding, lighted with secret fires. His imperial and his sharp-ended long mustaches pointing at a 45-degree angle are perfectly barbered, but his short, dark hair is rebellious and refuses to conform. The purposeful bronzed face is rather handsome, with a melancholy cast to the expression.

As a romantic-eyed, strong-chinned young soldier in Oaxaca, Díaz had begun his career aroused by the unfortunate lot of the Indians. At the feet of Juárez himself he had been imbued with liberal principles when he studied law under him. He had been tavern companion and camp brother to Indian peasant and *mestizo* small-holder. He had fought like a lion for his country and achieved the reputation of being one of the greatest soldiers Mexico ever produced. But he ended metamorphosed into a white man in a white society. Long before the end of his rule he had turned white, not because of the French creams he was alleged to use to lighten his complexion, but because he became a white man at heart. He seemed to renounce his darker blood, as if it were a misfortune, by shutting his eye to the Indians' needs and to his opportunity to help them.

When Díaz was fifty-one and a widower, he married a girl of eighteen, Carmen Romero Rubio, the daughter of one of the most powerful conservative politicians of the time. There was no more charming young woman in Mexico and none more aristocratic in feeling and attitude than Carmelita, as everyone called her. She had poise and intelligence. A delicate aura of glamor hung about her. Her influence on this husband old enough to be her father was extraordinary. With superb tact she set about to make a gentleman of him, though at times she almost despaired of making him comb his unruly hair. As her drawing room became a salon for the highest society Mexico could provide, Díaz took to the refining ways of culture, though he maintained an incorruptible dignity. There was nothing of the popinjay or martinet in him. He would have felt an egregious ass trailing imperial ermine like Iturbide or Maximilian. Like Juárez, he invariably dressed in black, but his clothes were cut by the best tailors and he learned to wear them well. By nine o'clock in the morning he was in his frock coat. He never let down, never let the Indian show through—least of all to his aristocratic young wife, whose approbation became a ruling factor in his life along with will to power.

Carmelita not only made him a gentleman, but she kept him young. When he was in his late sixties, strangers would guess his age as fifty. With his magnificent, deep chest and firm, muscular frame went an athletic agility. His walk had the casual grace and dignity of a puma. On his swarthy skin was the healthful glow of a man who had made the most of the out-of-doors. While little given to talking, his personality dominated any gathering. He listened to Carmelita, to bishops, to doctors of letters, to distinguished foreigners. He absorbed like a blotter and got his education through the ear. When he did speak his voice was mellow and friendly and it inspired confidence.

Following Maximilian by an interval of only a decade, Díaz found that upper-class Mexican society still relished the taste of court life the emperor had dished out to them. So he began giving banquets with pomp and ceremony to please local society as well as to impress foreign diplomats and capitalists. He and Carmelita had the Chapultepec palace elaborately done over in the hideous vogue of the last quarter of the nineteenth century. A conglomeration of ornate chandeliers, carved golden oak, flowered carpets, sentimental French paintings, Chinese teakwood, and decadent statuary were imported and installed, along with a few pieces of excellent taste. It was all as mixed and overloaded as a contemporary 1890 interior of a Fifth Avenue mansion of a Vanderbilt. But the Díazes were cordial and gracious in the new manifestations of foreign elegance, and a host of unaristocratic Mexicans now strove to be worthy of the honor of an invitation. High silk hats emerged on tens of thousands of heads. Waves of pretentious frock coats all but swept the blanketed, barefooted Indians into the gutters. In the social order of Mexico it came to be said that any occupation that could not be performed in silk hat and frock coat was deemed degrading.

The son of the rich went abroad now in shoals to the universities or to polish themselves off with a grand tour. The estate owners spent a brief period of the year on the *hacienda,* the rest in the capital or in Paris. Mexicans, having become conscious that the eyes of the world were upon them, wanted the civilized world to know how highly civilized they were. So they not only built railroads furiously, but with a great fanfare of dedication they opened art galleries, opera houses, and administrative buildings to the public, while half-naked Indians gaped wistfully and wondered why no crumbs fell to them from the groaning table of the new order.

Before Díaz brought prosperity to the land, he had made the maintenance of peace his prime objective, and he was prepared to resort to any means to achieve it. When he took command, the unstable country had been racked with strife for sixty-seven years. Most of it had been that peculiarly disrupting kind of civil warfare in which Mexico was compared to two clawing cats slung over a wire with their tails tied together. By shrewd as well as strong measures, Díaz brought order to a distracted land. If admonitions and favors could not win peace, Díaz would squash incipient revolutions by hasty executions. Having no high opinion of the Mexican character in general, the president used to say, "A dog with a good bone will not fight or steal." So wherever he could he gave jobs or privileges to would-be trouble-makers. He bought the loyalty of some by gifts of sinecures or concessions or *haciendas*. He secured support of others by creating jealousies and hatreds among lesser rivals. "Divide to rule" was his motto. He followed his own version of the Indian *cacique* system—supreme big chief, big chief, chief, little chief, tiny chief, each powerful in his own domain. He would play one general off against the other, make each suspicious of the other. He would make a friend of a potential enemy by appointing him governor of a state, and then he would send a general whom the governor loathed, to command the standing army in that province and to keep an eye on the governor. Whenever an army man or a prominent politician was about to become too popular, Díaz would knap him on the head and make him duck to more insignificant size. He would tolerate no potential rival near his throne. He was careful to select for his vice-presidents men whom the public abominated.

Newspapers that were too critical of his administration Díaz bought over or suppressed. A few irrepressible journalists were sent to meditate in damp, underground cells of fortresses without benefit of ink and paper. Rebellious Indians of the north were condemned to slave labor in the pestilential jungles of Quintana Roo. Díaz justified his harshest measures by saying publicly, "Better shed bad blood now to save good blood later."

The church caused him little trouble, because he winked an eye at the return to practices forbidden by the 1857 constitution. Catholic schools and nunneries were no longer raided. Religious processions were not chased off the streets. It was said, however, that no ecclesiastical appointments were made until Díaz approved the lists. The archbishop would be having tea with Carmelita. They would toy with names. Porfirio would drop in and nod or look dubious as names were mentioned. His intimations were most helpful to the archbishop in making prudent selections.

Díaz had his own original bag of tricks for winning friends and influencing individuals. One day a notorious bandit was brought before the president, a lasso about his neck. Díaz received the criminal in chilled silence. Taking his pearl-handled revolver from the desk, he methodically loaded all five chambers. Holding the gun in his left hand and pointing it at the culprit, he thrust out his right hand. Eyeing the man intently, he said, quietly: "Which do you choose? This hand with the five bullets or this hand with five friendly fingers?" The astonished bandit, who had expected to be shot on the spot, blinked but could not speak. Dropping to his knees, he grasped the right hand in fervent gratitude and turned out to be a most vigilant and loyal thief-catcher.

Díaz handled brigands who might have stirred up trouble against him by giving them positions of authority. He made them *rurales,* state mounted police. It was an occupation they could turn into more profit than by highway hold-ups and pilfering. The *rurales* got a good living off the countryside without having to point a gun. Wherever they went roast chickens and wine were theirs for the asking and the best horses they could straddle.

Like Napoleon playing on the vanity of little men with his ribbons of honor, Díaz made the mounted police proud of their job by giving them a cavalier-like costume that attracted attention in fashionable parks as well as on remote country roads. The *rurales* wore suits of suède in smoke-gray or russet brown, with silver silk embroidery on the bolero jacket and a vein of embroidered silver running down their glove-tight trousers. The sun and the moon high-lighted the silver on their sombreros, their saddles, their formidable spurs, the studs on their bridles. The devil-red blankets carried over one shoulder were like flaming badges of authority. Even the president himself, in gala uniform with his breast ablaze with medals, was a drab figure compared to commanding officers among the *rurales*. Their hats loaded with silver braid cost hundreds of dollars. One top leader had his saddle and equipment mounted in solid gold to the tune of $25,000. With their Mauser rifles, their lassos and quirts, their knives in silver sheaths and their pearl-handled revolvers, they were veritable "arsenals on horseback." Besides carrying weapons to withstand a siege, they carried their own supplies, their cooking pots and pans, their horseshoeing outfit. Some of them also carried guitars and would nearly madden village maidens with their romantic plucking of the strings. Superb and daring horsemen, they lived for hairbreadth escapes from death. Though they were like the matinee idols to some, the very name *rurale* had power to paralyze with fear. Some *rurales* took dogs along as scouts to smell out fugitives and track them down in places a horse could not go. The dog was also trained to hold his master's bridle like a groom when he dismounted to indulge in a passing *amour*.

For all his theatrical costume, a *rurale* had to be inordinately practical and resourceful. When he was told to get a man in storm-swept mountain or fetid jungle he was not given any other instructions or furnished with government maps. If the captive had talent for marksmanship and riding and wanted to serve the government, he was taken into service. If he had no special gifts he was shot down as useless to the commonwealth.

These knights-errant could be as ruthless and cunning as they were daring. And on occasions they could be wantonly cruel, as when they buried up to the neck in an open field a group of recalcitrant villagers who refused to give up their *ejidos*, and then charged back and forth sportively as if playing some kind of polo in which the object was to knock the stuffing out of skulls.

The *rurales* had another function, very significant in the Díaz days: They served as instruments of the *hacendados* to keep the peons in line. They searched out peons if they escaped, yanked them home, and often gave them a good lashing for having put them to trouble, as well as making them pay so much a day for the man hunt. Despite the excesses of the *rurales*, they did the country signal service in that for the first time in Mexican history roads were made safe for travelers. They played a part not only directly in *La Paz Porfiriano*, but indirectly in the new prosperity. The economic basis of the Díaz dictatorship was simple in pattern: By selling a host of concessions to foreigners Díaz acquired a money reserve which more or less freed him of dependence on Mexicans. Through the money obtained from foreign interests he was able to support his troop of *rurales*, who kept the nation's treasury from being disgorged on civil strife. Without the *rurales*, "The Hero of Peace"—as his admirers called Díaz—might not have been able to give Mexico a generation's breathing spell in which to build and expand. The economic progress under Díaz was spectacular enough to impress the world at large.

During the nineteenth-century expansion in the United States, Mexico had stood still, rooted in her colonial tracks. At the time Díaz took over she was noted throughout Europe as one of the most backward nations in the world. This *mestizo* from Oaxaca was the first Mexican administrator to possess a world-view, to give his country a place in the sun as a nation, and to win the respect of foreign powers. Though he was farsighted in realizing that Mexico would become enlightened only as she emerged from her seclusion and made contact with the world, he was woefully shortsighted in keeping the masses in a stupefying condition of peonage. To bring about the material prosperity he put his country's resources in pawn to foreign capitalists. In his policy regarding land ownership he turned Mexico back towards feudalism.

Under Díaz the concentration of land in the hands of a few became more exaggerated than anything Mexico had known. By 1892 one-fifth of the territory had passed into the possession of land companies. Millions of acres of public land were turned over to a small number of individuals, native and foreign. William Randolph Hearst's father got a hunk "about the size of Maryland and Delaware combined." The famous Terrazas estate in Chihuahua was estimated to comprise almost thirteen million acres. Vast tracts of public land were doled out as rewards to politicians who would strengthen the dictatorship. By 1910 almost half of Mexico belonged to less than three thousand families.

By the granting to land companies of the rights to national waters for irrigation and industries, the essential water supply of the village lands could be cut off by the grantees. After the waterless tracts had been abandoned they could be legally "denounced" and the companies could claim possession. When villages rebelled by refusing to obey the "denouncing" laws, they were often destroyed, and the land ownership passed to the federal government. Though the same Indian family had possessed the same strip of land since before the conquest, if the present head did not have hid away somewhere a title to it, the property could be "denounced" and bid in by a land company.

The *ejidos* grew so small that many family allotments were

reduced to a couple of furrows. As the rich, productive lands gradually passed into the wealthy landlords' hands, Indians were forced to seek sustenance in the rock-strewn mountain sides. At the close of the Díaz period approximately ninety-five per cent of the rural population owned no property whatsoever—not even six foot of grave space in which to be buried or a tiny plot on which to raise a mess of beans. As Wistano Luis Orozco wrote: "The millions of acres bought up by the land companies represented many more millions of tears, for it is not the powerful, not the great *hacendados* who have seen their millions of hectares fall from their hands, but the poor, the ignorant, and the weak."

The laws and the taxes seemed arranged for the benefit of the foreign companies and the few rich estate holders. In the state of Guanajuato, for example, the land tax levied on all the estates amounted to less than that paid by the street peddlers. The special privilege that existed in the second half of Díaz's administration was beyond anything that any country has known before or afterwards.

At the very time that Díaz was putting the ownership of Mexico into the hands of the few, a smart young redhead in London named G. B. Shaw was continually jumping up on soapboxes to denounce such practices in England. In 1884, the year he joined the new Fabian Socialist Society, he was warning the powers that be:

The practice of entrusting the land of the nation to private persons in the hope that they will make the best of it has been discredited by the consistency with which they have made the worst of it.

In this same year, Díaz was using his power to make everything as attractive as possible for the English oil companies to operate in Mexico. He stood godfather to the mining code of 1884 by which the surface proprietor was declared owner of the coal deposits and petroleum. This new decree supplemented the Ordinance of Aranjuez which had existed a century and one year

—since 1783—and under which the crown retained ownership of "all minerals including bitumens and earth juices." To private persons or companies was now granted absolute possession on condition that they worked the property and paid taxes.

In a tract published in this year of 1884, the youthful Shaw who discerned the sociological dangers far ahead tried to make his handwriting on the wall noticed by making it witty:

The most striking result of our present system of farming out the national land and capital to private individuals has been the division of society into hostile classes, with large appetites and no dinners at one extreme and large dinners and no appetites at the other . . .

But little more attention was paid to G.B.S. in England and the United States than in Mexico in those rampant decades of rugged individualism when money talked through brazen megaphones.

In the *fin de siècle,* while the Pre-Raphaelites in England were rhapsodizing on eternal verities and endeavoring to move in an ambiente as remote from sordid materialism as they could contrive, a group of young intellectuals in Mexico became powerful as apostles of scientific progress. They called themselves *científicos.* Like the English of the middle of the century, they twisted Darwin's theory of natural selection and the survival of the fittest to justify their class rule over others. They renounced the humanitarian liberalism of their fathers' and Benito Juárez's time, and put their faith in scientific efficiency and material evidences of civilization. They discredited everything Indian and believed the salvation of Mexico lay in complete white domination. These young creole lawyers and economists—there were less than two dozen in the inner circle—became a kind of ex officio "brain trust." They influenced Díaz to encourage and conciliate foreign capital to the utmost and to turn the culture of Mexico more and more towards Europe. Because of their efficiency and their honesty "within the law," Díaz let the lawyers among them negotiate with foreign companies. They put up a good front and through rich fees they lined their pockets well.

By far the most able of the *científicos* was José Ives Limantour, the natural son of a French adventurer who had dug for California gold in '49 and who had made a fortune by buying up church property cheap at forced sales. He was a thin, dapper, ascetic-looking man, with a skinny neck and a high, broad, intelligent forehead. By profession he was an economist-banker. In 1893, when still a young man, he was made minister of the treasury. For the next seventeen years he held the dominating position in the government. His power was second only to that of Díaz himself. The first year that Limantour was in control of the nation's finances Mexico balanced her budget for the first time during her independence. There was even a surplus of 2,000,000 pesos. With Limantour's financial genius to depend on, Díaz settled down to revel in the patent fruits of prosperity.

A network of railways now spanned the difficult Mexican terrain. As the miles of railway were extended from 400 to 15,000, telegraph lines stretched from 4,500 to 20,000 miles. New iron works, smelters, meat-packing plants, paper mills and breweries were flourishing. The total number of textile mills reached 146. Mexico became one of the great sugar-producing countries of the world. Mining in gold and silver advanced from an annual gross of $25,000,000 to $160,000,000. Harbor facilities were vastly improved. Exports increased fivefold. Imports augmented eightfold. The national income rose five hundred per cent under Limantour's shrewd administration.

Those who looked only on the façade of Mexico—at the palaces and boulevards, the imported elegance, the mounting commerce, the gay night life, the safe traveling—naturally saw the regime of Porfirio Díaz as the Golden Age of Peace and Plenty. There was peace for everybody and superabundance for the privileged. But the Indians shorn of liberty endured a penury more abject than they had known.

In their fervor for efficiency and progress the *científicos* made one gross blunder: They did not take into account what was happening to the less fortunate among their fellow countrymen. They considered the Indian a beast of burden and the *mestizo* "a mistake of nature." It was the *científicos* who cut the last bonds of affinity between the *mestizo* Díaz and the Indian cause. The common folk of Mexico—the backbone and ballast of the country—were by a false sense of economy left entirely out of the calculations of the new civilization and progress.

In 1900, when Díaz had been in power almost a quarter of a century, seventy per cent of the Mexicans over ten years of age were still illiterate. To improve the general intelligence, Díaz allocated the paltry sum of eight million pesos annually for education. Yet his last gala birthday party at the National Palace—September fifteenth, 1910—cost twenty million pesos. The equivalent of two and a half years of an entire nation's educational budget was consumed in one day and night of festivity.

In the midst of the flaunted prosperity the masses lived in incredible squalor. Four pesos and rations was the monthly salary of *hacienda* workers. In the middle of the Díaz rule the average daily agricultural wage was thirty-six centavos a day, valued in United States money then at about eighteen cents. Though wages remained the same for a century, prices of essential foodstuffs rose steadily. From 1810 to 1910 the price of flour increased some 100 per cent and beans almost 600 per cent. The price of corn from which the daily *tortillas* were made almost tripled. Virtually nothing was done in the way of scientific farming to increase the yield. Every year it was necessary for Mexico to import wheat and corn, and sometimes rice and beans.

On the bad side of the Díaz medallion was the vicious system of the "payroll store" where peons received not wages but merchandise. The peons were not permitted to trade at other shops, and they had to pay whatever price the storekeeper set. Sons and sons of sons were enchained to the plantation by debt. When the strictures against debt peonage in the 1857 constitution were pointed out to him, Díaz merely shrugged. The upper classes went on splurging in Paris and Madrid on the exploited labor of the frustrated peons. *Haciendas* were left in the hands of overseers, whose business it was to extract from the sweat of the laborers all the golden profit possible and to see that the lowly kept their place.

In "the good old days of Díaz" the Indian who had been lashed learned to kneel and kiss his master's hand in gratitude for the whipping. An oil worker who presumed to drink water from the cup reserved for foreign white bosses was shot down for his impertinence. In a textile mill that paid the highest dividends in the world a protesting group of unarmed workers were killed for presuming to question the authority of the managers. There were no recourse in the courts against the decree of privilege.

On the other hand, the foreign investors fared superbly. In the grand manner, Díaz had exempted the oil companies from paying taxes on oil. Prodigious profits were made out of Mexican petroleum by the Englishman, Weetman Pearson—created Lord Cowdray by the British crown when his fortune was sufficiently impressive—and by the Yankee, Edward L. Doheny, who in 1900 acquired enormous tracts of rich oil land not far from Tampico at the bargain price of less than a dollar and a half an acre. Not only did the Mexican people gain nothing in taxation from billions of barrels of their "black gold" enriching British and American coffers, but they were charged the same price for kerosene paid in England and the United States. However, a few cabinet ministers and senators profited from the shares of stock which the oil men were tactful enough to present with their compliments.

By 1910 the investment of United States capital in Mexico had swelled to a billion dollars and was greater than the capital stock owned by all the Mexicans themselves. High-powered interests in the United States possessed over fifty per cent of the oil fields and seventy-five per cent of the operating mines. In agriculture Americans owned great sugar, cotton, coffee, and maguey plantations, as well as vast cattle ranches. Because of his generosity to foreign business, Díaz became the idol of American business interests—the Guggenheims, the Rockefellers, and the lesser fry. In the early days of Theodore Roosevelt and his trust curbings, it was heard around Wall Street that what our great democracy needed was another Porfirio Díaz to head it.

At home, Mexicans were saying that Díaz had made Mexico the mother of foreigners and the stepmother to Mexicans. In lawsuit decisions Díaz let it be known that the foreigner must always be right, and judges so decreed. Many patriotic Mexicans began to resent the foreigners, and a grumbling murmur rose all about the country. Diaz's old ears refused to hear it or attach significance to rumors brought him by Carmelita or Limantour. There was a surplus in the treasury. One had but to glance at harbor activities or drive down a city boulevard to see amazing manifestations of prosperity. The army got its pay checks regularly. The bureaucracy was well fed and subservient. There could be no formidable opposition. Who would dare oppose him?

However, Díaz began to cool perceptibly to the United States. He himself saw that American interests were becoming too powerful. His most generous favors were shortly bestowed on British representatives. He even let the United States know, too, that he could be very cordial to Japan. He gave an order that some visiting Japanese seamen were to be received with ostentatiously gay demonstrations. United States business men began to notice clay feet on their idol. They began to speculate aloud that perhaps some ambitious man who had his fortune to make might best serve their purposes. The American journalist James Creelman went down to interview Díaz to see what was what. To the surprise of everyone, Díaz announced that he was willing to retire; his ambitions had been realized. He believed, he said, that Mexico now had the ability to develop into a true democracy. He professed to welcome an opposition. He wanted the people to choose his successor in a free and honest election.

Apparently, he had aimed the interview only at the American public and had disregarded any Mexican reaction. Creelman's story, printed everywhere in Mexico, created a hubbub and widespread opposition that emerged from underground. Some believed, however, that Díaz deliberately gave the interview to see who would spring forward in Mexico as the most eager for his place. But the "important" men prudently lay low and bided their time, for Díaz knew too well how to deal with rivals.

# 15. The Little Black Sheep

*"We poor visionaries—for then we were only that—had come armed only with the feeble experience of our books and our early ideals."*

MARTÍN LUÍS GUZMÁN

One of the most unlikely men in the land rose up as the leader of that opposition. At first he was no more regarded by Díaz and his cohorts than a stray voice piping in the wilderness. He was a little five-foot-two man, ill-shaped and delicate, with a high-pitched voice and a high-domed forehead and a receding hair line. But he was as noble in spirit as his form was lacking in impressive attributes. His name was Francisco I. Madero, and his prominent family had a strain of Jewish blood. His grandfather, who had been governor of Coahuila, was one of the wealthiest men in Mexico, owning some million and three-quarters acres of land and having extensive mining and banking interests. Francisco was like a changeling among the handsome, pleasure-loving, successful members of the Madero family. His father and brothers and innumerable relatives thought him a bit queer, and looked upon him affectionately as a ne'er-do-well misfit. He was one of those anomalies, a son of the rich turned reformer, the kind who loves to feed the hungry and give his coat to the shivering. When he was in school in Paris, where his father had sent him to get the notion of becoming a Jesuit priest out of his head, he literally spent all his generous allowance administering to the needy. Besides being a vegetarian, he was a dabbler in the occult. And like the militaristic Caesar and Napoleon and Cortés and Adolf Hitler who consulted astrologers, the gentle Madero played the ouija board and communed with departed spirits. After his return from Paris his family turned over to him the management of some agricultural properties. But he seemed far more interested in cultivating the toilers than the soil, and he delighted in gathering scores of peon children at his own dinner table to feed them nourishing dishes and teach them polite manners.

In 1900, when Francisco was twenty-seven, he surprised his family and friends by taking an active interest in politics and political reform in the capital. He helped to form the *Club Democrático Benito Juárez* and championed the introduction of American democratic methods into Mexican politics. His liberal views were first a joke, then a pain in the neck to his conservative, wealthy family. But though at thirty-two Madero was one of the leaders of the reform element, few important persons took either him or his movement seriously. The majority of the public was completely unaware of him until 1908, when he published a fair criticism of Díaz's administration called *The Presidential Succession in 1910.* The book mildly called attention to certain evils in the political and social set-up, and advocated a single presidential term and drastic suffrage reforms. He professed nothing against Díaz's having the presidency one more last time, but urged that the vice-president should be chosen by the honest vote of the people.

Madero's family was amazed to find that their little black sheep had become famous overnight. Francisco began making democratic speeches all over Mexico. Despite his frail, thin voice that would sometimes break into falsetto, his sincerity and logic and passionate zeal brought him converts as if he were an apostle of a new religion. Then in this land of restricted speech he had the temerity to found a liberal newspaper.

The old lion Díaz had no more taken the odd black sheep seriously than had Francisco's relatives. But as the public enthusiasm obviously waxed and crowds were turned away from Madero meetings, Díaz began to ponder. More out of curiosity than anything else, the dictator had it arranged for Madero to call on him. He listened with studied gravity while Madero told him that his mission was to stir the Mexican people to realize their responsibility to the ballot. He professed to be impressed with such a noble aim. As he regarded the enthusiastic young man with cool detachment, he was falsely reassured. He saw that Madero's right shoulder had a noticeable twitch, that in temperament the little fellow was as highly nervous as he himself was calm. The pragmatic meat-eater was even amused by the idealistic vegetarian. For all his acumen, Díaz could not discern that the weak body before him conserved a remarkable physical resistance. All the skill he had in judging human nature could not make him aware of the power of an ardent ideal. He believed, as did other practical souls, that "all armed prophets have conquered, and the unarmed ones have been destroyed." Since his frail adversary did not seem to possess so much as a slingshot, the giant little dreamed that he carried concealed a shining pebble of truth which would prove mortal to the giant.

When Madero had bowed his adieu, Díaz could not but smile whimsically at the earnest crackpot. He joked with his friends about the idiot's pretensions. No fortuneteller was there to warn him within a year the iron-willed man of action would bow in defeat to the apostolic dreamer.

Díaz continued to smile when Madero was nominated for the presidency by the anti-re-electionist party in April, 1910. But in May, when thirty thousand Madero adherents actually made a shouting demonstration before the National Palace, Díaz began to heed his advisers. The demonstration had come when Díaz announced his own intention to run for president once again. He decided it might not be entirely amiss to let Madero's zeal cool off in jail until the election was over. So in June he incarcerated his opponent in the prison of San Luis Potosí on the charge of plotting a rebellion.

Díaz had looked forward to the coming September fifteenth

as the apostheosis of his triumphal life. There was to be a gala celebration of the centenary of Father Hidalgo's *Grito de Dolores* and his own eightieth birthday. Five days previous to the fiesta, flies appeared in the ointment. A mob in sympathy with Madero threw stones at the Díaz windows. As a birthday present the old man was anonymously promised a bullet to end his rule on the night of September fifteenth. But Díaz, scorning the threat, looked down the corridor of the future to the end of his next six-year term, when he would be approaching ninety.

From early morning on September fifteenth the people jammed the great plaza, eating from the sidewalk brazier restaurants. Rainbow-colored streamers were strung on wires across streets from house to house. Colored pennants like silken tongues savored the early autumn atmosphere. Girls in sheer white dresses and net veils poured into the cathedral for communion, chaperoned by old ladies in fine black lace mantillas. The bullfighters wore their most expensive sky-blue satins and canary velvets ornamented with gold and silver braid. Bands played, horses cavorted, soldiers marched under the sun. And always at the edges of the picture was the *chiaroscuro* of sandaled Indians, grave, unwashed, yet unfailingly picturesque.

In the midst of the clamor of blaring bands and stamping horses, through the surge of humanity and motor cars and mounted police, an old Indian woman wearing a battered straw sombrero resolutely drove her flock of turkeys before her. She guided them with a long stick held in one hand, and grasped her red blanket tight about her with the other. Looking neither to right nor left, she took no notice of the paradeful splendor. She spoke her special language to her turkeys, touched them reassuringly with her stick, and passed through the madding crowd. An Englishman, observing her, murmured to his American companion: "Though dynasties pass, this will go on."

In the afternoon, historical pageants were staged with costumes as costly as in a de Mille spectacle. When night came the spires of the cathedral blazed with incandescent light. And the buildings surrounding the plaza, which had been strung with high-powered lights, were as bright as noon.

In the illuminated palace on the east side of the square, sixty distinguished representatives from among the world's great nations were seated at dinner. Ten huge candelabra spaced between tall silver urns spilling over with pink blossoms made dazzling the jewels on the powdered throats and arms of diplomats' assorted wives. The Maximilian silver glittered regally. The first eight courses were served on silver plates, the last two on plates of solid gold.

While Díaz's special guests were being sumptuously served, to the crowds out in the great square was offered music from sixteen bands, all playing at once and different selections. They were treated, too, to the most elaborate fireworks Mexico had ever beheld. Precisely at five minutes to eleven the sixteen bands stopped playing, the sparks from the fireworks turned to invisible ash.

There came a thickening hush as a spotlight played high up on the palace, where the liberty bell hung—the bell the white-haired priest rang in the early dawn of September sixteenth, 1810. Directly under the bell on the little iron balcony a canopy of purple velvet had been rigged up. The eighty-year-old Don Porfirio appeared before his people, stalwart and impressive. For a moment all human breathing seemed to have ceased. But no shot rang out. Then there was a concerted wave of movement. Hats came off. The bell was struck thrice, and the old dictator uttered Hidalgo's cry of liberty. A hundred thousand *vivas* rent the air. The church towers began to tremble with the frantic pealing of bells. About the cathedral, rosy clouds of smoke wafted heavenward like souls making ascensions in pillars of flame. Rockets rushed shrieking at the sky as if challenging the stars. Peons who were not already drunk rushed off to enjoy the liberty of drinking themselves insensible. In the palace the great ball was opened with a grand march led by Porfirio. Before sunrise twenty carloads of champagne had been consumed by the two-thousand guests.

Far from the fanfare a little, bearded man, not half the age of the old dictator, lay on his prison cot in San Luis Potosí and silently renewed his faith in his mission. Notwithstanding the centennial *vivas* and the congratulations from kings and queens that poured in to Díaz over cable and telegraph, Madero's revolution broke within two months.

In the first week of October the election returns were announced. The government counters had allowed Madero a consolation of 196 votes from the entire republic. Díaz found himself overwhelmingly re-elected for another six years. He would be in his eighty-seventh year when his new term was up. But if he purposed to retire then, he did not say so now. Safely re-elected, Díaz consented to release Madero on bail. Madero jumped his bond. On October seventh he crossed into Texas. At San Antonio he published his Plan of San Luis Potosí, conceived while he was in prison. Madero declared the recent elections fraudulent, and announced his provisional presidency. November twentieth was set as the date for general insurrection.

Dr. Vásquez Gómez, the vice-presidential candidate on the reform ticket, and Gustavo Madero, Francisco's brother, hurried to Washington to pull wires and win friends. When the day for the revolution came, Francisco crossed the border with high ardor. He was received by an army of fully two dozen men, some with guns. In his overwhelming disappointment, he returned to the United States and made up his mind to go to Europe. But great news from Chihuahua stopped him in New Orleans. On November twenty-seventh cowboy *insurrectos* led by a shop-keeper and a notorious bandit defeated state troops. The bandit was a former peon who had defied all efforts of the *rurales* to stop his cattle rustling. He was called Pancho Villa.

As the revolutionaries moved north victoriously, they cut the railway to the border. The success in Chihuahua stimulated desultory uprisings in other states. Madero re-entered Mexico in February to join the rebel forces in the north. The idealist and the bandit met for the first time. Beholding the tiny figure of a man with a bearded face illuminated by a pair of great, trusting eyes, the hulking Villa was dumbfounded. Was this the *hombre* who inspired revolt against the mighty chief? But he took to the little fellow at once with a big-brotherly affection and even a kind of awe. And Madero saw beyond the cruelty and lust and cunning of the outlaw, to the ideal he cherished in his heart. All the evil qualities in Villa he attributed to the misery of his youth when chained to debt servitude on a *hacienda*. He was gratified that Villa neither drank nor smoked; and he made no inquiries about his tempestuous sex life.

While master and disciple were becoming acquainted, the United States sent twenty thousand troops to camp along the border. Limantour returned from a mission in Europe by way of New York, and tried to make compromises with Gustavo Madero. He was also prepared to offer almost any concessions in Washington to prevent intervention. But the terms demanded by the revolutionaries were too stiff. The resignation of Díaz and the downfall of the *científicos* were only a part of the demands.

Amid the bold and vengeful talk and the sharpening of war blades, Francisco Madero was still hoping to effect the revolution without bloodshed. At heart he was an ardent pacifist. But in the hills west of Ciudad Juárez the *insurrectos* were eager to start the rebellion immediately. For heavy arms they were equipped with "a long gun that had been made in a machine shop and a little brass cannon that had been stolen from its ornamental position in El Paso's city park." Madero's headquarters were in an adobe one-room house near the river. Here leaders came daily to confer with him and to urge him to immediate attack. Madero vacillated. His companions said he was conferring with the spirits of his immortal advisers, Socrates, Napoleon, and Benito Juárez. "Without arriving in his troubled brain," commented war correspondent Timothy Turner, "at any definite course in all this terrible rumpus his eloquent oratory had stirred up." Turner, who was with Madero at El Paso, summed up at the very beginning the cause of the leader's subsequent failure. "He was too chicken-hearted. He couldn't bear killing and bloodshed. His hesitation was never from fear." But while Madero was trying to win over the enemy by persuasion, his more-of-this-world lieutenants, fed up with dallying and dubious messages from departed heroes, moved up on Ciudad Juárez and began to shoot and dynamite the town into subjugation.

The revolution was launched, and Madero had to try to get used to the bloodshed. On the tenth of May, Navarro, the federal commander, capitulated. While Villa was preparing for his execution, Madero graciously conducted the enemy across the border to safety. The bandit-disciple became so infuriated that he promptly arrested Madero for treachery. Madero appeared before the troops and spoke so appealingly that he won their tumultuous shouts of confidence. Thoroughly mollified, Villa hung his head and begged the little master's pardon for his own impetuosity.

At the beginning, the federal troops in the north had no medical corps. The dusky women camp followers were the haphazard Florence Nightingales. They tended the wounded and were wives, sweethearts, mothers, as well as nurses. These *soldaderas* had no official positions, but their presence was encouraged by the government both for the economic and psychologic factors. It was an old Mexican custom to take the womenfolk to war, to keep the men contented and to see that they had hot dinners. Some women went to the wars out of necessity and some purely *pour le sport*. They rode the tops of troop trains with their cooking utensils and bags of meal, their stolen chickens and pigs, and with their brood of brown children clinging to their skirts and *rebosas*. And when the army went on foot, the female auxiliary preceded them like royal purveyors, stripping fruit trees, rooting up vegetables, collecting hens and cocks as well as eggs. No farmer dared stand up against their patriotic onslaught.

The *insurrectos* at the beginning had doctors, but no camp followers. "But later on," wrote Timothy Turner, "they developed a competent corps of them, begetting many little *soldados* and *soldaderas* in proper army fashion." And there was nothing Madero could do about that. It distressed him to notice fifteen-year-old boys among his warriors living in companionable sin with "hard-tacks" old enough to be their grandmothers. But he knew better than to interfere with the romantic morality of Mexican soldiers.

The war's start was so insignificant that the keen-nosed Díaz could not detect anything worthy of his apprehension. Yet the little victory at the border town of Ciudad Juárez turned out to be decisive. It was to mark the speedy end of an era. All over Mexico driblets of insurrection against a generation's repression began to flow to make a swelling river of revolt. In the south, in Morelos, the peon leader, Emiliano Zapata, won a significant victory. Several state capitals were taken over by revolutionaries, supported by city mobs.

The government, which had first been incredulous and then alarmed and at last frenzied, could do no more than talk excitedly in ring-a-rounds. After the long peace of a third of a century the army consisted of less than twenty-five thousand trained soldiers. Many of his generals were nearly as old as Díaz and had become rusty with disuse. He had little comfidence in them. They were few he could really trust. So he stood before great maps spread out on the palace billard tables, and conducted the fight himself by telegraph.

Eleven days after that federal defeat at Ciudad Juárez, it was all over. Díaz promised to resign. Commissioners from both sides gathered to prepare articles of peace. Madero shyly requested that two Mexican spiritualists and one American be allowed to sit silently at the conferences. They were never introduced. They never spoke, but sit in the conference room they did. It was decided that the Mexican minister in Washington, Francisco de la Barra, was to serve as provisional president until an election could be held. Madero, of course, was to receive the presidency. On the night of May twenty-first the treaty was signed on the outskirts of Ciudad Juárez. The momentous paper was spread on a deal table out of doors, the scene lighted by the headlights of motor cars, the spiritualists hovering in the shadows.

When the news of the treaty was released in the capital, the streets became jammed as at another centennial. Crowds let off a pent-up repressed steam of years. Under his very windows in his house on Cadena Street the rabble shouted its demand for the old dictator's immediate resignation. But now Díaz decided he did not want to resign.

He was stretched out with a raging toothache. In his physical agony he would get up from time to time and pace the floor, while the mob was shouting its repudiation of his lifetime of labors. The anguish from the abscess in his jaw made it easier to bear the hurt in his breast. Carmelita, constantly at his side, pled with him to sign the drawn-up document of resignation. His doctor urged him for his health's sake. Those he called his closest friends pointed out that there was no other way. The old man clamped his jaw over his pain and stubbornly refused. He could not bring himself to relinquish the power he had held for a third of a century. In his bitter perplexity, his fever rose alarmingly.

A menacing crowd surged in the Zócalo. Soldiers from the National Palace fired into their midst. Men dropped and died in pools of their own blood on the paving stones. Some of the wounded crept or crawled away. Yet the crowd hung on. Bullets could not rout them. Finally rain came and sent them scurrying like sheep for shelter. They left the fresh corpses of their fellows behind on the crimson biers that turned to pinkish gray with the dilution of rainwater. Observers in windows counted two hundred stretched out dead.

The news of the massacre was brought to the house in Calle Cadena. Carmelita ordered the servants to pack. At last, worn down by sleeplessness and excruciating suffering, Díaz yielded to his wife's entreaties. In the black first hour of morning he took up the proffered pen and signed in a bold hand.

Despite the late hour most of the city, too, was still awake. The climactic news was received with tumult and caterwauling. Amid a fiendish clangor of pans and tin cans beaten by gangs of urchins, the Díaz household tried to settle down to a couple of hours' sleep. Soldiers thickly guarded the street. Solicitous friends tiptoed about the house and took their stations within doors, heavily armed against an attack. Just before sunrise on the twenty-sixth of May the aged president and his lady, accompanied by a few relatives and friends, were hurried into closed cars and rushed to the railway station. There they boarded a special train for Vera Cruz, where a ship was waiting to take them to exile in France.

Díaz wept manly tears at his departure. It was not only because he was a patriot saying good-by to a land that had nurtured him and which he had loved profoundly in his own ruthless way— he actually believed that Mexico still had need of him. In those who were to take his place he could not discern qualities equal to the job. "They have unleashed dangers they will not be able to control," he mumbled through his aching jaw.

Clear of brain and remarkably vigorous in body, Díaz lived on until he was nearing his eighty-fifth birthday. In the ease of sheltered elegance in Biarritz, he received news of great turmoil in Mexico. He read of Madero's murder. He learned that the dope addict, Victoriano Huerta, was slaughtering viciously to bring about reaction. Then from the north the forces of Carranza and Villa came fighting against the provisional government and in the south the barefoot peons of the firebrand Zapata defeated government forces and burned the *haciendas* of Morelos. When Huerta was routed from Mexico the fight continued; three groups of revolutionaries were at each others' throats. Worse than what Díaz had feared and prophesied had come upon Mexico. When he died in Paris on July second, 1915, his native land was as unpeaceful and bewildered as those two spitting cats slung across a wire with their tails tied together. Shaking his head sorrowfully, but with a kind of grim justification, Díaz could say to his wife and friends, "Ah, you see, I knew my Mexico!"

# PART SEVEN

# THE REVOLUTION

## 16. Martyr

*"I hoped to find a meadow at the end of the road, I found a swamp. Facts are bitter; so are men. . . . That bitterness eats your heart out; it is poison, dry-rot. Enthusiasm, hope, ideals, happiness—vain dreams, vain dreams. . . . When that's over, you have a choice. Either you turn bandit, like the rest, or the time-servers will swamp you . . ."*

MARIANO AZUELA

At Madero's triumphal entrance on the eighth of June, the trees and roofs were crammed with a jubilant populace. Boys clambered on statues, bestrode bronze horses, and perched on the shoulders of marble heroes. Girls hung perilously over balcony rails, waving colored silks at the street crowd as a prelude to the big show. As the engine bearing the private car of Madero puffed into the station, suddenly the ground began to rumble and the buildings to tremble. An earthquake shook the capital. The portent proved more malevolent than the sourest soothsayer might have predicted.

Yet when Madero was elected president in October with an honest, overwhelming majority, it would have seemed that Mexico was ripe for her regeneration. One of his enemies declared with sarcastic fury that Madero had supplanted the Virgin of

Guadalupe in the people's adoration. But too much was expected
—a miracle overnight, like a Hindu fakir's trick, where a mango
seed grows into a tree before one's incredulous gaze.

Madero had inherited a land steeped in political corruption,
illiteracy and ingrafted prejudices, a land where hate and jealousy,
special privilege and greed had long flourished like spurious
grasses in rank soil. The powerful forces of intrenched wealth
and reaction lay in ambush and in the open to obstruct him.
Foreign concessionaires, leagued with the Mexican conservatives,
were prepared to fight with relentless persistence to maintain
cheap labor and sordid conditions in industry and field.

Because of his exaggerated opinion of human nature, he attributed philosophical motives to the Mexican masses. He misjudged their fervor for his mission. Once when asked why he
did not divide his goods among the poor if he was so interested
in their welfare, he replied: "The people are not asking for bread,
they are asking for liberty." He would never learn what Bernard
Shaw professed to have found out in his first dealings with socialists—that "any revolution can be bought off for thirty bob."

As the prime specific for his country's ills, Madero stoutly and
unswervingly advocated a real democracy—a free state with a
free ballot and a free church. He believed that political and social
reconstruction could be achieved when based on nothing more
radical than the United States Declaration of Independence. He
was unprepared for human nature's resistance to such mild purgation. He could not fathom the code of ethics by which the gen-
tlemen-political-grafters plied their trade. He could not conceive
that governors and generals in Mexico expected large *pourboires*
beyond their regular salaries for doing the duties of their offices.
He had not figured on the politicians' putting their own personal
advantage above everything else in the world. He was shocked
to learn that they examined each move and change by the touch-
stone of "What is in it for me?" Such things as disloyalty and
duplicity were not easy for Madero to understand. He believed

that right eventually triumphed, and he assured the people that liberties would be recovered one by one.

When the millennium did not materialize with the magic celerity they expected, the needy masses began to lose faith in their apostle. The idealistic theories which sounded so well in speeches and on paper were not easy to put in practice. The politicians turned out to have small appetite for Madero's ideals; they were greedy for the fruity spoils of victory. Madero made the mistake of trying to conciliate the old regime, and congress endeavored to checkmate him on every move for reform. He could manage neither his cabinet nor his generals. By trying to secure harmony so that he could proceed with constructive work, he was accused of irresolution.

Finally, smoldering discontent broke into open revolt in various parts of the country. Two generals of his own party—but at opposite extremes in viewpoint—began to carve for themselves: Zapata with his peons in the south and Orozco with the estate owners in the north. The northern revolt was quickly squelched. But Zapata's agrarians could not be silenced. When Madero pled with the peasant leader to be patient and cease fighting, Zapata mounted a table in a mountain village and, with his innate sense of the dramatic, waved the Mexican flag and issued his Plan of Ayala, which a Morelos school teacher had composed for him. In it he announced to Madero and all Mexico that he and his men would never lay down their arms "until the *ejidos* of our villages are restored to us, until we are given back the lands which the *hacendados* stole from us during the dictatorship of Porfirio Díaz, when justice was subjected to his caprice."

Madero was anything but blind to the needs of the agrarians, but he had promised more than he could deliver in a short time. The peons had expected land immediately. The president saw that the whole land-division program had to be studied. He did not want the nation's economy to be completely disrupted while changes were being made. In certain northern states, where land was taken from some of the rich *científicos* and allotted to the Indian peons, the change had not worked out well. The Indian did not know just what to do with the land. Some of them promptly sold it to speculators for a handful of silver. Others transferred it for a little cash back to the *hacendados* from whom it had been taken, and asked merely to be allowed to continue to work for them.

The first casual land division proving a failure, Madero created a national agrarian commission to study the whole land problem. Their recommendations were not ill-reasoned. They drew up a plan of breaking up a large proportion of the great estates into small farms to be sold on a long-term payment plan financed by the government. (This was shortly done with great success in Finland and Scandinavia.) They advocated returning the *ejidos* to the Indian villages, where the transfer would not disrupt the immediate economy. They recommended new irrigation systems, forest conservation, road building and modern methods of farm cultivation. To put the plan into execution, an agrarian executive committee was commissioned.

Madero, like his contemporary Premier Branting of Sweden, was trying to find a middle way for Mexico. But both conservatives and radicals vehemently denounced his plan. The radical agrarians looked on it as an instrument to make the landowners rich in cash at the government's expense. They wanted the land confiscated without remuneration. The conservatives did not want any governmental interference whatsoever in their property rights. So both sides cried out against him.

In the field of education, Madero was blocked by immediate circumstances. He wanted to give the people schools as much as did those reformers who were vociferating demands. But there were few trained teachers and virtually no altruistic volunteers. The church could have helped more with education, but church schools were forbidden by law. Teachers would have to be trained. Until then, the semi-literate would have to lead the illiterate. In the meantime Madero appropriated from the shrunken national budget fifty per cent more for education than Díaz ever had, even when his treasury was bulging.

To get funds to meet the budget, Madero put a tax on the oil companies. A howl of indignation and dismay went up. Before this time, the foreign oil companies had not been asked to share their fantastic profits. The oil tax helped seal Madero's doom.

Because of his conciliating and trusting nature and his innate milk of human kindness, he was betrayed to right and left, before and behind. Not only was desultory brigandage loosed about the land with a vicious cruelty, but the powerful foreign colony, led by the ambassadors of the United States and Great Britain, definitely soured and began to sneer. Madero was beset on every hand by ill-wishers, whose malice and ridicule preyed upon him. The most vivid comment on how painfully he was affected by his unhappy situation is given by Edward I. Bell, an American newspaperman who interviewed the president during his last stressful months in office.

The interview took place in the innermost of the presidential reception rooms of the National Palace. Mr. Bell wrote:

It happened that as I entered, there appeared at the opposite end the undersized, frock-coated figure of Madero coming from his private office. In my mind was the impression of the immense and ponderous building stretched across the Plaza's eastern boundary; of the great stone stairway, its steps hewn for giants so that the knees of an ordinary person are lifted almost to his chin as he climbs panting in that rarefied atmosphere; of the long corridor, and dwindling series of reception rooms; and it seemed to me that I had walked down the diminished vista which one sees through a strong field glass reversed, and in the vanishing point of this perspective stood "the little man" dwarfed by his huge responsibilities, so desperately circumstanced, so pitifully doomed to failure and extinction. All illusions aside, he was greatly changed from that enthusiast who was my neighbor so little while ago and taught political economy to his curbstone pupils in the Calle Berlín. His cheeks, which used to curve smoothly from his broad forehead to his narrow chin, were now sunken and lined; his brow was wrinkled; a dozen years had been added to his apparent age, a fair half of them in the last seven days. He showed loss of sleep and was extremely nervous, with the impatient manner of a man who is trying to do too many things at once, and knows in his heart that they are none of them done well, but he had not lost a grain of his courage nor an atom of his essential self-respect.

"I do not want to kill my people to make them good," he declared in a shrill voice, at which a knot of Mexicans awaiting audience in a far corner of the room turned questioning eyes upon me as one who was being roughly lectured in a tongue they did not understand. "I could have controlled them," he went on. "I am preparing to open lands to them. I am arranging employment at good wages for all Maderista soldiers and many other men, on public works. Does your government suppose that I have given no thought to conditions here, or that extensive plans such as mine can be carried out by magic in a day? I ask of no man or government anything but a reasonable chance. Why is this unfriendly effort made to force me to violate my pledges against the shedding of blood? What influence is at work secretly to accomplish this injustice? Surely the United States has nothing to gain by making me a tyrant and a madman!"

Many of his own countrymen chose to regard him as a madman because he was so little of a tyrant. They despised him for his lack of force. Mexico needed a strong hand, they said, and instead with Madero she had got merely a soft heart. Madero refused to see that absolutism alone had ever succeeded in Mexico, that even the great democrat Juárez, who had had himself re-elected three times, ruled with an iron will.

But with opposition on every hand, Madero might yet have won his selfless battle for democratic principles if Henry Lane Wilson, the United States ambassador, had not tipped the balance against him. The idealist Madero had long been a thorn in the flesh of Wilson, who seemed to be the representative of certain American big business interests which resented the competition of the powerful Madero family in north Mexico. The president might still have survived the ambassador's animosity, however, if he had followed Porfirio's dictum, "Better shed bad blood now than good blood later." If he had allowed Felix Díaz, the old dictator's nephew, and a few other formidable trouble-makers to be executed, he might have saved himself. Felix Díaz had fomented a rebellion in Vera Cruz. Captured and con-demned, his death sentence had been suspended by the tender-hearted Madero. When he was released from prison in Mexico City by insurgent soldiers he became the leader of the rebellion that same day that General Bernardo Reyes met his death.

All during January, under the very nose of the president, prom-inent generals had been planning a *coup d'état*. Reyes, returned from his diplomatic banishment in Europe and now under a suspended death sentence for high treason, was looking forward to establishing a military dictatorship "along reform lines."

In the early morning of Sunday, February ninth, the soldiers of the Tacubaya barracks and the disaffected cadets from the military academy released Bernardo Reyes and Felix Díaz from their respective prisons. Reyes took command and proceeded to the National Palace, which he expected to capitulate without the firing of a shot. Gustavo Madero had dashed from Chapul-tepec just in time to persuade the Palace guards to give over their conspiracy and remain loyal to his brother. He switched the command to General Villar, a man of whose integrity he was sure. When Reyes rode forward to take over the Palace from supposedly friendly conspirators, he was met with a volley of fire that cost him his life and put his troops to flight. The rebel soldiers retired to the Ciudadela, and there Felix Díaz became their leader. Villar, unfortunately, had been so badly wounded that the loyal command had to be passed on to another.

When the president arrived at the Palace he put his fate in the hands of General Victoriano Huerta, a cunning and ruthless *mestizo,* who proved to be the prime unprincipled villain in Mexican history.

During the day Felix Díaz seized control of a greater part of the city and immediately became *persona grata* at the American embassy. As soon as Huerta ascertained that Henry Lane Wilson would back him in treachery, he, too, turned traitor, and formed a pact with Felix Díaz. By agreement, Huerta was to assume the provisional presidency until some sort of election could be held, whereby Felix Díaz was to be made president and bring back "the good old days" of his uncle, so dear to the hearts of foreign investors. The deal is known as "the Pact of the Embassy." The ambassador explained later that his support of the traitors was due solely to his desire for Mexico to resume its peaceful ways as quickly as possible.

For ten awful days—the period is called *La Decena Tragica*—the capital was thrown into the confusion and horror of civil strife. From a distance of a mile right across the heart of the city the forces in the National Palace and those in the Ciudadela bombarded each other. Residences and public buildings were despoiled in the ear-splitting cannonading. At nightfall the bombardment would cease by truce so that the dead could be removed. So many innocent civilians were killed that bodies were heaped in a pile, saturated with coal oil, and burned among the ruins.

Díaz and Huerta purposely made the days as hideous as possible so that the citizens would demand peace at any price. Huerta got rid of troops personally loyal to the president by sending them into attacking positions where they could do the rebels no harm but where they would be slaughtered systematically. February eighteenth was the day selected for the final blow. Huerta, mistrusting Gustavo Madero's persuasive powers, beguiled him to lunch with him far from the National Palace. Acting all innocence, he made himself unusually entertaining, while his detailed subordinates took possession of Francisco Madero and his vice-president at the Palace. When Huerta received a sign that the deed had been done, professing to be unarmed, he borrowed Gustavo's revolver for a fake meeting with a stranger requesting an interview. Then he arrested the unarmed Gustavo and hurried him off to the Ciudadela. There Felix Díaz's soldiers insulted him, slashed his face open for sport, and while he pled for his life for the sake of his wife and children, they cold-bloodedly shot him.

That evening Victoriano Huerta had a rendezvous with Felix Díaz and the leading followers of Reyes at the United States embassy. Wilson persuaded the dubious and hesitant to accept the provisional presidency of Huerta. Then he called in the foreign diplomats and explained the new set-up to them. He presented the villainous Huerta as "the savior of Mexico." In Washington, President Taft and the state department were somewhat nonplussed at the wording of the official telegram announcing the ousting of the gentle Madero. The wire said, "A wicked despotism has fallen."

On the solemn promise that they and their partisans would be immune from further harm, Madero and his vice-president, Piño Suárez, had resigned. On the medal of the Sacred Heart of Jesus, given him by his mother, Huerta had sworn that Madero would be allowed to retire to exile.

The fallen president expected to leave for Vera Cruz as Porfirio Díaz had done. His family was notified to await him at the railway station. They went there accordingly and waited and waited. But General Huerta, fearing the influence the ex-president might inspire in the United States—in spite of his own personal support by the United States ambassador in Mexico—hesitated to let him go. For three more days he held him prisoner in the National Palace. Madero's wife and several members of foreign legations begged Henry Lane Wilson to intercede with Huerta to spare Madero's life. Wilson, whose interference had been decisive in the Huerta machinations, now took the lofty attitude that it was not his mission to interfere in Mexico's internal problems. He gave Huerta *carte blanche* to do what he deemed necessary "for complete restoration of peace." In private he expressed the opinion that Madero belonged in an insane asylum and that shooting wouldn't be too good for Piño Suárez.

On the twenty-second—ironically, the embassy was celebrating George Washington's birthday—Huerta finished off his villainy with the murder of Madero and Piño Suárez. After dark, the president and vice-president were bundled hugger-mugger into a carriage and told they were to be transferred to the penitentiary "for better safety." Along the way, outside some stables, they were routed from the carriage and shot down "while attempting to escape." This is the story as it is generally written and most widely accepted.

The story that is told by many responsible persons on the conservative side is that Huerta in his perplexity struck the table with his fist and cried, "What am I going to do with Madero?" One of his aides, standing by, took it as a call for a loyal volunteer. Quietly he left the room. Securing Madero and the vice-president, he had them taken to the basement of the palace and summarily shot. Then he put their dead bodies in a carriage and took them to the place near the penitentiary where they were discovered. According to this version, Huerta was extremely upset about his faithful dog's impetuosity, because he feared the martyrization would react against him.

But in any case Ambassador Wilson professed to believe Huerta's story that the men had been killed by accident in an attempted rescue by armed friends. Brazenly he asked the United States government to accept the explanation and to recognize the Huerta administration.

Of course, not even one Mexican moron believed such a palpable fabrication. Without debate, however, Great Britain, Spain, and Germany recognized the Huerta usurpation. But though Henry Lane Wilson had smirked over the new cabinet in which one of the ministers was the attorney for a score of American corporations, the United States government hesitated. Even the reactionary President Taft, whose brother was attorney for a

British oil company, had grave misgivings and left the decision of recognition to the Democrats and Woodrow Wilson, who was to be inaugurated within a fortnight.

Francisco Madero was dead at thirty-nine. Many who looked kindly upon his memory regarded him at best as an honest failure. Critics have written so copiously about his failures that they would lead one to think that he must have been in power at least half as long as Díaz. The truth is that Madero was president only from October, 1911, to February, 1913. Sixteen months were allotted him by fate to diagnose Mexico's case and cure her of a hundred diverse ills inherited from centuries of bad habits. And during his brief charge the patient seemed possessed to defy the physician and let the ulcers grow. He was not a Strong Man with capital letters and Mexicans do like strong men. Yet, as the years go by, a greater glory illumines his historical figure. He stood at the crossroads pointing a new direction. After Madero, Mexico could never settle back completely to its wonted ways of beds of plush and contrasting beds of nettles. His failure came of his magnanimity and because he lived up to his democratic creed, which made him respect the free action of other men. But for all his Christ-like compassion he was not the fool and the weakling his detractors pretend. He saw clearly that political revolution had to come before any kind of agrarian or social revolution. His chief principle of "free suffrage, no re-election"— it was not new—was the only effective one to win adherents among a host of former Díaz supporters who would have denounced any radical reforms. Madero was the tender idealist who rushed in where hardened generals feared to tread. It took some such frail apostle to defeat the most formidable dictator of the age.

The scholarly Andrés Molina Enríquez, leader of the radical agrarians who forsook Madero in 1912, was to write his vindication in 1930, four years before Cárdenas: "The government of

Madero . . . should be considered the most agrarian that we have had. It lasted a year, and if it had lasted the four of his term, the agrarian problem would probably have been solved. The great masses of the nation have always thought so, and for this reason they weep at the tomb of Madero."

# 17. Avenging Winds from the North

*"Most men come down like cattle and will not be remembered either for the good or for the evil. But this you must know for certain, that this is not the true inheritance of man: Man was created to be a precious thing in this world, and a precious thing in the world to come. The problem is just this—if he is willing to win for himself the inheritance he was created to possess."*

THE KING'S MIRROR (THIRTEENTH CENTURY)

The counter-revolution, which had been welcomed with *Te Deums* in the churches, was straining to begin business in the good old Porfirian way. But the martyrdom of Madero did not restore order to the wretched land. Instead, like a ghost of vengeance, rebellion rose up within three days. Venustiano Carranza, governor of Coahuila, openly declared against Huerta's self-appointed government. And before many months four future presidents—Carranza, Obregón, de la Huerta, and Calles—were fighting against the usurper in one army called the Army of the Constitutionalists.

The American ambassador, Henry Lane Wilson, was to see nemesis overtake those who wished Madero out of the way. The man he had assisted to power was a sinister scoundrel whose talents lay principally in intrigue and battle cunning. Yet he had not only the support of the American embassy and American business, but that of the Catholic church, the landowners, and most of the army officers. The British colony led by Lord Cowdray, the millionaire oil magnate, professed to see remarkable abilities in the half-blooded Huichol Indian, who was a notorious dipsomaniac. The newly arrived British minister, Sir Lionel Carden, made much of him. But the few honest men in the Mexican congress who still hoped to get through reforms for the relief of the common man resigned in despair.

From the first, Huerta's entire energies were bent on building up a military machine powerful enough to crush his enemies. In governmental affairs the dictator tolerated no criticism. Several persons who openly defied him were murdered by hired assassins. At one blow a hundred and ten congressmen were imprisoned for daring to protest against the assassination of a fellow member, whose dead body was found bullet-riddled in a ditch in Coyoacán.

Huerta soon discovered that the boresome business of state administration interfered with his enjoyment of the fruits of victory. So he rarely allowed himself to be caught at the National Palace. Foreign envoys had to flag him down on the boulevards or search him out in some bar, if they wanted an audience. He professed to think more clearly after swilling cognac. Ministers and lesser dignitaries—when they were lucky enough to catch him—were forced to do business at some saloon table over brandy bottles. Often, when the president was located, he was in too sodden a state of intoxication to focus his eyes or his attention. At night he would occasionally summon his ministers to a hide-out in the suburbs, where, riotously drunk and full of song, surrounded by bizarre and dubious-looking companions, he would proceed to affairs of state.

Because of the brutality and chicanery of his military rule, plus his support from the church and foreign capital, Victoriano Huerta remained in power for seventeen months, one month longer than had Madero. He had soon lost the support of the American embassy, however, because ten days after Madero's murder another Wilson of a very different caliber became President of the United States. Woodrow Wilson was no more fooled by Henry Lane Wilson than he was by Huerta. The former was recalled, and the latter was never recognized by the United States government. President Wilson had admired Madero's integrity and was in full sympathy with his ideals. He refused recognition of the Huerta government on three grounds: The fate of Madero, the failure of Huerta to hold a real election, and the palpable fact that Huerta controlled only a small part of Mexico.

Through the London press, the British undertook to chide President Wilson for his chill attitude toward the Mexican usurper. And European bankers rallied to lend Huerta sixteen million pesos—at a usurious rate—when the United States refused to lend him a centavo.

Despite the British rebukes, which further endeared the British interests to Huerta at the expense of American capital, Woodrow Wilson remained uncompromising toward the usurpation. He expressed the belief that foreign concessions in Mexico were the root of revolutions. He pointed out that when foreign interests dominated domestic affairs conditions became critical, and that there could never be any peace in Mexico so long as the president was put in by one set of concessionaires, while another set out of favor was striving to pull down the government and establish another. He went further and declared, "Huerta must go."

It was what Mexicans were saying in every state in the republic, though in many places they only whispered the words that might too easily prove mortal if the Huerta spies overheard them. In the north they were more bold, where Carranza's army, under the command of Alvaro Obregón, a rancher and ex-machinist, was winning successive victories.

On the night of March thirteenth, the bandit general, Pancho Villa, who had escaped from prison into Texas, swam his horse back across the Rio Grande into Chihuahua with a rebel army of eight cow-punchers. By superlative bravado and a gift of ruse he began taking towns and collecting troops. Huerta tried to buy him off with a check for 100,000 pesos and the rank of divisional general. But Villa contemptuously spurned the bribes, inviting

Huerta to "swill up the cash in *aguardiente*," and pointing out
that his rank was higher than any Huerta could bestow; was
he not already Supreme Commander of Free Men? When Huerta
got rid of the progressive governor of Chihuahua by having him
thrown under a moving train, Villa became undisputed leader
in that northern state. His army grew with the impetuosity of a
desert sandstorm, and the federals fell and retreated before him.

In the late fall of 1913 the United States State Department
warned Americans to leave Mexico. A fleet of American gunboats was sent to cruise about in the Caribbean off the Mexican
coast. In February of the next year the government removed the
restriction against shipping arms across the border, and the forces
opposing Huerta soon had all they needed. Huerta had been getting plentiful arms from Europe.

In April there occurred one of the most unfortunate episodes
in the relations between the neighboring republics. Some American marines from the gunboat *Dolphin* tied up at a wharf in
Tampico, the oil town, to procure gasoline. Because the place
was within prohibited area, they were arrested by Huerta soldiers.
Later they were released with apologies. But the admiral in command of the United States ships in the vicinity demanded a more
ostentatious apology, a naval salute. Huerta said he would give
the order only if the Americans promised to return the salute
gun for gun. While the question was being hotly debated, the
rebels ran the federalists out of Tampico.

On April twenty-first, when news came that a German ship
was approaching Vera Cruz with a full cargo of machine guns
and ammunition, President Wilson ordered Josephus Daniels,
secretary of the navy, to seize Vera Cruz to keep the ship from
landing. In the seizure almost two hundred Mexicans were
killed and sixteen American marines. Though President Wilson
had given the order only to bring about Huerta's downfall
quickly and so end the chaos in Mexico, his action created profound mistrust throughout all Latin America. Many revolution-

aries, including Carranza, condemned the impulsive gesture as a violation of Mexico's sovereign entity. Huerta tried to unite the nation behind him now by blatantly threatening to recapture Texas and to substitute the Mexican eagle for the American eagle on Washington's capitol. But Villa sent Washington indirect word that Huerta should not be allowed "to use his satanic abilities to start a war with the United States."

However much publicly the rebels denounced President Wilson's well-intentioned but danger-charged move to help them, they made good use of the munitions pouring across the border. Some of the money to pay for them came from *haciendas* Carranza divided up and sold in the north. Some came from the Madero family, who reputedly gave a million dollars in gold to avenging the murders of Francisco and Gustavo.

As Villa with his "Army of the North" and Carranza with his "Army of the Constitutionalists" gathered momentum in their oblique southward drives, it became a race to see which would reach the National Palace first. With the two armies converging on the capital like a V-shaped wedge and Zapata's "Agrarian Army" circling up from the south, Huerta packed his bags. On July fifteenth he took the fugitive train for Vera Cruz. On a German boat he sailed to Spain. The next year he recrossed the Atlantic and entered the United States. He went to Texas, where immigration authorities arrested him. He was charged with "inciting a revolution in Mexico while on United States soil." Before his trial was called he died in the El Paso prison. It was rumored that he was killed by a vengeful fellow countryman.

The federal troops in the capital surrendered by telegram on August tenth, 1914. General Obregón entered the city five days later and took possession for the First Chief of the Constitutionalist Army, as Carranza entitled himself.

Almost as soon as Carranza was settled in the National Palace as provisional ruler, Obregón had to turn back north to mediate with Villa. For Carranza and Villa had immediately begun barking threats and accusations at each other. Villa had been halted in his march on Mexico City when Carranza cut off his coal supplies, and he swore diabolical vengeance. The mediators agreed that Carranza should retain power only until an election could be held. But complete peace was not to be in the interim. Obregón now had to rush to Sonora to settle a new civil war that was breaking out. Then he returned to the capital to inform Carranza he was not to be the next president. Carranza was surly and bided his time. Obregón doubled back to finish negotiations with Villa.

When he arrived this time, the burly bad man was in a furious mood. He announced that Obregón was to be shot at once. With cool logic the genial Obregón remonstrated. Such an action would besmirch Villa's honor and prestige. The ruffian patriot saw the point, dismissed the firing squad, ordered a fine dinner, and burst into tears. "Pancho Villa does not kill defenseless men," he declared emotionally, "and least of all, thee, little comrade, who art my guest."

But when Obregón and his aides took the first train out the next morning, they had not gone far when the Supreme Commander of Free Men decided he had better finish off his parting guest after all. He telegraphed to have the train stopped and he sent a squad of killers in swift pursuit. Obregón and his staff, suspecting the cause of the halt, rushed to the engine, seized control, speeded up, and effected their own rescue just as in a motion-picture thriller.

# 18. Whose Chair?

*"Villa? Obregón? Carranza? What's the dif-*
*ference? I love the revolution like a volcano*
*in eruption; I love the volcano, because it's a*
*volcano, the revolution, because it's the revo-*
*lution! What do I care about the stones left*
*above or below after the cataclysm? What are*
*they to me?"*
                                    MARIANO AZUELA

A convention to decide who should be elected president was
held at Aguascalientes in October. It was hoped that civil war
might be forestalled by the right choice. But the meeting was
at cross-purposes from the beginning, marked by plot and coun-
terplot, with a few fervent reformers vainly expounding socialistic doctrines. While Carranza sat glum and aloof in Mexico,
contemptuous of the whole proceedings, Villa gained ascendancy.
He surrounded Aguascalientes with his troops and made a great
show of his strength. He amazed the delegates with a spectacular
review of his magnificent Dorado cavalry. When a serious deadlock came between the opposing factions, Villa melodramatically
offered to commit suicide, if Carranza would do the same. Finally, when Carranza did not rise to the bait, the convention com-
promised on General Eulalio Gutiérrez as provisional president.
Honest and able enough, Gutiérrez lacked the dominating personality and the necessary heavy artillery which Mexico was
wont to demand of a leader. As the meeting broke up, the delegates began choosing sides in the inevitable civil war.

Obregón decided to stick by Carranza. Villa's army, which
now called itself the "Army of the Convention," shortly began
its march on the capital, accompanied by the provisional presi-

dent. As Villa drew near, Carranza withdrew his government and his forces to Vera Cruz, which the United States Marines had conveniently evacuated. The presidential chair was left without a sitter.

Before Villa could get to the capital, however, Zapata with his horde of peons arrived from the south to take possession. The citizens were more terrified than they had been in these last two exciting years of horror and flight. They expected to be burned out or murdered in their beds. For the *zapatistas* had been depicted as the most savage of all the cutthroats. Zapata was compared by the press to Attila. But, wonderful to relate, when the swarthy little commander occupied the city, November twenty-fifth, 1914, there was quiet and order. Shopkeepers and townspeople had hastily barred their doors and hidden their valuables where they could. But Zapata's men made no attempt to rob private shops. They did not even force their charity. Fear-shaken householders would hear a humble knock at their door and on opening would find a simple countryman, with hat in hand, asking politely for a little bread. Horses, however, were loot of another color, and they were promptly appropriated from any stable in which they could be found. A well-known Mexican polo player saved his entire string of ponies by bedding them for the duration of the occupation in a rented dwelling house next door to his own place. At night he sneaked food to them through a hole cut out in the masonry and concealed with thick, transplanted shrubbery.

As the peasant invaders stood ragged guard in the brocaded elegance of government buildings, they kept on their straw sombreros. From time to time they would walk up to the great gilt-framed mirrors and make shy grimaces at themselves. Officers in rag-tag uniforms regaled themselves by riding up and down the elevators in childish glee. In their rural innocence a group of *zapatistas* valiantly charged a fire engine, which was rushing with brazen clangor to answer an alarm. They thought it must be some new instrument of warfare. With their rifles they picked off the unlucky and astounded firemen as neatly as if they had been jumping jack-rabbits.

When Pancho Villa arrived in December, he conferred with Zapata at Xochimilco. The bandit conqueror from the north and the farmer conqueror from the south came to an agreement and made a spectacular double entry into the capital, riding on horseback down the Paseo to the National Palace. The boulevard was jammed with watchers; even the most timid ventured forth to see the sight. The expansive Villa in his general's outfit towered high above Zapata, but the small-boned little fellow from the south far outshone the blustering giant in glory. He wore a charro suit with elaborate silver buttons parading up and down his tight trousers, and on his head was an enormous white sombrero so garnished with silver braid that it shone like a magnificent full moon in the morning sunlight. His white charger was so superb that foe and friend alike sighed over his matchless beauty. Though the notorious big bad man grinned from ear to ear and bowed as if all the applause were for himself alone, the little man in the twenty-gallon hat stole the show.

At the National Palace, just for the fun of it, Villa threw his great bulk into the presidential chair crowned with the winged eagle in gold leaf, and posed for photographers, first in one position and then another, smiling with expansive satisfaction whichever way he sat. In a more humble chair at his left curled the wide-eyed tense Zapata, almost hidden behind his massive hat and looking as ill at ease as a woods animal caught in city traffic.

The presidential chair of Mexico was no easy or secure seat. Within the brief period between September, 1914 and February, 1915, the possession of the capital and the chair changed hands six times. Whenever there was a switch in control, arrests and executions followed as in the days of the French Revolution. Prominent men had to be very nimble with their legs or their tongues not to be shot for treason. Reprisals begat worse reprisals.

For a stretch of years conditions were so explosive that Mexico came to be called "the land where peace breaks out once in a while." The wife of the American chargé d'affaires wrote: "Posting a letter may mean literally going to the cannon's mouth."

What the citizens had expected from the *zapatistas* they got in choking measure from the *villista* generals. A saturnalia of debauchery and thieving held the city in appalling thralldom, while Villa made the provisional president, Gutiérrez, a virtual prisoner, surrounding him with a "bodyguard" of two thousand soldiers. Soon most of the honest-purposed men who had supported Villa at the convention had sneaked off to hideouts. In his conceit, believing himself now invincible, Villa turned his fierce energies to *amours*. He took his women where he found them, and almost created a crisis with France by abducting a young hotel cashier who happened to be a French citizen. In broad noon, before the gaping populace, the Supreme Commander of Free Men carried the struggling girl out of the hotel and dumped her into his car.

While Pancho Villa was cutting such undignified capers in the capital, Carranza was carrying on his own government at Vera Cruz and for the first time in his life was ready to take advice. Though his majestic figure, set off with a venerable white beard, gave his presence something of the distinction of a Viking chieftain, Venustiano Carranza was really a "stuffed shirt." His patriarchal appearance, together with his tremendous powers of endurance—he could ride hard for days without showing fatigue —made some men take him at his own consummate valuation of himself. But at base he was uninspired. In his notorious tenacity (inherited from a good Basque ancestry) he was akin to the Indian democrat, Juárez; but in nothing else. He had no apostolic mission like Madero. His real passion was not to uplift the downtrodden masses, but to attain a kind of paternalistic power like that Díaz had possessed. He could not abide any interference with his will. Several times already he had told the United States government he was not interested in alien advice. And what he desired most from his own people was simply obedience. But since he had found himself evicted from the capital, he was willing for expediency's sake to listen to the counsel of wiser men. Obregón and Luis Cabrera advised him to make a definite swing to the left. From Vera Cruz, Carranza promulgated a series of reform decrees, the most significant one dealing with the agrarian problem. In the meantime, Obregón won for him the support of the industrial laborers by promises and bargaining. By force of circumstances the Revolution now began to bear some constructive reality.

As sporadic fighting continued, intrenched local wealth and American business in Mexico simultaneously became dubious of Carranza and began to look with favor on the fantastic Villa as one easier to handle. There were rumors that Villa would be recognized by the United States government in exchange for the gift of Lower California. With the bandit chieftain in complete control in the capital and almost two-thirds of the country, it did look for a while as if he were the "strong man of Mexico," no matter how he behaved personally. While Wall Street urged Villa's recognition, Obregón shrewdly built up the Carranza popularity at home by proclaiming him as the real revolutionary and Villa as a secret tool of reaction.

As Villa continued to cavort among the primroses on gaudy paths of dalliance, Obregón gave the *villista* forces a thorough trouncing at Puebla. Then he marched swiftly over the moun-tain to take possession of Mexico City. Villa hastily withdrew to the north, and Zapata slipped back south. People everywhere were kept on the move, fleeing for their lives from *hacienda* to town, from besieged town to mountain refuge. Crops were neglected. Fields grew rank with weeds. Marauders roamed and ranged, raiding towns and holding up carriages and wagons. A passenger took his life in his hands on any railroad journey in 1914-15. Though Mexicans love guns and cannon, they have an especial passion for dynamite, and now they indulged it freely by blowing up trains. In 1915 typhus in virulent form broke out. In 1916 the peso dropped to two cents. Some foodstuffs advanced over a thousand per cent. In the empty markets of the capital dressed alley cats sold for thirty pesos.

Obregón had to work with terrific energy to save the distressed city from actual starvation. He endeavored to stop hoarding, and doled out rations to the poor. He caused emergency taxes to be levied on the merchants and on the church. When the church refused payment, Obregón conscripted one hundred and eighty priests for armed service. The upper classes openly cursed the *ranchero* Obregón and the *hacendado* Carranza and prayed piously for the success of Villa, the roughneck.

When the capital was once more set in temporary order and Carranza was again established in the National Palace, Obregón decided to settle the contention with Villa once and forever if possible. He marched his army as far as Celaya. There he set up his defenses. Having made an intense study of modern methods of warfare, he utilized miles of barbed wire and had trenches dug as was being done in the great war raging in Europe. In the front trenches he stationed the straight-shooting Yaqui Indians with their fearless wives and steady-nerved offspring beside them to reload the rifles. Of all the Indians in Mexico the little, well-knit Yaquis from Sonora have ever been the most terrific fighters. They liked the brave and *simpático* Obregón, who knew he could depend on them to the last death. But he put his main dependence in lines of machine guns, plentifully supplied with ammunition and arranged in a half loop.

Villa made the mistake of attacking. With vaunting bravado he ordered his hitherto invincible cavalry forward, all singing the lusty *La Cucaracha*. For three horrific April days Villa sent his horsemen charging the barbed-wire entanglements. The impaled beasts and men were slaughtered by the machine guns and the Yaquis' quick, sure aim. Obregón won a decisive battle. But he exposed himself too courageously and his right arm was shattered by a grenade.

Villa saved his skin, but when he fled he lost everything else. Obregón deliberately coursed the bloody tracks of Villa's troops, even before the wound of his own amputated arm had properly healed. Thrice Villa turned to give battle, and thrice his forces were cut to pieces. His spell broken, his army began to wither away like frost-bitten bean-plants. Each day desertions diminished his ranks, until there was nothing left that might be called an army. Villa was not only deserted, but he was tricked and robbed by his own men. At last, riding alone, he returned to old, familiar haunts in Chihuahua, where friends of his outlaw days still revered him as a kind of Robin Hood. Pancho Villa's fabulous career had come full circle. He was back where he started. But twice again he was to flare as a climactic troublemaker.

President Wilson formally recognized the Carranza government in October, 1915. This dispensation meant no more guns and bullets across the border for Villa. The former Supreme Commander of Free Men brooded furiously for a while and then he decided to smack Uncle Sam across the face. In January his men held up a train, lined up the seventeen American passengers, and shot them down one by one. The incident did not bring on a war with the United States; so he determined on a more spectacular and provoking feat. In March he made his notorious raid on Columbus, New Mexico, and shot up the little border town, again killing seventeen American citizens. Indignation was so hot and high in the United States that, with voices clamoring for intervention, President Wilson felt impelled to do something drastic. He ordered General Pershing to take ten thousand troops and capture Villa dead, if he could not bring him back alive.

With scouting planes and artillery to supplement cavalry and infantry, Pershing's caravan set off across the desert of Chihuahua in pursuit of a wily will-o'-the-wisp. Accompanied by carloads of journalists to satisfy the newspaper readers at home, the soldiers trailed Villa by the horses his men had ridden to death and abandoned, to the delight of the buzzards. Sometimes they lost the trail in blinding sandstorms, and cursed and spit sand and cried it out of their stinging eyes. They went two hundred and seventy miles before they actually caught up with Villa's forces, which had now swelled because of Mexican resentment against the punitive Yankees. They routed the Mexicans, but Villa escaped. They chased him seven thousand feet up into the snow, where winds cut like razors. All through the rest of 1916 the man hunt went on, the Americans following false rumors and twice barely escaping ambush.

An ominous friction rose between Mexico and the United States. Carranza began protesting in strong language against the "invasion and violation of sovereignty." Finally, his military leaders, though sworn foes of Villa, notified General Pershing that if he advanced a mile farther he would meet with federal armed resistance. Despite the United States State Department's assurances that there would be no intervention, Carranza began to concentrate troops along the northern border. The American National Guard was sent to line up opposite them. At the beginning of July war was imminent. The United States government again advised all its citizens to leave Mexico. But nothing untoward happened in the next six months of futile searching, and on January second, 1917, Pershing was ordered to give up the chase. There was a more significant mission for him in Europe.

On February fifth, the punitive expedition came home after eleven months of ranging. It had been a failure in every respect. It had cost the United States not only $130,000,000, but losses in friendship and prestige. Every faction in Mexico resented it. Carranza was more surly than ever about any proposal the United States made thereafter, and his pro-German sympathies grew.

Hunters had never had less fun, whereas the chief hunted had apparently enjoyed himself hugely. But Villa had failed to bring on a war with the United States, which by his exasperating high jinks he seemed bent on inciting. While the Americans turned their bellicose energies to the conflagration in Europe, Villa continued for a while to play the dashing hit-and-run marauder among his own people. In some towns he paused long enough to burn out the eyes of persons alleged to have aided General Pershing, and once he permitted his bored officers the diversion of tearing harmless Chinese shopkeepers asunder by roping them between four horses and then whipping the horses off in four different directions.

After a few years of making a mortal nuisance of himself, the old rapscallion was seduced into pastoral quietude when a high official presented him with a handsome estate in Durango. Here soon he seemed to take as much pride in showing off his tractor at work as he once did in reviewing his magnificent Dorado cavalry. He professed to be completely in love with private citizenship. He babbled enthusiastically of the school he had built for his laborers' little ones. His conversation again became emotional about the dream in his heart for uplifting the downtrodden. But in the summer of 1923 he was assassinated. While on his way into a nearby town for supplies, with two bodyguards, his car was riddled with bullets from an ambush and he died with his boots on. Supposedly, he was killed to prevent his rushing into public life again to oppose the presidential candidacy of his bitter enemy, General Plutarco Elías Calles. His funeral was without a touch of pomp. The stirring cry of *Viva Villa!* was never again to rouse the rabble, except in folksong.

# 19. A Great Constitution Is Born

*"The people have been mocked in their hopes."*

EMILIANO ZAPATA

To hold his power, Carranza had seemed willing to go to almost any length, except to truckle to the United States government. Like Díaz, he permitted strategic people who were useful to him to graft so outrageously that malicious wits substituted a coined verb "to Carranza" for the verb "to steal" and the public gleefully took it up. Though the president himself had no need to steal—he was already well-to-do and his social position was superior to that of his closest lieutenants—his government was palpably corrupt. But Carranza knew that if he precipitously checked theft and the spoils of victory he might be thrown out of office. He could be powerfully scrupulous in his defense of Mexican sovereignty, however. His enemies might call him the most obscene names in the Mexican vocabulary, but they invariably admitted that "Old Whiskers" could handle the international situation. They praised him as "a patriot who could save the nation from the Yankees." Now he was to be tested as a patriot who could save the nation from the Mexicans.

Pershing's punitive expedition had whipped up a surge of nationalism and made the Mexican populace eager for anti-foreign and anti-conservative legislation. When a convention met in November of 1916, to revise the constitution of 1857, such radical measures as were passed might not have been devised and accepted if there had been no invasion from the north.

The delegates met at Querétaro in the old Iturbide Theater, where Maximilian had been condemned to death. For seventy days the new constitution was abornin'. Carranza himself had laboriously prepared a mild document with the emphasis on political, not social, reform. But some delegates were determined that the constitution should do justice to laborer and peasant. Obregón, with his mildly progressive views, his seasoned common sense and his wide popularity, added potent weight to the force of the left-wingers.

When the constitution finally emerged on February fifth, 1917 —the very day the last American soldier marched out of Mexico —it proved to be one of the most important documents of modern times. By its articles it purposed to transform Mexico's social structure. It was a magnificent victory for the underprivileged and for the independent nationalism of Mexico—on paper. Though successive presidents and supreme court justices have wrangled mightily over the interpretation of the various subheadings of its articles, the constitution has remained a standard for testing every individual act of each government that followed.

The hero of the constitution was a youngish revolutionary general, Francisco Múgica, born the son of a rural schoolmaster in Michoacán. Stocky, strong-jawed, with disciplined dynamic energy, Múgica was the mainspring of the convention from the beginning. He had studied the Indian problem in the north and in the middle of Mexico and in Tabasco. He had come to the convention fired with intelligent and practical ideals of reform and the determination to put his ideas into concrete measures. Múgica had the unofficial aid of the brilliant Molina Enríquez, who worked with him in committee, though the latter was not an official delegate.

Around four articles controversy has raged, and by these same four Mexico has made its chief radical gains. The two most famous sections were Article 27 and Article 123. Article 27 concerned division of land and the property rights of Mexican citizens and foreigners. Article 123 is generally referred to as labor's

Magna Carta. Next in significance were Articles 3 and 130 which dealt with education and the church.

By Article 27 the state was to own all the subsoil wealth and have the control of water. Oil and mineral concessions to foreigners were to be limited. No foreigner could own land in a prohibited zone thirty miles from the seacoast and within sixty miles of the border. Such expropriation as was necessary for the public welfare could be demanded.

Section 1 (e) of Article 27 stated precisely: "The nation's ownership of waters and minerals is direct and imprescriptible; only the 'right of exploitation' of the nation's waters and subsoil may be conceded to private parties, and that only on the condition that the resources be regularly developed and the right legally exercised."

Section 2 (1) decreed: "Only Mexicans by birth or naturalization and Mexican companies have the right to acquire ownership in lands, waters and their appurtenances or to obtain concessions to develop mines, waters, or mineral fuels in the Republic of Mexico. The nation may grant the same right to foreigners, provided they agree to be considered Mexicans in respect of such property, and accordingly not to involve the protection of their government in respect of the same."

Section 2 (2) decreed that: "Churches shall have no legal capacity to acquire, hold or administer real property or loans on real property."

Besides thus dealing with foreign investors and the church, Article 27 set up "Principles and Procedures for the Solution of the Agrarian Problem." It established the meaning of *ejido*— "the waters, woods and lands which the village may need." It vested the title of *ejidos* in the village as a whole. It decreed that villages which had been deprived of their lands should have the lands restored.

The law further provided that the nation should undertake to recover the public lands and waters alienated under the Díaz regime in prejudice of the public interest. All *ejido* lands taken from the Indian villages since the Juárez administration were to be restored. The land hunger of independent peasants was to be satisfied by taking acreage from the *haciendas* and compensating the owners with government bonds.

Article 27 brought a howl from all conservative elements—foreign big business, the oil and mining companies, the large estate owners, and the church. Article 123 also dismayed capital, for it was designed to give Mexican labor a fair deal. It legalized the right of workers to form unions, to bargain collectively, and to strike. It established an eight-hour working day with double pay for overtime. It provided compensation for accident or occupational disease. It abolished labor for children under twelve. It provided special protection for women workers; no heavy work during the last three months of pregnancy and a month's leave of absence with pay following childbirth. Large industries were obligated to provide schools for employees' children. No man's children could be henceforth held liable for his debts.

Article 3 was devised principally against the Catholic church's influence in education, which Díaz had allowed to assume a pre-Juárez emphasis. Public education was to become strictly a government function. Any but secular primary education was declared illegal. By Article 130 there were to be no more foreign priests in Mexico. Henceforth all priests were required to register with the civil authorities. To the various state legislatures was granted the power to limit the number of priests within their jurisdiction.

"Mexico, in theory at any rate," as Eyler Simpson said, "achieved at one bound what many other countries have been struggling step by step to obtain." It is one of Mexico's many little ironies that the conservative Carranza—the nearest in spirit of all subsequent presidents to Porfirio Díaz—should have been the chief executive when the famous reform constitution of 1917 was passed. Forces with which he had no sympathy and which he could not even comprehend carried the day. But though he was persuaded to make use of the political strategy of reform, he purposed to handle the reform measures in his own dictatorial way. Of course, Carranza might have sabotaged the whole thing. It adds greatly to his stature that no matter how sour he felt towards various articles, he let the constitution pass with its full radical measures.

Amid wild enthusiasm, those of the masses who were literate read of the new constitution as if the millennium would come with the dawn. But Carranza considered the Revolution accomplished merely with his formal inauguration in March. He prepared to brush aside the "fanciful" ideas of the constitution and revert to the good old days after his own fashion. As a sop to the radicals, however, 48,000 families out of the millions of the land-hungry received land. Though Carranza expropriated vast tracts of private property from his enemies, only 450,000 acres were distributed among the people. Many single individuals still owned considerably more territory than the redivided total. As for labor, Carranza had no notion of letting the industrial workers get uppity. When an electricians' strike occurred in Mexico City, he called it treason, and the leader was sentenced to death. Though the condemned man was reprieved, many another striker about the country was lynched. In general, the new rights accorded workers were as ignored as if they had never been inscribed in the constitution.

Back in Morelos was Zapata, watching and waiting, with faint faith in Carranza's good intentions. He signed an open letter to the president in which he accused him of trying to convert the Revolution into a movement for his own gain and that of his little group of friends. "It has never crossed your mind," he declared bitterly, "that the Revolution was for the benefit of the masses, for that great legion of the oppressed which you aroused with your preachings. The *ejidos* have not been returned to the villages . . . nor have lands been distributed to the workers, the poor peasants and those truly in need . . . Your soldiers steal seeds, cattle and work-animals; in the small towns, they burn and loot the homes of humble citizens; and in the cities they speculate with the grain they have stolen." His stinging accusations were crowned by the cry, "The people have been mocked in their hopes."

So Zapata, a communist who had never read of communism, kept up his fight for the rights of the poor. His ragged army rallied again and again to the most stirring of all the Revolution's slogans: "Men of the South! It is better to die on your feet than to live on your knees." That was the voice of Zapata speaking from the heart, though he was hardly sufficiently literate himself to pen the words that were to become world-famous.

To still the accusing utterance and to break forever the peasants' revolt in Morelos, Carranza sent General Pablo González into the sugar state. González indulged in an orgy of earth-scorching. He burned down the miserable huts of innocent country folk, hanged and tortured non-combatants. Worst of all, he destroyed their meager makeshift farm implements. But no fury or havoc could break the power of Zapata. At last the *jefe* was caught by a devilish trick in which Col. Jesús Guajardo pretended to be converted to the agrarian side, and cold-bloodedly shot down a detachment of his own troops to prove it. Zapata was deceived. He consented to confer with the federal, who was to render him great assistance. He went for a rendezvous to a certain *hacienda*. With his visionary eyes aglow with his mission, he rode into the great courtyard to a flourish of welcoming bugles. He was met with a blaze of rifle fire. Zapata died literally on his feet, "still fighting for agrarian justice two years after Article 27 of the 1917 constitution had made land distribution a part of the basic law."

To prove that he and all he stood for were dead, the leader's mangled body was brought by muleback and displayed in the town of Cuautla on April tenth, 1919. But to the peasants who passed worshipfully by the bier the dead commander was metamorphosed into a deity. Though his wretched armies dispersed, his influence remained like an enduring light, and within a few years the peasants legally received the land they suffered so to obtain.

Carranza, who had become more and more unpopular with most factions, because of his stubbornness and conceit, determined not to relinquish control when his term was up. He dared not go so far as to stand for re-election, but he selected as his puppet successor a mediocrity who was currently the Mexican ambassador in Washington. The vast majority of the people wanted Obregón for president, the man without whom Carranza could never have reached the National Palace. For all of his natural amiability, Obregón had not been able to endure Carranza's petulance and domineering ways and his heavy intelligence, so he had retired from the earlier intimacy with the chief. To keep from being cheated, Obregón's indignant friends decided swiftly on revolution. The leader was Adolfo de la Huerta, governor of Sonora. His second was the able Plutarco Elías Calles. Both men had fought for Carranza under Obregón. Their cue came when the president sent federal troops into Sonora to break a railroad employees' strike. The revolutionists, claiming violation of state's rights, demanded the removal of Carranza and the appointment of a provisional president until a proper election could be held. As the rebellious bands from the north came south with a great singing, their army swelled into a tidal wave of allegiance to Obregón.

Carranza had ever known how queasy was his tenancy in the presidential chair. To defend it, under the somber dignity of his frock coat he had invariably carried concealed a long, black pistol. But when the hour came it did not save him. A single weapon could not halt a tidal wave. Realizing that he must flee, but hardly knowing which way to run, Carranza telegraphed to General Guadalupe Sánchez, to whom he had been as generous as a doting parent. The commander at Vera Cruz replied by wire: "President and father, though everyone else betray you, I shall not. If but one man remain loyal to you, I am that man."

The fugitive train for Vera Cruz was ordered prepared—or, rather, twenty-one trains were readied, for this flight was to be on the grand scale. Not only were the few real friends like the incorruptibly loyal Francisco Urquizo to accompany the president, but a group of self-seeking politicians as well as the cabinet, the supreme court and some of the congressmen. Twenty thousand soldiers came along to protect the public servants and the quantities of gold pieces and treasure variously estimated at between twenty-seven and a hundred million.

The flight began as a comedy of errors and confusions, and ended in disaster and tragedy. The trains were attacked shortly after they left the capital. Their artillery was lost; four trains got sidetracked. There were days of delays here and there along the short route. General Sánchez proved perfidious, went over to Obregón, who had entered Mexico City shortly after the exodus. Carranza's troops were defeated, his trains stalled. He knew there was no hope of reaching Vera Cruz by rail. On horseback he escaped into the mountains. A local chieftain named Herrero offered to be his guide and guardian over the rough terrain to Tampico. On the night of May eighteenth, in an Indian hut in the wilderness, as the tired old man was quietly sleeping, his guardian shot him dead and gave it out that Carranza had committed suicide. His body was brought to Mexico City six days later and buried in the Dolores cemetery with proper honor and ceremony.

By most commentators Carranza's administration is harshly condemned and considered remarkable for corruption in a country where political corruption has been exceeding rank. But it should be recalled that Carranza inherited Mexican chaos and managed to bring some order to the land. In any tribunal one

should not ignore the evidence that it was Carranza who instigated and led the rebellion against the villainous Huerta. He
ever stood out boldly for Mexico's national sovereignty. He refused to bow low to foreign capital or subscribe to any foreign
interference. And, however ingrown his personal, conservative
principles were, it was during his regime that the agrarian revolution won its decisive constitutional victory when the constitution of 1917 was conceived and passed, "as bold and statesmanlike an action as has been recorded in the annals of Mexico."

# PART EIGHT

# MEN FROM SONORA

## 20. The Happy Man with One Arm

*"Poor Mexico—so far from God and so near to the United States."*

PORFIRIO DÍAZ

The day after Carranza's funeral, Adolfo de la Huerta, a young-ish radical from Sonora, was made temporary president to finish out the six months of the unexpired term. He chose a liberal cabinet, including General Plutarco Elías Calles as minister of war. Obregón, who everybody knew would be the next president, did not fill a cabinet post in the interim, but he remained in the capital and maintained an office, "obeying the new regime," as he pleasantly expressed it. At the presidential elections that came in September there was no opposition. The one-armed hero was inaugurated president at the end of November.

Mexico as a whole was enthusiastically behind Alvaro Obregón. Perhaps there was no one then alive better equipped with common sense and force and kindliness to tackle the formidable job, to calm the nation after a decade of bewilderment and savagery, and to steer the destinies of Mexico out of the slough of semi-feudalism towards an enlightened prospect of democracy. Mexico needed just such a realist of the first order as the genial, hard-fighting Obregón.

Like Madero and Carranza, the new president was a creole, but he did not belong to the upper classes as they did. One set of his grandparents had come over from Spain—poor folk, "doubtless driven to emigrate by sheer hunger," as he himself said. The other set of grandparents were picked up in Mexico and though they were of a lineage which makes it impossible to say positively there was no strain of Indian blood, it is generally conceded that Obregón was pure white. He remained a rough diamond to the end, by choice. He despised folderol. There was nothing whatever paradeful about him. He was a farmer, a *ranchero,* not a *hacendado.* He was also a business man, a wholesale dealer in chick peas. His formal education was limited, but he had an unusually receptive mind and he was an astute judge of men. He knew values. He was hard to fool. He was not selflessly inspired as was Madero. He was a practical man of affairs, with ambition, a humanitarian outlook, and a healthy sense of humor. Despite his faith in himself, he was somewhat surprised to find that he possessed the military genius to become one of the greatest Mexican generals of all times.

A born leader, as engaging as shrewd, he was also an able organizer and executive. His sense of balance made him know when to compromise. He was never in danger of an ideal swaying him too far. Though a forceful and persuasive speaker, he was too earthy ever to become lyrical in his thinking. He found life an exciting adventure, and in his last years he warmed his one hand at its metaphorical fires with more satisfying ardor than most men could with twice their two hands. He took his drinks neat and plentiful, but he never had hangovers. His easy familiarity of manner was the same to men of every class. Little children adored him. Dogs instinctively trusted him. His smile was frank and warming, with sometimes a *soupçon* of amiable mockery. Even after he became president he was still careless of his dress, wearing unpressed suits and a weather-stained old panama. This was not affectation; he felt more comfortable that way. His conversation was as unconventional and casual as his clothes. His trick of always saying the unpredictable made him pungently entertaining and a "natural" for front-page copy. As a wisecracker he was unsurpassed among his fellows.

Though there was plenty of fun in this ruddy-faced, chubby new president, there was no more nonsense than there was illusion. He had a remarkably clear picture of the needs of the people of the time. He allowed the Mexicans just as much liberty as he thought good for them. He was determined not to let the peace be broken if he could help it. Unlike Madero, he knew they wanted bread more than freedom. He believed that the uplift of the masses must come by gradual evolution. To illiterate Indians could not be given middle-class responsibilities overnight. Economic welfare came next in importance after peace, and then as large doses of agrarian justice and elementary education as the country could afford.

Obregón's task was not only to make "an amicable adjustment between white Mexico and Indian Mexico," but to placate foreign capital, while suggesting to his people that he was being tough with foreigners. He had the misfortune to come into power at the same time that Harding became the Republican President of the United States, when Albert B. Fall and Edward L. Doheny, the oil sharks, carried such weight with the government.

Though the Harding administration looked upon him as a bolshevik of deepest crimson, Obregón was not even a socialist. He refused to make too wide a breach in the *hacienda* system. He did not believe land redistribution should come with a wrenching violent enough to disrupt the national economy. In his term of office he distributed 3,000,000 acres among 624 villages—not much, perhaps, but almost seven times Carranza's record. But he did not intend to risk crop shortages by giving too much land to Indians who might not work for themselves after they had it. Many would raise barely enough for their own families, and felt no responsibility as farmers to help feed the rest of the nation. Some who received twenty or thirty acres of land would cultivate one acre for themselves and let the rest go to weeds. Even in Morelos, where the peasants, shortly after Zapata's death, had got the land they had fought for, there was discontent. Among the new small freeholders, who had not yet the skill to manage for themselves, many pleaded openly for the return of the *hacienda*.

Though Obregón supported the labor unions and strongly urged labor to organize so that industrial wages would rise, he had no patience when labor troubles disrupted production. While giving protection to workers, Obregón astutely fostered native capitalism. He tried to instill some constructive energy into his people, and he saw the creation of native industries as a step towards the gradual supplanting of foreign capital.

For education he did far more than had ever been done by any preceding president. The famous José Vasconcelos, Obregón's minister of education, is really the father of popular education in Mexico. But it was Obregón who chose Vasconcelos to do the job, and he gave his minister vital encouragement and as much of the state funds as he could possibly allot at the time. Almost a thousand rural schools were built under the Obregón administration. Vasconcelos not only built schools and created libraries, but he tried to make the schools cultural centers of the villages, and he sometimes even fed warm breakfasts to the smaller children.

The practical Obregón winked at the surreptitious continuation of church schools, which had been outlawed by the 1917 constitution. "Of course we are not unaware of the menace of these Catholic schools," he confessed. "We know well enough their aim is to inculcate anti-government and anti-revolutionary propaganda. But the government hasn't the money or the facilities to teach all the children of Mexico. Church schools are illegal, yes; but it is preferable that children receive any instruction rather than grow up illiterate."

He was pleased that Vasconcelos never spoke of "the Indian

problem," but always of "the problem of ignorance." He liked Vasconcelos's way of putting it: "Ignorance made worse by the indifference and even the downright cruelty of those who, possessing wealth and education, have done nothing whatsoever to benefit their fellowmen." But he could not help but be amused sometimes at Vasconcelos's vision as compared with Mexican actualities.

Vasconcelos had the zeal of a redeemer. He decided the people should read and read the best, and he had vast editions of the classics printed to distribute among them. Verna Carleton Millán gives perhaps the most authentic version of a much-told story which casts a revealing light on the basic situation in Mexico:

Once, when Obregón and Vasconcelos had escaped from the presidential train which they were warned was to be attacked by rebels, they became lost in wild, unfamiliar territory. On horseback they pushed on for hours, and finally came upon a lone hut. The old Indian standing by the door was astounded to see strangers in his remote domain.

Obregón called to him with that friendly common-denominator manner that men rarely failed to respond to: "Friend, can you tell me where we are?"

The man shook his head.

"But what place is this?"

The man shrugged.

"What town are we near?"

"Who knows?"

"Were you born here?"

"Yes."

"And your wife, too?"

"Yes."

Obregón carefully enunciated his last question. "You and your wife were both born here—you've always lived here—yet you still do not know where you are?"

"No," the old man reaffirmed with unperturbed indifference.

The president turned to his minister of education and said, with amused irony, "Make a note of this man, José, so that you can send him copies of the classics you have just edited."

Though Obregón kept the peace, though Mexico was more prosperous than she had been for more than a decade, though patently he represented the great majority of the population, the United States under the Republican President Harding withheld recognition. Harding was hand-in-glove with the oil men who were still boiling with fury because the Mexicans had reaffirmed in the constitution of 1917 the ancient Spanish and Mexican legal principle that the nation's subsoil wealth belongs to the state. At the very time that a group of American oil men was hoping to possess eternally the oil of Mexico, this same group was trying to sell the United States oil reserve that belonged to the navy. The notorious Teapot Dome scandal which cost President Harding his reputation and perhaps his life was just brewing.

From the beginning, Obregón had insisted that Article 27 should not be retroactive. But the Harding government refused to recognize the government of Obregón unless the president signed a treaty to that effect, which would guarantee American property rights acquired in Mexico before May first, 1917. The United States administration considered the reform program in Mexico a threat to American vested interests, and demanded "adequate safeguards" in the form of a treaty. Secretary of State Hughes drew up a pact called a "Treaty of Amity and Commerce," which was presented to Obregón on May twenty-seventh, 1921, less than three months after Harding took office.

According to the authoritative Dr. Rippy, the crux of the matter lay in four provisions: (1) Assurance that nationals of either country residing in the other would enjoy all the privileges of native citizens; (2) reciprocal guaranties against confiscation and expropriation, except for public purposes, and after "prompt payment of just compensation"; (3) assurances against the retroactive application to American citizens of Carranza's agrarian decree of January sixth, 1915, and of the provisions of the 1917 constitution; (4) restoration to American citizens, whenever possible, of the property rights of which they may have been deprived since 1910 and adequate compensation for all losses suffered on account of such deprivation.

Diplomatic assurances were not deemed sufficient. The United States government demanded a treaty. Obregón refused to accept recognition on such high-handed conditions. He considered it humiliating to the national dignity to do so. Besides, no matter how he may have felt about the increased business that would come to Mexico with official recognition, he had to be wary not to make obeisance to Wall Street in the sight of his own people. The spirit of nationalism had been waxing ever since the Pershing chase after Villa.

The matter dragged on unsettled for almost two years. In a note of March thirty-first, 1923, from Obregón's foreign minister, Alberto Pani, to Secretary of State Hughes, it was pointed out how the Mexican supreme court had "defined in an unmistakable manner—in five cases of injunction—the nonretroactive character of Article 27 in that part relative to petroleum. The Mexican minister also cited statistics which revealed that the entire petroleum industry in Mexico was capitalized at $1,050,532,-434. Of this amount American and British interests owned 91.5 per cent. The Mexicans themselves held an insignificant 1.1 per cent of their own oil wealth.

Pani regretted that American citizens had suffered losses when the Mexican government granted some *ejidos* to the villages that had once owned the acreage. He regretted, too, that the crises of the times had not permitted immediate indemnity in cash. But, after all, he pointed out, Obregón had "extinguished a destructive agrarian revolt at the cost of serious injury to only a few landowners," including a mere twenty-six American citizens. In summing up Obregón's and Mexico's case, Pani wrote, with remarkable restraint: "Considering all this, the damages to the American agricultural properties will never justify the systematic resistance, worthy of a better cause, which the United States has been opposing to the currents of sympathy, created and developed under the protection of the goodwill of the government of Mexico."

It is believed that Secretary Hughes felt a bit ashamed of his course. At any rate, since Hughes saw that Obregón would not be coerced into signing the treaty, within a few weeks after the Pani note he changed his methods and sent two commissioners to Mexico to negotiate for recognition. Certainly, public opinion in the United States was against the Harding and Hughes attitude to Mexico, and many business men and bankers were clamoring for recognition.

From May fourteenth to August fifteenth the two American commissioners conferred with two Mexican commissioners. At length they arrived at what passed for a satisfactory mutual agreement. But the impasse was really broken only because of Obregón's cleverness in playing the American bankers off against the oil men, in causing the bankers to press for recognition so that they could begin collecting interest on loans. To insure a peaceful presidential succession, Obregón had felt that United States recognition would be worth whatever compromise he might make from the standpoint of expediency. He made some slight concessions, agreed to pay compensation for the revolution's damages to American property, and reaffirmed that Article 27 would not be interpreted as retroactive. A storm of protest from a portion of the Mexican public greeted the announcement of the terms. Obregón's enemies found excuse to accuse him of selling out to the United States. On September third, 1923, after Obregón had been president for almost three years, the United States recognized his government.

The belated recognition helped avert a complete overthrow,

but it did not circumvent a revolt. With his astute judgment, Obregón had chosen Plutarco Elías Calles, his secretary of interior, for his successor. Calles was recognized as a man of uncommon ability, but he was not generally popular, because he refused to waste energy in winning friends. And because he professed socialism, the generals with a passion for loot, as well as estate owners, the Catholic church, and the British oil companies, straightway created an opposition and backed Adolfo de la Huerta, Obregón's long-time friend and the incumbent minister of the treasury, a former radical who had become progressively more conservative. Soon another counter-revolution was in full blast. It took three bloody months to squash it. Again there flared the traditional betrayals and flagrant displays of callous opportunism. In Obregón, however, there was none of Madero's chicken-hearted compassion for troublemakers. He ordered every captured rebel officer above the rank of major to be shot.

"But you can't shoot me," cried a young reactionary attorney, Francisco Treviño, who had been caught with the de la Huerta forces. "I am not even a soldier. The penal code does not prescribe the death penalty for insurrection." Obregón's bluff minister of war, Francisco Serrano, with tragicomic grace immediately signed an order appointing Lawyer Treviño a "General in the Mexican Army." At the bottom of the page he added a mordant postscript: "Shoot General and Lawyer Francisco Treviño."

Adolfo de la Huerta was more fortunate; he escaped to California and became a singing teacher. His little flair of self-gratification as a tool of the reactionaries had cost his hard-up nation sixty million pesos. A vast deal of Obregón's constructive work had been sabotaged by the unworthy rebellion.

Obregón's record, like that of all Mexican rulers, is a subject of controversy. But unquestionably the Revolution had gone forward. Under him, Mexico was the first of the so-called "back-

ward" nations of the world to allow labor to organize. He gave
Mexico a taste of democracy by permitting the press to go un-
censored. He let the opposition rail against him in congress. He
himself went about unarmed and without a bodyguard. It was
a brave practice, for Obregón was bitterly hated by the "outs,"
who resented his favoritism. Of course, he did some spoils-divid-
ing. He was over-indulgent with his friends—it is said he would
sometimes even pay his minister of war's gambling debts out of
the national treasury. "All of us are thieves, more or less, down
here," he engagingly joked with Blasco Ibáñez. "However, the
point is that I have only one hand, while the others have two.
That's why the people prefer me."

The people had preferred him because he was the best material they could find at the time for the job, because he was a man
of sound sense, without the arrogance and absurdities of the
logician, or the rapt fantasy of the visionary. They liked him
because his smile won their hearts and because he was fearless
and clever.

Except for the bothersome revolt of de la Huerta and the
meanness of the Harding government in withholding recognition, Obregón had enjoyed his arduous administration. He had
set Mexico on the road to achieve modern democracy. But, with
his unflinching estimate of human nature, he knew that the road
would not run straight, that it would twist to right and left,
and make time-wasting detours both ways. He knew, too, the
brakes that lay submerged in each revolutionist. He knew himself. "We can get rid of clericalism," he said with a half-wink,
"and we can get rid of capitalism, but who is going to get rid
of us?" And again, in the same vein, he said more seriously:
"The bitter fruit of all our previous revolutions has been that
we could not rid ourselves of the liberators."

But when Calles, the one-time rural school teacher, was elected
president, Obregón did not try to run the government. He went

back to the private life of a *ranchero* and a wholesale dealer in chick peas. Still he kept a more than casual eye on the presidential chair and was prepared to occupy it again when Calles went out—if the people really wanted him and if it could be arranged.

# 21. Big Boss

*"The Mexican Revolution is not over yet, nor will it take less than a century to accomplish fruition."*
WALDO FRANK

President Calles carried the Revolution farther than Obregón. The sincerity of his original ideology can hardly be doubted. Some of his statements call to mind words of Franklin D. Roosevelt when the latter launched the New Deal almost a decade later. Calles wrote:

The ideal of my government is to save the great masses of the population from misery and ignorance, to raise their social standard, to teach them to eat better, to give them schools and culture, to raise them to a higher level of civilization, so as to construct a homogeneous nation, closing the existing gulf between a handful of Mexicans who enjoy comfort, refinement and well-being, and the great mass of Mexicans, exploited by every tyranny, abandoned by every administration, buried in misery, darkness and suffering.

I prefer . . . to carry on this humanitarian task—even if by so doing my Government is marked with the name of Bolshevist which propaganda is giving it. I leave to time to pass the difficult final judgment.

Time passed a very different judgment from the one Calles had in mind when he penned his eloquent credo. Though he accomplished much for Mexico, as the years ticked by the young radical socialist appeared to go the way of all flesh. At the end of his rule he had become a plausible conservative. Like Prime Minister Ramsay MacDonald, who was beguiled into giving over the Socialist cause in England, Calles, by his actions, seemed to renounce the constructive principles of some of his most pro-

274

gressive work. At any rate, he himself halted the Revolution. "So far and no farther," he at length decreed.

Like Obregón, Calles came from the rugged northern state of Sonora. The birthplace was a very humble house in the pretty seaport town of Guaymas. His mother was part Yaqui Indian, and the tale often goes that his father was the "improvident son of an itinerant Armenian." But there is no more truth in this report than in that which says he is Jewish. Calles's blood is predominantly Spanish. Because of a near-East cast of his features, Plutarco earned his nickname of "El Turco." Without being what the Latins call *simpático*—as Obregón was and as Franklin Roosevelt is—the man had a dynamic fascination. His was a highly intelligent, dark and subtle face that came to be deeply lined and prematurely aged. The close-cropped mustache added a kind of distinction. His piercing hazel eyes seemed to accuse one of dubious motives. The jaw was square-cut, strong like those of his Yaqui ancestors. Because of a fundamental vein of hard metal in his character, this grim and taciturn man won the title of the "Iron Man" of revolutionary Mexico. A born organizer, he had something of that relentless will which dominated both Juárez and Díaz. But, though a master craftsman in politics, he had less camaraderie than Díaz and a more flexible intelligence than Juárez. By sheer force of ability and statecraft he was able to maintain power from his inauguration on December first, 1924, to beyond the ascendancy of Cárdenas in 1934, though there were three other presidents in the interim.

Calles was named Plutarco Elías, but as a boy he lived with a relative of his mother named Juan Calles, and he adopted the name of his foster-father, which was also the name of his mother. His education did not extend to college, but it was sufficient to secure him a position as a rural elementary school teacher when he was seventeen. Early life was largely a typical Mexican struggle against poverty. Young Calles tried farming, journalism and bartending to keep the pot boiling for his wife and children. In his mid-thirties he turned to the more lucrative politics, and became a frontier chief of police at Agua Prieta. From here he gravitated into the Revolution, rising swiftly under Obregón from lieutenant to general. Calles's authority was such that men instinctively obeyed him, not out of affection but because of an aura of determination and superior judgment that hung about him. He was a man more respected than loved. However, the orphans at the Cruz Galvez Industrial School, which he built for their protection and education, affectionately called him "Papa Calles," because he would "encourage them with broad smiles, as he praised a specimen of a girl's needlework or of a boy's cobblery," and because he would himself take the orphans' handiwork to sell in the cities to raise money to keep the school going.

After serving as military commander of Sonora in 1916, Calles became governor of the state. When Obregón was elected president he brought Calles to the capital as secretary of interior, the chief position in the Mexican cabinet. And finding him the ablest and most dependable of his ministers, he began grooming him for the presidency.

The upper classes and business men were horrorstruck at the thought of such a radical in prime control. "God help us if that bolshevik Calles becomes president," they cried. Unlike Obregón, Calles at first made no attempt to conciliate the capitalists. In fact, he well aired his hatred and contempt for them. His support came from laborers and farm workers, intellectual radicals, and the middle classes. The estate owners, the church, and big business opposed him with vehemence and vituperation. And when he assumed the presidency he straightway sheared all three groups of a vast deal of power and privilege.

From the first, Calles intended to be a benevolent dictator. He was as chary of too much liberality as he was zealous about progress. Being a remarkably astute politician, however, he played his cards with as much skill as vigor. He demanded efficiency of his chosen officeholders and spoke so feelingly of honesty that the officials who did steal were very careful to be unwontedly moderate in their rake-offs. Though he had to keep the army in an amiable state of mind, he brought about some drastic reforms. He purged it of its incompetents, but to these he gave land and farm implements and some financial assistance to start them off. The peacock-splendid uniforms of the officers were abolished. Gold and blue and magenta gave way to sober khaki, which officers were forced to buy for themselves. Fifteen thousand illiterate soldiers were taught to read and write and reckon. Barracks became schools, just as rural schools became realities. "Universal elementary education," Calles declared, "is Mexico's crying need."

The new president made it clear that the chief purpose of his administration was "the bettering of the Mexican people," but he warned them not to expect a millennium. "It is a task," he said, "that requires in many cases the laying of new foundations and of building upon them slowly and steadily, stone upon stone." Though the de la Huerta rebellion had left the nation's treasury worse than empty, by his shrewd economy the president was able to show extraordinary achievement at the end of his first fiscal year. He had made up a deficit of almost fifty million pesos, paid some internal debts, resumed payment on foreign debts, balanced the budget, and established a national bank with a reserve of more than sixty million pesos. No one else since Limantour had revealed so much talent for finance.

Not only did Calles reform the army set-up, build four thousand schools, strengthen the nation's financial position, and discharge twenty thousand government employees, but he encouraged labor and gave his special presidential blessing to the *Confederación Regional Obrera Mexicana* (CROM), which more or less corresponded to the American Federation of Labor. He considered trade unions indispensable to the capitalistic system. "The trade unions," he said, "stand or fall by capitalism. But they should never intervene in political matters. Their sphere is purely economic, and once they meddle in politics they lose their character and their significance."

Calles did more road building than any precedent chief executive. Modern macadam highways were laid with an eye for scenic beauty as well as practical engineering. A series of irrigation projects were instituted. In less than three years after his inauguration Calles had brought the budget for public health to fourteen times the figure allotted by Porfirio Díaz. The record in general looked good.

In land reform, however, the president fell far short of pleasing the radical agrarians, though in his four years in actual office he redistributed some eight million acres among fifteen hundred villages. Calles, for political reasons, had proclaimed himself the heir to Zapata. To make every peasant a proprietor is the best way of avoiding revolution and political unrest, he said. Many of the estates which had swallowed up vast tracts of land under Porfirio Díaz were now made to disgorge. The lands expropriated were paid for in government bonds at ten per cent above the assessed tax valuation, which meant that the government got the land dirt-cheap. But in title adjustments Calles came up against the old Adam in human nature. The village politicians often proved tricky and rapacious. For the new home-owners he created agricultural banks to lend them money. But the local banker-politicians betrayed their humble fellows and lent most of the money not to the poor, but to the rich estate owners in the district who would be sure to repay and who would advance the money lender politically. It was partly his disappointment in the villagers' inability to get along together and their lack of interest in national production that made Calles finally halt his agrarian reform program.

In his triple fight against the *hacendados,* big business, and the church, it was the church that proved to be his most formidable enemy and the stoutest impediment to the success of the

Revolution. From youth Calles had been anti-clerical, and, reviewing history, he had convinced himself that the Roman Catholic church constituted "a perpetual menace to the Mexican state
and a permanent obstacle to social progress." He knew the full
extent of its power over the peasantry. In his first year in office
he wrote out a statement for the press in regard to his attitude
to the church: "I am an enemy of the priestly class which considers its position in the light of privilege and not of evangelical service. I am an enemy of the political priest who tries to
keep our people submerged in ignorance, the priest who is allied
with the landlord to exploit the peasant, and the priest who is
allied with the employer to exploit the worker. I declare that I
respect all religions and all creeds so long as their preachers do
not meddle in our political conflicts, spurn our laws, and allow
themselves to become tools of the powerful in the exploitation
of the weak."

The showdown came in 1926, when the Archbishop of Mexico
declared in a public statement that the church did not and could
not accept the religious provisions of the constitution of 1917.
Calles immediately instituted strengthening legislation to enforce those provisions as set forth in Articles 3 and 130. The
clergy refused to obey that part of the constitution which limited
their numbers and which forbade foreign priests from entering
Mexico. In answer to their defiance, Calles began deporting
foreign-born priests and nuns by the hundreds. Monasteries were
turned into public schools. The church was deprived of legal
standing; it could not make use of private property, real or
personal.

In retaliation, on July thirty-first, 1926, the church announced
its refusal to hold any services whatsoever. The priestly sit-down
strike continued for three years. Masses and christenings were
bootlegged in private homes. But committees of private citizens
were made responsible by the government for keeping the
churches open, so the people could go and pray when they

would, and never were they to be asked to contribute a centavo.

A few ill-advised priests began to stir up fanaticism among the Indians. The most sensational of the protesting groups called themselves the *Cristeros* or "Men of Christ." They made depredations on rural schools, sometimes murdered innocent school teachers and covered their mangled bodies with crude banners proclaiming "Christ is King." Their most spectacular display of banditry occurred in April of 1927 when they dynamited the Mexico-Guadalajara express and a hundred passengers were killed outright or burned to death. Priests caught with the vengeful mob declared they were there in the capacity of chaplains, not dynamiters. But Calles hustled six bishops across the border into Texas, and put a price on their heads if they dared to return.

In the reprisals, several army generals took occasion to do some raiding on their own. They tore down images in churches and rode their horses defiantly up to the very altars. The excuse they gave for their shocking sacrilege was that the destruction of a saint's statue before the eyes of the populace would prove that God did not care. They professed that their purpose was to cure the Indians of superstition instilled by the priests, to show them that God did not take the side of the clergy. Only by such drastic measures, they affirmed, could they break the spell laid upon the ignorant during four centuries of conversion and thralldom. Many priests had told the simple countryfolk that it was as sinful to be an agrarian as an adulterer. Now hordes of bewildered peasants decided to risk owning their own land, particularly since the saints did not seem to resent being broken into shards.

The state of Tabasco, under pressure of the tempestuous radical governor, Tomás Garrido Canábal, closed its churches and made it virtually impossible for a Catholic priest to celebrate the rites of his church. The publicity-loving governor decreed that only married men should be priests and they must have passed their fortieth birthday. He shouted in public places there were too many bastards at large already, that if the priests wanted offspring they must assume responsibility for their upbringing. A cry of furious indignation arose against such implications as well as the indirect extinguishing of all priesthood in Tabasco. But Garrido Canábal was unrelenting, and grinned as school children on their way home from school made a pastime of knocking out a brick or dislodging a stone from a village church that only yesterday had been a symbol of holy awe.

Powerful foreign pressure was brought on Calles to soften his attitude toward the church. The Knights of Columbus reputedly sent a million dollars to help the *Cristeros* to keep the guerrilla warfare going. Some agencies accused Calles of wanting the religious belligerency prolonged to prove to the world his justification for harshness against religious orders. Imperialistic William Randolph Hearst, who owned an extensive domain in north Mexico, mobilized his newspapers to call for intervention. United States oil men found themselves fired with such a sudden pious zeal that even Methodist and Baptists among them forgot their unreasonable antagonism to Roman Catholics and urged a holy crusade to save Mexico from the infidel. Something more sacred than sweet religion was being endangered—holy capital. But even with the world press against him, Calles would make no compromise. In the end the church had to come to terms with the government. Rome decreed that the clergy should register with the civil authorities.

In his second year after taking office, Calles turned some attention to foreign business interests, and inaugurated his slogan "Mexico for Mexicans." He proceeded to enforce certain anti-alien clauses of Article 27 and decreed that those who owned oil fields must exchange their titles for fifty-year leases. Sizzling but noble-worded notes from Washington were answered by cool, noble-worded notes from Mexico. Some American big business with capital invested in Mexico filled Washington's administration halls with lobbyists urging armed intervention on mundane grounds. This was in the very heyday of Wall Street—1926-1927—when the so-called vested interests could not conceive of any forces that could halt their sway. The Hearst papers went so far as to accuse four liberal United States senators of taking million-dollar bribes from Mexico's government to prevent intervention. But the loud-mouthed cries for intervention of the Honorable Edward L. Doheny and the Honorable Albert B. Fall, protagonists in the oil scandals under Harding, acted as boomerangs. United States public opinion said, "No intervention."

President Coolidge now did one of the most inspired acts of his prosaic life; he sent Dwight W. Morrow to try sweet reasonableness on the grim-jawed Calles. It was an extraordinary choice, since Mr. Morrow was a partner in the House of Morgan and an avowed exponent of the capitalistic system. Some Mexican leftists immediately labeled him a gilded debt collector. Yet no man could have made a more impressive success. Morrow was no trained diplomat, but he was a generously endowed human being, possessing innate charm as well as tact. He was the first significant United States ambassador who endeavored to understand the Mexicans. He developed a genuine fondness for Mexico. He won the confidence and the friendship of President Calles, who had been strongly anti-United States in his sentiments, and at the same time he won the admiration of the general public because of his persuasive sympathy. He became sincerely interested in Calles's program. Over ham and eggs at breakfast at the Morrow house in Cuernavaca, informally, man to man, Calles and Morrow would discuss little incidents of daily living among the people as well as affairs of state.

Calles was impressed with the ambassador's uncommon receptivity as well as his integrity, intelligence, and genuine naturalness. Morrow cared as little for precedent and protocol as did Calles. But he knew how to flatter far better. He invited the world's most admired man of the hour, Charles Augustus Lindbergh, to visit Mexico. And shortly came America's most engaging personality, homespun Will Rogers, to help win friends.

The radiation of Morrow's good will warmed the republics of the southern continent clear to Tierra del Fuego. Though he was personally liked as no other United States envoy to Mexico had ever been, leftist liberals began to cry out warningly that he was beguiling Mexico out of the Revolution. Within a few months after his arrival, Mr. Morrow's gentle persuasion had been so effective that the Mexican supreme court pronounced the Calles oil legislation unconstitutional. Aliens who possessed land before 1917 were to retain full rights of ownership, with all the subsoil wealth.

Morrow remained as ambassador for three years, ever taking an unfeigned interest in Mexican affairs and bringing the two countries much closer together. But when he departed Plutarco Calles could no longer be called a socialist. He had become more and more conservative as he became richer. He had built himself a glittering white mansion with a vast front window two stories high, not far from the charming ancient house Morrow had bought in Cuernavaca. Not only had he become a wealthy landlord, but many of his ministers and associates garnered greater fortunes, as reassured foreign capital poured into the republic. The street in Cuernavaca where some of them built sumptuous summer homes became known to the wags as "Ali Baba Street" and the "Street of the Millionaire Socialists."

But the full flowering of the Calles metamorphosis did not come until after his term of office was over. As the end of his term came near, Calles decided that no one was so well qualified to be his successor as Obregón, who had remained completely outside politics during the Calles incumbency. So the constitution was changed whereby Obregón could again become president, with the term of office lengthened from four to six years.

One cogent reason for Calles's final conciliatory attitude toward the oil men, on the advice of Morrow, was that he feared the United States might throw support to some candidate not of his choice. On the announcement that Obregón would again stand for president, two opportunist generals promptly plotted *coups d'état,* but they were captured and promptly executed. Because the traditional military revolts were nipped in their incipience, Obregón was the only candidate. In late June he was re-elected. But the foreshadowed spectacle of Calles and Obregón forever offering the presidency to each other was dramatically and swiftly dissolved. On July seventeenth, while dining with friends at a restaurant in San Angel, Obregón was shot to death by a seedy young artist who approached him on pretense of doing a free-hand sketch of him. The entire truth of the assassination has never come to light. The young killer was a Catholic fanatic, named José de León Toral, and a nun was accused of being the direct instigator of the crime. High-up churchmen hinted that some of Obregón's own comrades at table sent a few extra bullets into his body for good measure. A few even accused Calles of shedding crocodile tears as he walked bareheaded and unescorted in the funeral procession. Certainly, the death of Obregón left Calles the undisputed Big Man of Mexico. However genuine his grief for Obregón, it was doubtless tempered by his realization that in the whole broad Mexican landscape there was none now of his caliber. Yet it is something without parallel in Mexican annals that these two Strong Men, whether they really liked each other personally or not, had remained loyal since the first year Calles served under Obregón in battle.

Not only in his obvious loyalty to Obregón had Calles been unusual in the Mexican chronicle, but he now refused to let himself be drafted for re-election. His enemies said it was because he did not dare throw suspicion on himself as the real destroyer of Obregón. When he called the state governors and generals to a conference and the generals were speculating among themselves and smacking their lips over prospects, Calles announced positively that there would never be another *caudillo.* The end had come for chiefs and military dictators, he said. Mexico was ready for democracy. For president, Calles proposed the name of a lawyer from Tamaulipas, Emilio Portes Gil. It proved as satisfying a compromise choice to all sides as could have been made at the time. Calles retired to ostensibly private life; but, unlike Obregón, he took a psychic position directly behind the presidential chair and for the next six years, during a succession of three presidents, he played the proverbial rôle of the power behind the throne. Whatever may have been Calles's real intentions of retiring into private life, the political machine he had created could not function without him. From his villa in Cuernavaca he pulled strings in the capital and spoke words that came out of presidential lips. His cohorts would not let the *jefe maximo* retire. Whether he was still essential to his country can be endlessly debated. That he was indispensable in his own four years of administration is not to be doubted by any who read the records without prejudice. If the fatal bullets had gone into Calles instead of Obregón, the judgment of history would have been emphatically favorable to Calles, even though he was never beloved by the populace. Continuing to dictate from behind the scenes for almost seven more years, the stars in his historical crown dropped out one by one, and the luster of his early achievements for Mexico became tarnished by subsequent events.

## 22. Three Mouthpieces and a Six-Year Plan

*"Whatever the cause, the idealists who fight for the under dog always end by fighting one another for the place of upper dog."*

JOSÉ RUBEN ROMERO

Calles not only gained tremendous prestige by declining further tenure of the presidential chair, but he broke all precedents by being Mexico's first political boss who was not the chief executive. The lawyer, Emilio Portes Gil, whom Calles had tranquilly manipulated into office, had headed the Calles cabinet as minister of interior. He was a politician of ability as well as contradictions. It so happened that in taking advice or orders from Calles he was not compromising with his principles, because he and Calles still saw virtually eye to eye at the time. Early in his career Portes Gil showed uncommon promise. Like Calles, he had been a school teacher in his teens. Later, as a rising young attorney, he became a reformer in his native state and fought convincingly for the rights of peasants and labor. From his youth he was an ardent practicing prohibitionist, who once amazed the tipsy at a political banquet flowing with champagne by rising and delivering a passionate temperance speech. A stout opposer of the church's influence in politics and education, it was he who put the sharpest teeth into anti-clerical legislation. He had the shrewdness to draw the *obregonistas* and *callistas* closer together so that a new political party could be formed into a permanent organization which would consolidate the powers of the ruling clique. With Calles's aid he drew into the organization every significant political organization in the country, except the Communist Party.

In May, 1929, at a national revolutionary convention at Querétaro, Calles organized the *Partido Nacional Revolucionario,* known as PNR. Its announced purpose was to break forever the supremacy of the army in Mexican politics, and it purported to revive the era instituted by Madero, "Apostle of Mexican Democracy," and "to lay foundations for civilian regimes of peace and liberty in the nation." The principles were declared to be social-democratic, much like those of the most potent party in the Scandinavian countries. But the organization was undemocratic in that an airtight system was established by which the government in power could absolutely control elections.

Besides the formation of this powerful political organization, two events of special significance took place in the short regime of Portes Gil: On June twenty-ninth, 1929, church bells rang out again for regular service for the first time in three years, when the clergy gave up their sit-down strike; and the federation of labor, CROM, lost its official protection. Portes Gil deliberately backed the unions that had maintained their independence, until he broke the power of CROM's dictator, blatant, squash-bellied Luis Morones, former plumber and electrician.

Morones is one of those incredible cinematic characters who make noisy splashes in Mexican social life. For some sixteen years he was the chief dynamo in the labor movement. He took the lead in 1918 when CROM was formed. Possessing native cunning as well as political sense, he had the energy to project his personality and his ideas. When Obregón ran for president, Morones formed the Labor Party to support him. Later, Calles and Morones had backed each other, and Calles had elevated him to a cabinet post. As the revolutionary *callistas* emerged into "millionaire socialists," Morones followed his betters' lead and became a millionaire proletarian. He learned to be a sharp, hard trader. He was alleged to make industrialists respect his ability to forestall strikes. He bought estates, apartment houses, a hotel. He invested in stocks and bonds in his own name and that of friends. He developed a penchant for glittering motor cars and a passion for diamonds that equaled Peggy Joyce's, but he wore his with less grace.

For relaxation from the proletarian grind, he built himself a suburban pleasure palace at Tlamplan, lush with luxury, and complete with *frontón*. His week-end parties with their spiced foods, heady wines, and luscious girls became notorious. Tired, old-rich business men mingled genially with tired new-rich proletarians on the spreading silken couches and in the imperial swimming bath. Morones's henchmen learned that what was sauce for the upper classes was sauce for the top underdogs.

At labor meetings, however, when the sad-eyed, flat-bellied workers would scowl at Morones's flashing diamonds, he would defend himself with a wink and a laugh. "I do this just to show those bastard bourgeois that we laborers can wear diamonds too." When they glanced with oblique accusation at his long, shiny automobiles, he would plead, "Would you believe more in my sincerity if I came on burro back?"

But the stench of corruption grew so offensive that great blocks of the union men did quit believing in his sincerity. In fact, they came to think that the silk-shirted leader was leagued with their employers to keep them in their lowly places, even though in earlier years he certainly did achieve shorter hours, better wages, and somewhat better working conditions for the factory toilers. Some began to put their faith in the flamboyant Morones assistant, a refined, intellectual young man, physically slight and somewhat ascetic looking, but one who could turn into flame in public speech. Since 1926 he had been the Morones one-man brain trust in CROM. His name was Vicente Lombardo Toledano. He was born in the town of Tezuitlán in Puebla on July sixteenth, 1894. His grandfather had come from Italy in 1850, and made a small fortune in copper. No man in Mexico was better educated. Vicente earned a degree in law, and afterwards became a master of arts and a doctor of philosophy. Now, while he worked with Morones, he was concurrently professor of law and philosophy at the National University. Between these oddly contrasted key men, labor began choosing sides secretly before there was an open split in 1933, the year in which Lombardo Toledano was ousted from his professorship for his radical preachments. In the regime of Cárdenas, the ex-plumber Morones was to suffer total eclipse, while the scholar was to rise higher than any labor leader in Latin America.

The last event of significance in the Portes Gil administration was the temporary obscuration of the erudite José Vasconcelos, one of the strangest anomalies in Mexico's vast gallery of paradoxes. It was Vasconcelos who had first recognized the dynamic abilities of the youthful Lombardo Toledano and who had made him director of the National Preparatory School, an extraordinary honor for one in his twenties. It was Vasconcelos who, as Obregón's secretary of education, organized Mexico's ministry of education, and who made his influence felt throughout the entire South American continent. It was he who divided the department of education into three sections: Schools, libraries, and fine arts. It was he who stimulated native painting and secured the first government commissions for the great muralists, Rivera and Orozco, who were to keep revolutionary ideals before the people and to bring the art of Mexico to international prestige. Vasconcelos had a touch of genius, but, as with many other geniuses, his sense of reality was often vague. But whatever his failings and his surprising reversals in political ideology, he unquestionably helped "to mold the future of a race."

Born on February twenty-eighth, 1882, in Oaxaca—the native state of Juárez and Díaz—José Vasconcelos early revealed his brilliance as lawyer, writer and public servant. At the beginning of his career he was considered an ardent socialist, and he lectured convincingly against "the two social plagues—great estates and military dictatorships." He actively attacked political corruption, and at the risk of his life he openly opposed Calles, when the *jefe maximo* assumed extraordinary powers. He proclaimed the Calles dictatorship more intolerable than that of Díaz, and he attacked commercial and industrial aggression from the United States. He warned the nation against the beguilement of Dwight Morrow. When Calles selected a mild conservative named Pascual Ortiz Rubio, a former ambassador to Brazil, to succeed Portes Gil, Vasconcelos ran against him as an "anti-re-electionist" candidate. Because of his wide popularity with the masses, to whom he had distributed copies of the classics, Vasconcelos fully expected to be elected. A poor man, who made his living entirely by scholarship, he paid his campaign expenses by the unprecedented expedient of charging admission to the halls where he spoke. He made exciting use of Calles's phrase, "Mexico for the Mexicans," and everywhere turned away crowds. Yet when the official results were announced the widely-known Vasconcelos was allotted twenty thousand votes to the virtually unknown Ortiz Rubio's million plus.

Believing that eighty-five per cent of the Mexican people were really with him, Vasconcelos lingered in Sonora and then crossed into Texas to wait for the revolution that would put him in power. But there was no uprising whatever, and Vasconcelos found himself Mexico's most distinguished exile. The puling mob had let him down. He became bitter and cynical. Then gradually he seemed to revamp his whole political philosophy. He emerged into a kind of Catholic mystic. The story of his metamorphosis he has told with utter frankness in a many-volumed autobiography which will doubtless live as one of Mexico's great works of literature.

The regime of Ortiz Rubio was notable chiefly because it was conducted by telephone from Calles's gleaming villa in Cuernavaca. Under Ortiz Rubio the Revolution went definitely backward. Four months after his inauguration, in February, 1930,

Calles announced the failure of the agrarian program and his own renunciation of it. The news was a bombshell to many a liberal. Calles was branded turncoat. But no doubt he was as honest in his reasoned convictions as Dwight Morrow had been in pointing out the bad features of the plan. Production of essential foodstuffs had decreased, Calles said, because of the careless inefficiency of the peasant proprietors. The large-production plantations were the only ones that really paid off to the good of the national economy.

"The happiness of the peasants cannot be assured," the "Iron Man" now declared, "by giving them a patch of land, if they lack the preparation and the necessary elements to cultivate it. . . . On the contrary, this road will carry us to disaster, because we are creating pretensions and fomenting laziness." He pointed out the great number of *ejidos* in which the land was not cultivated after it had been given to the people. "Still it is proposed to enlarge the *ejidos;* why?" he demanded bluntly.

So redistribution of land stopped under Ortiz Rubio. Calles had his way about everything else. Cabinet ministers and foreign diplomats found it more expedient and conclusive to drive to Cuernavaca than to call on President Ortiz Rubio at the National Palace. The president chafed helplessly under the neglect and the jibes of the press and the music-hall comedians. Fuming with indignation at a rank slight to his authority, he determined to assert himself. He removed some of Calles's confidential officials. Whereupon the Big Boss promptly announced the resignation of the president. Ortiz Rubio was thunderstruck to read of it in the newspaper at breakfast. He choked with rage. Then his trembling hand reflectively rubbed the jaw that had recently been injured by a would-be assassin's missile. By the time the first interviewer arrived he had come to a decision. He confirmed Calles's announcement. Shortly afterward he left for the less strenuous precincts of New York City to recover from the executive grind. "Being president of Mexico is a very, very trying and exhausting business," he told a metropolitan reporter.

To finish out the last two years of Ortiz Rubio's term, Calles selected a practical business man. Abelardo Rodríguez was youngish, robust, energetic. He had been a professional baseball player and a revolutionary general. He was a proprietor of notoriously successful gambling joints near the California border. He was also a banker and a multi-millionaire. As his business associate he had made a neat little fortune for Calles. As a state governor and a cabinet minister he had proved an able administrator. On the whole, the Rodríguez regime was prosperous. Commerce expanded, real estate boomed. With the 1930 governmental swing to the right, reassured foreign capital had poured in. Labor activities were halted or shushed. The watchword now was, "Foreign capital must not be molested or frightened."

President Rodríguez took up polo, spent much time with alien capitalists on the golf links, laughed at being known as "the country-club president." But underneath the playboy surface he kept his eye on the ball of public sentiment. And in his last half year in office, when he saw the gathering resentment against some of the more obvious reactionary moves, he discounted the menace by a sudden reversion to his original revolutionary inclinations. He summarily revived land distribution. All the "stop" laws of Ortiz Rubio were discarded—and the road for more *ejidos* was cleared. In the brief period from February twentieth to July thirty-first, 1934, almost eighty-two thousand heads of families received land. Twenty million pesos were turned over to the National Bank of Agricultural Credit to assist the *ejiditarios* to get a decent start.

Many liberals consider that the best thing Rodríguez did was to appoint a young leftist lawyer named Narciso Bassols minister of education. Bassols looked at education scientifically. He regarded the Indian's school work as valuable in improving his economic life. He undertook to educate the parents of children at the same time. He acquainted them with the new types of agricultural and industrial activities that would bring with them the possibility of a new standard of living, an "indispensable requisite if the Indian is ever to emerge from his traditional misery."

Before Bassols, Calles had directed his attention chiefly to anti-clerical influence in primary schools. Bassols insisted that secondary schools should be taken from the influence of the church. On his advice, in December, 1932, President Rodríguez decreed that all education in secondary schools should be secular.

The Archbishop of Mexico straightway announced that "all parents must hereby refrain from sending their children to the lay secondary schools." Despite his power, the order was not carried out. The majority of students continued to attend the state schools. The clergy fought furiously to discredit Bassols' work. They attacked his so-called "sexual education," and created such a furore that in the end they did force his resignation. Bassols believed that children should be taught the "facts of life" in an intelligent and decent way. He deplored the thousands of illegal abortions and the quantities of illegitimate children born to girls in their early teens, because out of religious scruples the parents had kept them in ignorance. The sexual education was hardly more than a course in physiology and hygiene. But whispered tales were blown into horror stories. It was rumored that men teachers made a practice of seducing little girls to teach them by laboratory methods. Some declared that boys and girls were stripped like artists' models while the teachers lectured on bodily functions. Others claimed that cocks and hens were brought into the schoolroom for demonstration.

Though none of the outrageous stories could be proved, and it was always someone else's child to whom something had happened, a wave of fanatical excitement swept over the parents. Mothers dragged their offspring from the schoolhouses, broke windows, attacked teachers who were forced to flee from their fury. The hysteria won out. In May, 1934, the parents' association instigated a strike among the children. Bassols resigned, and was immediately elevated to the position of minister of interior. Though seemingly the work of Bassols in education had been sabotaged by his enemies, his name will live as that of one of the advanced forces in Latin American education.

After a decade's supreme command, Calles was astute enough to foresee that he must play a trump card dramatically if he were still to continue pre-eminent in the game. He played it at the PNR convention which met at Querétaro in December, 1933. "The time has come," he said, "to formulate a detailed plan of action for the period covered by the next six-year presidential term."

When the convention opened, some of the leftists took stock of the agrarian achievement. In the two decades since Madero, less than twenty million acres had been distributed to the villages. Over three hundred million acres still belonged to *hacendados* and *rancheros*. Eighty per cent of this belonged to the estates of more than two thousand five hundred acres. Half of Mexico was still owned by two thousand families. The Revolution was lost in a quagmire. The left-wingers decided the time had come to rescue it, clean it up, and set it on the road again. Sniffing the prevailing local wind which carried an unmistakable scent of Russia, Calles determined to make concessions in such a way that he himself would seem to be the inspirer of all new good to his people. He conceived the idea of a "Six-Year Plan." The very term subtly implied something to go beyond the communists' working dream that promised so much at the end of five years.

Though the plan was something for the underprivileged to tie their hopes to, yet it was reassuring to the conservatives. For Calles proclaimed it would be a program "based on calculations, on statistics, on the lessons of experiences." "We must study what we can accomplish," he said, "given the possibilities of our budgets and our reality." And he roundly denounced "more criminal radical programs that make social experiments at the expense of the masses' hunger."

The crux of the plan was a state-directed national economy, with state arbitration in labor disputes. Labor was to receive new benefits, but business was to be protected. Co-operatives were to be fostered. The section on agrarian reform was broad. The distribution of land and water rights was to be continued "until the needs of the rural population were satisfied." Everybody of good will in the republic was to benefit by it. All in all, the plan was an extremely clever conception.

But in committee the plan had gone much farther to the left than Calles had intended. However, like Carranza in regard to the radical 1917 constitution, Calles had little notion that its specifications would be carried out wholly.

In the choice for a new president, Calles realized that he had to please the left wing. After the last few years of the ribbing of "the millionaire socialists," Calles knew that the next candidate must be "a poor man's choice." He had to be a man who had fought well in the revolutionary forces, who was liked by the army officers, one who was not well-to-do, one who appealed to farmers and laborers alike, and one who could not be labeled a Calles stooge.

Thirty-eight-year-old Lázaro Cárdenas, a man known for his honesty and humanitarian principles, fitted the specifications. As governor of his native state of Michoacán, General Cárdenas had pleased the masses by his handling of land reform and by his educational program. In 1930 he had been made president of PNR. Then Calles had chosen him for two cabinet posts in quick succession, and he had proved uncommonly able in both. He was popular with his fellow officers. Despite an intense vitality, he was quiet mannered and gravely *simpático*. Cárdenas was the choice.

There was at least one man in Mexico who took the "Six-Year Plan" in profound earnest. That was Lázaro Cárdenas. He made his public pronouncement: "The agrarian program will be completely solved. Aid will be given for the organization of the United Front of Labor so that the raising of the standard of living may become a reality. The educational program needed by the masses will be carried out. And, in short, there will be realized in its totality the doctrine for which General Calles has been fighting, to make Mexico a strong and responsible country." Throwing the credit to Calles flattered the Big Boss and to a degree fooled him, though it was merely Cárdenas's tactful way of urging Calles to return to his earlier socialistic attitude.

Politically, the nomination of Cárdenas could not have been better calculated to please the party and the populace. Of course, the election was in the bag. There could be no opposition to Calles's shrewdly conceived and manipulated PNR with its present radiant program. But no sooner was the nomination of Cárdenas a fact than that amazing fellow rushed off on a terrific seven-month campaign tour, as if he were running against the devil and Porfirio Díaz himself in league with the United States government. By train, by car, by muleback, and afoot he covered eighteen thousand miles—some admirers say twenty-five thousand. He sought out villages so remote that it was hard to find their trail. He asked questions, listened to requests and prayers. He gave advice. "What are your needs? Of land, of water, of schooling, of seed, of roads, of physicians?" He made manifold promises. "If it is possible," he said solemnly, "I shall give you what you require."

Some of the people looked upon this man with the burning eyes, the hearing ears, the homely eloquence, as the new messiah. By his complexion and earthy knowledge he was one of them, he spoke their language, but never had they seen his like. Some of them had heard rich speeches before, but never words with such heart-striking sincerity. Here was a leader worth the following. He had given them a sudden faith in themselves and in their government. He made them feel citizens already.

At first Calles smiled wryly at such tumultuous outpouring of energy. Perhaps it was good for young Cárdenas to let off steam before getting into harness. Let him dash over the broad pastures and through the wood-lots and feel his oats. After the inauguration would come the time for breaking, for that smooth, steel-gripped handling of which Calles was past-master. But yet— There was flickering foreboding in Calles's calculating brain. He might have a little trouble with a man who had learned so much about a whole nation's outer and inner life. Sometimes knowledge is a dangerous source of power, and Lázaro Cárdenas knew more about Mexicans and Mexico than any other man alive. But Calles did not dream that Cárdenas really meant every word he said, without a scintilla of the customary discount on Mexican rhetoric. The modest man from Michoacán was both too forthright and too subtle for the Big Boss.

Elected in July, 1934, Cárdenas was inaugurated on the last day of November. He did not demur when the old dictator selected for him a cabinet which included five Calles supporters and his own son Rodolfo. During his first weeks in office Cárdenas listened with polite attention to the Big Boss's advice. The wealthy *callistas* went on with their play and their business, with easy minds. And then they woke up to the fact that Cárdenas was in earnest about the agrarian program. He even laid a vigorous finger on the acreage of some of them. He had the temerity to padlock the lucrative gambling saloons of others. To some factory strikers he dared to say, "More power to you, men! Strike! Unite!"

Calles warned him he was going too far. When Cárdenas would not scare or be intimidated by telephone, Calles pointedly held court at Cuernavaca with some powerful senators. He condemned Cárdenas's attitude towards strikers, and casually mentioned the resignation of Ortiz Rubio. Cárdenas struck back so swiftly that he staggered the chief. He threw out the Calles cabinet and put in a new one predominantly for broad reform. Yet he was smart enough to choose for his secretary of agriculture a flaming reactionary and a passionate Catholic devotee, old General Saturnino Cedillo, who had risen from rags to feudal riches. Cedillo placated the clergy and temporarily stilled the privileged groups. The plausible Portes Gil aided Cárdenas greatly in switching *callistas* in the Cárdenas group. Important officials stopped driving to Cuernavaca to take orders or pay court. The desertion turned into a stampede. Mexicans of high integrity blushed for their politicians' shameful haste and hypocritical servility.

The Iron Man was utterly unprepared for such a reversal. His bluff had never been called before. He fell ill. He went to California for medical care, and lay abed in a Catholic hospital and was tenderly nursed by nuns. After six months he felt strong enough to return to the capital and reclaim his power. He brought the discredited Luis Morones with him. But Cárdenas had everything under control. Calles's only recourse now was to call his presidential choice a communist, as he himself had been called bolshevik in his time. The old revolutionary cried out for the nation to beware of the radicals. He urged workers to support the diamond-splurging Morones and "conservative labor unions." Cárdenas remained wrapped in a mystical and dynamic silence.

When the Mexico-Vera Cruz train was dynamited and thirteen passengers were killed, the *callistas* were blamed. A mass demonstration before the National Palace demanded the exile of Calles. Cárdenas decided it would be best for the country's health if the old chief were on alien ground. One April night at his ranch, as Calles lay propped up in bed recuperating from influenza, wearing black silk pajamas and reading *Mein Kampf*, he looked up from his book to see a general and three soldiers standing in his room. He wondered if he were to be taken before a firing squad. But he was bundled off to the nearest airport. In the dawn of a Texas April his plane landed at Brownsville. Unshaven, his mustache ragged, his complexion greenish, Calles stepped out into exile. The Iron Man of Mexico looked so broken that the reporters who approached were oddly tongue-tied. "I am exiled," Calles announced bitterly, "because I opposed attempts to implant a dictatorship of the proletariat." But nothing he had to say mattered much now.

# PART NINE

# REDEEMER OF FORGOTTEN MEN

## 23. The Way of the Redeemer Is Hard

*"But if any other things oppose thee, go on according to thy powers with due considera- tion, keeping to that which appears to be just. For it is best to reach this object, and if thou dost fail, let thy failure be in attempting this. He who follows reason in all things is both tranquil and active at the same time, and also cheerful and collected."*
MARCUS AURELIUS

Though he is an avid reader, it may be doubted that Cárdenas ever read Seneca. Yet across the ages he seems to have appropri- ated a leaf from the stoic's book. "Would you rise in the world?" Seneca said. "Then you must work while others amuse them- selves. Are you desirous of a reputation for courage? You must risk your life. Would you be strong morally and physically? You must resist temptations. All this is paying in advance; that is prospective finance. Observe the other side of the picture; the bad things are paid for afterwards."

Lázaro Cárdenas was born one of eight children into a poor but well-thought-of *mestizo* family in the little town of Jiquílpan, Michoacán, on May twenty-first, 1895. In 1895, the acme of the Golden Age of Díaz, his birthplace was a typical Mexican small town, without benefit of physician or sewer or mill to grind meal for the *tortillas*. Water for drinking and washing had to be carried from the one well in the plaza. But the Cárdenases were not peons. The father, Dámaso, was among the four per cent of Mexicans who owned land. His tract, however, was small and rocky. But here, with his own horse and a wooden plow, he grew the family corn. Besides, he ran a small grocery shop where drugs also were sold. And to add to the meager budget, he once operated a one-table poolroom.

Lázaro was a serious child who took to book-learning with curiosity and diligence. Though not a general favorite with his playmates in the town school because of his grave temperament, he was looked upon quite naturally as a leader. Legend repeatedly tells how his schoolmaster, a liberal in advance of his time, predicted he would some day be governor of Michoacán. Lázaro's formal schooling stopped at the equivalent of the sixth grade, when he was eleven, at the very age at which Juárez's began. The primary school did not go beyond the sixth year, and there was no secondary school in Jiquílpan. His father could not afford to send him away to study for a career. So he got him employment with the proprietor of the town's printing shop, a *politico* who was also the district tax collector. Lázaro's daily wage was half a peso. The two jobs of printer's devil and helper in the tax office gave the lad his initiation into the arcana of Mexican politics. Noting his alert, eager mind, his employer lent him books and periodicals. He became an inveterate reader, and at sixteen he was writing for a liberal newspaper called *El Popular* devoted to Madero and the *maderista* cause. At eighteen he was appointed town jailer, but he was too honest to make anything out of the potentially lucrative sinecure. Soon he determined to join a guerrilla band against the usurping Victoriano Huerta, who had killed Madero. Lázaro gave his sole prisoner a gun and took him along for company.

Young Cárdenas's promotions were as swift as his own forced marches. His habit of early rising served him well in battle, for he was expert at what Mexicans call "dawning"—surprising the enemy at dawn before they are awake. In less than a year he was a captain of cavalry under Obregón. Moved by Villa's flaming championship of the common people, Cárdenas took a significant portion of his cavalry over to him in January, 1915, and was made a lieutenant-colonel. Two months later he reappraised Villa and took some five hundred of his men over to General Calles, who made him a full colonel. He lacked some weeks of being twenty.

At the time that he switched between the constitutionalist army and the forces of Villa, both were fighting against the common enemy Huerta. When Obregón became president in 1920 he elevated the twenty-five-year-old Cárdenas to brigadier-general and made him provisional governor of his home state, Michoacán. It was a wondrous rise for a small town boy with only a sixth-grade education. In the intervening years he had been entrusted with important military posts in Tehuantepec and Guanajuato, and for three years he was chief of military operations in Huasteca, the jungle coastal region where a gigantic oil boom was in full swing.

In his movement about Mexico, young Cárdenas had seen his countrymen in all their humiliating poverty. He had lived where there were no schools, no medical aid, and where many existed touch-and-go with starvation. In Huasteca the contrast between the foreign oil men's pleasant, well-screened houses on the hills and the workers' sodden huts on the pestilential swamp edges made a searing impression on him. "Why is it not the right of every man of any race to have an adequate shelter to call home?" he asked himself.

The contempt of the white foreigners for the dark-skinned Mexicans also burned into his soul. Not that the managers weren't most polite to the military commander of Huasteca. They were so delighted to have him among them that he had hardly unpacked when a brisk official came to pay his respects and, for a calling card, left a handsome new Packard as a gift. It was just an old oil-company custom to welcome new commanding officers with shiny cars—as insurance that the docile workers would remain unprotesting. Cárdenas's aides were enchanted with the Packard and voluble in its praise. (At the time he possessed only a wheezing jalopy, an ancient, second-hand Hudson.) They choked with disappointment when the commander coolly declined the car. A few days later their hopes rose again—the jalopy sputtered its last and was done for forever. The Packard was offered again. Like boys begging for a pony, his aides urged their young chief to take it. Again he declined. He purchased a democratic Dodge on the installment plan.

Foreign capitalists learned early in his career that Lázaro Cárdenas could not be bought. Mexican politicians and citizens, rich and poor, learned, too, that he was never to be swerved from principle or purpose. He first gained his reputation for honesty when he repaid a loan of 20,000 pesos which the business men of Vera Cruz had made to help General Obregón. This was considered most unconventional behavior. But he caused downright consternation among the military when he returned to the paymaster general 93,000 pesos out of the 100,000 allowed him for "extraordinary military expenditures." By returning the unspent portion he implied he could be loyal without the traditional general's fee for loyalty.

Six years after he had served the brief term as provisional governor of his home state, Cárdenas ran for the office and was elected by a big popular majority. He was now thirty-one. As governor of Michoacán he carried out with vigor the agrarian program of the Revolution, giving land to the Indians according to the prescription. When the wealthy *hacendados* would promise him all sorts of things if he would spare their property, he would reply quietly, "It is my duty to carry out the ideals of the Revolution." In an effort to save her estates, a beautiful and fascinating Mexican lady who had married a Spanish *marqués* crossed the ocean and sought an interview with the young governor. She was received with grim courtesy. Highly intelligent as well as charming, the *marquesa* talked with convincing ardor for two hours, pointing out advantages to the workers and to the national economy if Cárdenas would let her keep her land. She had constructive plans, she would do this and that for the workers, she insisted. Throughout the interview Cárdenas answered every argument with the same sentence, "It is not the idea of the Revolution." Sometimes he spoke indistinctly, looking off. Sometimes he looked at her with direct candor and spoke forcibly. But always the same refrain: "It is not the idea of the Revolution." The lady had less effect on Cárdenas than the dubiously glamorous Princess Salm-Salm, pleading for the life of Maximilian, had had on Juárez. She was left the *hacienda* house and barns and some three hundred and thirty acres. The tens of thousands of acres went to the men who had worked the land. The *marquesa* hates "that stubborn peon," as she calls him, to this day.

Not only did Cárdenas give land to the peasants, but he encouraged and advised them in person. He armed the new small holders and taught them to defend themselves against the "white guards" of the *haciendas*. He dinned accusations into the ears of the well-to-do estate owners: "Don't you know it is the duty of the rich and the fortunate to help the poor?"

Uplifting the Indian became the supreme purpose of Cárdenas's life. He made trips into untraveled parts of his native state. Squatting before their humble huts with the Indians, he listened to their needs. Breaking all precedents, he was extremely accessible. The lowliest might come to the governor's mansion to present his case. Cárdenas gave a new impetus to education. He emboldened labor to demand and get better wages and living conditions. He brought running water to villages. What he did to help the "forgotten men" in his home state he was to do on a large scale six years later for the whole of Mexico.

When his term of governorship was up and he was off to

Puebla to take the post of military commander, Cárdenas had to borrow money for the journey. He had not squandered his salary on himself; he had given it away to those whose needs were urgent. An infinitesimal portion of it he had spent on courtship. For at thirty-three he had fallen in love with a sixteen-year-old girl from his home state. She was Amalia Solórzano, and she came of a good, middle-class family of some means. Very pretty, demure in manner, but uncommonly independent in her thinking, she was being educated in a convent in Mexico City. Her parents, who opposed the match at first, considered her safe with the nuns. Because convents were operated against the law, however, the bewildered sisters did not dare refuse to let Cárdenas come to call, for fear he would padlock the nunnery. They were afraid, too, to intercept the love letters that passed between them. When the nuns would deny Amalia some privilege, she could say, "If Lázaro should hear of this!" and the poor women could only cross themselves repeatedly and grant her request. Shortly before his nomination for the presidency the pair were married.

The early-rising, hard-working Cárdenas had not reached his fortieth birthday when he was inaugurated president of Mexico. His idol Madero was the only other important Mexican who became president in his thirties. In this century only two men have made a new spirit in Mexico. Each had the apostolic soul. One was Francisco Madero. The other was Lázaro Cárdenas. Madero made a new political spirit. Cárdenas made a new social and economic spirit. He stands out as the most radical administrator ever to occupy the presidential chair. In the January twenty-third, 1939 issue, the editors of *Life* magazine, in the fifth year of his regime, offered a most apt summation of the man himself: "Cárdenas is probably the first completely fearless, honest and unselfish politician to appear since Madero (assassinated in 1913)."

Like Madero, Cárdenas was something unique in Mexican politics—with a greater difference. Unorthodox and unpredictable, he was as enigmatic to the Mexican press as to foreign correspondents. His imperturbability and intuition were attributed to his Tarascan ancestors. In print he was often spoken of as "the Indian," though it is doubtful if his blood is Indian by half. But his oddly shaped head, which rises in the back, does give his profile a resemblance "to figures in Mayan *bas relief,*" as the Weyls have said. The face is longish, the jaw strong, the chin slightly receding and stubborn. The Indians consider him handsome; some white Mexicans consider him homely. In photographs the most outstanding feature of his face is the mouth, with its protruding, sensuous lips, surmounted by a thick but closely cropped black mustache. When one comes into the presence of the man himself it is the eyes alone that seem significant. They are unforgettable eyes that see through and beyond, while observing the minutest detail at close range. They seem to seek the best in a man or a situation, and yet they are by no means incautious. In color, too, the eyes are extraordinary. They are green, or greenish hazel, flecked with gold. But the lashes are so black and thick that sometimes under emotional stress the eyes appear to be fiery black. At times they seem to illuminate the glowing, light copper-tinged complexion, while holding communion with some mystic force.

Above medium height, Cárdenas is impressive in figure. His muscular physique gives the impression of prodigious vitality and elasticity. In the rare interviews he gives, his manner is alert and earnest. If he likes his questioner, he puts him at smiling and even familiar ease. If he does not find him *simpático* he can assume a mask of Indian impassivity. His voice is of good quality, pleasant, deep, vibrant and tempered. He is not a natural-born public speaker, but what he utters comes so sincerely from the heart that he can stir his audiences to passionate allegiance and they remember what he says. His inherent personal magnetism is of such quality that both friend and foe speak of his "political sex appeal." His aura is one of dynamic serenity, but there is a tenacity in his make-up as durable as the grain of ironwood. His roots go so deep into his native soil that opposing whirlwinds cannot uproot him.

At the beginning of his regime Cárdenas kept as completely out of the limelight as possible. He granted almost no interviews and so attracted little attention as a "personality." But someone ventured to write prophetically of him as "a figure of great promise and unlimited uncertainty."

In his direct, unspectacular way, Cárdenas straightway began breaking precedents, both public and private. Eight days after his inauguration he announced that the national telegraph company would transmit free of charge, every day between twelve and one, messages from the public explaining to him their urgent needs. In the office and at home he often reversed the accepted order and received the tattered and darker-skinned first. He weakened the control of professional politicians like Emilio Portes Gil by taking into the fold of PNR representatives of labor unions and peasant organizations. He was the first president to advocate woman suffrage and the independence of women. "Women must organize," he said, "so that the home shall cease to be looked upon as a prison to them." He refused to make his own home in Chapultepec Palace, the official residence of presidents since Maximilian. He transformed that historic building into a museum so that the lowliest could enter freely where only privileged feet had trod before. He and his young wife took an unpretentious, attractive house in the suburbs. Instead of appearing before diplomats in the conventional black, he wore well-tailored business suits of some gray or brownish tweed mixture. His own needs being more than met by his salary, Cárdenas divided his lemon farm in Michoacán among the workers, giving each a share and reserving one like share for his little son. And at the reading of the will of his father-in-law he persuaded his wife to deed her portion of the land immediately to the workers who lived on it. These two latter private actions the general public has not even heard of.

Lázaro Cárdenas would have delighted the heart of Thorstein Veblen, because he scorned the "conspicuous expenditure" of the leisure class and discarded superfluities right and left. He let it be known that his was not to be a society regime, with great dinners, and that no liquor was to be dispensed in his house. Because he is so remarkably virile and enjoys the simple things of life with such gusto, Cárdenas scorns stimulants as much as he despises affectations. Not only does he neither drink nor smoke, but he disapproves of bullfights. He did not attend a single fight while he was president, and he will not permit his little son to wear toreador costume as do the neighbor boys. He looks down on prizefighting as degrading. On one of his visits to Oaxaca, when the reception committee had arranged a program of boxing matches for his entertainment, Cárdenas asked if they could not substitute some Indian folk dances, which they did.

Despite his condemnation of public display of brutality or cruelty in any form as deleterious to the national character, no one has ever accused him of being soft. His endurance is so nearly superhuman as to be proverbial. Four or five hours of sleep suffice to keep him in trim. He can outride, outswim, and outwalk any of his aides.

His bitterest enemies pay tribute to his personal courage. He has never carried a revolver except in war, and he has steadfastly refused to have a bodyguard. Once in the north, in his chief enemy's stronghold, someone in the crowd began shooting at his presidential train as it was pulling away from the station. Cárdenas immediately ordered the train to be stopped and backed up. Then, descending alone and unarmed, he walked swiftly up to the bystanders and asked who had fired the shots and why. There was no confession, no answer, only a general emotion of shame. But by his impulsive bravery Cárdenas had turned enemies into friends.

The one time Cárdenas is known to have gone into a church during his presidency he risked his life. On a Sunday in a small town in Guanajuato, an open-air educational program was in process in the plaza. According to the story, the priest, resenting the competition, incited his communicants to break it up. In their zeal they killed a young lecturer, and they were about to finish off the other performers when Cárdenas happened to arrive, in the midst of the turmoil. "Put up your knives and get back into the church," he commanded the fanatical; "I have something to say to you." When the muttering worshipers were reassembled, Cárdenas walked down to the chancel, turned and faced them. "You should be ashamed of yourselves," he said with cool passion. "Those people out there were doing no harm. They were sent by the state to teach and enlighten. This house was made to speak the truth of the religion which says 'Love your neighbor.' It was not built for its priest—like that cowering coward in the corner there—to send people out to kill their brothers."

Cárdenas broke precedent in never killing a political enemy while he was president. Because he hated the aggressive implications of the word "war," he changed the name ministry of war to ministry of national defense. He decreed complete freedom of the press, and let anti-administration criticism fly about as unrestrained as from the soapboxes of Hyde Park.

Though he soon began to be called a cloud-dweller, Cárdenas possesses an uncommonly clear mind. And before his first year was out, the visionary had plucked up by the roots an entrenched dictatorial clique without having to kill anyone. He had accomplished a bloodless revolution. Where Calles had said, *ex cathedra,* "The Revolution has gone far enough," Cárdenas said, "It has just got started." The Revolution had promised redemption to the peon and industrial wage-earner. It had promised to break up the great estates and give land to the land-hungry. It had promised education and better health to the masses. Cárdenas accepted as his bounden duty the task to make good all the lapsed pledges. "The main road of the new phase of the Revolution," he said, "is the march of Mexico towards socialism." By his own definition, though, this movement "departed equally from the anachronistic norms of classical liberalism and from those which are proper to communism that is undergoing an experiment in Soviet Russia." He admired above all the social democracies of Scandinavia. But he studied the needs of his people in relation to their temperaments and potentialities and Mexico's resources and *mores,* and he used common sense as well as humanitarian principles to motivate his reforms.

Many of those things José Morelos had planned for Mexico in 1814 now began to work in 1935. Morelos, a century and two decades ahead of his time, had conceived an advanced democracy. What Cárdenas attempted to do in six years caused men to say, variously, "Cardenas is twenty-five, fifty, a hundred years ahead of his time." At the core of Cárdenas's program, as at that of Morelos, was the desire to moderate penury and luxury in Mexico. He looked upon the Indians as a race disinherited from its own country. He opposed the typical upper-class ideology that says the Indians need a master, that they fare best when treated as children and worked humanely as slaves. He determined to help them in their struggle for the minimum of human rights. "We want fewer Indians and more Mexicans," he said.

Cárdenas's main objectives were four: (1) To give land to all peasants who needed it; (2) to raise the living standards of workers; (3) to give every one a chance at an education; (4) to improve the health of the country. He was determined to get at the psychological and material roots of the people's problems. When he did not seek them out, he let the Indians come to him and speak their tales of woe. And despite his tense, nervous temperament, he listened with saint-like patience while they talked in their hesitant, roundabout way. "These people have such needs," he said, "I cannot give them everything. But I can at least give them patience." He could not promise all they wanted, but he promised what he could. "You shall have the bridge." "A water pipe will bring water to the village." "There shall be a little co-operative mill to grind the corn for your *tortillas.*" "A road shall be built so that you can get your produce to a bus line." "You shall have a doctor in this district." "The school house shall get a new roof." "No, I cannot give you all fountain pens." Cárdenas went to the people and the people went to him. The politicians in between counted for so little. This was his greatest innovation of all—direct government.

A wit conceived a joke, which circulated widely, revealing where Cárdenas put the emphasis in administration. The president was concentrating on work at his official desk one morning when his private secretary presented him with memoranda of urgent business. "Crisis with the railway workers." "Pass it on to the minister of communications," said the president. "Sisal production in Yucatán under par." "Tell the minister of agriculture." "Important message from the United States State Department." "Tell the minister of foreign affairs." "Big bank scandal imminent." "Inform finance." The procedure was interrupted by one of the free telegrams from a remote village, Santa Maria del Tule. It was signed Juan Diego. "My corn perished with drought, my burro lay down and died, I have malaria, and my wife is having a baby." Brushing documents aside, Cárdenas rose with alacrity. "Order the presidential train. We go to Santa Maria."

If they heard in advance that he was coming, the proud and grateful people would erect flower arches for Cárdenas to walk under. But he preferred to have his visits unheralded—no reception committees, no banners, no bands. He generally just "appeared" in a town, walking along the streets with the crowd. He would sit on a bench in the public square and talk with folks. The word would spread, "Lázaro has come to help us."

And the townspeople turned out and the country people would pour in to look at him. He visited schools, jails, hospitals. In the charity wards he would stop for a word of cheer among the worst sufferers. It never occurred to him that his ways were unorthodox.

Hubert Herring well describes what happened when Cárdenas visited a town: "They crowd in upon the president, everyone would touch him, some would embrace him, the children hold flowers up for him. And for all a greeting, a clasp of the hand, a word of affection . . . The startled pride, the hungry joys of the people have a religious quality."

Cárdenas never seemed to weary of the strain. "It actually seems to rest him to have lots of Indians hovering around him asking for things," one of his secretaries said. His ministers and senators were exhausted when they returned from inspection tours with him. He could be up at five and going strong until midnight day after day—looking, listening, making decisions, giving orders. If it was necessary to go by horseback the presidential party went that way, and walked the last miles when riding was impossible. Cárdenas could relish the humble food of the peasants and a blanket spread under the stars. His party often had little taste for his rough-and-ready regime. Once when the presidential train was resting at Pátzcuaro and the hungry senators aboard were just about to sit down to a dinner the chef had prepared with especial pride, an Indian dashed up on horseback to beg Cárdenas to come to his village over the mountains to settle some big trouble. "Come, we must all go at once," Cárdenas said to the dismayed party. "But my beautiful dinner?" wailed the chef. "Serve it to those hungry-looking people gaping in at the windows," Cárdenas said. "But what about us?" howled the senators. "We'll eat beans and *tortillas* with the Indians."

The men close to Cárdenas learned that they had to live most abstemious lives to keep up with him. "You will kill yourself," his friends would say to him; "you can't keep up this pace." He would answer: "There is so much to do, so little time—. If I am used up in six years, what does it matter?" Cárdenas knew he could only begin many reforms and public works. He knew that it required time as well as long patience to transform a social structure. But, working on the manifold businesses at hand, he ever kept a vision of the future.

Like Disraeli, Cárdenas believed that "the health of the people is really the foundation upon which all their happiness and their powers as a state depend." But he knew that health could not be achieved merely by constructing hospitals and creating more physicians. It had to begin with a basic education. So he ordered rural primary schools to be built as quickly as possible, and at least two thousand new ones a year came into operation during his regime. The figures for schools stood between seven thousand and eight thousand when Cárdenas became president; the number of teachers between nine thousand and ten thousand. When he left office Mexico could boast of twenty-one thousand schools, forty-four thousand teachers, and almost two million pupils.

In 1935, through the ministry of education, he published a plan of action in regard to the primary "socialist" school. Education was to be compulsory; free; co-educational; scientific—to give an evolutionary concept of the world; of a welfare nature when essential—so that poor children suffering from malnutrition should have food; integral—to co-ordinate physical, intellectual, and social education. A children's bill of rights was drawn up; its ideals lay close to Cárdenas's heart. Children, it declared, had the right "to be born of healthy parents, with the means to bring them up properly. They had the right to receive proper nourishment, to develop their talents and abilities regardless of race, creed, economic or social position. They had the right to well-equipped, well-ventilated school rooms, with plenty of time for recreation in the fresh air." As to responsibilities, it was their duty "to work for the betterment of the general welfare and to serve the nation and humanity in the fight for social justice."

Like missionaries going into the wilderness, teachers were sent forth to spread the blessings of a new gospel. The path of the Cárdenas rural-school teacher was not one strewn with wild flowers. The landlords feared the power of the peons if they were educated. The church frowned on these new secular schools as communistic and anti-religious. Many of the Indians, speaking only their ancient dialects and bound to ancestral superstitions, were distrustful of anything new. In various parts of Mexico two hundred teachers were killed, women as well as men. Some were shot in the back; some, hanged; one or two, burned alive. Others were tied to automobiles and dragged on rocky roads until there was no power in their mangled bodies to impart any knowledge whatever. In an Jaliscan village one teacher's murdered body was chopped into mincemeat and flung out into the fields like manure.

Often village officials were in the pay of the landlords and would do nothing to protect the teachers. So Cárdenas provided revolvers for the teachers and they went to their duties armed. To encourage the faint-hearted, the president visited numerous schools himself, sang the national anthem with the children, shook their grimy little paws, reassured their parents. As fresh, dauntless spirits continued to take the places of the murdered ones, finally the landlords and the religious fanatics gave up the fight and let the schools carry on. In 1939 Cárdenas awarded pensions for life to the dependents of teachers who had lost their lives in spreading rural enlightenment.

The teaching of hygiene was one of the most important works of the rural schoolmaster, and sometimes he had to be both physician and nurse, at the risk of his life. Teachers who distributed and administered the free quinine, vaccines and serums supplied by the department of health were menaced by the Indian witchdoctors.

Every good innovation in Mexico has had a struggle, and has demanded its crop of martyrs. But Cárdenas was determined to make the masses health-conscious, in order to try to halt the annual toll from infant mortality, gastric infections, malaria, tuberculosis, and dysentery, that most prevalent and accursed of all diseases in Mexico.

In a survey the president had made in 1936, there was found to be only one physician for each nine hundred and fourteen square kilometers in rural Mexico, one for about each seven thousand persons. The proportion varied with the states. At the bottom was Querétaro, with only one doctor for fifty-two thousand persons. Some sixty per cent of the population of Mexico received no scientific medical attention whatever. So, in spite of all opposition, traveling ambulance units, like mechanized knights-errant, proclaimed the new way to health wherever roads went. When roads ended, the pioneers of mercy made up burro cavalcades.

The Indians resented health units tampering with the village well. Evil spirits in the water tanks were what bred dysentery— not those unseen things called germs. The backwoods people believed in curative brews as weird as the mess in the witches' caldron in *Macbeth*. One supposedly infallible medicinal tea was made from powdered woodpeckers' heads. Another special nostrum required "tears from a widowed sow." As groups of health officers descended on villages with their vaccinating needles, the people fled to the woods as if escaping a legion of stinging ants. Quarantines were utterly unknown even in sizable towns, and often the army had to be called on to enforce a quarantine in times of epidemic.

An excellent native motion picture called *The Forgotten Village,* for which John Steinbeck provided the running commentary, told a typical story of the struggle to bring health instruction and remedial agencies into the backwoods. Like the school teachers, some pioneering physicians and nurses met death at the hands of parents incited by the jealous charm healers. So the government ordered the young physicians to carry revolvers in their medical kits.

In 1936, at a congress held in Morelia, Mexico's medical service in rural districts submitted a project in group medicine, to be partially government financed and partially paid for by the people. In group medicine the fee for complete medical care for an entire family was to be as low as twelve pesos a year ($2.40). Cárdenas supported the idea with all his might.

He gave orders for eleven military hospitals, to be constructed "in strategic centers of operation," and for forty regional hospitals. When he could not find the money for provincial town hospitals, his imagination led him to various workable expediencies. For instance, in Pátzcuaro he built a large motion-picture house for the municipality, and the profits he used for financing the conversion of a disused monastery into a charity hospital. As monthly profits mounted, the very latest surgical equipment, X-ray machines, and sterilizers were installed. The hospital is a cheery place, spreading around a fountained patio filled with flowers. Its directing nurse was formerly a nun who had been brought up in a druggist shop in Morelia where her father was the leading apothecary.

But it was far easier for Cárdenas to create new hospitals than to dissolve the charlatanism and bureaucratic red tape and favoritism that existed in medical circles. That discouraging story Verna Carleton Millán tells with vivid authenticity in *Mexico Reborn*. She knows the story as perhaps no other does, for she has been married to the distinguished Mexican physician, Dr. Ignacio Millán, for ten years. Her husband, who was recently made the head of Mexico's cancer clinic, fought side by side with Cárdenas against incredible odds and all the traditional reactionary attitudes of the Mexican medical profession.

Cárdenas listened to the advice of Dr. Millán, who is widely recognized as another selfless patriot. In Mexico's crying need for physicians, Millán's plan was to recruit rural doctors from rural districts; to take the cream of those students who were able to finish vocational science courses and to give them a medical education at government expense. In return for this free education, the students were pledged to practice in rural districts for five years.

In 1938, Dr. Millán's school of rural medicine was opened at the Polytechnic Institute. The funds were so scant that the noted physician taught half a day for twenty dollars a month, but he was able to recruit a competent staff at the same meager salary. The penniless students received allowances for living expenses. The medical course was stepped up to five years instead of six, and in 1943 the first class of doctors was graduated.

To make as many ignorant people health-conscious as quickly as possible, another excellent idea was promulgated by the faculty of the medical college. Instead of the graduates becoming interns in city hospitals, they were sent for six months into communities that had never known a doctor. Medicine was free, fees were nil. The salary was ninety pesos a month. The physician novices had to train their own nurses and set up their clinics where they could. At the end of the period, for their thesis they were to write a tabulated survey of their community—the kind of people, climate, sanitation, diet, income, and special diseases of the region. On completing their six-month rural internship and their thesis, they receive their degrees. Not only has the plan been of eminent value in its compilation of essential information, but in revealing to the young physicians the terrible needs of their less fortunate compatriots. Many students from well-to-do families, who heartily resented their primitive assignments, became interested in the humanitarian aspects of the work and of their own volition returned to the regions of their novitiate for further practice and study.

Along with the coming of the pioneering student doctors, the first drugstores were opened up in remote towns. And in every village there were tacked up posters that told stories, as obvious as comic strips, in which Germs and Dirt were the personifications of man's mortal enemies. A tabloid paper, *Hygiene,* was distributed free about the land. In Mexico City a building on Calle Juárez was rented and turned into a museum of health for public instruction.

Cárdenas saw the health statistics improve, infant mortality decline. But he had known that Mexico could not become a healthy country by education and medical care alone. A prime cause of Mexican sickness lay in poverty. The people did not have enough to eat and they could not afford to buy the proper food. Cárdenas was determined to eradicate malnutrition if he could. First of all, men had to have soil on which to grow their food. He had tried from the beginning to remedy this basic deficiency by giving land to the land-hungry.

# 24. Tierra

*"He and his fathers have been serfs; it takes
time for him to walk erect as a free man."*

HUBERT HERRING

As the crux of the Cárdenas ideology was the belief that a man
who desired land and who would work it should have it. "No
man can be a citizen unless he walks on something of his own,"
the president said. So he proceeded to give land to men, to make
them conscious of citizenship. At the end of his third year in
office Cárdenas had distributed among the peasants six million
more acres than all the preceding administrations together. On
July twenty-first, 1939, during his fifth year, the president summed
up the land distribution of his previous years; thirty-seven million
acres in all had been re-divided. In his farewell address to congress on September first, 1940, he presented the final figures of
land distribution under his regime; the total area amounted to
45,330,119 acres.

Of course, the problem was not so simple as merely giving
land to the hungry peasants. There were matters of credit, tools,
seed, farm animals, agricultural guidance, to arrange. All of
these factors Cárdenas met as well as he could with the human
material he had to work with and the slimness of the national
treasury. And nature, like human nature, in Mexico is uncommonly unaccountable. Droughts were obstacles to success, as well
as was corruption in some bank clerks and laziness in some peasants. The president had to warn the farmers against being cheated
when they sold their produce. His agronomists had to struggle
to make them take up new methods.

But when Cárdenas went out of office it was absurd to deny

the economic betterment of the peons who received land. The most superficial observer, if not blind with prejudice, could see improvement in the houses, the clothes, and the daily food. But from Cárdenas's viewpoint, more significant was the change in the people's psychology "from servility to independent worker."

On October sixth, 1936, Cárdenas, the audacious innovator, made high and wide head-lines when he expropriated at one blow about a million acres of land in Coahuila and Durango. The district was known as Laguna, and was the finest cotton-growing land in the country. In 1936 almost three hundred thousand acres were under cultivation. For decades the region had paid handsomely the dozen families who owned it. But the thirty thousand peon families who worked the land were among the most pathetically poor in the whole republic. No tales of ruthless dispossession of workers at the introduction of modern machinery, no reports of callous indifference to starvation in unproductive seasons, have been surpassed by those in the Laguna. The worker's daily wage—when he was employed—was one peso, and sometimes it dropped as low as eighty centavos. Work hours were as long as in the blackest days of slavery.

When Lombardo Toledano's labor union, CTM, was created with Cárdenas's blessing in 1936, the workers in the Laguna fields and their fifteen thousand desperate, dispossessed brothers had a chance to be redeemed. In August, thousands of agrarian laborers throughout the Laguna struck. As to wages, they asked only one peso seventy-five centavos a day, with a seven-day payment for six days' work. But they also demanded medical care, schools, and decent houses to replace their miserable shacks. All of these demands were quite within the law. The landlords, however, considered them preposterous and confiscatory. In the deadlock, the entire Mexican cotton crop was in jeopardy. Calling his economic advisers together, Cárdenas made one of his climactic decisions. He signed an expropriation decree, and then proceeded

in person to Laguna to advise with the agrarian commission and
to help direct the parceling of land.

Production in Laguna was to be an experiment in scientific
and collectivized farming. Nothing like it in scale had ever been
attempted in this hemisphere. The lands were allotted to newly
created *ejidal* groups, each a separate co-operative society. Machinery for co-operative use was ordered. Technical advisers were
employed. Methods were devised to control and distribute the
the waters from the rivers that overflow in the autumn. Construction of an enormous dam, El Palmito, was ordered begun.
It was to be the largest dam in the Western Hemisphere south
of Boulder Dam. It represented an investment of twenty-five
million pesos and was to be completed by 1940. Special imple-
menting work in the Bank of Ejidal Credit was inaugurated
to provide the workers what money was immediately needful in
commodity production and for their daily living. When the harvest came in, the *ejidatarios* were to pay off their debt to the
bank and receive their share in the profits. Despite the curses
and sabotage of the naturally furious landlords, it began to look
as if the experiment in co-operation was to have a successful first
season. But an unexpected enemy wrought havoc. Perverse nature blighted the region with one of the worst droughts it ever
experienced. The crop was a failure. And because there was no
profit, many of the disappointed *ejidatarios* blamed Cárdenas
rather than the rainless season.

In 1938, however, the crop was middling good. The Ejidal
Credit Bank distributed over three million pesos in profits, after
setting aside twenty-seven million pesos for past expenses and
the next year's sowing. Four hundred tractors and fifteen thousand plows were purchased. New, neat, well-windowed schools
sprang up. At the end of 1938 the total of rural schools in the
Laguna region was close to three hundred. Mills for the co-
operative grinding of meal were established, and chicken runs,
to be managed co-operatively, were arranged. A modern well-

equipped Ejidal Hospital was soon in operation in Torreón, the town in the heart of the district. Group-medicine membership shortly reached over thirty thousand. The *ejidatarios* began to buy shoes and the kind of groceries and clothes they had never known before, and even radios and stoves. Many left their straw mats to sleep in beds for the first time. Merchants in Torreón, bidding for the rustic trade, began to address the *ejidatarios* as "señores." The old manager of Torreón's single moving-picture house in 1936 had wailed that the new order would ruin him, that never again would he have those fine motor cars of the well-to-do lined up in front of his place, that he would have to close. But in 1938 so many truckloads of peasants were arriving to see the movies that he could not accommodate them. By the end of 1941 Torreón could boast of seven cinemas instead of one.

Enemies of the Revolution—those who have never visited Torreón and Laguna, or not since 1937—still maintain that co-operative *ejido* farming in the region is a failure. They say that the *ejidatarios* merely swapped masters, the government bank in exchange for the *hacendado*. But despite the dubious features of the new order and some bureaucratic corruption and ineptitude that seem inevitable in Mexico, the *ejidatarios* are far better off than they ever were before. Not one would dream of returning to the old ways if he could.

Cárdenas had expected mistakes to be made, but these errors, he said, would in time be rectified or eradicated. At first the agents might not always buy the seed best adapted for a proper region, or the proper machinery. An inferior system of marketing might have to be revised. When graft and bureaucratic incompetence were detected, however, he promised that offenders would be removed and punished. Let the critics censure, he said, after four years of experiment.

Four years later, in February, 1941, Avila Camacho's very able minister of agriculture, Marte Gómez, made a frank report on Laguna. Admitting freely all failures and miscalculations, he pointed up the indubitable success. Now one hundred and seven million pesos of the original one hundred and twenty-six million had been liquidated. And though the *ejidatarios* had received only nine million pesos in profits, they had the inestimable benefits from good schools, water-supply systems in the villages, and medical care and hospitalization. Men had become proficient in new skills, in mechanics, in electrical plants, in operating tractors, in accounting. "The prosperity is established," said Gómez. "The optimism of the region is reborn. That optimism is not illusory. It is a prosperity based on the riches of the soil and on the hard work and spirit and enterprise of the men of the Laguna."

In 1942 and 1943 some of the more fortunate *ejidatarios* were able to pay off all their debts and offered to pay for the land the government had given them. But, of course, the land already belonged to them, they were told. With the profits they were to continue to raise their standards of living and their qualities of citizenship.

Cárdenas is one of those persons who perceives the "elements of magnificence in plain men." He believes in the possibility of building greatness by the routine labor of every day. But he had to fight first for the minimum of human rights. He threw his weight into helping the industrial workers of Mexico to help themselves. To fortify him, he had the authority of the 1917 constitution's Article 123. To help him push immediately the cause of the working man, he had one of the most intelligent and forceful personalities ever to rise in the labor unions of the hemisphere, Vicente Lombardo Toledano.

By Article 123 collective bargaining, minimum wages and hours, and compensation insurance were all prescribed. But in practice everything had fallen far short of the conditions envisioned by the authors of the article. Judged by any standards, the demands of labor seem little enough. Two years before Cárdenas became president, the wages were scandalously low.

The millionaire Abelardo Rodríguez, as Calles's minister of industry, commerce, and labor, had been profoundly shocked at the results of his own investigations. A few months before he himself became president, he wrote that he was convinced that four pesos a day was the minimum wage on which a man might live and support his family. He found that a salary of hunger was almost universal; that only occasionally did it reach the category of bare necessity; and almost never of comfort. He found the minimum wage to be about one peso and six centavos, and he discovered sections where the daily hire for ten hours was as low as sixty centavos.

Rodríguez, the capitalist, had said four pesos should be minimum. The radical Lombardo Toledano had a struggle to get the minimum to three pesos fifty. And for all his dynamic vigor and spell-binding oratory, Lombardo Toledano had tremendous difficulties in getting labor to stick together. Labor disputes often led to deadly organizational conflicts. In 1935 and 1936 seventy-two textile workers were killed in inter-union feuds. Cárdenas pled for harmony. In eight states the president personally used his influence to bring disputing factions together. "In union lies strength," he repeatedly told the workers. "Quit your petty bickering among yourselves. Each quarrel within labor strengthens intrenched capital." Then he put the matter more cleverly: "Only organized labor can force me or any other citizen in power to satisfy the needs of the people."

During Cárdenas's first three years there were several hundred strikes a year. The wage scale could not remain static, because of changes in the cost of living. Almost as soon as a strike had brought about an increase of fifty centavos, the advanced living costs would obliterate its value as real wage. Mexican courts began to favor labor in almost every dispute that reached them. The proletariat grew in strength. Wages for textile, oil, and mine workers increased sixty per cent in Cárdenas's first four years.

In February of 1936 Mexican workers combined in the largest organization that had ever existed in Mexico. The new federation was formed on a basis of industrial unionism and was called the *Confederación de Trabajadores Mexicanos* (CTM). Its initial membership went beyond half a million. Lombardo Toledano was, of course, its head.

By 1938, CTM was claiming to affect the lives of approximately a million workers. It organized an excellent sports program to relieve industrial fatigue. It became a political power in state and national elections, throwing its influence towards that candidate who promised to help labor. Its social and economic victories were significant. It proved to be a potent instrument in bringing about some of Cárdenas's social reforms.

Cárdenas met his most formidable opposition in the heavily industrialized Monterrey region. But he unequivocally declared that his revolutionary regime favored the weaker side in the struggle. Strikes were legitimate weapons, he maintained; the lock-out was unpatriotic. He warned Monterrey industrialists not to organize against labor. He pointed out the danger of armed strife if they made "political capital out of anti-union agitation." "If employers grow too weary of the social struggle," he said, blandly, "they can always hand over their factories to the workers or the government—that would be patriotic."

Regarding it as anti-social for machinery to remain idle, the president would not permit the Monterrey factories to close down. He announced his intention of leasing all idle factories and giving them to the workers to run as co-operatives, under state direction. "When a factory refuses to obey labor laws or decisions of arbitration boards or when it ceases operations," Cárdenas said, "it can by law be expropriated and turned over to the worker." A law was passed in 1936 to empower the president to take over any property "required for social utility." The expropriated property was to be paid for on the basis of assessed valuation, within ten years. Cárdenas did not desire to take over any private industry for either the workers or the government; for he realized neither was trained sufficiently in socialism to succeed. But with private enterprise fighting him bitterly and refusing to co-operate, the threat of expropriation was his most potent weapon.

Cárdenas and Lombardo Toledano were an amazingly powerful combination. They worked well together and did much for labor. Though both were striving for the betterment of the common man's lot, there was a basic difference in their motives. Cárdenas's motive was selfless; his ruling principle was never a will to power. Lombardo Toledano was believed to be profoundly interested in his own personal career.

The two dynamos were not always in ideological accord. Lombardo Toledano had undergone considerable change in attitude after an extended visit to Soviet Russia. When he was dismissed from the University of Mexico in 1933 for his "unwelcome Marxist views," he straightway formed his own university where there would be no censorship of his curricula. It became known late in 1935 as the Workers' University. Lombardo Toledano was the rector. The teaching had a predominant communist slant. But though he printed and distributed series of leftist pamphlets and spoke warmly in praise of Russia, he ever denied any direct affiliation with Stalinist communism. He called himself a Marxist. The thousand-odd students under his tutelage came mostly from industrial workers, though some were peasant boys. They received a good education at the smallest possible cost. The proletarian university was supported partially by government funds, and endowed with Cárdenas's good will. But no pressure from the socialist student committees could persuade Cárdenas to recognize and establish diplomatic relations with Soviet Russia.

Cárdenas approved of Lombardo Toledano's aim, through the Workers' University and his newspaper *El Popular,* to make labor so unified in spirit that it would remain strong regardless of pro- or anti-labor sentiments of Mexico's chief executives. But he stopped considerably short of some of the labor leader's more radical theories. As much as he liked Lombardo Toledano, he did not think it prudent to permit one man to be too powerful. When the labor leader attempted to seize too much power for himself by incorporating the farmers' union with his CTM, Cárdenas said, "Hands off! The peasants have their own leagues which serve them very well." When Lombardo Toledano began to militarize CTM and asked its members to put in a certain number of hours a week in drilling, Cárdenas set the peasants' organization to drilling.

In January, 1937, Cárdenas's government granted complete freedom of the press. And when Lombardo Toledano organized a mass demonstration against the reactionary papers, Cárdenas refused to support it, and it fizzled. Its leader was extremely dubious about Cárdenas's general amnesty of February, which permitted the return to Mexico of all political exiles, an esti- mated ten thousand, virtually all of whom were of conservative bent. But the CTM's leader and the president were in accord in June, when the foreign-owned National Railways of Mexico were expropriated "for reasons of public welfare." The roads were greatly in need of repair, and the rolling stock was in a perilous condition. Wrecks had been frequent. No foreign capital could be obtained. So the federal government had to do the financing. In August the management of the railways was promised to the workers. And on April twenty-first of the next year the senate approved the bill to turn them over to the workers' administra- tion. It was a bold experiment and it proved a failure, even as certain union leaders had feared.

On the most publicized and controversial issue of the entire administration, the oil expropriations, Lombardo Toledano sup- ported Cárdenas with all his eloquent might.

# 25. Heroic Madness

*"Twenty or thirty years ago the heroic madness of Cárdenas in expropriating the oil properties could not have succeeded."*

FRANCISCO CASTILLO NÁJERA

In May, 1937, seventeen thousand oil workers struck. They returned to work on condition that the labor arbitration board would investigate the economic condition of the companies, to determine their capacity to pay increased wages and to create certain social services. The deplorable housing and disgusting sanitation conditions of the workers were documented by photographs and charts and displayed by government agents. The board's report was presented in August. It showed that the Mexican oil worker's wage was less than one-third that paid in the United States. It reckoned the production costs for a barrel of crude oil in Mexico as less than one-fifth that in the United States. In relation to capitalization, the board found that the profits from 1934 to 1936 amounted to an average of a little more than thirty-four per cent. "Experts investigated the books," wrote Dr. Alfred B. Thomas, "and found that the companies had made a clear profit in these two years (1934-1936) of 168,783,529 pesos." Whether the figures were accurate or not, on the basis of the investigations the board awarded to the oil workers wage increases and welfare benefits to an amount of something over twenty-six million pesos annually.

The oil companies protested with accusations of prejudice and exaggeration. In the end they agreed to an increase of some twenty million pesos for everything. But they refused adamantly to grant closed shop to all except the chief executives, and they refused to agree to allow any workers' representative to have any part in the administration. The companies denied the validity of the labor board's awards, and took test cases to the circuit court; lost every one; took them to the supreme court, and again lost every decision. But they seemed completely unperturbed about conformance. Finally, March eighth, 1938—seven months after the original awards were made—was fixed on as the date of reckoning and active compliance. At first one of the managers had said, "We cannot and will not pay." Now the oil officials still refused to abide by the decisions, but said, more tactfully, "We are unable to comply." They were confident Cárdenas would not call their bluff. Had they not won out against Obregón and "Iron Man" Calles? The latter, coaxed by Dwight Morrow, had let the Mexico supreme court reverse his own decree. Cárdenas, too, would knuckle under. He would hardly dare invoke the wrath of both His Majesty's Government and the United States. The oil men did not reckon maturely with their opponent.

By the authority of the law of the land, the oil workers had the right to enforce the supreme court's decision by calling a general strike. But an oil-union strike would have stopped all production, and might have created a hazardous crisis in industry. It was imperative that production continue. Cárdenas gave the companies ten days of grace to mediate and come to terms. The oil companies gradually raised their offer to within half a million dollars of the total award—and then said, "No more." But they refused to grant closed shop for all but the chief executives. Though they had dropped defiance, they still bluffed. And a few of the most incorrigible imperialists among them actually believed that when all else had failed they might "whistle for the gunboats."

Cárdenas certainly did not want to expropriate the oil. He had expected the directors to realize that he was not bluffing, and to abide by the supreme court's decisions. Mexico was in no way

prepared to handle production and marketing efficiently. Reper-
cussions from expropriation might have a most deleterious effect
on the national economy. Not a single economist or cabinet minister would have dared to urge the president to so drastic a
course. But Ramón Beteta, the young under-secretary of state,
whom Cárdenas intuitively trusted more than he did anyone else
in the republic, was close beside his chief with inspiriting moral
support as well as a trained knowledge of economics. He pointed
out to the president that the international oil alliance would most
likely create a world-wide boycott of Mexican oil. Cárdenas faced
the prediction. To him, not only was the sovereignty of Mexico
at stake, but the whole future of its dealings with foreign business and foreign powers. He took the full responsibility and
decided the matter alone on the inner promptings that are said
to come to him in times of stress and crisis.

At ten o'clock on the night of March eighteenth, 1938, he
stepped up to the microphone in a national hook-up and quietly
announced that the properties of the seventeen American and
British oil companies in Mexico had been expropriated. He explained that the oil officials had created a national emergency,
and "in behalf of the general welfare as against narrow private
enterprise" the government had taken over. The companies were
to be indemnified within ten years. He made it clear that the
expropriation was exceptional, saying, "It will not be extended to
other activities of the country which the government views with
sympathy and considers necessary for the national development."

The Mexican public was as wonder-struck as were the oil
officials, who had at the very last hour come across with a promise of the full amount, proving their capacity to pay all the time.
Virtually to the last man, the nation was with Cárdenas. Never
had any Mexican's prestige been higher with his own people
than was his on that night of March eighteenth. The oil expropriation was the most daring move any Latin American execu-

tive had ever made against the capitalistic might of Great Britain and the United States. All of the nineteen other Latin American republics were jubilant. The imperialists gasped. But a couple of Englishmen, heads of other British-owned concerns in Mexico, said to their oil compatriots: "Damn fools, we told you so. We told you Cárdenas was not bluffing. You brought this all on yourselves. You deserve expropriation. Now there's no telling where this thing will end." As business men, the British and American managers—with the exception of Harry Sinclair—had proved themselves unastute and bull-headed. The stockholders were to pay for their executive bungling and for the expensive propaganda campaign they were to launch to try to recover their lost control.

For three days the nation was ecstatic to the bursting point. The multitudes demanded to see Cárdenas, to hear his voice. On March twenty-second, two hundred thousand assorted persons bearing a multiplicity of banners paraded for six hours. Bands played tunes of victory. Church bells pealed as joyously as if Cárdenas were a communicant. The great plaza became a solid mass of excited humanity. Mexicans had never felt so good about themselves, their nation, and their leader. When the voice of Cárdenas sounded out over the crowd, the people went wild.

Though the ovation could not be halted, Cárdenas continued to speak. He announced an internal loan to pay the indemnity. Few could possibly have heard him, but word got around that they must collect money to pay off the oil companies. Contributions were brought to the Palacio de Bellas Artes, large checks, small checks, and even pennies from ragged children. Country folk brought hens and suckling pigs. Society women gave up discarded jewelry. The hundred-million peso aim fell considerably short of being reached, but the giving relieved the tension. "The expropriation of Mexican oil," wrote Virginia Prewett, "was as bold and brilliant a political coup as has been brought off in modern politics. Mexico, without money, friends, or arma-

ment . . . suddenly rose up and unceremoniously kicked out
the powerful American, and the doubly powerful British, oil
interests. It was more than a case of the mouse defying the cat,
it was the mouse cracking the two neighborhood champions'
heads together."

But the president did not become heady with his people's
demonstration or lose his grasp on realities. More than anyone
else, he knew the monkey wrenches which angry, powerful nations could throw into the machinery of small nations. His
brain remained steady in its functioning. If the big powers
stopped short of intervention—no matter what else they did—
Cárdenas still felt confident he could win out in the end. When
ten days passed and no gunboats had arrived, Cárdenas said
smilingly to a friend, as if a crisis in a dread disease had passed,
"The conflict is won."

But though he had not believed that Washington would take
such an unneighborly action, he had considered the possibility
and was willing to risk the landing of marines. He had even
planned to meet intervention with more than scorched earth in
the oil fields. He would have dynamited everything connected
with the oil industry to oblivion. He was determined not to
sacrifice Mexico's self-respect by permitting foreign powers to
run the expropriated business.

Cárdenas had acted completely within the laws of the land.
From a decree of King Charles III of Spain in 1783, all subsoil
wealth, including all minerals, bitumens, and "earth juices" belonged to the state. The Mexican constitution of 1857 reiterated
that the nation's subsoil wealth belonged to the government.
And though Porfirio Díaz had denied it and decreed that subsoil wealth might belong to the owner of the surface, the constitution of 1917 was very explicit in reverting to the constitution
of 1857 and stating categorically that the government alone had
title to the subsoil wealth. And by that law, passed under Cárdenas on November eighteenth, 1936, the Mexican president was

empowered to take over any property "required for social utility."

Cárdenas was prepared for a bitter reaction from the foreign capitalists, but not for the extent of their claims and reprisals. He had hoped the oil executives might be reasonable, considering the unrestrained exploitation they had enjoyed for three and four decades. It is impossible to know accurately the vast sums from Mexican oil that had poured into alien pockets, but it is generally assumed that the total profits earned by the oil companies exceeded a billion dollars. One company, El Aguila, was paying its stockholders a sixty per cent dividend in 1920.

Now in their fury the oil companies were bent on throwing Mexican finance and industry into confusion, and their lobbyists brought intense pressure on the United States government. Though Washington sent no punitive expedition, it struck Mexico a severe blow. The United States treasury suspended its regular purchases of Mexican silver, which it had been buying since 1934 at an artificially stimulated price of 44¾ cents an ounce. Silver was perforce thrown on the free world market at a considerably lower price. The value of the Mexican peso dropped alarmingly. In finding it necessary to defy United States patronage, Cárdenas had to risk economic collapse. Hardly expecting this blow, though it had been threatened, he took it with fortitude. Coming just when it did, a few days after the expropriation, it certainly suggested retaliation.

Cárdenas's immediate reaction was not recrimination, but a desire to forestall bitter anti-American sentiment on the part of his people. With cool wisdom, he announced: "It must be taken into account that the government of the United States of America has announced that purchases by it of a part of Mexico's output as heretofore made are going to be canceled as from April first next. [The date was only five days off.] We are keenly desirous now that this fact be known to the nation, that it judge said action calmly and correctly." Cárdenas was scrupulously careful not to let a hint of condemnation escape him, for he knew the fiery temper of his people. Paradoxically, the troubled president took it as his bounden duty to still the anti-United States feeling that was simmering hotly with all the recrudescence of past resentments.

On March thirtieth, the tension was relieved when Secretary of State Hull announced that Mexico was within her legal rights in expropriating oil properties, proper indemnification being the only condition to be satisfied. President Cárdenas was so pleased that he invited the American ambassador, Josephus Daniels, to his office to express his gratitude in person. And in the formal message of appreciation to Daniels, which was printed in all the newspapers the next day, Cárdenas said, among other things: "Today my country is rejoicing. It quietly celebrates the proof of friendship which it has received from your country, and which it will treasure up in its heart."

Though the ambassador had dutifully exerted a little pressure on President Cárdenas against the possible expropriation early in March, it was generally believed that his sympathies were all with Mexico. A goodly proportion of Cárdenas's success in liberal reform had been due to the co-existence of Franklin D. Roosevelt's New Deal administration, for both governments were ostensibly working for the same ends—the alleviation of the sufferings of the underprivileged. One of the greatest boons bestowed on Cárdenas was the ambassadorship of Josephus Daniels, who had proved a staunch ally of his social program. But when the Mexicans had first heard of his appointment in 1933 many were wrathful. They remembered that it was Daniels who, as secretary of navy, on Woodrow Wilson's command had ordered the marines to take Vera Cruz in 1914. "Dirty swine, both, Franklin D. Roosevelt and Josephus Daniels," the anti-*gringos* cried. Some tried to wreck Daniels's train. Others threw stones at the embassy. An American who really knew Daniels and who witnessed the stone-throwing said with assurance, to his companion, "The time will come when they will be throwing roses to him."

Soon the people learned to their gratification that back in the United States Mr. Daniels was considered a champion of the underprivileged and that he had fought Standard Oil. Before the first year of Cárdenas's administration was ended, the common people had accepted the ambassador as a friend. They even said, "He considers the rights and happiness of alien masses as important as the pocketbooks of his compatriots." He seemed in complete accord with the tenet of the Cárdenas regime that "the end of production is not more goods but the most efficient satisfaction of human necessities." He did not delight the privileged, however, but he grinned amiably at their disapproval and sipped his tomato juice, while they drank their martinis. When he left Mexico he was more popular with the citizens at large than any American ambassador had ever been, not even excepting that most able and charming gentleman, Dwight Morrow. And his feelings for Lázaro Cárdenas were best expressed in his last telegraphed message to him: "You have made your place in history alongside of Benito Juárez." Cárdenas had great need of the American ambassador's friendship and faith in the two critical years that followed Secretary Hull's reassuring note of March thirtieth, 1938.

Mexico's right to expropriate having been publicly reognized by the United States government, now the problem was the indemnity. How much? That question was to be the focal point of much grief. The companies now demanded four hundred million dollars for indemnification. Such an absurd and staggering amount was obviously beyond the power of Mexico to pay. Cárdenas sent the noted economist, Jésus Silva Herzog, to examine the companies' books and arrive at a reasonable figure for just settlement. As a basis of appraisal Silva Herzog accepted the companies' own declared valuation for taxes as of December, 1936. This was like a blow beneath the belt to them. Then, calculating this shrunken amount, together with unearthed sums of back taxes due and unpaid compensation to workers under the existing labor laws, he figured that Mexico owed the companies no more than fifty million pesos. From these two poles, naturally a deadlock ensued, to last for three years. However, to the rage of the others, one of the American companies, Sinclair, was smart enough to settle rather promptly for eight million dollars, the arbitration figure arrived at for the value of buildings, machinery, and equipment. Some of the other American companies and all the British not only held out for an absurd valuation on their material properties, but also demanded compensation for subsoil wealth to be taken in the future.

On April first, 1938, President Roosevelt announced that the basis of just indemnity would be measured by the actual unamortized investment. The oil companies laughed sardonically—and flooded the newspapers with their claims for more than four hundred million dollars. At the same time, the propagandists spread the insinuation that Mexico was economically bankrupt and unable to pay anything at all.

On May fourteenth, Cárdenas himself offered a solution of the oil indemnification problem. "Inasmuch as forty per cent of our oil production is consumed on the domestic market," he said, "there remains sixty per cent for export. After deducting production costs, the balance will be left as a guarantee for the payment of the oil indemnity over the ten-year period fixed by the corresponding decree and the expropriation law." This was exactly what was done three years later. The truth is, of course, that the oil companies did not want to arrive at an arbitrated figure. They did not want to be paid. They wanted the oil fields returned to them.

The economic situation in Mexico grew more critical. And then the American owners of the Mexican silver industry brought pressure to bear on Washington. Shortly, news came that the United States would resume purchases of Mexican silver but at the regular New York market price and not at the preferential figure paid to Canada and formerly paid to Mexico.

Though oil agents lobbied for intervention, New Deal Washington with its "good-neighbor policy" never considered such a measure. President Roosevelt looked upon Mexico and Cárdenas with especial warmth and cordiality. A moderately well-disposed neighbor to the south was imperative. War clouds were gathering in Europe. And all South America was watching the Big Neighbor. Secretary of State Hull, who had promptly acknowledged that Mexico was within her rights as a sovereign state to expropriate, contended that expropriation should be met with immediate compensation. Cárdenas wanted to pay. But, with his depleted treasury, to pay cash at once would have meant the rupture and perhaps the destruction of his whole social program. Mr. Hull sent a few reminding notes to Mexico. Gradually, as months passed, they became sharper in phraseology. Mr. Hull scolded, as was natural and to be expected for policy's sake. He was even accused of hounding, which the Mexican government had not expected.

The tone of the first diplomatic notes from England infuriated the Mexican government, but they were answered with restraint by the foreign minister. The British were more incensed than the Americans. They had more to lose. The American wells were less valuable and contained only a few more years' supply. The British-owned Pozo Rica was the second potentially richest in the world; it had only recently been tapped, and was currently producing about two-thirds of the total oil. In April, His Majesty's government said it had reached the conclusion "that the real reason for expropriation was the political desire of acquiring permanently for Mexico the advantages of the property and the oil fields; that the expropriation was equivalent to confiscation carried out under the appearance of legality based on labor difficulties." They intimated that the return of the British-owned properties would be the only satisfactory solution.

On May eleventh, His Majesty's Government sent a communication of protest, weighted with demands. It listed all the arrears in interest and principal on damage claims on British property in the revolutionary decade 1910-1920, plus the railway debt and the land-expropriation claims. It also suggested its right to examine and analyze Mexico's internal situation. In somewhat stodgy syntax the note expressed pained surprise tinctured with British disdain.

"His Majesty's Government cannot but regard failure of the Mexican Government to discharge even their existing obligations as in itself rendering unjustified an expropriation, an essential condition of the validity of which would be the payment of full and adequate compensation amounting in the case of the oil expropriations to a very large sum. . . . My government must in any case request the immediate payment of the sum of 370,962.71 pesos which fell due the first of last January."

Cárdenas replied immediately by sending the demanded check for the exact amount, including the seventy-one centavos. In his accompanying reply he denied categorically Great Britain's right "to analyze the internal situation of Mexico." With cool sarcasm he reminded His Majesty's Government—without directly mentioning the famous war debt to the United States—that "even powerful states cannot always pride themselves on punctual payment of all their pecuniary obligations." With that caustic farewell to England, he recalled the Mexican ambassador and severed diplomatic relations. Again Cárdenas had broken precedent, but he had added prestige to Mexico's national sovereignty. "After all," as Virginia Prewett remarked, "you can count on your fingers the men who have ever been in a position to slap the British Empire in the face—and get away with it."

In April of 1938 the Mexican government had found itself involved in big business in a big way. First, units sabotaged by the oil companies had to be restored as best they could. Then, millions of pesos went into building decent houses for the workers. Other houses were painted; toilets were installed. Man-agers' spacious private homes became workers' clubs. Cinnamon-colored and orange-brown children were permitted in the company swimming pools formerly kept exclusively for whites.

At first the oil workers outdid themselves in an effort to make a success. They worked overtime without extra pay. The runs even became longer. The storage tanks filled. But where was the market?

In his message accompanying the decree, Cárdenas had said that Mexican oil would not be available for fascist countries. A week after expropriation Cárdenas announced that Mexico hoped to sell all her oil to the democracies. He said he wanted especially to trade with the United States. He feared that any greatly increased commerce with Germany might tend to heighten Nazi political influence in Mexico, which he ever distrusted. "We need the help of our neighbors," he said, "and if our neighbors do not help us, we will have to manage as best we can by ourselves."

But the democracies were not in the market for Mexican oil. Moreover, when Mexico tried to sell her oil elsewhere, there were no tankers available. The international cartel had seen to that. An Associated Press dispatch from London on May third stated: "A complete boycott of Mexican oil is reported to have been ordered by Shell, with a threat of refusing to have any further dealings with any concern which ships, purchases, or otherwise handles Mexican oil." In Mexico, Shell agents began spying to ascertain the movements of tankers, so as to impose full penalty on anyone who disregarded the boycott. Fearing reprisals from England, the little nations with tankers dared not transport Mexican oil at any freight rate. When a few loads of Mexican oil did arrive at Swedish ports, British agents there claimed the cargo and held up the unloading. England attempted to embargo boats carrying oil to France. United States oil machinery and supply companies that sold to Standard declined to sell the necessary equipment to the Mexicans. They returned certified checks to the Mexican government and frankly said they dared not deal with Mexico for fear of Standard's wrath. In May, 1939, a contract for twenty-eight large trucks to be supplied from American manufacturers was canceled because of pressure brought by enemies of Mexico. Other companies refused credit. When Mexico had tankers built in Italy, Great Britain refused to permit delivery through her blockade. Rather than let Mexico use the tankers, she stupidly let them be confiscated by the Italian government after the World War was on.

The screws of relentless economic warfare were turned on Cárdenas without mercy. But he managed to endure and come through the ordeal incorruptible and unbowed. With no cash and no market, Cárdenas—completely against his desire—had to turn in the end to Germany and barter oil for machinery parts. The Axis powers only would buy Mexican oil—and they bought well below the world market price. So the great democracies literally threw Mexico into the orbit of Axis influence. Mexico's imports from Germany went up by leaps and bounds as United States exports to Mexico fell. In 1939 Mexico's economic survival depended on trade with Germany, Italy, and Japan. Oil-company propaganda had the nerve to denounce the Mexican government bitterly for aiding the Axis war preparations—at the very time that United States boats were groaning under cargoes of scrap iron for Japan. "We were made to appear traitors and scoundrels," said a righteously resentful Mexican, "because we sold oil to the totalitarians so that our people could eat bread, after the markets of the world had been closed to us. What did the United States and England expect us to do with the oil? Drink it for sustenance?"

The ejected oil companies desired above everything else to bring about the fall of Cárdenas. Certain American journalists admitted freely that they had come on assignment to launch

a campaign against the Mexican government. They were interested in only one side of the controversy. They made no effort
to ascertain the truth. They tried to implant the idea in the
United States that Mexico was in a chaotic and anarchistic state.
By their falsifications and exaggerations they temporarily ruined
the tourist trade. They did incalculable harm in creating mutual
distrust and hatred between the next-door neighbors.

The most harmful propaganda was the attempt to create the
impression that Cárdenas intended to confiscate all foreign business. He had no intention of doing anything of the kind. Cárdenas was sufficiently realistic to know that foreign capital was
a necessity to Mexican economy. He only asked that foreign business be willing to abide by the laws of the land, which are
extremely generous to foreign business. Never once did Cárdenas
voice an intention of destroying free enterprise. He would fight
to the death an out-and-out government control of business, for
there was no assurance that control might not swing back to
the conservatives. To foreign investors he said, unequivocally:
"Mexico is a sovereign nation. Those foreign businesses which
respect the laws will be undisturbed. Those who defy the laws
must risk the consequences."

In Mexico, the oil propagandists strove to turn the nation
against Cárdenas, to blame him for all crop failures, to implant
the idea that his faulty sense of economics had impoverished the
country. With the loss of taxes from the *haciendas,* as well as
those from foreign business, the government finances were in a
critical position. Local business men in Mexico soon took occasion to conduct a "grudge fight" with plenty of malice behind
it. The upper-class enemies of Cárdenas made the confused opinion more confounded by saying everywhere, "Cárdenas is the
Great Destroyer of Mexico."

But the oil companies continued to bring pressure on Washington and the Democratic administration to do something more
drastic. In its later notes the State Department said less about the

oil, but began pressing Mexico to pay the agrarian claims, amounting to some ten million dollars. The claims over which Washington pretended to be so agitated were mostly made in behalf of a few very rich American landowners. In the days of astronomical New Deal figures, certainly a paltry ten million dollars could mean little to the United States, whereas it was a significant amount to Mexico. While the claims were being validated by a commission, Mexico agreed to pay a million dollars a year towards the final indemnification.

As the election year of 1940 came, the United States administration seemed to feel it had to do some appeasing of that part of the American public which had been lured by propaganda into taking the oil companies' side. On April third, 1940, the State Department sent the stiffest note of all, not only asking that the oil question be submitted to international arbitration, but suggesting that unsettled matters of seven decades past be arbitrated. Mexico's experience with international arbitration had not been too agreeable, for when the Chamizal territory question was arbitrated in Mexico's favor in 1911 the United States declined to accept the decision.

Relations between the neighboring republics became more strained, but Cárdenas was firm against any anti-American demonstration. He seemed to be trying to give his people the idea that Washington's unfriendly acts were "innocent errors into which the oil trusts had forced her." A few Mexicans interpreted the matter differently and said, with a wink, "Both governments are playing the same game."

José Vasconcelos, who was in self-exile in the United States at the time, created a mild sensation, though it hardly rose above the whispering stage, by suggesting that Washington did not look on the oil expropriations with unadulterated disfavor. Since Great Britain had controlled more than two-thirds of the Mexican output, was it really so sad that she had been ousted from her strong position? Might not the United States come in reasonable time—by indirect if not direct methods—to have complete control of Mexico's oil? Whatever lay behind Vasconcelos' supposition, however angry his temerity in voicing such an idea made the United States State Department, the fact is that today in 1944 many Mexicans are inclined to accept the interpretation.

Without any thought whatever of the British holdings, certainly the average United States citizen questioned on the street in 1938 sided with Mexico. Despite the mighty machinations of the oil corporations, Cárdenas, backed by Mexico, had really won in his two-and-a-half year war with them, and the majority of the American public were glad of the fact.

"The act of expropriation," wrote Professor Alfred B. Thomas at the time, "bids fair to create in 1938 Mexico's economic independence to parallel her political independence initiated in 1810." If on first thought the view seems too sanguine, it may be remembered that real political independence had not been won a whole century later. Cárdenas's act in throwing off the yoke of the oil companies pointed the beginning of the end of what the Mexicans speak of as "colonial economic servitude." And this economic independence is a consummation which the epoch-making principle of the "good neighbor" is committed to furthering, regardless of the notes the State Department sent in policy.

# 26. Unorthodox

*"They are at the mercy of their own natures."*

D. H. LAWRENCE

Shortly after the severance of relations with Great Britain, old General Saturnino Cedillo let loose his expected rebellion. The aggrieved oil men as well as the Nazis were accused of encouraging and supporting it. A German, Baron von Merck, had been employed to give military instruction to Cedillo's peons and his political sycophants, and everyone knew that the chieftain maintained a private army as well as a private chapel. Cedillo, an illiterate and tricky Indian, who had begun his career as a land-hungry *zapatista* and had become a millionaire landlord, was one of the "personalities" of the Cárdenas regime. Shrewdly, for political reasons and to conciliate the alarmed clerics, Cárdenas had chosen this anti-Calles, pro-Catholic *cacique* to fill the atheistic Garrido Canábal's post as minister of agriculture in 1935. Cedillo stayed in the high position long enough to disprove utterly his pretended championship of agrarianism. Cárdenas, who knew that Cedillo was trying to plot his downfall, kept such a wary eye on him that he could hatch no mischief. The chieftain stuck it out until August of 1937, and then resigned to return to San Luis Potosí, where he was as much a "kingfish" as Huey Long was in Louisiana.

On May fifth, 1938, less than two months after the oil expropriation, the San Luis Potosí legislature, which was bought and paid for by Cedillo, formally withdrew recognition from the Cárdenas government. Cárdenas made a characteristically quick move. He ordered the presidential train. Despite disturbing news of wrecks and blown-up bridges, and with a somewhat nervous staff, he proceeded straight to the city of San Luis Potosí. Cedillo with his troops took to the nearby hills. As if all were peace and brotherly love, Cárdenas established himself in the administration building and received petitioners. Ownership of the vast holdings of Cedillo was to be transferred in parcels to the peasants who worked the land. New schools were ordered. The town was to have running water in all districts. Streets were to be paved and sidewalks made. Public assistance was to function in reality as well as name. Cárdenas was greeted with cheers wherever he appeared.

In a public address, the president exhorted Cedillo and his rebels to return to ways of peace and patriotism. He was the old brigand's best apologist—"the general is not a well man," he said. As a defiant answer, the airport was bombed. One bomb dropped close to Cárdenas's place of residence. Leaflets, too, fell from the air, urging all people to join the rebellion. Cárdenas now lost patience and sent federal troops to bring back Cedillo *alive*. He offered amnesty to all rebels who confessed the error of their ways. Except for some few hundreds of insurrectionists hiding in the hills, the revolt evaporated. Cárdenas returned to Mexico, leaving the social aspect of San Luis Potosí marvelously transformed. Twenty days after the abortive beginning, the disturbance was over. In a skirmish between the federals and the *guerrilleros,* Cedillo met his death. "It's too bad the old man got killed," Cárdenas said, regretfully. All the captured offenders he pardoned.

One sidelight on the critical time was of especial significance. When in the midst of the rebellion Cárdenas spoke from San Luis Potosí on world peace, talking over a hemispheric radio hook-up, he was introduced by the counselor of the United States embassy. It was like a personal reassurance from Washington that no matter what the United States was doing to him in regard to oil expropriations, at heart the New Deal administration was still his "good neighbor" and was going to stand by him. Another illuminating sidelight on tne revolt was that the church supported the radical, unorthodox Cárdenas against the militant Catholic Cedillo.

In the midst of the general unrest over the rebellion following the oil crisis, the Archbishop of Mexico counseled his people to support their government wholeheartedly in the hour of crisis. It was a gracious as well as a sagacious gesture. For though Cárdenas had not indulged in the church persecution of former administrations, he was known to have little faith in the benefits of organized religion as practiced in Mexico. To the horror of the clergy, Cárdenas had once said: "Men have enough trouble here on earth without adding heaven's troubles." But his attitude towards the church problem was quite different from that of Calles. It is not in Cárdenas's nature to persecute. And in his first year in office he had proved his determination to permit no bloody strife between anti-Catholics and Catholics—even at the expense of exiling a friend. The man who was punished for anti-clerical agitation was Tomás Garrido Canábal, that flamboyant one-time dictator of Tabasco whom Cárdenas had made his secretary of agriculture before Cedillo.

When Cárdenas visited Tabasco during his presidential campaign he had been impressed with many of the social reforms and services Garrido Canábal had established. In the election he had cast his complimentary vote for the Tabascan governor. But he had not counted on his minister bringing a troop of his clergy-baiting Red Shirts with him to the capital. When they created a horrible disturbance by killing five persons coming out of church in suburban Tacubaya, Cárdenas shortly dispensed with Garrido Canábal's services and sent him to Costa Rica on a vague "agricultural mission" which was tantamount to exile. In 1938, when sanguinary riots followed the reopening of a Catholic church in Tabasco, Cárdenas told the local authorities to repeal the state's drastic anti-church legislation and to permit a limited number of priests to hold services. He assured the clergy they might appeal to the courts for protection if there should be any further persecution.

Though Cárdenas was gentle in dealing with the church, he was not uncritical. He was thoroughly aware of the church's costly retardation of the whole revolutionary program. He held the clergy guilty for a great percentage of the backwardness of the masses, for much of the miserable exploitation they had suffered through centuries. But as long as the church did not actively try to interfere in politics he was content to let it be.

Cárdenas wanted to get the people, psychologically, off their knees. It pained him to see the fanatically devout crawling up the hill to the shrine at Guadalupe with cactus spines bloodying their bared chests and backs. One could be humble and even worshipful, he said, without prostrating oneself on the pavement of the church. When the Archbishop of Jalisco told the members of the Catholic labor unions that "God does not look with compassion on those who are discontented with their fate," and that "the Saviour loves those who are resigned and submissive," Cárdenas had a counter charge: "Every hour spent on your knees," he said, "is an hour stolen from humanity." And when a delegation of Indians told him they believed in him and his social program, but that they could not give up their saints, Cárdenas smiled indulgently and said: "If you must worship God in church, go ahead. But don't let yourselves be exploited in the process."

Whatever the kingdom of God might be, Cárdenas could not subscribe to the idea that it was symbolized by robed pageantry and ostentatious ritual. The kingdom of God, as he saw it, could be found only in nature and in the hearts of men. The spirit of conciliation was, of course, a segment of it. He would be conciliatory up to the point where conciliation would not work against the general welfare of mankind. In his compassion for humanity, in his unselfed devotion for serving his brothers,

Cárdenas, the unbeliever, approached some phases of the Christ ideal as closely as good pastors do.

The new liberal archbishop, Luis Martínez, who came from Cárdenas's home state of Michoacán, did his part to bring about a rapprochement between church and government. He went so far as to say to his people: "It is charity for man to want to realize the will of his fellow man as if it were his own, and it is a greater good to achieve concord and harmony among our brothers than to achieve realization of the highest ideals and holiest aims."

Cárdenas was grateful. Relations between church and state steadily improved. Church festivals became publicized. The press began using photographs of weddings, christenings, communions. The most vehemently anti-clerical states allowed the reopening of a limited number of churches. The cornerstone of a brand-new church in Mexico City was consecrated. The four hundredth anniversary of the miracle of the Virgin of Guadalupe was celebrated with magnificent pomp. High churchmen from South America helped to officiate, and the entire diplomatic corps attended one gala celebration. Cárdenas himself did not appear at any of the festivities. He could not bring himself to lend his presence to a religious ceremony of even such national and Indian significance. He knew his appearance would have been misinterpreted as either sanction or political hypocrisy.

But by no means was Cárdenas opposed to any religious activity which he deemed helpful to his people. He could not subscribe to dogma, but he virtually said: "Though I cannot be bound by any forms, if you propose a free church, where Christ is a living reality, and where brotherhood is the only creed, I shall give you my full support." By chance he found a nondenominational religion he could approve of, in the faith of an American linguistic missionary.

One day reports came to the president of something uncommon going on in the Aztec-speaking village of Tetelcingo, near the town of Cuautla, where Zapata is buried. A man had planted vegetables in the village square and was encouraging the Indians to eat something besides corncakes and beans. The man was also teaching Spanish to the Indians and learning Aztec himself. Cárdenas called for his automobile and went to investigate.

He found a soft-spoken, sandy-haired fellow with a soft-spoken, sandy-haired wife living in a trailer at the edge of the dirt plaza. The man, whose name was Cameron Townsend, came originally from California; his Swedish wife, from Chicago. They were nonsectarian missionaries. Townsend was a teacher of linguistics and the gospel of Jesus Christ. He was not an ordained minister; he had studied philology and sociology in college, but not theology. His meager support and that of his missionary student workers came from numerous churches in the United States. He had taught in Guatemala and had translated the New Testament into one of the most difficult dialects prevalently spoken. When questioned by Cárdenas, Townsend modestly explained that his objective was a desire, prompted by Christian convictions, to serve his fellow man. He was interested in the welfare of humanity and especially of the Indians of Mexico, and he had come to live among them, to have a small part in the Mexican government's movement in behalf of the Indian peoples. He had discovered that at least two million of them were completely foreign to the life of the nation as regards language, customs, social standards and economic progress. Another desire was to have those portions of the Biblical testament of good will and brotherly love translated into and published in all the Indian languages.

When Cárdenas asked him why he had chosen Tetelcingo, Townsend answered smilingly that he had heard it was the dirtiest and most backward village in the state of Morelos. But the town authorities had been hospitable and had permitted the strangers to locate their trailer and erect a bamboo shed in the square between the town hall and one of the seven Catholic churches. The ministry of labor in the capital had been helpful.

Cárdenas found the plaza had been planted out to trees, flowers, and vegetables, and now served as an experimental station for new crops, as well as a park. Beets, carrots, cabbages, and turnip greens were flourishing. The surplus water which had formed bogs for breeding mosquitoes had been utilized for irrigation. Pipes had been laid to introduce drinking water into the sections of town that had none. Townsend had obtained an old truck to teach the Indians how to drive, so the village women would not have to go so many miles on foot each day to Cuautla to sell their *tortillas*. A campaign to exterminate the ant pest had been initiated. An edition of ten thousand copies of the Townsend method of teaching the illiterate to read in Spanish was on the press in Mexico City, and an Aztec primer was being prepared. Privies, entirely unknown before, were being built. As an inspiration to cleanliness, some houses had been whitewashed inside as well as out. Two cows had been provided for a community dairy, and Townsend had taught some of the older boys how to milk and care for the animals.

Cárdenas was impressed with the practical aspects of the missionaries' work, and he was assured of the sincerity of the strangers when he saw how the well-bred Mrs. Townsend, with a serious heart disorder, could live in a bamboo hut without essential comforts. He liked the articulate religion of the Townsends because of its social message. He liked its simple teaching of the gospel of brotherly love. Here, he said, was something worth supporting; whereas, for him, a church which preached largely the gospel of "charity among the rich and patience among the poor" was moribund. He determined to make things as easy as possible for the fifty-odd student missionaries from the United States who had been trained by Townsend and who were going into the hinterland in pairs to study the Indian tongues, to translate the New Testament, and to bring some enlightenment to the primitive.

The first thing the president did after his surprise visit was to send a doctor to Tetelcingo. (There was no medical care whatever when the Townsends came; the witch doctors professed to cure by breaking eggs over the patient and then placing the shells on an ant-hill.) Cárdenas next sent five thousand budded orange trees to be planted out to provide both vitamins and profit for the population. Then he lent practical assistance to the young student missionaries in their dangerous and arduous work in the remote mountain districts. When his presidential term was up, his interest in the Townsend program did not flag, and "the unbeliever" and "the man of God" have remained fast and intimate friends.

All went happily enough, too, between the government and the Catholic church until the very end of 1939, though with the fall of the Spanish republic in April, 1939, Catholic activities in Mexico began to assume an aggressive attitude. At the end of December, congress passed the bill for socialistic education in the primary schools, as an amendment to the famous Article 3 of the 1917 constitution. The principal points of the bill were as follows:

1. The object of education is to prepare the younger generation for the advent of a social regime in which the means and founts of production belong to the nation.
2. Primary education is defined as "The sum of knowledge indispensable to permit citizens to play an active part in the transformation of society."
3. Education must be socialistic, because it must fight for the progressive and conscious socialization of riches and the means of production.
4. For exactly the same reason it must be co-operative.
5. No school directed, supported or financed by foreign diplomatic representatives will be permitted to continue, even if it already exists, for the purpose of imparting instruction.
6. Any building in which religious instruction is imparted will be confiscated, and its director liable to two years in prison, and its teachers liable to six months' imprisonment.

7. Any person promoting religious instruction shall be liable to two months' to two years' imprisonment.
8. Socialist education will embrace the whole formation period of the youth, from replacing occupations that take up the children's time with those of professional instruction.

Private schools, however, were allowed to teach religion under special permission from the federal ministry of education, but they were required to exclude all intervening or economic assistance of religious bodies or institutions, under the penalty of one thousand pesos fine and revocation of license.

Ezequiel Padilla, among others, had warned the government against the dangers of going too far in antagonizing the religious element of the people. "Extremes may beget extremes," he said. Though the church had been told to keep hands off education, the clergy created a tempest of protest. There was bitter opposition among the people, too, and demonstrations against the socialistic education program were held in the capital and many of the other cities. Fortunately, though, both President Cárdenas and Archbishop Martínez were devout lovers of peace, and at the time proved the moderators for the extremists on both sides. But the pendulum was to make its great backward swing in the next regime.

In one policy Cárdenas would not compromise a whit even for the sake of unity. His government stood out as the only one among the twenty Latin American republics to support the Spanish loyalists against the fascist Franco. More clearly than the great democracies had he seen the danger and world threat of fascism in the Spanish struggle. Against high protests from the Catholic hierarchy, and against the disapproval of all the other Latin American governments, he sent active help to the loyalists in guns and ammunition. And in spite of dismayed opposition, he offered Mexico as an asylum for loyalist refugees, after the might of Germany and Italy had proved too strong and the democratic government of Spain had fallen.

Charges of being leagued with Soviet Russia were hurled at him. But he had proved their falsity by admitting to Mexico in 1937 Stalin's arch-enemy, the exiled Leon Trotsky, and he still absolutely refused to recognize the Soviet government.

As to the existence of any communistic government in Mexico, Cárdenas denied it categorically. "Our government," he said, "is democratic and liberal, with a few moderate traces of socialism which affect landownership, principally for restitution, and in the laws which refer to the relationship between capital and labor, but which are not nearly so radical as those of other democratic countries, or even of others which are monarchies. . . . Our revolutionary movement was born of the hopes and needs of our country. It is not proper to attribute to it any similarity with existing social movements in other parts of the world, except those whose principles are common to any movement seeking proletarian justice and the cultural and economic improvement of the oppressed."

To quiet fears, however, Cárdenas began to call a halt on the the redness of revolutionary phrases. Even the word "socialism" was heard less and less. The word "democracy" began to take on new emphasis in 1940, after the European war was on.

On June twenty-second, 1940, realizing the approaching magnitude of the conflict, the peace-loving Cárdenas asked for compulsory military training. It was the first time in her bloodstained history that the Mexican government had made such a drastic move. Cárdenas saw that Mexico's active help might be needed. But he also had in mind something beyond national defense: The education and health values Mexican youth would receive when supported for a year at government expense.

Though Lázaro Cárdenas had defended the international dignity of his country with uncompromising courage, integrity, and devotion to a greater extent than any preceding president, the opposition propaganda among his own countrymen continued until the very hour he went out of office. Cárdenas answered his critics honestly. "The cause of social unrest," he maintained, "must not be sought in the existence of communistic groups, which merely constitute minorities without influence on the country's destiny. Unrest arises out of rightful aspiration and needs of the working masses, as yet unsatisfied, and out of non-compliance with labor laws. Fanatics who murder school teachers or who oppose enforcement of the labor laws and of the revolutionary program have done more harm to the nation than the communists."

Yet Cárdenas was by no means blindly partisan in the cause of labor. He warned the proletariat against excesses that might prove suicidal. He broke with the extreme leftists in labor. He brought thirty strategic members of the oil-workers' union to the National Palace, and accused them of rank ingratitude. He ordered dismissals, and demanded payment to the government of two hundred and twenty-two million pesos' deficit of the oil companies caused by internal corruption and carelessness. Then he presented them with a cleansing plan for reorganization.

In his last important speech to the nation Cárdenas again admonished the extremists in labor that their advances might be lost. By contrast, he emphasized social gains which would not be canceled: The land given to the peasants, the financing by the Ejidal Bank, the public works under construction. "The multiplicity of schools," he affirmed, "the free expression of thought, the respect for human life, and the international policy of Mexico are conquests and new standards which the Revolution has given to the people and which the people consider their own." Naturally, he did not say that an overwhelming proportion of these benefits had been achieved by himself alone. He said, "the Revolution has given." His future biographers will be able to say, without straining truth, "Cárdenas gave these things to the people." It is what the masses say today.

The president admitted unreservedly the government's limitations in the completion of its program for "economic, material, and moral construction." He confessed freely the government's inability to solve all the needs of the country, "though using every resource and struggling against the power of international finance." "But," he asked his critics, "what program of economic recuperation do you propose as a substitute?" And challenging both the muttering reactionaries and communists, he demanded, "What does the opposition offer?" He answered for them: "Only a new era in which the hatreds and resentments of a few people will seek to revenge themselves."

Cárdenas is the only Mexican revolutionary chief executive who did not turn more or less conservative before he went out of office. When his six-year term was ended, he was of the same opinions as when it began. At the end of his regime, on being asked by an American writer if the Revolution were over, the president looked profoundly grave at such a question. "As long as there are villages without water, as long as thousands of villages are asking for land," he said, "how can we stop the Revolution? As long as forty per cent still work at starvation wages on other people's property, the Revolution must go on."

## 27. Passport for the Future

*"No individual, public or private, in these current years has more magnificently or more significantly served the Indian—and therefore more has served human justice and the spirit of mankind—than President Cárdenas."*

JOHN COLLIER, COMMISSIONER OF
INDIAN AFFAIRS OF THE UNITED
STATES GOVERNMENT.

To bring some coherence to politics, and to find a suitable successor for Cárdenas, the PNR was reorganized into the Party of the Mexican Revolution—PRM. It was reorganized on the basis of men's classes and occupations: Farm, labor, army, and a group called "the people." Each sector was to fill certain offices. The sectors were to select their own candidates and support them in the elections. For a man to be a presidential candidate at least three sectors had to agree on him, before the choice was official. As its guiding principle, the new organization stated "without any reservation whatsoever we accept the democratic form of government."

The search for a successor was earnest, sincere, and thorough. But in the length and breadth of the land there seemed to be no one of the caliber of Lázaro Cárdenas. Finally the choice was reduced to a handful of generals, and then to two. One of these was by far more colorful than the other, and he had played a much bigger rôle in the Revolution. He was Cárdenas's close friend Francisco Múgica, a defiant leftist, eleven years his senior. It was Múgica who had been the chief begetter of some of the best features of the 1917 constitution. The other candidate was also a personal friend of Cárdenas, an unexciting, dependable man, just his age, and his current minister of defense. He was Manuel Avila Camacho.

Although Avila Camacho was a brigadier-general before he was thirty, because of his unobtrusive personality a Mexican wit dubbed him "the unknown soldier." In war he had made a reputation for fighting by persuasion, for gaining victory over his enemy not with the sword but with words. Cárdenas had found him invaluable as a trouble-shooter. In temperament and background the two men were in high contrast. Avila Camacho had only a trace of Indian blood if any, and he had none of that psychic understanding of the Indian which Cárdenas possessed. He had never known poverty. He was completely bourgeois-bred. His parents were well-to-do. His older brother, Maximino, a horse fancier, was rich. His own favorite sport was polo, where his rating ranged between two and three goals. But he was not at all what might be called a "society man," and, like Cárdenas, he did not drink. Rarely was he to be seen at social functions. He was a homeloving family man, who adored his wife and who relished good and plenteous food. His aura was bland and amiable, but reserved. Conciliatory as he was, there was no outward mark of the politician about him.

Cárdenas would take no active part in choosing between the two likely candidates. Though closer to Múgica and owing much to him, Cárdenas felt that Múgica's emphatic leftist tendencies might work against the success of the party. And he also felt that with the world in turmoil and Mexico in a critical economic situation, it would perhaps be better to slow up and consolidate the social gains and revolutionary accomplishments than risk too far.

The disjointed time was not right for Múgica's candidacy.

And his kindness to Trotsky, the bitter enemy of Stalinist Lombardo Toledano, had turned the powerful CTM from him. When the more moderate National Farm Confederation (CNC) came out with surprising alacrity for Avila Camacho, its action put Lombardo Toledano on the spot. If he now supported Múgica, the popular front would be split. For him, it was a difficult choice. Lombardo Toledano and Avila Camacho were born in the same little town, Tezuitlán, in Puebla. They had been boyhood friends and desk-mates, and were still on friendly terms. Lombardo Toledano was entertained at the Avila Camacho ranch and there "an agreement was reached," although the labor leader had misgivings about the tie-up. The most extreme radicals among his union members immediately began to lose faith in him. But with war threatening to engulf the globe, Lombardo Toledano himself was not averse to a harmonizing act.

The PRM nominated the bland, stolid Manuel Avila Camacho. His opening campaign speech was steadying and reassuring. There was not a hint of fireworks or even inspiration, but the words were good if not forceful. The candidate declared that "the people's conquests, the guarantees and rights of the peasants and working masses, are already an established fact that continues to progress in reality, law, and national consciousness." And "these substantial conquests"—the land grants to rural workers, benefits to trade-union workers—he affirmed to be "the foundation of our economic organization."

However lacking in specific statements, the speech presaged stability. How right Cárdenas had been in fearing Múgica's leftist candidacy was proved by the fact that even the moderate Avila Camacho, who seemed uncommonly conservative compared to Cárdenas, was not rightist enough for a large portion of the electorate, who demanded a complete change. The church, big business and small, former *hacienda* owners, and all the dissatisfied and disgruntled groups, were eager to back some candidate not sponsored by the PRM. They found a strong one in General Juan Andreu Almazán of Monterrey. He was able, conservative, very rich. His expansive, smiling personality was the sort to catch the popular imagination. He was nominated for the presidential candidacy by the Committee for National Reconstruction, which emerged as PRUN.

Almazán was a good campaigner. He won votes whenever he appeared. His speeches were better than Avila Camacho's. And they, too, were middle-of-the-road in most aspects. Almazán said he would not please "those enemies of the Mexican Revolution who wish to make me a tool for a reactionary program that will return to them their abolished privileges." His program was statesmanlike. He promised to give personal title to those *ejidal* lands turned over to the peasants. He declared a generous appeasement program to the church. In regard to organized labor he said: "Class war should exist, but it must be carried on within the law, with the resolve to find the road of co-operation." To business he said: "It will be necessary—and fortunately the Mexican Revolution is ripe for it—to encourage the national spirit of enterprise, surrounding legitimate investors with the guarantees amply compatible with the generous laws of the Revolution."

As the opposition watched the public response to the Almazán sentiments, more and more of his ideas seemed to take root in the speeches of Avila Camacho. By March third, Almazán was accusing PRM of stealing his thunder. "They no longer speak of radicalism, of social education," he said. "They are no longer proclaiming the dictatorship of the proletariat. . . . They predict harmony. . . . They pretend to be defenders of the family, of the small property owners, of the freedom of worship, and they repudiate communism."

But Avila Camacho had always been an enemy of communism and a defender of the small property owner and a believer in freedom of worship. His ruling passion was to create harmony

It was because of his harmonizing qualities that Cárdenas felt comfortable about his nomination. Still, as the winds blowing from all quarters foretold a coming counter-revolution whoever won the elections, Avila Camacho did direct some of the thunder to his own uses.

It was the women, though, who nearly defeated him. Cárdenas had advocated votes for women and had just missed achieving his aim. If woman suffrage had been granted and the women had voted, Almazán would have swept the country with such an overwhelming majority that PRM with all its energy and in-genuity would hardly have had the face to claim victory. The women were for the church and against socialistic education. Beyond that, they hardly stopped to think. It was Cárdenas who had made them rights-for-women-conscious. And though they could not cast a ballot themselves, they campaigned for Almazán, they held meetings, they arranged luncheons, they hung out ban-ners and threw flowers whenever their hero appeared. Priests praised and blessed their work. Many husbands knew no peace until, to stop the women's babble, they promised to vote for Almazán. When election day came the churches could not ac-commodate the female devotees at early Mass. And when Mass was over the women surged to the voting booths. They risked bricks and bullets. They formed cordons of encircling arms to prevent *avilacamachistas* from voting. They stood as a barricade to protect *almazanista* machine gunners. Some met their death. Some with unabashed unscrupulousness encouraged their teen-age sons to vote, not only once, but several times. Aristocratic old dowagers who had rarely set their high-arched feet on city pavements mingled freely with streetwalkers who hoped for the good old days again. Judy O'Gradys and colonels' ladies were more than sisters under the skin that day. Religious feeling in outdoor politics proved a great leveler. "Don't you see," said a realist, as he studied the crowd, "why we can't have complete democracy here? The Archbishop of Mexico would be elected president every time."

The election of July seventh was a noisy, bloody, shameful affair. Sirens shrieked like judgment day as ambulances rushed through the streets to collect the wounded and the dead. Both sides were flagrantly guilty. Both sides cheated and stole and shot and maimed their opponents. Cárdenas himself could not get to vote at his own chosen balloting booth in Calle Juan Escutía. A PRM general had "seized the box" and closed the polls to prevent several hundred *almazanistas* from voting. Cárdenas hung around for forty minutes. While he waited the people enthusiastically shouted, "Viva el General Cárdenas!" But they told him frankly, "We want Almazán; you promised free elections." Cárdenas felt a bit sheepish; he had promised free elections and he could not even vote himself. "If Almazán wins," he said, "he'll be president." By nightfall, after he had witnessed bloodshed and trickery at many polling centers, Cárdenas shook his head. "I'm afraid Mexico is not yet a democracy," he said, wryly.

But Almazán was not the next president, though many people one meets in Mexico think he was elected, and will always think so. The popular Miguel Alemán, who managed Avila Camacho's campaign, is willing to admit that Mexico City may have gone for Almazán, but he stoutly maintains that the country at large was behind Avila Camacho. The most telling witticism on the question came from Cantínflas, Mexico's great music-hall comedian. In a skit, Cantínflas announces to his stooge that he has decided he will be the next president of Mexico. "Why, who would vote for you?" scoffs the stooge. Cantínflas, grinning, comes back at him, "Who voted for Avila Camacho?"

On the "official count," released on July twelfth, the PRM officials rather overstated their claims. They gave their candidate a seventeen-to-one victory, 2,265,199 for Avila Camacho, 128,574 for Almazán. The PRM committee pointed out that "the impromptu ballot boxes" set up by the *almazanistas* had been ejected. What the real figure which represented the mandate of the people was, no one knows accurately. But everyone acknowledges that Mexico proved herself not mature enough to permit an honest election. True democracy was something still to be defined for Mexico.

Almazán had said, boldly, "If the will of the people is not recognized, I will know what to do to see that it is respected." To many of his coherents this was tantamount to threat of revolution. In the weeks that followed, Mexico was in that tense state of nerves that precedes civil strife. In the traditional way, Almazán had sailed for Cuba six days after the election returns were released. He had said to his cohorts, in farewell, "I shall return within a month to take my place as your leader." He was reported to be laying his case before the United States officials assembled at the Latin American Conference in Havana. For precaution, a mild purgation and strategic shifting of *almazanista* officers in the army took place. Some prominent men accused of plotting rebellion were arrested and temporarily stowed away in prison. A plague of rumors infested the nation. Innumerable dates were set for the beginning of the fight.

When the atmosphere was charged to the point of combustion, Cárdenas made one of his unexpected moves. He went to the little town of Dolores in Guanajuato, where Father Hidalgo had launched the struggle for independence in 1810. It was near the heart of *almazanista* territory. There on the night of September fifteenth he uttered the *Grito del Dolores* and made an address which was broadcast throughout the land. His words had a sobering effect. Six days later, in an authorized interview, President-elect Avila Camacho said, "I am a believer." The simple words were like holy oil cast upon tempestuous waters. Except for that scurrilous villain, Victoriano Huerta, no Mexican president since the enactment of 1857's anti-clerical laws had made a public confession of faith. As the Catholics sent up grateful prayers of thanksgiving for the president-elect's confession, the revolutionary spirit ebbed. When the surprise news came in mid-November that the Vice-President of the United States himself, Henry A. Wallace, would come to witness the Avila Comacho inauguration, the potential revolution was dead.

Almazán had not yet returned to lead the revolt. Belatedly, after four months of expectation, he arrived by plane on November twenty-first. His followers had by now lost their zest. They had been ready to shed blood for his cause, and he had let them down. Almazán put the blame on the United States government. The youths from conservative families cried out in disappointment and resentment, "It has come to a pretty pass when our meddling neighbor won't even let us have a nice little revolution when we want to." But many older heads, who had endured revolutions in Mexico, had decided weeks before that time that peace and Cárdenas's candidate were better than bloodshed and Almazán.

Almazán had lost his chance to be a popular hero, but he had wisely followed the course of discretion rather than valor. Though contemptuously condemned by the militant in his party, he had proved himself a bigger man by holding the war dogs in leash.

The pro-Nazis, however, turned the Almazán renunciation into a field day of resentment-stirring against the United States. The tack taken was that Almazán had made a heroic sacrifice to forestall Yankee intervention. They now determined to poison the Wallace welcome. But their agitation in the subsidized press and with mobsters reacted sorely against them. Wallace's visit was a triumph from the minute he crossed the border. The Mexicans found him natural and *simpático* and took him to their hearts. He knew more about agriculture, by which seventy per cent of the Mexicans made their living, than they did. Before he came, he had studied Mexico's economic situation and needs.

And he had gone to the Berlitz School in Washington and learned Spanish, so that he could speak with them in voice as well as spirit. His progress along the new Pan-American Highway was a prolonged ovation.

In frenzied exasperation at the way things were going, Nazi agents and certain *almazanistas* made up a mob to spoil Wallace's entrance into the embassy. The street crowd was as deceptively quiet as an expectant welcoming committee at first, and then at a signal burst forth with staccato shrieks of "Down with Wallace! Death to the *gringos!*" Wallace, who had been slipped into the residential entrance on Calle Londres, was happily unaware of the disturbance before the main entrance on the boulevard, where the late-arriving military and naval attachés had to do some slugging with their fists when attacked with blackjacks. Some bricks were hurled, and hundreds of Nazi handbills were passed out. Prominent Germans were seen skirting the edges of the crowd to watch the success of their handiwork. They laughed to see the anti-American missiles fly, but they laughed out of the wrong side of their mouths. The Mexican press condemned them in strong ink. The capital outdid itself in honoring Wallace.

On December first, the inauguration took place. After Cárdenas had placed the silken insignia of office about the shoulders of the new president, the friends embraced with sincere and manly emotion. Then, not remaining for the official luncheon, Cárdenas merged immediately into private life and political silence. At forty-five his work as chief executive was done.

The year before, in 1939, the magazine *Life* had registered its opinion of "Cárdenas's bloodless Revolution" as "the kind that remakes the world without violence or spectacle." Its editor had said: "If it works, the United States will eventually have a prosperous neighbor, a huge, natural market for American manufactured goods. And a beginning will have been made in giving the submerged masses of Latin America a share in their governments.

If it fails, Mexico will careen back into bloody, picturesque making civil warfare."

As to whether the Cárdenas Revolution was a success, the second taxi driver an American observer chanced upon in Mexico in
December, 1941, answered the question to the American's satisfaction. "How can anyone," the chauffeur said from his heart,
"deny Cárdenas's good work? Now the poor people have something to start life on! And they have shoes to put their feet in.
Cárdenas brought clean running water to the small towns, water
that comes out of a faucet. Can you, a *norteamericano,* dream
what that means to the mothers? Cárdenas made free education.
I myself had only two years in school. At the age of seven I had
to withdraw to work so that my little sisters could have some
schooling. Now my own son already has thirteen years of education and is advanced in chemical engineering at the university.
You understand the difference? The Indian is ambitious for the
first time. Is that not good for the future of Mexico?"

Go almost anywhere within the width and length of Mexico
today in 1944 and ask, "Who did this?" "Who did that?" The
answer is so overwhelmingly "Cárdenas" that it almost seems
there was never any other chief executive. "The beautiful road
to Acapulco?" "Cárdenas." "The spectacular highway to Guadalajara?" "Cárdenas." "This bridge? That dam?" "Cárdenas."
"Those irrigation works in progress?" "Cárdenas began them."
"That hospital? That orphanage? The children's playground?"
"Cárdenas." He gave and gave—the little things mounted up in
alleviation of man's distresses. A pipe line here, a district nurse
there, a sanitary engineer, a thousand budded orange trees for
this village, chemicals to purify water in another, scholarships
for bright sons of poor soldiers. But, beyond all these material
benefits, he gave the "forgotten man" a new hope. He led the
common people out of a bondage that was centuries in arrears
of contemporary civilization. Despite the shortness of time and
world events and the opposition of malicious forces mightier than

the Pharaohs, he brought his people within sight of a promised land. Then, without bidding them farewell, he retired, leaving them to pursue their own destiny under other leaders. As a passport to the future he had presented each with an imponderable gift that might be called "vision."

# PART TEN

# HIGH PLACE IN THE HEMISPHERE

## 28. A Good Left Hand

*"We are here to deliberate on the fate of the Americas."*

EZEQUIEL PADILLA

A sound, well-integrated, and conciliatory man was precisely what Mexico needed in this critical transitional state—this emergence from daring socialistic experimentation into temperate consolidation. With his uncanny instinct, Cárdenas had chosen for chief executive that man best calculated to keep the pendulum from describing too drastic an arc to the right. By nature, Avila Camacho was nothing of an extremist or an experimentalist. He possessed none of Cárdenas's flashing genius. "Equilibrium," said one of his admirers pointedly, "is far better than genius in administrative politics. Genius is good for a writer, a musician, a painter. But it is apt to be dangerous in politics."

Avila Camacho stood almost squarely in the middle of the road. But that road was very different from the Mexican road of 1910. It was a road that had been three decades in the process of construction, ever since Madero offered the first plans for a section of it. It was a road laid out for the general welfare, and had been reinforced and extended through successive administrations, sabotaged under Victoriano Huerta, pushed ahead feverishly under Cárdenas. But though Avila Camacho's feet were planted firmly in the middle way, his heart was undoubtedly on the left side with Cárdenas.

When he took office three outstanding objectives of the Revolution had already been accomplished. Except in isolated cases, agrarian feudalism was a thing of the past—sixty million acres had been cut off from big estates and allotted to peasants. The power of the Catholic church had been radically restricted. So many rural schools had been built that Mexico had definitely begun its march toward total literacy.

The new president did not consider the Revolution finished, but he knew the time had come for it to check up on itself, to measure solid gains against flaws, errors, abuses. As soon as he was in power he began to speak much of "evolution." After a tempestuous reign of three decades King Revolution was dead. Long live the King Evolution!

Where Cárdenas had overwhelmingly put the emphasis of his government on uplifting the common man, Avila Camacho promised "to govern for all." Since as a school boy his ruling principle had been a desire for harmony, now into his cabinet the new president brought a remarkable fusion of allegiances and ideologies. Close friends and followers of ex-presidents were given portfolios. The opulently gifted, world-visioned Ezequiel Padilla, whose eloquence had often caused him to be chosen as his spokesman by President Calles, was made minister of foreign affairs. Level-headed Francisco Xavier Gaxiola, former private secretary of the business-man president, Abelardo Rodríguez, became minister of public economy. Portes Gil was represented by the progressive new minister of agriculture, Marte Gómez. But Cárdenas men got the majority of cabinet positions. The only one of first importance, however, who remained precisely in his place was Eduardo Suárez, the astute minister of finance under Cárdenas. The brilliant, intellectual Ramón Beteta, former undersecretary of foreign affairs and the personal adviser to whom Cárdenas was most devoted, was shifted to the post of undersecretary of finance. Another close personal friend of the ex-president, the forceful Francisco Castillo Nájera, was left in his strategic post as ambassador to the United States. The most conservative member of the cabinet was the president's own brother Maximino, who shortly was made minister of communications. The top place, that of minister of the interior, went to the youngest among them, the personable, energetic Miguel Alemán, who had conducted the Avila Camacho campaign.

Important positions outside the cabinet were divided among those of diverse persuasions. The erudite, pro-Spanish, intensely Catholic José Vasconcelos, who had exiled himself under Calles and who had been permitted to return to Mexico in 1939 under Cárdenas, was made director of the National Library.

In his first year, many advisers urged the new president to pursue what they called "energetic policies." But to Avila Camacho that was another name for violent measures hurtful to human liberty. He was determined to rule by persuasion. "That which is not obtained by good will is negative," he said. At the beginning of the revolution, he confessed, it had been necessary to fight—even to use 75-mm. guns—just as a growing child needs the rod from time to time. But Mexico had now entered the educational stage of its development. "The whole republic demands now," he said, "a material and spiritual consolidation of our social conquests in a prosperous and powerful economy."

Despite some significant changes in policy, the first two years of the Avila Camacho regime were on the whole characterized by an unprecedented outward harmony. Almost every faction found his administration not unpleasing. "So far he has done nothing wrong" was on millions of lips. Of course, he could neither charm the incorrigibly reactionary who still prayed for another Díaz, nor could he satisfy the communists. Both of these groups would have been content only with a complete overthrow of democracy. Yet even both sets of malcontents grudgingly admitted, "Perhaps he is the best we can do under the circumstances." Watching him handle the various factions in the nation, as a bullfighter plays the bull with his cape-draped left hand to get him into whatever part of the arena he desires, the people began to murmur delightedly, "He has a good left hand."

The president's first "reform" act, within a fortnight of his inauguration, was a pronounced modification of the Cárdenas agrarian program, though there was no indication that Cárdenas himself disapproved of it. Avila Camacho decreed that the acreage the government had given to the peasants in communal possession should pass into personal ownership. Almost a million and a half heads of families were to become private owners of the *ejidal* plots. But the new peasant proprietors were to be protected from themselves as well as from unscrupulous speculators—something Benito Juárez had neglected to do. Ownership was not transferable; the acres could neither be mortgaged nor sold. The land was to remain in the family in perpetuity or until death wiped out the family. Financial assistance from the government was to continue where necessary. The large-scale co-operative farms, such as those in Yucatán and the Laguna, were to continue their co-operative methods and management. But the collectivist Russian way was not to be the agrarian way of Mexico. This was a deliberate blow to the adherents of Stalinism.

The next anti-communist move was to take the National Railways out of workers' control and put them back under government management. The workers had failed miserably, and the severe reprimands of Cárdenas had not caused them to mend their ways. But, by way of conciliation, labor retained three of the seven seats on the board.

One of Avila Camacho's most significant reforms was an amendment to the nationalization of properties law, by which the courts, not the ministry of finance, received the power of expropriation or confiscation. This measure was brought about largely by pressure from the church, so that any acquired church property would have some degree of legal protection. Although Cárdenas had nationalized petroleum, Avila Camacho proposed that private Mexican enterprise be permitted to engage in new oil industry.

While promising labor that all previous gains and reforms would be strictly protected, the new government had the labor code revised to forbid illegal strikes. The first serious strike in the regime had a compromise settlement. Employees of the British-owned Mexican Tramways struck for wage increases and participation in the management. They did not get the latter, but they did the former. To make possible the increase in pay—the company had not been able to pay a dividend for years—Mexican Tramways was allowed to raise certain fares. Here was a settlement that betokened protection for labor, but also protection to capital.

Industrialization took new heart with Avila Camacho. The stepping down from the key position in labor of "that scourge and terror of capital," Lombardo Toledano, was an added stimulus to business. When his term as secretary-general of CTM was over in the spring of 1941, Lombardo Toledano was succeeded by a labor leader considerably less radical. The strong-jawed Fidel Velásquez lacked Lombardo Toledano's dynamism and intellect, but he seemed to be the harmonizer Mexico needed in its readjustment. By no means, however, did Lombardo Toledano retire from the public scene as Cárdenas did. He still retained two significant positions. He continued as director of the Workers' University, where laborers study economics, political science, languages, psychology, and Marxism, for a peso a year. Here his influence on the thinking of contemporary and future Mexican labor is still profound. Moreover, he retained the headship of the Confederation of Latin American Workers, that recent organization which holds tremendous potentialities, even though its activities are necessarily curbed for the war's duration. Though Lombardo Toledano has unquestionably lost a great deal of his popularity with the Mexican workers and though his motives are still suspect with many of them, he remains the outstanding labor leader between the Rio Grande and the nether tip of Chile.

The liberals in Mexico had little quarrel with the reform moves Avila Camacho made during the first nine months of his regime. They had no cause for apprehension until the leftist minister of education, Dr. Luis Sánchez Pontón, was relieved of his office and a rightist, Octavio Véjar Vásquez, succeeded him. This appointment seemed brought about by clerical pressure. For soon the new minister was saying in public that Mexican education should have the sign of the cross behind it, and he began clearing the ministry and the schools of those even suspected of sympathy with socialism. Here was a complete right-about from the socialistic educational program which had left religion completely outside its operations. A law forbidding co-education in state schools was passed. Cárdenas had fostered co-education not only for economy but because he believed it would accelerate woman's advancement in civic rights and responsibilities. But girls were henceforth to be educated "principally as mothers"—the old cry of the Nazis and Fascists, as the leftists quickly pointed out. Liberals as well as communists now began to fear a return of clerical domination in education and thence a tie-up between the church and the army, followed by clerical meddling in politics. And when Vejár Vásquez restored to the Jesuits a huge block of property which Cárdenas had expropriated and turned into four large schools, the liberals were completely convinced that the new minister was a menace to the general welfare of Mexico. "Educational progress has been set back half a century," they declared.

It now seemed that Cárdenas had been ill-advised in getting congress to pass the bill for socialistic education as an amendment to the famous Article 3. The ministry of education, which had more and more come under the control of communist sympathizers, had pushed Cárdenas's ideals far beyond any "scientific" intentions and had become too imitatively red. Teachers who sneered at the symbol of the cross as no more than two pieces of wood fitted together were often congratulated by school inspectors. But when the youngsters' heads were stuffed with the notion that they were equal to their parents—"all, all are equal"—and taught they must never say, "Good morning, mamma," "Good morning, papa," but simply, "Good morning, comrade," it was more than parenthood would stand for. So some of Véjar Vásquez' so-called retrogressing in education was by no means unpopular with many mothers and fathers. And despite all the attacks on the private church schools, many a parent who considered himself an advanced liberal in ideology preferred to send his offspring to one of those private schools run by nuns. The sisters were often better trained as teachers than those to be found in the federal schools. They spoke better Spanish and seemed more thorough in their teaching and more devoted in improving the manners and morals of their charges.

The church bells, which had rung gently, almost furtively, for so many years, soon began to peal with triumphant vigor in the counter-revolution. The well-to-do members of the Falange and coteries of upper-class refugees from Catholic European countries began to make churchgoing in the cities fashionable again. In provincial towns, too, citizens of every social and economic category surged to the services and knelt indiscriminately on the stone floors.

This swing back to Catholicism was greatly augmented by the activities of two rightist organizations, which came from widely different economic groups. Both served Axis interests, directly or indirectly. The first was the Falange, whose members were adherents of Franco and exponents of his much-publicized dictum: "The foreign policy of Spain is dedicated to the spiritual reconquest of Latin America." The members of this group in Mexico numbered about fifty thousand. Their magazine *Hispanidad,* which disseminated their propaganda, was characteristically pro-Axis, anti-Semitic, anti-United States. Many of their members affected black shirts. Though the organization's work had been considerably curbed by the fact that Cárdenas had never recognized the Franco government, it had got in some telling propaganda against the Allies' war effort before it was officially outlawed and sent under cover.

The other suspect organization was not a transplantation from Spain; it evolved out of Mexico. The movement called itself *Unión Nacional Sinarquista,* "without anarchy." Though direct connection with the Axis has not been proved, the Axis liberally aided the movement with contributions. Like the Nazis, the members have a characteristic salute, the difference being they extend their right arm diagonally to the left. Fanatically pro-Catholic and intensely anti-communist, *sinarquismo* declares for what it calls "the restoration of the Christian Social Order." Though its acts of violence have been denied, the movement is alleged to be a revival of the *cristeros,* who rose up in the time of Calles and dynamited and stabbed "in the name of Christ the King."

The *sinarquistas* consider the "liberal democracy" as practiced in Mexico as dangerous to their "Christian order" as is communism. They oppose bitterly any idea of collectivism, even in agrarian matters. They seem determined to have the government repeal the anti-clerical laws and to give the church the full license that existed before Juárez. Though Cárdenas was careful not to enforce the anti-clerical laws too rigorously and Avila Camacho made public confession of faith, the *sinarquistas* say the laws must be wiped from the statute books. The power of the *sinarquistas* was attested in their effective backing of the church's stand against socialistic education and co-education.

As communism flourishes almost exclusively in urban districts among industrial workers, the strength of *sinarquismo* lies principally in rural regions. In those parts of Mexico where the priests have ever swayed the Indians, the members are most numerous. Some villages are one hundred per cent in the movement. One liberal critic has said every parish house in Mexico is being turned into a *sinarquista* club.

Though a man named Manuel Torres Bueno is now the confessed chief of the movement, since Cassius-lean Salvador Abascal was demoted for talking too much, the direction of the organization is secret. Complete obedience is demanded of its members. The power of the discipline is evidenced by the way in which its adherents have renounced alcoholic beverages, including the national drink of *pulque*. The leaders are strong advocates of family life. They cry out for rural education, as if the idea had originated with them, as if Cárdenas had not made education of the poor peasants his most important work. Their program sounds entirely virtuous. It has one great flaw—it is antidemocratic. Its members take orders, just as communists take orders from Stalin and Nazis from Hitler.

When a new colonization by *sinarquistas* in Lower California was condemned by the chamber of deputies as fifth-columnist, the president averred that he himself had approved of their establishing such a colonization. He said he did not believe that the *sinarquistas* constituted any danger to the country. His minister of interior, Miguel Alemán, whose business it was to eradicate the fifth column, went on record to declare he had not been able to discover anything subversive in its activities. Leftists accuse Avila Camacho of not being averse to the increasing power of the movement, because it might serve him as a political check on other groups. The *sinarquistas* claim they are not political and that they do not intend to participate in politics. But liberal politicians watch their growth with speculation and misgivings. In five years the movement has grown into a potentially formidable organization estimated to have eight hundred thousand members.

No one can say how far the power of *sinarquismo* may reach. As yet no dynamic leader has revealed himself. His enemies murmur that the scholarly José Vasconcelos is a secret force in the movement. Though presumably shorn of his one-time political influence, Vasconcelos holds not only the significant position of director of the National Library, but he is head of a private college of his own. A man of subtle and brilliant intellect, he is a disarming personality and a stirring speaker. If he ever emerged to show himself as a political leader of some branch of the counter-revolution, he might indeed create a stir.

Vasconcelos insists today that he is a "Christian revolutionist" and has always been one. "I will fight to the death the anti-Christian," he declares. "I was reared a Catholic. I left the church because it supported Huerta. Calles's persecution of the church sent me back to it. I have always been with the persecuted. When grafters and criminals are your enemies they accuse you of being reactionary."

Liberals shake their heads over José Vasconcelos. They speak of him with some perturbation as "our clandestine minister of education." They distrust his influence. He is idolized by a group of zealous religionists and pro-Falangists among the students at the National University. If being strongly pro-Catholic and pro-Spanish makes a reactionary in Mexico, Vasconcelos is a reactionary. But he is a highly honorable one and must be reckoned with as a leader among the intellectuals.

While affairs at home were taking up most of the Mexican government's energies and attention, the wars in Europe and Asia became a specter of global menace. Mexico had just begun to co-ordinate her agricultural and industrial activities. She was hoping to forge, as the president said, "an economy capable of sustaining the enormous program of education and hygiene which the material and moral well-being of her citizens has so long demanded." But by the spring of 1941 the subversive work of the Germans and the Japanese had caused the government to consider the dim possibility of an invasion that might strike at some part of the western hemisphere.

In May, the president ordered military maneuvers in Puebla,

his native state. On the outskirts of Puebla, the capital city, where many bloody battles had been fought in the past, eleven thousand troops went through their paces for a fortnight. For the climax a spectacular sham battle was staged on the hallowed ground of the *Cinco de Mayo* victory over the French in 1862. Despite the excitement and enthusiasm and some marvelous feats of the Mexican cavalry, the impact of the maneuvers was in the bare-faced revelation of Mexico's military weakness. Since the time of Juárez the main purpose of the army had been to keep order within the boundaries of the republic. The personnel of the Mexican forces was quite adequate for peace-time operation, but there were only forty-two thousand first-line combat troops and some sixty thousand *agraristas,* rural volunteers whom Cárdenas had armed mainly for their own protection. The shortages in equipment were appalling. The army planes—not more than thirty could be sure even of take-off—were five years old or more. The nation's anti-aircraft guns numbered one.

At the conclusion of the May maneuvers, however, President Avila Camacho, with a broad, bland smile, said cheerfully to the press: "There will never be any danger of an attack on the United States by any other nation through Mexico."

The magazine *Time's* observer, while paying tribute to the daring and endurance of Mexican soldiers, felt less assured. "The equipment with which Mexico must defend 764,000 square miles," he wrote, "does not equal either in quantity or quality that of the National Guard of Connecticut."

The following September, to reassure the citizens of the capital, Mexico's six thinly plated four-ton tanks were sent forth in parade. At the corner of López and Articulo 123 Street a taxi driver turned sharply and crashed into one of the instruments of war. The tank was so badly damaged that wreckers had to assist it to a repair shop. The Chevrolet, however, proceeded on its own power to jail and court, where the unlucky cab driver was fined "for damaging state property." The incident brought hilarious delight to the Mexican crowd.

While there was not the faintest doubt that Mexico would fight fiercely to protect her shores from invasion from the east or the west, she could hardly protect herself without matériel. Her ministry of national defense went into conference with a vitally interested and welcome defense mission from the United States. Mexico had virtually no money to put into war gear. Mexico could not think of diverting her small budget from education, swamp drainage, and public-health improvement to spend it on total defense, which would still be no guarantee against a concentrated Axis invasion. So it was necessary that the United States materially assist in the Mexican defense measures.

Three weeks before Pearl Harbor the United States State Department had tried to make generous amends for the sharpness of its notes in regard to the oil expropriation and agrarian claims. On November nineteen, United States-Mexican agreements were signed in Washington by Secretary of State Hull and Ambassador Castillo Nájera. The agreements greatly clarified the diplomatic atmosphere and brought back a cordiality into the term "good neighbor" that had gone a little sour in 1938.

Mexico assumed the obligation to settle the oil companies' claims. The two governments were each to appoint an expert to determine just compensation payable. In earnest of good faith, the Mexican government deposited $9,000,000 on account of the compensation to be paid. This was hardly more than a cupful in a bucket to the valuation the American oil companies set on their seized properties—reputedly $175,000,000. The difference between this figure and the $11,500,000 the Mexican economic investigators had claimed they were worth in 1938 would ordinarily have called for super-human arbitration. The crisis of the times, however, boded well for Mexico and ill for the coffers of the corporations. The date set for the announcement of the decision was April twentieth, 1942. The oil companies became resigned. They knew their claims must be sacrificed to war effort.

The two governments next agreed to negotiate a reciprocity-trade pact. The United States treasury devised a method of financial co-operation that would make transactions easy on Mexico. To stabilize the peso, it agreed to make $40,000,000 immediately available to the Bank of Mexico. To expedite the final construction of the Pan-American Highway through Mexico, the Export-Import Bank arranged substantial credits and announced that it would consider other requests for credits for economic development not only by the Mexican government but by private enterprise guaranteed by the government.

The treasury revealed a radical change of heart about the silver purchases which it had stopped in March, 1938, a week after the oil expropriation. It agreed to buy Mexican silver direct from the Mexican government at the preferential rate of thirty-five cents per ounce that had been paid previous to the expropriations. This meant the purchase of some six million ounces of silver a month, at approximately $25,000,000 a year.

In full settlement of the agrarian claims for American-owned property damaged by revolutions or expropriated under the revolutionary laws of the land, Mexico agreed to pay $40,000,000. Already she had paid $3,000,000 on this account. The remainder was to be paid in annual installments for fifteen years.

American conservatives protested that the United States had been out-traded on almost every issue. Much of the credit for the maneuvering went to the astute Mexican ambassador. Much belonged to the suave, far-sighted foreign minister, Ezequiel Padilla. A big price had been paid for good will. But it proved sound business on the State Department's part, for the United States had imperative need of some striking demonstration of the good-neighbor policy. The generous settlement fortified that idea of continental solidarity which was soon to be put to a dramatic test at the Pan-American Conference at Rio de Janeiro. It gave

Dr. Padilla the trump ace he urgently needed in the game he was playing in Mexico against pro-Axis sentiment. When he rose in the Mexican senate to comment on the agreements, Padilla was already addressing all Latin America.

"This marks a change in the international policy of the United States," he said, "not only towards Mexico but towards all the countries of America. The supreme values of co-operation and good will have been substituted for the dictates of imperialism and force . . . The signing of the agreement was one of the most eloquent demonstrations of the new American spirit. It is a moral triumph for American solidarity."

According to the Mexican press, Ezequiel Padilla became the man of the hour in Mexico. Within two months he was to be toasted as the man of the hour in the Americas.

While Avila Camacho pled for unity and harmony on every front and went all out for complete co-operation with the United States and the Allies, Axis agents worked openly and under cover to rupture the happy relations.

The news of Pearl Harbor came as a great shock to Mexico, as well as to the United States. On first reaction, some *gringo* haters were jubilant that the little dark men had slapped Uncle Sam so viciously in the face. But on second thought they, too, were confounded to realize that their long Pacific coast line was exposed to the danger of invasion. The Japanese navy knew that coast thoroughly; it had sent "fishing expeditions" repeatedly into every cove. There was only one tiny gunboat to guard the harbor of Acapulco. Anti-aircraft protection was non-existent. Regardless of the sentiment of some of her citizens, the Mexican government did not hesitate to stand firmly by the United States. She promptly broke off diplomatic relations with Germany, Italy, and Japan. She took possession of Axis shipping and froze bank deposits. Axis nationals were shortly removed from the coastal regions and settled in the interior where they could be closely observed. (There were a little fewer than 7,500 Germans in Mexico, some 5,000 Italians, and 4,300 Japanese.) Axis business concerns, like the German hardware and chemical firms and the coffee plantations of Chiapas, were taken over by state administrators, the profits to be paid into blocked funds in the government-owned Bank of Mexico. However, many alien nationals working for allied concerns were not disturbed. Intelligent discrimination was practiced. For instance, Orestes Cabutti, director of Thos. Cook and Son in Mexico, a cultivated Italian who had lived for eleven years in the country and who was not only extremely popular but highly respected for his integrity and his services to Mexico, was left at his post and unrestricted in every way.

Immediately on hearing the news of Pearl Harbor, General Cárdenas offered his services to the president. They were promptly accepted, and he was put in command of all the defenses of the vulnerable west coast. Within a year and a fortnight the national emergency had brought Cárdenas from his retirement back into the public life. He went straightway to that exposed, barren tongue of land known as Lower California and began construction of essential military roads. On January twelfth, 1942, President Roosevelt and President Avila Camacho announced the creation of a commission to consider the joint defense of Mexico and the United States, while Ezequiel Padilla pondered the imperative need of a unity of all the Americas and prepared to plead, at the imminent Rio Conference, for real hemispheric solidarity.

The success of this Pan-American conference was by no means a foregone conclusion. Several of the Latin American governments were fascist sympathizers. Others feared the Axis might and preferred to stay neutral and not risk material loss. At the beginning of 1942 there was considerable doubt that the Allies would win. Germany was then victorious almost everywhere her troops went. The Japs had proved their strength as well as their viciousness. England was losing colonial possessions at many

points of the compass. War-material production in the United
States was making slow headway. Despite repeated good-neighbor
manifestations in Latin America, the position of the United States
there was somewhat equivocal. Argentina's government was
known to have little love for the northern republic. No one could
say positively who were the passive enemies.

Under Secretary of State Sumner Welles, the United States representative to the congress, was deeply concerned. If the republics
split now it would be catastrophic to the structure he had labored
so arduously and skillfully with Cordell Hull to erect. But this
was not the time for the United States to take the lead in persuasion. The telling initiative should come from some Latin American statesman. On the urbane Brazilian foreign minister, Oswaldo Aranha, Mr. Welles could absolutely depend. But Brazil
was already known to be the United States' best friend south.
Mr. Welles needed a new imagination-stirring spokesman—someone from a quarter that had hitherto not been an avowed admirer
of the United States. He hoped Mexico's foreign minister would
prove to be that man. Dr. Padilla had the distinguished presence,
the intelligence, the force, and even the charm such a leader
needed. And he was flushed with the encomiums of his own
people because of the success of the extraordinary agreements
with the United States. To many of the Latin American delegates
and the international press men Dr. Padilla was only slightly
known. Though Mr. Welles admired him and knew his strong
democratic loyalties, he was not fully aware of his magnetism
with an audience. He did not know that Demosthenes had been
Padilla's hero of heroes since his youth. When the time came for
Mexico's representative to speak, things had been going stuffily
in the sultry atmosphere of a Brazilian summer. Padilla, looking
very handsome in a double-breasted suit of coffee-colored silk,
measured his audience sympathetically and began to speak quietly.
"We are here to deliberate on the fate of the Americas."

At the end of his first sentence a spell-like silence fell over the assembly. Perspiring delegates stopped fanning themselves with their programs. Hardened newspapermen felt prickly sensations along their backbones. Women in the gallery caught their breaths as their hearts skipped a beat.

The voice continued, though the people sensed the words rather than heard them. They felt the personality, the controlled fervor behind the words. "Japan's attack on the United States was not only an attack on the United States, it was an aggression by the totalitarian states on the world's democracies . . . it was an attack made by a totalitarian power on the whole of America."

The representatives of republics not in accord with the United States began to squirm as the voice increased in volume. "The men who have fallen gloriously on Wake Island and in the Philippines . . . have not fallen to defend the honor and sovereignty of the United States alone. They have also fallen to defend human liberty and the free destiny of America."

As Padilla paused, the place broke into an emotional pandemonium. Sumner Welles dabbed his moist brow lightly with an immaculate handkerchief and breathed with relief. The new spokesman was a tremendous success.

The Mexican went on reinforcing with logic and feeling the necessity of hemispheric solidarity and pointing out its future blessings. "If we can in this war manage to organize not only an economy but also an American moral entity, we shall be able to show that in our resolutions we are not only interested in the building of shipyards and the building of airplanes, but also that there is something higher that we are eager to build—and that is the Free Man of America." The cheers shook the glass in the window frames. Never in Pan-American history had a speaker received a more spontaneous and tumultuous ovation.

The strength and passion of Padilla's conviction carried more influence than his oratorical periods. And just as effectively as in the public hall, his persuasive eloquence carried weight in the privacy of committee rooms. In his shirt sleeves he stayed up half the nights pointing out, in a voice of gentle reasonableness, the perils of disunity.

At the January twenty-third meeting he was ready with his second prepared speech to recommend a collective rupture with the totalitarian countries. All the other republics except Argentina and Chile were in accord. He aimed his words at those two reluctant nations.

"This is without doubt a moment of tremendous historic importance. It is itself an episode of the war," he began. Again he had his audience spellbound. "We have not come here to argue with the words of peace, but to speak in terms of continental security, which is now so gravely threatened. . . . This is no time to defend material wealth"—his gaze fell on the Argentinian delegation—"it is time for sacrifice." He drove the point home. "It would be ignoble to pretend that others should defend the heritage of justice, the unity of America which we so loudly advocate, while we shelter ourselves in selfishness and false security. We are all of us in the same boat. Time will save none of us alone. All of us on this continent shall be crushed together or all of us be saved beneath the banner of American unity."

When the applause subsided, Padilla spoke soothing words to Argentina's representative, Dr. Ruiz Guiñazú, who was sweating profusely: "If there has been indecision—no matter, the constellations take form with the advance of night." Then he again applied the goad: "We are all in danger, and when the time comes for conscience to awake within this all-American unity, our two great sister peoples, Argentina and Chile, will make their conclusions known and, with their fraternal decision, brighten the union of all our flags assembled face to face with the tragic fate that menaces humanity."

No man could have done better—even if the Argentinian and Chilean delegates were willing to do no more than to recommend to their governments a rupture of diplomatic relations with the Axis powers. The signatures of the representatives of all the twenty-one American republics gave an appearance of complete unity. Mexico's prestige had never been higher with her sister republics. She had supplanted Argentina as Latin America's co-leader with Brazil. While Padilla's way was literally strewn with flowers wherever he moved in Rio, the unhappy Argentinian delegates got painful bumps on the head when their departing plane dropped into Guanabara Bay just after the take-off. "The plane was not overloaded," explained the jesting Oswaldo Aranha; "oh, no; it was Dr. Ruiz's conscience that was too heavy."

On the whole, the conference had come off well. Sumner Welles was gratified. Here was reward for years of labor for a cause that lay close to his heart. Being a good neighbor had paid another imponderable dividend. And if the United States had not been on most friendly terms with Mexico, and if Mexico had not had a foreign minister with such vision and oratorical virtuosity, it is conceivable that the proceedings might have fallen flat.

# 29. Counter-Revolution

*"What Mexico needs is economic help that will
not imply the sale of her freedom nor the slavery of her people."*

WOODROW WILSON

By the time Padilla returned to Mexico wreathed with laurels,
big money from the United States had arrived to implement the
Mexican defense. Fortification of harbors was soon under way,
and plans were completed for the construction of landing fields,
like the vast one at Ixtepec in the strategic Isthmus of Tehuantepec. Vessels of the United States and all the other American
republics were granted access to the harbors, and warplanes were
permitted a twenty-four hour stop-over on the airfields. The local
manufacture of small arms and the production of essential minerals were accelerated.

Throughout the spring of 1942, however, until the fourteenth
of May there were few visible signs of war-like activities in
Mexico. But on that date the Mexican oil tanker *Potrero de
Llano* was torpedoed by the Germans off the coast of Florida.
Several Mexican sailors lost their lives. There was some vengeful
shouting in the streets, and on June first Mexico officially declared war on Germany.

But by no means was joy ubiquitous when Mexico's decision
to enter the war on the side of Great Britain and the United
States was announced. Mexico had galling historical grudges
against other great powers—England, France, and the United
States—but none against Germany. Of all alien nationals the Germans had made themselves the most agreeable to the Mexicans.
Their business representatives—before Hitler's barter system—
had played fair with the Mexicans. Their traveling salesmen had

learned Spanish and gone into hinterland villages, selling their hardware and their drugs, giving toys to the children, often doctoring sick animals free, making friends for themselves and the German nation. Even the blondest German was not considered a *gringo* in the same category as a *norteamericano* or an Englishman. Many Germans had married into good *mestizo* families and had become accepted as Mexicans. At the large family gatherings so common in Mexico, if the radio played the Mexican national anthem it was the German in-laws who knew the words better than the Mexicans themselves and sang them more lustily.

It had been impossible to turn Germans into hated enemies within a few hours after their Japanese partners had bombed Pearl Harbor. Now it was not easy to make every Mexican believe that Germans would blow up a tanker and kill Mexican sailors. Only six months before Pearl Harbor, in a poll taken of the eighty students in a high-class business school in the capital, seventy-two had confessed their pro-Axis sentiments. Many Mexican youths still treasured the buttonhole German eagles and the little swastikas the German embassy had given out by the thousands the day France capitulated. The pro-Allies sentiment in Mexico came from the middle classes, the professional men, the more literate adherents of Cárdenas and from the radical labor unions, which had swiftly changed their tune about the imperialist war when Germany forced Russia to change sides.

Whether the Germans did or did not blow up a score of tankers, many of the well-to-do white Mexicans were speechless with rage at the war declaration against Germany. And in country districts some of the peasants had been so conditioned that for half a century the only foreign enemy they could conceive of fighting was the Yankees. When the war declaration was announced over the radio, tipsy fellows in the *pulquerías* and *cantinas* shouted gleefully, "Death to the *gringos!*" Some had to be shaken sober to make them realize that Mexico was on the side of the *gringos* and they then became more dazed than when drunk.

The masses were mightily bewildered. Through the press and the radio, the government had to devise a strenuous campaign to recondition the people's minds. Street singers were sent through villages giving the tidings in both Spanish and Indian dialects, dinning into the public the fact that Mexico could not survive if the United States were defeated. How could Mexicans relish a German victory, citizens were asked, when most of them were a *mestizo* people? If the Nazis got into control, the mixed-blooded population would be made politically impotent by "the master race," while the Indians would be used solely for exploitation. The people listened stolidly, but few felt an urge to get involved in a foreign war.

In August, 1942, President Avila Camacho decreed military instruction for all able-bodied males. In many districts there was sullen reaction. *Sinarquistas* agitated against submission to compulsory military training. Three towns were descended upon by armed bands that broke up troops of conscripts drilling in the plazas, wounding many, and in Miguel Auza killing the mayor and his son among others. Opposition in some places was so stubborn and cunning that the government had to pledge itself —as President Roosevelt did—that no boys would be sent overseas. The pledge was printed on leaflets and dropped into the recalcitrant hinterland by aviators.

There was only one way to make the peasants believe in the sense of being on the side of the *gringos* and against the Germans, whose peddlers had always been so polite. That was to set up their idol where all could see where his sentiments lay. So as Moses uplifted the symbolical brazen serpent in a time of great tribulation, Avila Camacho brought ex-President Cárdenas back to the capital as minister of national defense and made him the nation's top-ranking general. Cárdenas spoke to the people. His voice still held all the old magic for them. They began to murmur philosophically, "If Lázaro says it is right, it must be so."

The situation in Mexico was not without its special ironies.

The republic had not been involved in a foreign war since the 1860's, when she was attacked by the French of Napoleon III. Here, fourscore years later, she was lined up with the two imperial powers she had most feared and hated since that time. And the two most avidly peace-loving national figures since Madero—Cárdenas and Avila Camacho—found themselves with the chief responsibility of conducting a war effort on the home front to its effective conclusion.

The Nazis had spent millions in anti-United States propaganda and in various fifth-columnist activities. Mexico's war declaration now served to expedite the elimination of Axis influence between the Rio Grande and the Panama Canal. While Germany was professing contempt for the military set-up in Mexico, which Goebbels said was too feeble to make any impression whatever in the war, Cárdenas set about vigorously to reorganize the army. The whole army machine down to the most inexpert cook felt the vibrancy of the new force in command. Cárdenas built brand-new barracks and turned old colonial buildings into well-equipped quarters for the men. Not only did conscripts receive intensive training in arms, but also scholastic instruction to make them better citizens when the war was over. Thousands of eighteen-year-old Indian lads who spoke only their native tongues now had their first lessons in Spanish. Many of them had adequate food for the first time in their lives, the first warm clothing, the first dental and medical care, the first knowledge of hygiene.

Cárdenas shifted zone commanders, impressed them with the necessity for efficiency and expedition. His presence at the head of the war effort was felt in the mines, where men worked overtime to produce strategic materials for the American factories. Drugs, vegetable oils, industrial alcohol, mahogany, chick peas, henequen, and the entire crop of the rubber-bearing guayule plants loaded the freight cars and moved steadily across the border to be processed into needed war products. Virtually the whole output of silver, copper, antimony, zinc, tungsten, manganese, lead, mica, mercury, arsenic, and feldspar was placed at the disposal of the United States.

Mexican women threw to the winds the church taboos about woman's place being in the home, and took their places with men in the factories and did the work of men. Courses for women in telegraphy, welding, and mechanics were inaugurated. Some volunteered for target practice and map reading; others learned first aid and nursing. Three mornings a week women practiced military drill in the army stadium under the direction of two captains. In cities, towns, and remote villages, defense committees came to life. Men of all ages and professions drilled in the plazas or the playgrounds or the open pastures. School children of both sexes substituted drilling for their recess games. Although the government was equipped to train only fifty thousand eighteen-year-old conscripts a year, its professed purpose was to create eventually a reserve force of some two million trained men. How far Mexico was from that goal at the beginning of 1943, however, is shown by one succinct remark of Cárdenas. On being asked if his soldiers would fight outside the hemisphere, the general countered, "With what? Arrows? Rocks?"

When the anniversary of the *Grito del Dolores* came in September, 1942, the *Plaza de la Constitutión* before the National Palace was filled as it had never been filled except when Cárdenas spoke on the oil expropriations in 1938 and when the octogenarian dictator Díaz had struck the liberty bell in 1910, the centenary of Mexico's first bid for independence. Not only was this the first Independence Day celebration in seventy-five years that had found Mexico involved in a foreign war, but an extraordinary spectacle had been promised to the populace. As all eyes were focused on a platform before the palace, the people still gave doubtful credence to what they had been told to expect. But at the scheduled hour, on to the platform came President Avila Camacho, followed by six ex-presidents of Mexico—Cárdenas, Calles, Rodríguez, Ortiz Rubio, Portes Gil, and de la Huerta. Ranged side by side in unity, seven living men who had served as chief executive of their nation made a striking sight for all Mexico and the world to witness. Avila Camacho called for the full collaboration of his people with the United Nations in their fight against the Axis powers. The crowd shouted itself hoarse. If these seven men of varying political philosophies—two of whom had exiled another, one of whom had made a rebellion against another—could make accord for the national emergency, then there was hope for a real harmony. "A good left hand our president has indeed," the spectators murmured among themselves approvingly.

The time of stress and danger had also drawn the governments of Mexico and the United States closer and closer together. War had brought Mexico completely within the commercial orbit of her northern neighbor. In 1941 the United States had taken ninety-one per cent of Mexico's total exports and furnished eighty-four per cent of her imports. In 1942 the United States purchased 519,000 tons of strategic materials, compared with 221,000 tons in 1939. According to figures made public by Banco Nacional de Mexico in March, 1944, Mexico's exports increased from $138,000,000 in 1942 to $213,000,000 in 1943.

Avila Camacho had made it clear from the day of his inauguration that he welcomed foreign capital and assured it guarantees of fair dealing. Deposits which had been fearfully withdrawn from Mexican banks at the time of the oil expropriation poured back into Mexico. From October, 1940, to October, 1941, alone, Mexico had repatriated forty million dollars. And after the signing of the agreements with the United States, business had really begun to boom. To swell the stream of capital pouring into Mexico were the millions brought in by rich European refugees. A portion of the huge amount of United States capital that had gone into South America this past quarter of a century came to Mexico. Since 1911 American investors had felt safer in investing in those South American republics whose governments were more conservative. But now the anterooms of Eduardo Villaseñor, the astute director of the Bank of Mexico, were crowded with American capitalists seeking advice about Mexican investments.

Though the Revolution was ruthless enough about expropriating acreage, it had exhibited a special awe of banks. During the most radical times they were protected. As Villaseñor says, "The steadfastness of banks is very appealing to the large investor." In Mexico, banks continue to enjoy peculiarly high benefits. Many of the bank stocks pay dividends of fifteen and twenty per cent. Mexicans delight in bank stocks, but the investments they prefer above all others are those in rentable houses and buildings. The majority feel real security only in improved city real estate. They incline to the *rentier* mind of the French, and prefer to draw their interest of twelve to fifteen per cent from assured rents. Until recently Mexicans have never been heavy investors in industry. It is not in their nature to venture boldly in business, as it is in that of the *norteamericano*. Though they play the horses and buy lottery tickets, Mexicans are not eager gamblers in big business. They generally wait cautiously for foreigners to start and develop new industries, to furnish the capital and the technical skill, and then they will buy stock where they can. But with so much returned capital in 1941 and 1942, Mexicans began to create many new industries on their own.

By the third year of Avila Camacho's administration, the impress of paradox that has run all through Mexico's turbulent history was again strikingly noticeable. Progress in social reform seemed to have halted so that economic development could catch up. The sudden inpouring of capital due to the exigencies of the times had brought with it all the abuses of maldistribution of wealth. In the midst of Mexico's greatest boom, hard times had come to the poor man. War had helped to stack the cards in the hands of the counter-revolutionists. Daily the rich got richer, while the expressions on the faces of the poor became grimmer.

As their wages bought less and less, the underprivileged felt the pinch in their bellies. Prices continued to rise as the quality of things went down. By the summer of 1943 the price of many foodstuffs had doubled over 1941. The cost of clothing had more than doubled. Corn, sugar, and beans, Mexico's most easily raised essential commodities, were far from sufficient at any price. Other shortages, too, were serious. Frantic housewives and servants stood in line for half a day waiting to buy a little charcoal to cook the next meal. The price of charcoal was fixed by the government, but it often fluctuated according to whether or not a policeman was nearby. Sometimes there was none to be had even at black-market prices. The wildest sort of speculation in various commodities played havoc with Avila Camacho's earnest effort at price control.

Profiteering was on the rampage. And while the president struggled arduously to curb the inflation, some of the under men in his own ministeries were accused of graft "in the realm of priorities and such." A young aristocrat who had gone into the manufacturing of Venetian blinds in a small way was desperately in need of wood from the United States. When he had repeatedly failed to get it, a man from one of the ministeries telephoned him, and said, "I hear you need a certain kind of wood from the United States; I have a carload of it, which I will sell you at such and such a figure." It was more than twice as much as the young manufacturer could pay and remain in business. "How on earth," he demanded indignantly, "did you, a public official not in business, get hold of the wood?" "Never mind that; will you take it, at my price?" "I can't afford to; and I will lose my whole business before I'll submit to such extortion."

It was abuses like this one that prompted Senator Butler to allege, in his fantastically exaggerated figures of accusation, that a big portion of our lend-lease aid was going into grafters' pockets. It was what some of the Latin Americans themselves charged. But, naturally, in a program of such magnitude there was bound to be some dishonest seepage.

Certainly the flush times in Mexico which brought such reckless joy to the "haves" brought privation and apprehension to the "have nots." In some remote communities people faced actual starvation. An investigation revealed that eighty per cent of the public-school children in the capital itself came to school after an inadequate breakfast of coffee substitute with watered condensed milk, and a piece of bread. A worker with the minimum wage of two and a half pesos (fifty cents) a day or one with even four pesos cannot afford milk for his children at half a peso a liter.

Early in the Avila Camacho regime the English widow of a Mexican engineer found herself with three children to support. Bilingual and attractive, the best she could do at the time was to get a job as night cashier in the bar of one of the better hotels. Her hours of work were six P.M. to six A.M. Her pay was three pesos a day—sixty American cents—the price of two cocktails. In two years her pay doubled, but so did the cost of living. "We see the fruits of the boom everywhere," she commented stoically, "but the people hardly get a nibble."

As the counter-revolution advanced of its own momentum due to the abnormal circumstances, many of the people began to blame their hardships on the *gringo* neighbor. It is true that private American agencies had not only tried to buy up the scanty Mexican food—the government just did stop the sale of the bulk of the rice crop—but they bought so many blankets and *huaraches* and tablecloths that in many places there were none for the Mexicans themselves. On the other hand, American factories, which had been converted for war needs, were unable to supply Mexico's needs in agricultural tools and machinery. With seventy per cent of the wealth of Mexico normally coming from agriculture, the pinch caused by the lack of farm equipment was critical.

In the summer of 1943, while unrest among the workers and

white-collar employees simmered, the capital took on an air of almost contemptuous gaiety. Visitors to Mexico were impressed with the glittering façade of prosperity, the new smart shops catering to luxury trade, the crowded restaurants, where patrons sometimes stood as in breadlines waiting to get a table. They noted the new residential subdivisions with the hideous houses shrieking their gaudy new-richness. Whereas in the time of Cárdenas the emphasis in building had been on relieving the distress of the people—on practical apartments for working folk or small houses with good plumbing—now construction was concentrated on ostentatious living quarters for the wealthy. In spite of a three-year building boom, rents in Mexico City soared. Much undeveloped property quadrupled in value. The American head of the largest real-estate company in Mexico City stated privately, in August, 1943, that his company was selling a million pesos' worth of building lots a month in the fashionable Lomas de Chapultepec. Most of it was being bought by Jewish refugees, he said. "It isn't conceivably worth a third of the price, but if they want to throw their money about, we sell it to them." To help relieve the swollen pockets of the new gilded middle class, a vast and extravagant race track, El Hipódromo de las Américas, was built, partly with American capital, partly with Mexican. Plushy new night clubs with elaborate decórs (some owned by shady Americans) opened their doors. Mexico City became a rendezvous of international pleasure seekers, while labor demonstrators threatened to kill and eat the race horses at El Hipódromo if the price of meat did not go down.

"Where is this great social revolution we've been hearing about?" casual tourists in the cities commented. "We don't see signs of it in the kind of building now booming. Certainly not in wages, where good carpenters are getting eighty American cents a day and government road workers fifty cents."

"The feared dictatorship of the proletariat?" mused better-informed tourists. "The red menace inspired by that thunderbolt hurler Lombardo Toledano? The total ruin of the rich by that 'Great Destroyer of Mexico,' Cárdenas, who gave land and literacy to peons and who taught great empires to respect Mexico's sovereignty? Where *is* the Revolution?"

Thoughtful men of good will looked about with wry smiles on their faces and odd feelings inside them. Some laughed, not at the efforts of the honest idealists who had sought to uplift mankind, but at the irony of it all. The abundant life promised to the masses was too obviously absent. What had happened was not in the least in the intention and desire of the good president, Don Manuel. "The Revolution is not dead," he apologized, when questioned. "It is merely dormant temporarily, lying low under the stress of war."

Throughout history in times of crisis, wonders have often been likened to the handwriting on the wall at Belshazzar's famous feast. In Mexico, on February twentieth, 1943, in the little valley of Cuityúzero in Michoacán, a most strange thing occurred. While a peasant named Dionisio Pulido was placidly plowing his cornfield, the earth beneath him groaned faintly and a wisp of smoke burst out of a new furrow. The astounded farmer wondered if he had plowed too deep. After a brief pause, he rushed to the spot and attempted to beat out the fire with his palm-straw hat. But the path of smoke widened, and suddenly, with a roar, the earth opened and vomited fire, stones, and ashes into Dionisio's freshly plowed acres. The terrified man turned and fled as if he had looked into the mouth of hell. Other peasants, hearing the noise and seeing the incredible sight of hurtling fire and flames rising out of their quiet earth, prayed with all their breath. But soon they were snatching up what household goods they could and were running for their lives, as hot rocks began to drop on their frail-roofed shacks. The fiery accumulation in Dionisio's cornfield increased. It formed a hillock, then a hill, and at last grew into a mountain. As if drenched with poison gas, vegetation withered, leafed trees turned into lead-colored skeletons.

The countryside for miles about looked as if blanketed with black snow. The people's pleasant valley had become as awful and as desolate as a scene in hell. While Dionisio continued to bewail his loss, crying over and over, "Oh, my cornfield. My poor little cornfield!" scientists from all over the world began their journeys to behold one of the most remarkable phenomena to occur in this hemisphere since the 1780's.

The volcano was named Paricutín, after the nearest village. The nearest large town is Uruapan, where the most beautiful lacquer ware in the continent is made by a secret process handed down from parent to offspring. Wrapped in a murky fog of ashes when the wind blew that way, its streets an inch deep in black volcanic dust, its blossoms begrimed, Uruapan soon became overcrowded with scientists, photographers, tourists, and mere holiday makers, who used the town as the base for exploratory trips to the mountainous inferno.

In the midst of the hubbub, in the face of the evil magnificence of the volcano by day and the breath-taking grandeur by night, the scores of homeless folk like Dionisio Pulido went on imploring the saints for mercy and praying to the mountain to cease its havoc. Quietly on the scene arrived Lázaro Cárdenas to observe and speak with the unfortunate. A practical as well as a big-hearted man, without waiting for the processes of governmental relief Cárdenas hired trucks and sent several of the most needy families to a small estate of his in Michoacán, where he gave them the land for their own. In due time, governmental agencies made provision for the other small farmers whose houses and *milpas* lay irrevocably buried under lava and black dust.

As the crater of Paricutín widened fantastically and its stark cone towered heavenwards, men began to read symbolic meanings into nature's outburst. One Mexican magazine editor wrote, "It might be said that the fire of Paricutín acts as a purifying agency in the hearts of men." A revolutionary observer who had been much disheartened by the aspects of counter-revolution nodded his head before the spectacle and said to his companion, "Let them heed the warning." Then he quoted aloud a passage from the novelist José Rubén Romero that ran through his mind: "The struggle has been unequal, I know; but one day an earthquake will arise from the courage of the humble and in that time not one stone will remain upon another."

While Paricutín continued to make good reading in the press, even if its activities no longer were worthy of the front page, the scarcity and high prices of necessities of life were played up with emphasis in the liberal press. For several months the radical papers put on a campaign of pointing out abuses, demanding relief measures for the common man's distress. While never unfriendly to the president himself, the editorials stung furiously at his government. Then, in June, 1943, the editors suddenly softpedaled their accusations and warnings. Some of the extreme leftists said their leaders had sold out to the capitalists. But the radical writers were only acceding to an appeal from the president to withhold their fire while the government devised some workable means of making the ends of income and living costs meet.

In late September, 1943, Avila Camacho took positive measures to increase corn and sugar production. He ordered a quarter million acres in the tropical coastal region to be planted in corn. Corn was thereafter to be purchased not by private wholesalers but by the government, which also was to arrange distribution. Another attempt was made to freeze basic food prices. Wages were to be increased from five to fifty per cent for persons who made under ten pesos a day. They were to be frozen thereafter. Unauthorized strikes were strictly prohibited. Severe penalties were decreed for price violators. Employers who disregarded wage-increase orders were threatened with jail sentences and governmental operation of their business.

Even in normal times the chief administrator of Mexico has one of the toughest jobs of any executive in the world. "A slow river runs better," men had said hopefully of Avila Camacho when he was inaugurated in December, 1940. They could no more foresee than could he the sudden tributaries and cataracts that were to pour into the river of government to affect its channel and flow. Yet through all the unwonted factors occasioned by the war, Cárdenas's successor had not lost sight of the most essential peace-time job in Mexico—to raise the living standard and the purchasing power of the twelve million underprivileged in his republic.

In October, 1943, a young Russian-born radical close to Lombardo Toledano said in private conversation, "I believe that Avila Camacho would have pursued the social revolutionary course of Cárdenas if the pressure of world events had not disturbed his plans." In December, 1943, at the close of the first half of his six-year term, Avila Camacho began to speak again publicly of the revolution. "In spite of any external pressure," he said, "the underlying principles of the Revolution will be advanced."

# 30. Counter Counter-Revolution

*"In all your negotiations fear not to give
strength to that republic; Mexico can never
be an enemy, it ought to be made a friend, of
the United States."*
ABRAHAM LINCOLN

With the coming of 1944, though the unprecedented prosperity
inflation did not abate, the liberals noted with joy that the swing
to the right had touched its high mark in 1943 and was moving
back to the left. The collective sentiment of the nation had so
directed the turn. The president now made some significant
changes among his collaborators in government, putting in places
of maximum responsibility men chosen solely for their merit and
ability, not for the expediency of satisfying the reactionaries.
Jaime Torres Bodet, the progressive, intellectual under secretary
of foreign affairs, supplanted Véjar Vásquez as secretary of education. It was the latter's appointment to that important office
which had dismayed the liberals more than any other act in
Avila Camacho's regime. In no sense could Torres Bodet be
classified by the rightists as a radical, or by the leftists as a reactionary. He was moderate and balanced, a man of the world, a
poet and a critic, as well as a diplomat who had ably served his
country in so important a post as the ambassadorship to Brazil.
His appointment brought an enthusiasm and collaboration of the
various elements in one of the most vital ministries of government. And according to the magazine *Acá,* "he accomplished
in two weeks in office what Véjar Vásquez could not do in two
years."

Another popular leftist appointment was that of the distinguished lawyer Ignacio García Téllez, formerly Cárdenas's min-

ister of interior, as the head of social security, in a department which in time is expected to prove "one of the most fruitful conquests of the Mexican proletariat."

An ardent revolutionary, Silvano Barba González, former governor of Jalisco who had created a stir by denouncing Axis agents within the clergy in February, 1942, was selected to head the *departamento agrario*. Here he supplanted Fernando Foglio Miramontes, of whose work in agrarian affairs a liberal paper commented that it had been "so little brilliant that it seemed it had not existed."

These three governmental moves to the left, which brought renewed hope to the populace at large, were accompanied by ever-increasing public appearances of ex-President Cárdenas by the side of President Avila Camacho. By March, 1944, doubting Thomases were beginning to believe what Lombardo Toledano had tried to impress upon them during the critical unrest of March, 1943; namely, that Avila Camacho is as devoted personally to Cárdenas as he is to his aims. "I who have known President Avila Camacho all my life," the labor leader said, "know perfectly well that when the public applauds Lázaro Cárdenas in the presence of the actual president of the republic it pleases Manuel Avila Camacho more than if they were applauding himself."

"This determined turn of the majority to the left by the beginning of 1944," wrote an editor in February, "was accompanied by the government's moving in the same direction, so that it can now perform its functions with efficacy and confront not only the immediate problems, but also those perceived on the future's horizon."

Events were promising well for the general welfare, in numerous manifestations early in 1944. By New Year's Day the Inter-American Highway in Mexico extended 1,087 miles from Laredo to Oaxaca. Unfinished gaps between Oaxaca and the border of Guatemala numbered only four hundred miles. Work was to go forward on these last difficult stretches, the president announced. He also announced that road construction in Yucatán and on the vital Guadalajara-Nogales Highway and the Mexico City-Tampico Highway would continue in 1944.

In regard to railroad construction, the president said that the building of the Southern Railway would proceed, linking the Tehuantepec line of the National Railways with the United Railways of Yucatán, thus giving Yucatán rail connection with the interior of Mexico for the first time in history. At the end of March, to keep operations in order and schedules on time, the president took an unprecedented, firm stand on labor, and removed the last vestige of union control. According to governmental decree, management now has complete power to employ and dismiss workers, to disregard all union regulations which "slow up, impede, or impair" operation. Thus, railway management in Mexico now has more power than that in the United States. Avila Camacho's determined move to forestall any labor disruptions of any branch of the railroad service proved again his care for the general welfare.

As to his pet project, irrigation, the president announced in January that Mexico would spend $16,000,000 on its irrigation program in 1944. The appropriation placed at the disposal of the National Irrigation Commission is being used for works under way which will irrigate some 260,000 acres. By the special six-year program of the commission created in 1941, it is intended to improve irrigation in 653,000 acres and to open up an additional 1,081,000 acres to cultivation. Optimists estimated that by the end of 1944 more than a million persons would directly benefit from Mexico's achievements in irrigation and that national agricultural production in 1944 would be double that of 1941. However roseate such hopes may be, the president himself declared in February that ten million acres of corn would be cultivated in 1944—more than at any other time in Mexico's history, despite the extensive diversification in farming that Mexico has been attempting these past few years.

In the spring of 1944, though the man in the street blamed the United States for the inflationary prices of necessities and luxuries, relations between the United States and official Mexico had never been more cordial. A precedent had been broken in April of 1943 when President Roosevelt paid a state visit to President Avila Camacho in Monterrey, and had the visit promptly returned in Corpus Christi, Texas. In the first neighborly meeting, Don Manuel had gently referred to certain "negative memories" that Mexico still bore in regard to the United States, and both chief executives expressed fervent hope that future relations would be so happy as to dissolve them completely. The most significant outcome of the meeting was the presidents' agreement to create a Mexican-American Commission for Economic Co-operation. The commission met in both capitals between May twenty-first and July second. Out of the conferences came the creation of the Mexican-American Industrial Commission which held its first meeting in Mexico City in the late fall of 1943. By the time of this meeting the United States had already spent $771,000 in rehabilitating the Mexican railroads to keep moving the stuffs of war and in preparation for the future exchange of trade. By the end of 1944, if conditions continue, it is estimated that Mexico will have a $600,000,000 trade balance in her favor— money to spend in the United States as soon as there are articles to sell which Mexicans need and want.

A controversial negative memory was soothed on October first, 1943, when the Standard Oil of New Jersey officially announced a final settlement of all its publicized claims. The company was to receive a total of $22,332,484. The amount was hardly twelve per cent of the original claims. The officials advisedly refrained from comment as to whether or not they were satisfied. But on the same day the Mexican ambassador in Washington paid a visit to Harry Sinclair, president of Sinclair Oil, and presented him with a check for $1,500,000, Mexico's final installment on the $8,500,000 agreed upon in direct negotiations in 1940. Completely contrary to the attitude of the Standard executives, Mr. Sinclair blithely recalled that he had said from the outset that his agreement with Mexico was a satisfactory one and that he had been confident it would be scrupulously carried out.

The American public, as well as the press, was glad the oil expropriation ruckus was ended. It had long since become a bore, and in the face of a world war and astronomical monetary figures, its whole significance had become dwarfed. As far as the future of any foreign oil operations in Mexico was concerned, the most telling factor in the settlement was the categorical recognition that the subsoil wealth of Mexico belonged to the nation.

If the United States government had given Cárdenas in his last two years only a portion of the co-operation and material aid it has given Avila Camacho, much grief would have been avoided. But to appease Standard Oil and political agitation, the New Deal administration had felt it necessary to withdraw some of its active support from Mexico's New Dealer. What happened —and, worse, what nearly happened—because of the government's surface attitude towards Cárdenas, should forcibly remind the citizens of the United States of the necessity of making the good-neighbor policy work in times of peace as well as in the crisis of war. When the urgency of mutual-defense aims subsides and activities assume the wonted ways of peace, then will come the real test of the policy.

In a contest conducted by the liberal magazine *Tomorrow* early in 1944 on the theme "Latin America in the Post-War World," approximately ninety-eight per cent of four hundred and fifty-nine articles submitted by Latin American writers expressed awareness that the United States would emerge from this war as the real leader of Latin America. And all of these writers believed that the Latin American people and governments should co-operate with the United States. But with a great hope expressed, there were a strong mixture of cynicism and a fear that economic depression and chaos might result in the post-war era if the United States failed to carry out the precepts of the Atlantic Charter and of the good-neighbor policy.

From the first, President Avila Camacho pledged complete accord with the good-neighbor policy. But the United States has yet to prove to the satisfaction of all Latin Americans that that policy was not created largely as an insurance against the menace of war looming on both sides of the eastern hemisphere. "Will the good-neighbor policy outlast Franklin D. Roosevelt?" they ask south of the Rio Grande. Of course it must, no matter what name the program goes by. All level-headed Republicans as well as Democrats agree that the time has passed for imperialistic connotations or dubious interpretations of the Monroe Doctrine. According to the Mexican diplomat, Dr. Luis Quintilla, in the last quarter of the nineteenth century and the first quarter of the twentieth the Monroe Doctrine had been a monologue, in which sixty acts of aggression or intervention in the name of that doctrine have been chalked up against the United States. "Pan-Americanism"—which he used as another name for the policy of the good neighbor—"is a dialogue; in the future only dialogues will prove popular and beneficial." Some kind of collective economic order for mutual benefit will have to be wrought, and new methods of financing and exploitation instrumented.

For the post-war period the Mexican government, like most of the greater Latin American nations, has its determination set on a program of gradual industrialization. It has confessed to an urgent desire for some of the abounding technical resources of the United States to be placed at the disposal of the manufacturers and farmers of Mexico "in order to give them better opportunities for organization and development." Mexico must have factories to produce agricultural implements. She needs packing houses, ice plants, and hydro-electrical plants. She needs to manufacture

cheap clothes for her people. Honest foreign capital which desires to participate in this industrialization will be warmly welcomed. But it shall know that its managers must respect the
industrial laws of Mexico. Above all else, Mexico desires to abolish the unilateral exploitation which formerly transported wealth
out of the country and nourished a continual spirit of discord
within. In the future, Mexico will rightly expect a higher proportion of the profits to remain within her own borders. She
looks to industrial development to help improve, collectively and
individually, the general standard of living—to assist in the de-
pauperization of her impoverished.

Due considerably to the investment of capital from the United
States, Mexico's light and heavy industries have forged ahead during the Avila Camacho regime despite the difficulty of obtaining
the proper machinery. The 1940 census reported 12,711 industrial
establishments already in operation with a capitalization of $520,-
000,000 and over 330,000 employees. During 1942, sixty brand-
new industries were established with a total investment of
$38,000,000, a large portion of which came from the United
States.

The very able United States ambassador, George S. Messersmith, has assured the Mexicans that the good neighbor will
continue to be an effective and honest business man. He has
given repeated assurances that it is entirely contrary to the intention of the United States to frustrate Mexico's industrialization
after the war. He has told the citizens that unquestionably the
United States will assist her neighbor in the post-war industrialization.

But if by some unlikely mischance in governmental policy the
United States should be reluctant, Great Britain will be only
too eager to oblige immediately, as will other European nations
when they recover from the ravages of war. Whatever comes,
Mexico should be in a fortunate position for bargaining.

So far as the United States is concerned, the very core of the heartland of her future geopolitics lies in the high central plateau of Mexico. Somewhere within Mexico's boundaries might be located the center of the land mass known as the Western Hemisphere. And within its latitudes may be found a microcosm of the manifold conditions and potentialities of the twenty republics to the south. From the United States viewpoint, Mexico is the show window or the vestibule or the first front of all Latin America, call it what one will. With no other country is friendship more essential. In constructing a zone of hemispheric security for the United States, Mexico is the territory and the nation of prime importance. That importance is attested to by the fact that the United States maintains a larger diplomatic corps in Mexico City than in any other city of the world except London. And the State Department was careful to choose for its latest ambassador one of its very top career diplomats, the seasoned Mr. Messersmith.

In the summer of 1943 the supershrewd Stalin acknowledged this strategic geographical and political position by sending as his ambassador to Mexico his ace diplomat, the astute and charming Comrade Oumansky. Stalin did not offer to a small country like Mexico the very best diplomat Russia had to present to any nation merely as a gracious gesture in gratitude to the country which had refused for over two decades to recognize the Union of Soviet Socialist Republics. And the dictator was certainly not unaware that in the Western Hemisphere he had no more ardent admirer than Mexico's Lombardo Toledano, the head of the Latin American Confederation of Labor, the power of which organization is still to be tested. Some of Lombardo Toledano's enemies have jestingly called him the "interplanetary labor leader." But though no one may expect these jesters to prove complete prophets, within the jest there may lie a pinch of potent yeast. For the force of Lombardo Toledano and labor throughout the Latin American republics may swell to unconsidered proportions in the approaching decades.

Mexico, like all Latin America, is pregnant with future. And, like harbingers of approaching events, like vital links between the now and the soon-to-come, are the increasing networks of inter-American air transportation. In February, 1944, work on the huge new *Aeropuerto Central* in Mexico City was begun on a site adjacent to the present air field. (Before the plans were drawn the Mexican designers visited the best airports in the United States and consulted with American technicians.) Mexico will soon have one of the safest and most modern airfields in the world. The area is almost twice as great as that of La Guardia Field in New York. The very magnitude of the undertaking, the "looking ahead by half a century" in this gateway between the United States and South America, are warrant enough that close friendship between the next-door neighbors is imperative.

Just as there is a bond between all men of good will who desire something better for human society than *laissez faire* capital in the past seems to have done for it, so there is a bond between those citizens of Mexico and the United States who promote harmony and friendship and mutual gain. Lázaro Cárdenas has stated with conviction, for all his compatriots to hear, "Mexico's success depends upon a firm friendship with the United States."

It is not always easy, however, for the best intentioned of Mexicans and *norteamericanos* to make friends quickly. Besides the difference in tongues, which can be surmounted, there are those psychological barriers involving the whole background of Spain and the Indian blood-stream on the one side and the Anglo-Saxon heritage and modern American rhythms on the other. Not many persons in either republic are so blessedly constituted that they can dissolve such barriers at once and pierce directly beneath all custom to the essential heart of man.

The American who goes to Mexico in an attitude of criticism, who is quick to express adverse comparisons, does corroding damage to the cordial relations between the two nations. Mexicans resent, too, the crusading spirit of smug persons who are so sure they know what proper civilization should be. Often unseasoned business men from the north become slightly insane at the Mexican lack of punctuality. They fume and fulminate and determine to teach those fellows lessons, to make them understand that time is money. But Mexicans have different ideas of time's worth and they already have a plenitude of good precepts to guide them. Could a man from north of the border conceive a better gem of a sermon on punctuality than the one inscribed on a church door at San Miguel Allende? "Punctuality is the virtue of saints, the courtesy of kings, the duty of gentlemen, the need of men of business, and the custom of men of sound judgment."

Lack of rigid punctuality is with Mexicans by no means a sign of intentional discourtesy or unfriendliness. On the whole, Mexicans of every class are more than ready to offer friendly response to friendly approach. With them, courtesy is a quality descending both from their Indian and Iberian heritages. As the distinguished American priest, the Reverend Francis Clement Kelly said, "The Mexican peon is perhaps the only gentleman in rags on earth." From the lowest in estate to the highest, Mexicans are peculiarly sensitive to bad or unperceptive manners. They know better than do most citizens of the United States the truth of that old Spanish maxim, "In honoring others we amply honor ourselves." More than imperialistic bullying or greedy exploitation, it is decades of wounded sensibilities that lie back of Mexican resentment to *gringos*. Since it is as necessary to keep friendships in good repair as it is to keep harbor defenses in condition, good manners are no less significant in profitable alliances than reinforced concrete. As Stark Young says so happily: "Manners are the mask of decency that we employ at need, the currency of fair communication; their flower is a common grace, and their fruit not seldom friendship." And manners of the northern visitors are often scrutinized and silently chalked up plus or minus in the Mexican's conception of the composite *norte-americano*.

"One of the principal dangers to guard against," warned a perceptive American at a recent banquet for business men, "is the myth that Latin America is inhabited by docile peoples, eagerly waiting for Yankee energy, ingenuity, and leadership to make it blossom like a rose." Commenting on this timely admonition, Rafael Heliodoro Valle, dynamic managing editor of Mexico's famous *Excelsior,* wrote something to be remembered: "Although we recognize the excellent example given us by the United States with respect to devotion to work, a sense of responsibility, organization, and imagination at the service of human welfare, and tolerance for ideas and beliefs of every kind, we must still take into account the fact that life is different here. We are convinced that we are young nations which, in spite of many vicissitudes, have demonstrated their desire to improve. Only those who have studied our historic past can appreciate that the evils from which we still suffer are the result of political and economic conditions against which we must continue to struggle. Only a genuine, sincere understanding of this past will render possible the understanding, co-operation, and friendship of all American countries."

In our future relations there is a lurking danger to harmonious co-operation that Mexicans for their part should face squarely. The more the United States complies with Mexico's invitation to make capital investments, the more suspicious and jealous some of her citizens may become of us. With each million from the United States that goes into a new Mexican factory or into the opening up of a mine, there are those persons who will cry out that the Yankees are seeking to get an imperialistic stranglehold on them, that the good-neighbor policy is an instrument to keep them in a colonial state. On the other hand there are those naïve others among them who frankly expect the United States to rehabilitate their railroads, furnish money and materials to build their roads and drain their swamps, just because *norteameri-canos* are big-hearted saps. There are too those chronic blamers of the United States for all that goes wrong in Mexico. Finally, there are a few bitter souls who would relish some anti-United States tie-up with Argentina, some who even look to that unlikely day when Argentina, backed by certain European powers and other Latin American republics, may battle with the United States for the leadership of the Western Hemisphere. But these belong in the category of those misguided men who would throw their country into black confusion and misery to get their side or their ideology into power.

On the Monday after Easter, 1944, occurred such an ill-boding attempt. As President Avila Camacho got out of his automobile in the courtyard of the Palacio Nacional, a young artillery lieu-tenant approached, drew a .45-caliber revolver, and fired. The bullet went through the president's coat and vest and burned the shirt over the heart. But, miraculously, Avila Camacho was un-hurt. He grappled with his assailant, pinning his arms, until guards rushed up and disarmed the fellow. Then coolly the president asked that the officer, who was quite well known to him, a compatriot from his own state of Puebla, be brought up to his office that he might learn his grievance. The lieutenant, who had been educated for the priesthood, protested against the army regulation which forbids men to attend church in uniform, and kept repeating, "There is no justice." Through a spokesman, Avila Camacho gave out to the press that his would-be assassin was "a Nazi sympathizer." Throughout Mexico there were mut-tered accusations of Falange and *sinarquismo,* and a recalling here and there of the religious fanatic who had assassinated Obregón. Whatever the officer's motive, personal or group-directed, Avila Camacho begged the nation to make nothing of the unhappy incident and in no wise to let it stir up fresh unrest or bring division to Mexico.

The truth may forever remain a mystery, for at the military

barracks where he was incarcerated that same night the lieutenant was mortally wounded. According to the commander of
the Sixth Regiment, he was shot by guards as he attempted to
escape. On Wednesday the papers announced his death from
peritonitis. Was this the end of an isolated deed, people asked,
or did the lieutenant's crime presage something sinister in flux?
In a land as unpredictable as Mexico no one could ever say with
assurance what might or might not happen. One could only take
hope from the consensus of opinion that never in Mexican history had a president struggled harder to govern for all, and none
had been so loyally supported by so many diverse factions.

Yet, as affecting the immediate morale of Mexico, there is one
peculiarly disturbing sign that observers note among many young
men of the towns. It may be merely a phase rather than a trait
ingrained, but it is none the less to be deplored. It is a kind of
indifferent and contemptuous cynicism that seems more unhealthy because it is so resigned. Ask any young Mexican from
eighteen to thirty—soldier, taxi driver, lawyer, or shop assistant
—about the future of his country. The chances are he will reply
with a grimace, a shrug, a disillusioned turning down of the
mouth. Perhaps he will answer with some bitter quip about graft
or the political machine or the control of the national finances
by an alien world more powerful than Mexico. Howsoever he
expresses himself, one senses a frustration that seeks release in
mockery or irresponsibility or plain apathy. And sometimes, in
deeply thoughtful young men, that frustration has assumed a profound melancholy, like that of a young infantry captain who
spoke from his inner heart when he said, "Anyone who loves
Mexico stays with his heart broken."

This captain, who had been educated in the United States, was
referring indirectly to the betrayal of Mexico and the Revolution
by the revolutionists themselves. "Mexicans have been victimized
often enough by aliens, God knows," he went on to say, "but
they are victims just as often of their own natures. It is the

native political *conquistadores* who turned corrupt and broke faith with the people; these fellows undermined the Revolution. Our honest leaders like Cárdenas and Avila Camacho have had to make use of so much rotten timber. What you in the United States call 'graft' grows in rank soil here. Though we don't do it in such spectacular millions as sometimes you do across the border, it is a rooted and prevalent thing with us. It is not only winked at, but its success is often envied and even admired. For the first half of Cárdenas's administration, political graft was curtailed and slashed, from that of cabinet ministers to that of the smallest provincial *político*. Under the influence of Cárdenas, bureaucratic jobs went, wherever possible, to young men with a reputation for ideals. But with so much authority and so much money passing through their fingers, young men also succumbed in time to the old Latin temptation of lining their pockets while in office. Too many fine men who start out with honest purpose end up as slick politicians. That's the pity of Mexico. That's what breaks the heart of sincere patriots."

The theme of the most important novel to come out of Mexico recently—*Sunburst,* by Mauricio Magdaleno—bears out the captain's lament. It depicts the betrayal of his rural compatriots by a risen *político,* an Indian like themselves, a man who had suffered hardship with them and whom they trusted as a savior to bring them some sustenance from the Revolution. But the glittering politician exploited his old friends as trickily and callously as any *hacendado* or foreign *conquistador* from whom they expected nothing.

The purging of graft from the ranks of public servants, like tax assessors or policemen, cannot be successfully achieved until their salaries are raised to give them a respectable standard of living. And salaries cannot be increased unless the income taxes and property taxes are considerably raised. No government, not the most radical, has dared to decree a high income tax. On businesses, taxes are kept low to attract the foreign investor. And it is the custom of business firms, great and small, to keep a double set of books: one accurate, for the directors; and another for the authorized examiners, who, instead of asking to see the correct books, graciously demand their *mordido,* or bite, in pesos, from ten to several thousand, according to the ability to pay and the resistance to scaring.

*Mordidos* are considerations to be worked out within the national consciousness, just as every other country has its own peculiar problems to resolve. Only as abuses in one country affect international relations and good will should they be the concern of another country. And it is no more the business of *norteamericanos* to preach against the widespread petty dishonesty in Mexico than for the Mexicans to put on a campaign to clean up the appalling juvenile delinquency in the United States. Unhealthy moral conditions may be deplored, but they are not to be reformed by strangers.

When the war is over there will possibly be a contagion of disillusion or discontent among young Americans to be combated, as there is in Mexico today. In both cases they are problems to be faced on the respective fronts. But in regard to relations between the two nations, in the critical aftermath of war and in the post-war era, both governments and both peoples might profitably recall the Galilean's second great command, "Love thy neighbor as thyself." For, mankind being in an unredeemed state, Mexico and the United States may each be greatly tempted. Mexico could conceivably become a center of intrigue from distances as remote in space and ideology as the Union of Soviet Socialist Republics and Argentina. Leaders without integrity, or merely misguided, might create havoc in the nation by a foolish gesture. If big business in the United States should ever again attain its pristine "rugged individualism," bludgeoning "go-getters" among its ranks might try to urge the revival of a big-stick policy under another name and undo all the good neighborly work of the Franklin D. Roosevelt regime. As for a most desirable attitude of the post-war government towards Mexico, its leaders might happily take a leaf from Abraham Lincoln's book. In instructing his envoy to Mexico, more than fourscore years ago, the sagacious humanitarian wrote: "In all your negotiations fear not to give strength to that republic; Mexico can never be an enemy, it ought to be made a friend, of the United States."

It has taken a long time for succeeding chief executives to see the wisdom of Lincoln's sentiment. But more and more Americans of sound business sense are becoming convinced that today our interests coincide. Men of honest intelligence and kindly heart in both nations quite naturally desire perpetual amity between the neighbor republics. The *modus operandi* of maintaining that blessed condition would be easy indeed if the citizens north and south of the border could bear in mind a simple definition of Benito Juárez. "Peace," the great Indian said, with classical economy, "is respect for the rights of others."

# Acknowledgments

In 1934, immediately after I had finished writing a history of Cuba, I began doing research on the history of Mexico. During the decade between 1934 and 1944, although I published two other books, I continued to read and digest a prodigious amount of printed matter about Mexico, including hundreds of magazine articles listed in *Poole's Index* from 1811. I made several trips to Mexico, traveling extensively over the country. My last visit there consumed the summer of 1943.

In the late spring of 1941 I began the actual writing of *Timeless Mexico*. Naturally the most difficult and yet the most fascinating part of the work has been to get the story into one volume. Each specialist may doubtless feel that I have unduly telescoped those parts of the Mexican story he knows most thoroughly. I have had long debates with myself in the selection of events and details, in forming a judgment between two or among twenty different accounts of the same happening. I have followed one authority in one matter and another in another according to my own appraisal and set down what seems right to me. My main conclusions, I am afraid, will please neither reactionaries nor communistic sympathizers in Mexico or the United States. And my Catholic friends in the United States may deplore my account of certain clerical activities in Mexico. But perhaps they think only in terms of American or European Catholicism, which is something different from the religion that stemmed from Inquisitional Spain and mingled with Indian superstition.

For the English language world, real interest in literature on Mexico began just a hundred and one years ago. On October first, 1843, William Prescott signed the preface to his monumental *History of the Conquest of Mexico,* and in that same memorable

419

year Madame Calderón de la Barca published her delectable letters under the title *Life in Mexico*. Both books achieved great success on both sides of the Atlantic, and each remains today unexcelled in its special field.

Every decade since the 1840's has brought forth a fresh harvest of books on Mexico—and a large crop of magazine and newspaper articles. Among the wheat there have been tares, but even the tares have their own peculiar value, and often good grain is to be found among spurious matter.

It is interesting and cheering to note that since 1920 the American authors of the best-known books arrive more or less at the same conclusions. Virtually all these works have a definite liberal tone, though some obviously have a more radical bias than others. Among the imperatives for those really interested in Mexico are the works by Gruening, Parkes, Priestley, Chase, Rippy, Tannenbaum, Herring, Beals, Simpson, Plenn, Wolfe, and the Weyls. The contemporary American women who write with most significance of recent events are Anita Brenner, Verna Carleton Millán, Virginia Prewett, and Betty Kirk. Erna Ferguson has written entertainingly of the *fiesta* and Frances Toor has done an interesting job in the field of folkways. Bertita Harding and Blair Niles have each produced, in different manners, fascinating accounts of the Maximilian and Carlotta interlude, which is good for many retellings. In the field of archeological research some of the Americans who have distinguished themselves and whose writing on the subject is most commendable are George Vaillant, Herbert S. Spinden, E. L. Hewett, Sylvanus Morley, Frans Blom, Gilbert Médioni, Thomas Gann, T. A. Joyce, and J. E. Thompson.

In fiction Katherine Anne Porter has transcended all other American writers in portraying subtleties of Mexican character and atmosphere. For charm as well as acute observation, Gertrude Diamant's *The Days of Ofelia* should not be missed. By all odds the best book of personal recollections after Madame Calderón de la Barca, is *Viva Mexico!,* which Charles Flandrau wrote in 1908 in the last flare of the Díaz glory. But with many lovers of Mexico the favorite of all the books remains Bernal Díaz's account of the Conquest as he saw it with his own eyes and helped to achieve with his own fighting arms.

To all of the American authors mentioned above, as well as to scores of others whose volumes are listed in the selective bibliography, and to the Mexican and Spanish and English authors of books, and to the writers of hundreds of magazine and newspaper articles, I am indebted in one way or another. To Ellen Maury Slayden in particular I am grateful for many of the details of Mexico's centennial celebration in 1910.

From eye-witnesses I have attained much information that is not in the newspaper files or the books. I have talked with many who helped or who are helping to make the history: Plutarco Elias Calles, Lázaro Cárdenas, Manuel Avila Camacho, Ezequiel Padilla, José Vasconcelos, and Lombardo Toledano, foremost among the names of those still living. I have talked with soldiers who fought with Villa and with Zapata and with Carranza. I have spent an afternoon with the widow of Madero and mornings with aging persons who were intimates of the Díaz household back in the nineteenth century. I have talked with Englishmen, Germans, Frenchmen, and Swedes who have lived in Mexico from one to six decades. I have listened to Diego Rivera's original interpretations of Mexican history, and to his fellow great artist, Orozco, who will tell what happened but not what he thinks (except in his canvases), and to Rufino Tamayo, the Indian artist from Oaxaca, whose brooding eyes flash fire when he speaks of uplift for his brothers. And for having once painted that strangely evocative picture "La Cita," which I purchased in Mexico and which hangs above my living room fireplace, I shall ever be grateful to Carlos Orozco Romero. Among the Mexican historians and biographers I am particularly indebted to José

Valadés and Rafael Muñoz for their hours of answering questions.

For hospitality and for arranging interviews with the accessible and the seemingly inaccessible I am uncommonly grateful to the United States Ambassador George Messersmith and to the former Ambassador Josephus Daniels. For receiving me and for being most generous with their time I am profoundly grateful to President Manuel Avila Camacho, and to ex-President Lázaro Cárdenas and ex-President Plutarco Elías Calles, and to five current cabinet ministers: Miguel Alemán, secretary of government; Ezequiel Padilla, secretary of foreign affairs; Eduardo Suárez, secretary of finance; Francisco Xavier Gaxiola, secretary of economy; and to General Francisco Urquizo, secretary of national defense. For especially helpful assistance I am indebted to Ramón Beteta, under secretary of finance, to Eduardo Villaseñor, director of the Bank of Mexico, to Alejandro Carrillo, editor of *El Popular,* to José Vasconcelos, director of the National Library.

The list of other persons in various parts of Mexico to whom I am grateful for hospitality or glimpses of Mexican family life or reminiscences or access to memoirs is far too long to be printed here. But among those who were peculiarly helpful in one way or another must be mentioned the following: the Marquesa de Mohernando, Inés Amor, Orestes Cabutti, Verna Carleton Millán, Fred Davis, Roger Wolin, José Rojas, Amalia Rovzar, R. Fernandez del Castillo, Mrs. Robert Frazer, Gunnar and Margit Beckman, Sr. and Sra. Mario Casasus, Felipe Pomar, William Spratling, Sterling Dickinson, Wilbur Barker, Salomán de la Selva, Andrée Zozias, Antonio Pérez, John Robertson, Fernando Barbachano, José Patrón, Carlos Corres, Capt. Victor Esperón Urbina, Cameron Townsend, Pedro A. Chapa, Lucas de Palacio, Josué Sáenz, Don Miller, and Raleigh Gibson, first secretary of the U. S. Embassy.

To the Julius Rosenwald Foundation I express gratitude for a fellowship in 1943 to facilitate my work.

To four of my colleagues at the University of Alabama I am indebted for their reading and criticizing parts of the manuscript: Dr. A. B. Thomas, Professor of Latin American History; Professor Marshall Nunn of the Spanish Department; Professor George K. Smart and Mr. Edward Kimbrough of the Department of English. For indefatigable assistance in research I am grateful to Olli Durchman. To President Raymond R. Paty and Dean Charles H. Barnwell of the University of Alabama I am deeply indebted for encouragement and practical assistance. And as usual I am indebted to my wife for her unflagging help and indispensable criticism, and for her many typings of the script.

# Bibliography

Ackermann, Carl William: *Mexico's Dilemma*. New York: 1918.
Aiton, A. S.: *Antonio de Mendoza*. Durham: 1927.
Alamán, Lucas: *Historia de Méjico*. Mexico: 1849-52.
Anderson, Alexander Dwight: *The Silver Country*. New York: 1877.
*Aspectos del Pensamiento Michoacano*. Mexico: 1943.
Bancroft, Hubert Howe: *History of Mexico*. New York: 1914.
Barker, Eugene Campbell: *Mexico and Texas*. Dallas: 1928.
Barranco, Manuel: *Mexico; Its Educational Problems*. New York: 1915.
Barron, Clarence: *The Mexican Problem*. Boston: 1917.
Batres, Leopoldo: *Exploraciones de Monte Alban, Mexico*. Mexico: 1902.
Baxter, Sylvester: *Spanish Colonial Architecture in Mexico*. New York: 1910.
Beals, Carleton: *Mexican Maze*. New York: 1931.
—— *Porfirio Díaz*. New York: 1932.
Bell, Edward I.: *The Political Shame of Mexico*. New York: 1914.
Beteta, Ramón (and others): *Economic and Social Program of Mexico*. Mexico: 1935.
Biart, Lucien: *The Aztecs*. Translated by J. L. Garner. Chicago: 1913.
Blakeslee, George Hubbard: *Mexico and the Caribbean*. New York: 1920.
Blasco Ibáñez, Vicente: *Mexico in Revolution*. New York: 1920.
Blasio, José L.: *Maximilian, Emperor of Mexico—Memoirs of His Private Secretary*. New Haven: 1934.
Blom, Frans: *The Conquest of Yucatán*. New York: 1936.
Born, Esther: *The New Architecture in Mexico*. New York: 1937.
Brenner, Anita: *Idols Behind Altars*. New York: 1929.
—— *Your Mexican Holiday*. New York: 1932.
Brenner, Anita and Leighton, George: *The Wind That Swept Mexico*. New York: 1943.
Bulnes, Francisco: *El Verdadero Juárez*. Mexico: 1904.
—— *La Guerra de Independencia*. Mexico: (1910).
—— *The Whole Truth about Mexico*. Mexico: 1916.

Calderón de la Barca, Frances: *Life in Mexico*. Boston: 1802-82.

Callahan, James M.: *American Foreign Policy in Mexican Relations*. New York: 1932.

Callcott, Wilfred H.: *Liberalism in Mexico*. Stanford: 1931.

—— *Santa Anna*. Norman: 1936.

Calles, Plutarco Elías: *Mexico Before the World*. New York: 1927.

Caso, Alfonso: "Monte Albán, Richest Archaeological Find in America," *The National Geographic Magazine*, Vol. 62. Washington: 1932.

—— "Reading the Riddle of Ancient Jewels," *Natural History*, Vol. 32. New York: 1932.

—— *The Religion of the Aztecs*. Mexico: 1937.

—— *Twenty Centuries of Mexican Art*. Mexico: 1940.

Chase, Stuart: *Mexico; a Study of Two Americas*. New York: 1931.

Chávez Orosco, Luis: *Historia de Mexico*. Mexico: 1934.

Clark, Marjorie: *Organized Labor in Mexico*. New York: 1934.

Clavigero, Francisco Saverio: *The History of Mexico*. Translated by Charles Cullen. 2 Vols. London: 1787.

Cortés, Hernán: *Letters of Cortés*. Translated and edited by F. A. MacNutt. 2 Vols. New York and London: 1908.

Creelman, James: *Díaz, Master of Mexico*. New York: 1911.

Dawson, Daniel: *The Mexican Adventure*. New York: 1935.

Díaz del Castillo, Bernal: *The True History of the Conquest of New Spain*. Translated by A. P. Maudslay. Hakluyt Society. 5 Vols. London: 1908-16.

—— *Historia Verdadera de la Conquista de la Nueva España*. Madrid: 1904-05.

Dromundo, Baltasar: *Emiliano Zapata*. Mexico: 1934.

Dunn, Harry H.: *The Crimson Jester, Zapata of Mexico*. New York: 1934.

Durán, Diego: *Historia de las Indias de Nueva España y islas de Tierra Firme*. 2 Vols. Mexico: 1867-80.

De Sahagún, Bernardino: *Historia General de las Cosas de Nueva España*. 3 Vols. Mexico: 1829.

Egon, Count Corti: *Maximilian and Charlotte of Mexico*. New York: 1928.

Enock, C.: *Mexico, Its Ancient and Modern Civilizations*. New York: 1909.

Fergusson, Erna: *Fiesta in Mexico*. New York: 1934.

Flandrau, C. M.: *Viva Mexico!* New York: 1908.

Gage, Thomas: *A New Survey of the West Indies* (*1648*). London: 1929.

Gaither, Roscoe Bradley: *Expropriation in Mexico; the Facts and the Law.* New York: 1940.

Galindo y Galindo, M.: *El Gran Década Nacional.* Mexico: 1905-06.

Gamio, Manuel (ed.): *La Población del Valle de Teotihuacán.* Mexico: 1929.

Gibbon, Thomas E.: *Mexico Under Carranza.* New York: 1919.

Gonzaga Urbina, Luis: *La Literatura Mexicana durante la Guerra de la Independencia.* Madrid: 1917.

Gruening, Ernest: *Mexico and Its Heritage.* New York: 1928.

Guzmán, Martín Luis: *El Aguila y la Serpiente.* New York: 1928.

Hackett, Charles W.: *The Mexican Revolution and the United States, 1910-1926.* Boston: 1926.

Harding, Bertita: *Phantom Crown.* New York: 1934.

Herring, Hubert C. and Weinstock, Herbert: *Renascent Mexico.* New York: 1935.

Herring, Hubert: *Mexico, The Making of a Nation.* New York: 1942.

Holmes, William H.: *Archaeological Studies Among the Ancient Cities of Mexico, 1895-97.* Chicago.

Humboldt, Alexander von: *Essai Politique sur le Royaume de la Nouvelle Espagne.* Paris: 1811.

Ixtlilxochitl, Fernando de Alva: *Horribles Crueldades de los Conquistadores de México.* Paris: 1838.

—— *Obras Históricas* (XVI century); Relaciones, Vol. 1; *Historia Chichimeca,* Vol. 2, 1891-92. Mexico.

Jackson, Joseph Henry: *Mexican Interlude.* New York: 1938.

Jones, Chester L.: *Mexico and its Reconstruction.* New York: 1921.

Kelley, Francis C.: *Blood-drenched Altars.* Milwaukee: 1935.

King, Rosa: *Tempest Over Mexico.* New York: 1935.

Kingsborough (Viscount), Edward King: *Antiquities of Mexico.* 9 Vols. London: 1830-48.

Kilhum, W. H.: *Mexican Architecture of the Vice-Regal Period.* New York: 1921.

Kirk, Betty: *Covering the Mexican Front.* Norman: 1942.

Kirkpatrick, F. A.: *The Spanish Conquistadores.* New York: 1934.

Lawrence, D. H.: *Mornings in Mexico.* New York: 1934.

Lumholtz, C.: *Unknown Mexico.* 2 Vols. New York: 1902.

Lummis, Charles F.: *The Awakening of a Nation.* New York: 1893.

Manning, William R.: *Early Diplomatic Relations Between the United States and Mexico.* Baltimore: 1916.

Martin, Percy F.: *Mexico of the Twentieth Century.* New York: 1907.

Mayer, Branty: *Mexico; Aztec, Spanish and Republican.* Hartford: 1852.

Médioni, Gilbert: *Art in Ancient Mexico.* New York: 1941.

Millán, Verna Carleton: *Mexico Reborn.* Boston: 1939.

Molina Enríquez, Andrés: *La Reforma y Juárez.* Mexico: 1906.

Motolinía de Benavente, T: *Historia de los Indios de la Nueva España.* Mexico: 1914.

Muñóz, Rafael F.: *Santa Anna.* Madrid: 1936.

Musser, John: *The Establishment of Maximilian's Empire.* New York: 1918.

MacFarland, C. S.: *Chaos in Mexico.* New York: 1935.

MacNutt, Francis A.: *Hernando Cortez and the Conquest of Mexico.* New York: 1909.

McBride, G. McC.: *The Land Systems of Mexico* (Research Series, American Geographical Society, No. 12). New York: 1923.

Nicolson, Harold: *Dwight Morrow.* New York: 1935.

Niles, Blair: *Passengers to Mexico.* New York: 1943.

Noll, Arthur H.: *A Short History of Mexico.* Chicago: 1890.

Orozco y Berra, Manuel: *Historia Antigua y de la Conquista de Mexico.* 4 Vols. Mexico: 1880.

O'Shaughnessy, Edith L.: *Intimate Pages of Mexican History.* New York: 1920.

Padilla, Ezequiel: *Tres Discursos.* Mexico: 1942.

Palavicini, Felix F.: *La Estética de la Tragedia Mexicana.* Mexico: 1933.

Parkes, Henry B.: *A History of Mexico.* Boston: 1938.

Parsons, Elsie C.: *Mitla, Town of Souls.* Chicago: 1936.

—— *Mexican Martyrdom.* New York: 1936.

Pereyra, Carlos: *Tejas.* Mexico: 1935.

—— *Hernán Cortés.* Mexico: 1931.

—— *El Obra de España en América.* Mexico: 1925.

Pinchon, Adgcumb: *Viva Villa.* New York: 1933.

Plenn, J. H.: *Mexico Marches.* Indianapolis: 1939.

Porter, Katherine Anne: *Flowering Judas.* New York: 1935.

Prescott, William H.: *The Conquest of Mexico.* 3 Vols. New York: 1843.

Prewett, Virginia: *Reportage on Mexico.* New York: 1941.

Priestley, Herbert I.: *The Mexican Nation.* New York: 1923.

Puig Casauranc, J. M.: *Juárez, su Interpretación Humana.* Mexico: 1928.

Rabasa, Emilio: *La Evolución Histórica de México*. Mexico: 1920.

Radin, Paul: *The Sources and Authenticity of the History of the Ancient Mexicans*. Berkeley: 1920.

Redfield, Robert and Villa, Alfonso: *Chan Kom, a Maya Village*. New York: 1934.

Redfield, Robert: *Tepoztlán, a Mexican Village*. Chicago: 1930.

Reed, John: *Insurgent Mexico*. New York: 1914.

Rippy, James F.: *The United States and Mexico*. New York: 1926.

—— *The Rivalry of the United States and Great Britain over Latin America*. New York: 1929.

—— *Joel Poinsett, Versatile American*. Durham: 1935.

Rivera, Diego and Wolfe, Bertram: *Portrait of Mexico*. New York: 1937.

Rives, George Lockhart: *The United States and Mexico, 1821-1848*. New York: 1913.

Robinson, Fayette: *Mexico and Her Military Chieftains*. Philadelphia: 1847.

Robinson, Henry M.: *Stout Cortez*. New York: 1931.

Robinson, W. D.: *Memoirs of the Mexican Revolution*. 1904.

Roscher, W. G. F.: *The Spanish Colonial System*. New York: 1904.

Ross, Edward A.: *The Social Revolution in Mexico*. New York: 1923.

Saenz, Moises: *Some Mexican Problems*. Chicago: 1926.

Sahagún, Bernadino de: *Historia General de las Cosas de Nueva España*. 3 Vols. Mexico: 1829-30.

Sedgwick, H. D.: *Cortés the Conqueror*. New York: 1926.

*Seis Años de Gobierno al Servicio de México (1934-1940)*. Mexico: 1942.

Sierra, Justo: *Juárez, Su Obra y Su Tiempo*. Mexico: 1905-06.

—— *México, Su Evolución Social*. 3 Vols. Mexico: 1900-02.

Simpson, Eyler N.: *The Ejido, Mexico's Way Out*. Chapel Hill: 1937.

Smith, J. H.: *The Annexation of Texas*. New York: 1911.

—— *The War with Mexico*. New York: 1919.

Spence, Lewis: *The Gods of Mexico*. London: 1923.

Spinden, Herbert J.: *Ancient Civilizations of Mexico and Central America*. New York: 1928.

Spratling, William: *Little Mexico*. New York: 1932.

Stucken, Eduard: *The Great White Gods*. New York: 1934.

Tannenbaum, Frank: *The Mexican Agrarian Revolution*. New York: 1929.

—— *Peace by Revolution*. New York: 1933.

Taylor, John M.: *Maximilian and Carlotta*. New York: 1894.

Teja, Alfonso Zabre: *Guide to the History of Mexico*. Mexico: 1935.

Thomas, Cyrus and Swanston, John R.: *Indian Languages of Mexico and Central America and Their Geographical Distribution*. Bureau of American Ethnology, Bulletin 44. Washington, D. C.: 1911.

Thompson, Edward Herbert: *People of the Serpent*. Boston: 1932.

Thompson, J. Eric: *A Correlation of the Mayan and European Calendars,* Chicago Field Museum of Natural History, Anthropological Series, Vol. 17, no. 1. Chicago: 1927.

Thompson, Waddy: *Recollections of Mexico*. New York: 1847.

Thompson, Wallace: *Trading with Mexico*. New York: 1921.

—— *The People of Mexico*. New York: 1921.

Tompkins, Frank: *Chasing Villa*. Harrisburg: 1934.

Toor, Frances (ed.): *Mexican Folkways*. Mexico: 1935-36.

—— *Guide to Mexico*. Mexico: 1935.

Torquemada, Juan de: *Monarchía Indiana*. 3 Vols. Madrid: 1723.

Townsend, W. Cameron: *The Truth About Mexican Oil*. Mexico: 1940.

Trowbridge, Edward D.: *Mexico Today and Tomorrow*. New York: 1919.

Turlington, Edgar W.: *Mexico and Her Foreign Creditors*. New York: 1930.

Turner, Timothy G.: *Bullets, Bottles and Gardenias*. New York: 1915.

Vaillant, George C.: *Aztecs of Mexico*. Garden City: 1941.

Valades, José C.: *Santa Anna y la Guerra de Texas*. Mexico: 1936.

Vasconcelos, José: *Indologia*. Mexico: 1926.

—— *Ulises Criollo*. Mexico: 1935.

—— *La Tormenta*. Mexico: 1936.

Vásquez Gómez, Francisco: *Memorias Políticas*. Mexico: 1933.

Velásquez Chávez, Agustín: *Contemporary Mexican Artists*. New York: 1937.

Veytia, Mariano: *Historia Antigua de Mexico*. 3 Vols. Mexico: 1836.

Walling, William E.: *The Mexican Question; Mexican and American-Mexican Relations under Calles and Obregón*. New York: 1927.

Ward, H. G.: *Mexico in 1827*. London: 1829.

Weyl, Nathaniel and Sylvia: *The Reconquest of Mexico*. New York: 1939.

Whitaker, Arthur P.: *Mexico Today*. Philadelphia: 1940.

Zayas Enríquez, Rafael de: *Juárez*. Mexico: 1906.

# Index

431